The Genesis of
Modern Management

To Freda

The Genesis of
Modern Management

A Study of the Industrial Revolution in Great Britain

SIDNEY POLLARD
Professor of Economic History, The University of Sheffield

HARVARD UNIVERSITY PRESS
Cambridge, Massachusetts
1965

Printed in Great Britain by
W. & J. Mackay & Co Ltd, Chatham, Kent

Contents

	Pages
Chapter 1. Entrepreneurship and Management: The Limits of the Inquiry	1–24
(i) The limits of 'Management'	2
(ii) The scope of 'industry'	6
(iii) Management and the size of firms	9
Chapter 2. Large-Scale Enterprise on the Eve of the Industrial Revolution	25–60
(i) The landed estate	25
(ii) The domestic system	30
(iii) Subcontract	38
(iv) Experience abroad	48
(v) Some forerunners in large-scale industry	51
Chapter 3. The Course of Structural Change in Industry	61–103
(i) Mining	61
(ii) Metallurgy	75
(iii) Shipbuilding, building, civil engineering and public utilities	84
(iv) Textiles	89
(v) Pottery, glass, chemicals and other industries	96
(vi) Summary	100
Chapter 4. The Managers	104–159
(i) Formal educational provisions for managers	104
(ii) The practical training of managers	122
(iii) Technical training and the beginning of professionalism	126
(iv) The numbers of managers	133
(v) Payment and social status of managers	136
(vi) Conclusion: the rise of the industrial manager	156
Chapter 5. The Adaptation of the Labour Force	160–208
(i) The recruitment of labour	160
(ii) Training within industry and mass education	174

Contents

		Pages
(iii)	The creation of the new work discipline	181
(iv)	The assault on working-class morals	192
(v)	The factory village	197
(vi)	Summary	206

Chapter 6. Accounting and Management   209–249
(i)	Origins of accounting: landed estates, merchants, and putters-out	209
(ii)	Accountancy as an aid to regularity and honesty	215
(iii)	Accountancy as an aid to sectional costing	219
(iv)	The failure of total costing	223
(v)	The failure of capital accounting	233
(vi)	Accountancy as a tool of management	245

Chapter 7. Conclusion: Management in Theory and Practice   250–272
(i)	The first stirrings of theories of management	251
(ii)	The systematizing of management practice	259
(iii)	Management and the process of industrialization	270

Notes	273
Abbreviations	325
Index	326

Acknowledgements

The costs of the research embodied in this study were largely met by a grant by the Trustees of the Houblon-Norman Fund, to whom thanks are due for their generosity and forbearance. The author is also happy to acknowledge the further financial support provided by the Knoop Fund of the University of Sheffield.

A work of this kind cannot be attempted without the active co-operation of many librarians and other keepers of archives and their staff, and the author has reason to be grateful for much kindness and helpfulness beyond the call of duty on their part. To name only a few would be invidious, and to name them all would take up too much space; but the main institutions and collections which have been pressed into service must be recorded. They include the British Museum, the Public Record Office, the British Library of Political and Economic Science, the Sheffield Public Library (Spencer-Stanhope, Arundel Castle, [by permission of His Grace the Duke of Norfolk, E.M., K.G.,] Wentworth-Woodhouse and Wharncliffe Muniments, and Bagshaw Collection), the National Library of Wales (Tredegar, Cyfarthfa, Nevill MSS, MS 'Tours' of R. E. Yates, H. P. Wyndham, T. Martyn, and other papers), Birmingham Public Library (Boulton & Watt MSS), Birmingham Assay Office (Boulton & Watt MSS), The Royal Cornwall Polytechnic Society, Falmouth (Boulton & Watt MSS), The North of England Institute of Mining and Mechanical Engineers (Dunn's MS. History, Wm. Brown's Letter Book, Buddle Collection Accounts, etc., Quaker Lead Company Minutes, and other MSS), Cardiff Public Library (Pontrhydyrun MSS, Rhymney Ironworks MSS, Clutterbuck's 'Tour'), Newport Public Library (Caerleon Mills MSS), Newcastle-on-Tyne Public Library (Crowley MSS), Brotherton Library, Leeds (Marshall Papers, Gott Papers), Nottingham University Library (Galway of Serlby, Manvers of Thoresby, Middleton of Woollaton MSS), Liverpool Public Library (Herculaneum Pottery, Garston Vitriol Works MSS), University College of North Wales Library (Mona Mine MSS), British Transport Commission Archives (London and York), Friends' House, London (Kelsall MSS, Norris MSS, Lloyd MSS), Glamorgan Record Office (Dowlais MSS), Messrs. Newton Chambers (Archives), Mr. F. L. Harris, Redruth

(Tehidy Estate MSS), Mr. T. R. Harris, Camborne (Tehidy Estate MSS), Dr. J. E. Williams (Shipley Colliery Accounts) and Dr. John Rowe.

The author also wishes to acknowledge the facilities provided to read the unpublished thesis in the care of the librarians of the following Universities: Sheffield (theses by G. G. Hopkinson, E. S. Dane, E. D. Bebb, R. A. H. Page), Birmingham (P. S. Bebbington, J. E. Cule, B. L. C. Johnson), London (N. K. A. Rothstein, John Thomas, K. T. Weetch, O. Wood), Manchester (Frances Collier, J. R. Harris, Edith Malley), Nottingham (A. D. Insull), Oxford (R. M.Hartwell, J. R. Immer, R. A. C. Parker) and Wales (D. G. John, D. Pritchard, John Rowlands).

The editors of the following journals were kind enough to give permission to include in this book, in substantially unaltered form, large sections of articles published by them:

The Economic History Review: 'Factory Discipline in the Industrial Revolution', (2nd Ser., XVI/2, Dec. 1963).

The Yorkshire Bulletin of Economic and Social Research: 'Capital Accounting in the Industrial Revolution', (XV/2, Nov. 1963).

The English Historical Review: 'The Factory Village in the Industrial Revolution', (LXXIX/312, July 1964).

Studies in Romanticism: 'The Genesis of the Managerial Profession: The Experience of the Industrial Revolution in Great Britain', (IV/2, Winter 1965).

Last, but not least, thanks are due to a succession of typists who succeeded in producing order out of chaos. These miracles were performed by Mrs. A. Couldwell, Miss V. Wild and Miss H. Trippett.

1 / Entrepreneurship and Management: The Limits of the Inquiry

The Industrial Revolution in Great Britain, like all historical events of world-shaking importance, attracts a new body of historians to interpret it afresh in every age. If the interpretations change from generation to generation, it is not merely because new facts have been brought to light in the meantime, and the pupils can correct the mistakes of their masters, nor yet simply because each generation views history from a different set of prejudices; it is largely because each generation asks a different set of questions.

Today, much of the impetus for the re-appraisal arises out of the practice of looking upon the British Industrial Revolution as the prototype of the industrialization process which many countries have undergone since, and others are undergoing, or are about to undergo, at present. Since this approach seeks to help to forecast, and pave the way for, the next steps to be taken by living economies, it has a severely practical basis; at the same time, one of its incidental results is that new light is thrown on some aspects of this period in British economic history not merely by historians and economists, as in the past, but also by sociologists, by management consultants and by others of different backgrounds.[1] Inevitably, their uncomfortable questions point to gaps in our knowledge and our interests hitherto.

One of the most glaring gaps is the story of the genesis of modern industrial management. It is now twenty years since the doyens among British management consultants complained that 'we have as yet little knowledge of the standard and methods of management during the various phases of the industrial revolution'.[2] 'It has been possible', they go on to state, 'to deal with only a few firms about which specific data have been preserved'; but while there has been a whole series of valuable, detailed histories of firms and industries published since, and more manuscript material has been made available to scholars, the gap on management has remained. It is a gap which has become all the less justifiable since it not only concerns a field of human endeavour and attitudes which, like so much else in the industrial revolution, made its first appearance ever, in its recognizably modern form, in eighteenth-century Britain, but at the same time it covers precisely the kind of topics which demand practical answers today. This book is written in an attempt to fill part of that gap.

I

The title of this book may be considered to be too ambitious, since the chapters which follow do not deal with all aspects of management. Indeed, the limits of 'management' as such are not very easy to draw. If we begin by attempting to distinguish it from entrepreneurship, it is because, in doing so, we shall, in fact, have drawn very approximately also the limits of this study.

The concepts of entrepreneurship and management do themselves change with the changing structure and purposes of industry. Today, in an age of giant corporations and companies, whose survival as such is assured, managers rise by manipulating resources *within* their firms, rather than by shaping their firms and their industries themselves, as they did in the industrial revolution. As a result, the stress in management is on the efficient use of resources within the firm and, more recently, on the creation of a proper institutional and human framework to make this possible; while the simple emphasis on the cash nexus, characteristic of the early stages of industrialization,[1] has long been sublimated. The setting up of the organizational structure has become the highest task of management. Organization building

> is the most difficult of all managerial functions. It requires a concept of organization building and a philosophy of management.[2]

By contrast, risk-taking, the handling of uncertainty, the decision on the objectives and the direction of the firm, and innovation, all of which are the traditional entrepreneurial functions within the concepts of such different thought systems of those of Schumpeter, Knight or Shackle, for example, are given a much smaller weight in modern management literature.

Those who are accustomed to occupying their thoughts with the developing, pushful firms of the past, rather than with the ponderous oligopolies of today, would term all the above, functions of *entrepreneurship*, not of *management*, and would stress the dynamic aspects among them. Thus one recent study of entrepreneurial functions during the industrialization process emphasizes that during phases of growth, investment strategies rest on positive action directed towards modifying and expanding market structures and, in fact, towards shaping, to some degree, the whole economic environment.[1]

Arthur H. Cole, who has furthered perhaps more than anyone the study of entrepreneurship in the past, lists six spheres of action of the entrepreneur, which include not only such fields as determining the objects of the enterprise, the securing of finance, the development of markets and relations with public authorities, but also 'the development and maintenance of an organization, including efficient relations with subordinates and all employees', and the maintenance of the technical equipment in an efficient state, which were often in the past, and are certainly now, held to be subjects for management. For an entrepreneurial history, he goes on, we would want to know the entrepreneurs'

> origins, their burdens of uncertainties (with the collateral facts regarding their accountancy, controls, etc., or regarding ancillary institutions), the sources of their business information, the availability of counsellors, or their attitudes towards business and economic problems of their times.[2]

Other authors would, in the past as today, describe many of these as subordinate management functions.

We therefore have to choose a working definition of the limits of management. If we adopt the definitions provided by G. H. Evans, Jr., it is not in order to make them necessarily valid for all times and places, but merely as most appropriate for the period studied here. According to him, entrepreneurs have the

> task of determining *the kind of business to be operated* . . . the kinds of goods and services to be offered, the amounts of these to be supplied, and the clientele to be served.

Once these decisions have been made,

> Other 'top level' decisions become essentially management decisions,—that is, decisions designed to achieve the goals set by the entrepreneurial determination of the kind of business to be operated.

In Redlich's terms, while the entrepreneur makes strategic decisions, the manager makes tactical ones.[3] This book is intended to deal with the problems on the management side of the divide, with the achievements of the 'creative manager', and ignore those on the entrepreneurial side.

3

It may be felt that this limitation unduly restricts the scope of this study. The reasons for it are only partly theoretical. They are in part pragmatic and are all connected with the fact that the main gap in knowledge is to be found on the management side. As far as entrepreneurial problems are concerned, they have always attracted much of the interest of historians, whether they are dealing with the period as a whole, with separate industries, or with firms within it. The origins of the entrepreneur, the source of his capital, his adoption of technical innovation, and his methods and success in expanding his market have been among the main questions discussed in the literature. The wider social impact of the entrepreneurial class on their society has also been explored from time to time, including their influence on legislation, on tariffs or controls, on trade-union activity or factory acts, their resultant pressure for political rights and influence, and their social ambitions after achieving commercial success. It is fair to say that, by contrast, problems of internal management, the method by which entrepreneurial decisions are enforced, have received very little attention indeed.

Yet these problems are not without interest. Above all, they were new to the industrial entrepreneur, who had to deal with them as they appeared for the first time in history, and who could not in this field, as in most others, base his experience to any extent on that of the merchant or the putting-out master who preceded him. An accountant, for example, looking at the new tasks with which the new industrialist had to deal, might note that he would have much fixed capital; that he would require large stocks of raw material, sufficient to prevent any hold-ups due to shortages, yet not too much to waste capital; that he would have a large body of labour to be watched; that he would have to check expenditure, output and efficiency of different processes, in absolute terms and against each other; he would have to prevent fraud and protect his payroll; he would have to evolve a system of accounting to deal with depreciation, in order to establish his profits for the year, and his minimum variable costs, in order to know his minimum selling price in slumps. And in addition there were problems of techniques, of transport, of 'organization and control, planning production, co-ordinating departments', among others.[1]

Others would stress the particular problems, new to history, of managing a sizeable labour force:

> A small trader or money lender can operate with a few, and often without any, permanently employed assistants; whereas the industrial entrepreneur (provided he is more than a crafts-

man) typically must hire a group of men whose labour he must organize and direct. In addition to being motivated by the expectation of profit, and his capacity for applying innovations, he must have managerial abilities and, above all, the ability to command and organize. The chief characteristics of a small industrial entrepreneur are not so much his venturesomeness, nor his motivation to make profits, but his capacity to lead other men in a common undertaking, and his inclination to introduce technical innovations; and, in the early stages of industrialization, the vast bulk of these innovations are of a technological nature requiring the direct and immediate participation of the entrepreneur.[1]

Others, again, have been struck by the substantial increase in the sheer amount of managerial activity and skill which becomes necessary when large-scale modern industry first appears. In a developing country,

> an appreciable amount of managerial skill may be required to initiate and operate an import and export trading concern, a medium-sized bank or insurance establishment, a freight-forwarding company, or a large marketing organization;

more skill is required in transport, communications and the public utilities; but

> the most complicated organization to manage is the sizable industrial establishment. Here technical know-how, marketing ability, financial and administrative skills are all required. The manager of the industrial enterprise must have the capacity to plan and integrate the work of a hierarchy of specialists, and through them he must be able to recruit and develop a labour force which possesses both the motivation and the skills for efficient production. . . . *The size of the organization* and the *type of activity* in which it is engaged, therefore, have a direct bearing on the requirements for managerial ability and high-talent human resources.[2]

These skills, so highly prized and so scarce in the developing countries today, seem to have been taken for granted by historians of the British industrial revolution. It is arguable that since industrialization did take place in this country, management could have been no problem, and management skill could not have constituted a bottleneck; alternatively, it might be held that it was precisely the abundance of managerial talent which produced the industrial revolution, in Britain rather than in France, in the eighteenth century rather than the seventeenth. Even this argument, however, would require support from concrete investigation.

For practical purposes, only four major aspects of 'management' will be treated at length in this work, each forming the subject of one chapter. The first is the creation and training of a class of managers (Chapter 4). The second concerns the recruitment, training, disciplining and acculturation of labour (Chapter 5). The third aspect to be examined is the use made, by employers and managers, of accountancy, and other information available about the profitability of their enterprises, in the rational determination of their decisions (Chapter 6). Finally, we shall attempt in Chapter 7 to examine how far a theory and practice of 'management', as distinct from ad-hoc and unrelated decision-making, developed at all in the industrial revolution.

II

It is not universally accepted that the whole field of industrial management was, in fact, novel, and the claim that there was here a major innovation in individual thought and social practice will have to be further buttressed. After all, did not the ancient Egyptians build their huge pyramids, or the Chinese their wall, or, more recently, did not Louis XIV inaugurate a magnificent system of main-road building in France? If the control of large masses of men was in question, had not generals controlled many more, over the ages, than the manager of even the largest industrial company? If it was a matter of deciding rationally on the uses of large quantities of capital in order to maximize profits, had not merchants been engaged in just such activities for centuries? Or if the innovation lay in manufacture, had not the royal manufactures of France, the handicraftsmen and outworkers of Europe in the eighteenth century shown the way?

All those developments, it must be admitted, preceded the industrial revolution, often by several millennia, and it is equally true that the entrepreneurs and managers of the industrial revolution learnt one or the other aspect of their work from them. The innovation, and the difficulty, lay in this: that the men who began to operate the large new industrial units in the British economy from the middle of the eighteenth century onwards had to combine these different objectives and methods into one. Like the generals of old, they had to control numerous men, but without powers of compulsion: indeed, the absence of legal enforcement of unfree work was not only one of the marked characteristics of the new capitalism, but one of its most seminal ideas, underlying its ultimate power to create a more civilized society. Again, unlike the builders of pyramids, they had not only to show absolute results in terms of certain products of their efforts, but to relate them to costs, and sell them competitively. While they used capital, like the merchants, yet they had to combine it with labour, and transform it first, not merely into saleable commodities, but also into instruments of production embodying the latest achievements of a changing technology. And about it all there lay the heavy hand of a hostile State and an unsympathetic legal system, which they had to transform, as they had to transform so much of the rest of their environment, in the process of creating their industrial capitalism.

According to Nef,

> the industrial plant owned by private capitalists, who employed in it dozens and sometimes scores and even hundreds of workmen, was not the novelty it was once believed to be. Evidence has been piling up to prove that large-scale industry, in this sense, was common in mining and many branches of manufacture long before the middle of the eighteenth century.[1]

Even if this statement were strictly true, the problems of management in a partly immobile environment, with a fairly static technology, in the enjoyment of an actual or legal monopoly or of vast orders from non-commercial buyers, like Courts or armies, were very different from those of the eighteenth- and nineteenth-century market economy. It calls for one type of order and supervision, but it is very different from the flexibility and the opportunities within which entrepreneurs in the industrial revolution operated. While the older employer had few variables,

> rational capitalism, on the contrary, is organised with a view to market opportunities, hence to economic objectives in the real sense of the word, and the more rational it is the more closely it relates to mass demand and the provision of mass needs.[2]

> The real distinguishing characteristic of the modern factory is in general . . . not the implements of work applied, but the concentration of ownership of workplace, means of work, source of power and raw material in one and the same hand, that of the entrepreneur. This combination, was only exceptionally met with before the 18th century.[3]

This conclusion by Weber is preceded by a penetrating analysis of the development of rational self-interest as the motive force, and of

7

a social system creating individual independence to make it possible.

Far from antedating the rise of modern capitalistic industry to some period before 1700, it should rather be stressed how much of the older system was left in the interstices of the new factory organization, making adjustment easier and postponing, to that extent, the development of modern management techniques. The survival of subcontract, which at once reduces the problem of management to that of the workshop size, is perhaps the most important, and will be treated at greater length in Chapter 2. In the West Riding woollen industry the large factories of Benjamin Gott were the leading examples of the new industrialism and the pathmakers of the new manufacturing organization. Yet even by 1820, twenty-seven years after its erection, three-quarters of the labour force in the Bean Ing Works still used hand processes.[1] W. H. B. Court, in a most perceptive article,[2] has stressed the difference between the complete transformation of the primary processes, like iron smelting, into bulk producing industries, and the very different history of the final goods industries, like nailing or toolmaking, which merely multiplied similar units with rising demand, or at best introduced better organization, on the model of Adam Smith's pin factory, without fundamental technical change. In the sequel we shall pay much attention to the difference in the management problems between the two.

Again, Urwick and Brech have pointed out that while 'control' over labour could be transformed at an early stage, as it could build on older relationships, such as the obedience of apprentices, or the orders given to outworkers, the roots of other aspects of management, such as planning or co-ordination, are much more difficult to trace and were probably much more recent.[3] Gras has drawn attention to the monopolistic elements in the situation of the early industrial innovator, who had to compete against handicraft producers so much his inferior that cost details and mistakes of management could safely be neglected, until the second phase of the industrial revolution, at least. Finally, Ashton has noted a further distinction. There were firms in existing industries in which, as a result of the mere growth in size,

> new classes of technicians, machine-makers, book-keepers, and supervisors appeared in the manufacturing areas. As, after the introduction of steam, the metal mines of Cornwall became deeper, the captains became salaried managers and the tributers foremen. In coal-mining the charter-masters tended to become what are now called deputies.

By contrast, in the new industries which began on a large scale, without a craft or domestic background, such as distilling, brewing, sugar-refining and soap-boiling, men were employed direct from the beginning and supervised by the firms' foremen.[1]

The discussion on these limitations will also have shown the fields which this study excludes. It is not concerned with merchanting, an activity in which the staff to be controlled is normally small, or may even be dispensed with entirely by trading in claims only without actually moving the goods. It also excludes all transport undertakings, all purely financial firms, and all others not engaged in production or construction of some kind. It is also, except for comparisons, not concerned with enterprises in which the profit motive is absent, such as Government departments, even though in other respects they might be like other larger productive enterprises. Finally, and here the distinction is most difficult to draw, it attempts to exclude, and draw clear distinctions from, enterprises consisting of outworkers linked to a putter-out, where the work is clearly performed 'out', that is to say, outside the direct management control of the employer.

What is left is the group of manufacturing and building industries in which control over large productive enterprises led to problems of management in Great Britain in the period 1750–1830. Specifically, this includes the textiles, the metal-smelting industries and the production of metal goods, mining, brewing, large civil engineering works, and some individual large works in such industries as pottery, chemicals, glassmaking and papermaking, and in such assembly trades as shipbuilding and coachbuilding.

III

Inevitably attention has to be directed towards size as such, though our real interest lies in organization. Problems which are easily soluble in a workshop become major difficulties in a factory; above all, it is only with a certain size that the entrepreneur loses the ability to maintain direct contact with his labour force and has to make use of an intermediary management staff. This study is therefore concerned with 'large' firms only, though in some cases, as in the development of accountancy, where size has no direct bearing on the problem under discussion, some examples will be drawn from smaller firms also.

How large is 'large'? For our purposes a firm is large if its management has to some substantial extent to be delegated and becomes a problem. The actual size at which this occurs, and its measurement —by output, labour or capital—will differ from age to age and from industry to industry. J. R. Immer, writing about Birmingham in 1851, concluded that

> it was a city of large industries. The term, 'large', is taken to refer to factories of such size as to involve serious problems of organization, labour concentration and capital requirement. Although these factors vary with the type of manufacturing carried on, three hundred workers constitute the level at which these problems become more acute. It is also the level beyond which one man finds it exceedingly difficult to supervise his supervisors and finds it expedient to employ an intermediary in the form of a factory manager, a superintendent or a partner.[1]

G. C. Allen, also referring to Birmingham in the years leading up to 1860, defined a 'large' factory as one 'employing upwards of 150 persons and making an extensive use of power-machinery'.[2] His line of division was, however, less concerned with management than with the firm's ability to conduct its own marketing and obtain credit direct from the banks. For our period, with its lack of experience, we have set the limits nearer the lower of these two figures. In textile mills, perhaps the easiest to manage and the most subject to accepted routine because of the example of other firms, the lower limit is 200 workers. In other industries, employing many skilled and more differentiated male workers, or more capital, or, as in mining, simply difficult to organize on a large scale because of their very nature, the limit has been set lower still, at about 120–50 workers. These are the firms within which the problems of modern management in their totality first reared their heads in the industrial revolution.

The growth process itself is of some importance. It is by no means certain that larger size was always considered desirable, or could even theoretically be defended as being superior. On the contrary, organization theory itself suggests that while there may be technical, financial or marketing advantages in growth, management difficulties tend to work in the opposite direction, towards a lower optimum size. This limitation was felt in the industrial revolution also, even if not always consciously. It was generally only the overwhelming pressure of other factors making for larger size which broke down the wish to keep units small on grounds of the managerial optimum and forced British industry to introduce modern industrial management.

10

The Committee on the Woollen Manufactures of 1806, for
example, did not rate the advantages of large factories very highly,
at least for the West Riding. By continuing in the outworking tradition the merchant would save much capital investment, they alleged,
and would not need to 'submit to the constant trouble and solicitude
of watching over a numerous body of workmen'. 'It may well have
seemed rank folly', adds Heaton, 'to add to [commercial problems]
the worries of getting wool, handling labour, providing power,
buying machinery and risking riots.'

> The modern factory system [he stated in a different context] is
> based on the economy of the accumulation of machinery and
> the application of power; it embodies the use of capital, the
> congregation of workpeople, the division of labour, and the
> exercise of supervision. Each of these factors has great value in
> itself, but the major part of the economic advantage of the
> factory springs from the use of machinery capable of performing
> very quickly, and the use of power which can make the machi-
> nery go at high speed. Until these elements of speed become
> possible, the factory system did not possess any very great
> advantage over the cottage industry.

> Even in those industries where techniques demanded some
> concentration of work [the historian of the paper industry con-
> curs], the slowness of processes, the low productivity, the
> notorious unreliability of water- or wind-power, and the diffi-
> culty of securing capital combined to provide the maximum
> inducement to keep the plant small rather than large. Only
> where the nature of the product was such as to demand close
> supervision and the concentration of highly skilled workers was
> there normally any real economic incentive for large workshops.[1]

Again, we may notice the dual line of advance. For while in some
industries, as in textiles, it was the need for power and for co-
ordinated machinery which made size desirable, though management was the limiting factor, reducing the possibilities of greater
efficiency by expansion,[2] examples can be found, as at Soho or
Etruria, or in Adam Smith's pin factory, where on the contrary it
was organization and management which demanded the larger size.
It was in this connection that Gras traced the evolution of the 'central
workshop' quite independently of power machinery:

> It was purely for purposes of discipline, so that the workers could
> be effectively controlled under the supervision of foremen. Under
> one roof, or within a narrow compass, they could be started to
> work at sunrise and kept going till sunset, barring periods for

rest and refreshment. They could be kept working six days a week. And under the penalty of loss of all employment they could be kept going almost throughout the year. . . .

Secondly, there was division of labour:

There were workers on the one hand and foremen on the other. Some men did one kind of work, while others were put to something else. In time, considerable specialised skill would arise.[1]

Even here, however, in what H. D. Fong called the 'immature factory',[2] organization and management, while not the limiting factor, was a problem demanding a difficult solution. The entrepreneur could not simply go out and buy then, as it is alleged he has been able to do in more recent times,[3] ready-made systems of management, trained staff or office equipment. The pressure for size came from the need for competitive efficiency in a progressive economy, and size was thus to some extent the solution to a problem: but at the higher level it created new problems, the kind of problems which this study sets out to explore. If we are inclined to underrate them, because, after all, in historical fact they were solved in one way or another, it is salutary to remind ourselves that from the Continental point of view they help to explain why the economy of those other countries in Europe, equally far advanced in many respects in the eighteenth century, failed to take the next step to a factory system.[4]

There is here a further factor to be considered, which loomed much larger in eighteenth- and early nineteenth-century minds than in our own, but which ought on that account not to be entirely neglected. That was the view, based on bitter experience as well as on fashionable economic reasoning, that a system of large-scale management was to be avoided at all costs because managers who had to be given any measure of power or responsibility were not to be trusted.

Adam Smith, denying in a famous passage the ability of salaried managers to administer honestly and well any but the most routine and easily checked business, argued, as usual, not merely from philosophical principles, but from a wealth of practical experience relating, in particular, to joint-stock companies.

The directors of such companies [he accuses], being the managers rather of other people's money than of their own, it cannot well be expected, that they should watch over it with the same anxious vigilance with which the partners in a private co-partnery frequently watch over their own. . . . Negligence and profusion . . . must always prevail, more or less, in the management of the affairs of such a company. . . . The only trades which it seems possible for a joint stock company to carry on successfully, without an exclusive privilege, are those, of which all the operations are capable of being reduced to what is called a routine, or to such a uniformity of method as admits of little or no variation.[1]

Elsewhere, joint-stock companies, with their implied reliance on exclusive privileges, would be harmful, and break the 'natural proportion . . . between judicious industry and profit'.

This conclusion was echoed by the equally experienced Dean Tucker, with specific reference to the fact that chartered companies had in the past normally had some sort of monopoly:

> These *exclusive* Companies *cannot* trade, *if they were so inclined,* upon so *easy* terms, as *private* Adventurers *would do,* were the Trade *laid open.* So many *Directors, Supercargoes, Storehousekeepers, Factors, Agents, Clerks:*—and all the *Pickings* of their *several Dependants:*—so many *Fees, Sweetnings,* etc. from the *Manufacturer,* or *under Merchant,* that *his Goods* may have *the Preference* to *others,* —and the *Expenses of carrying* many Sorts of Goods from *distant* Ports of the Country, *where* they *are manufactured,* up to the *Metropolis,* where to be *Shipped* off, instead of being exported from the *next convenient* Port: *Expenses* of *Warehouses,* etc. etc. make it *impossible* for any *Corporate* Company to trade upon an *equal Footing,* with *private* Adventurers. . . . For this Reason it has been *always* found, that if *private* Adventurers shall be *permitted* to *engage* in the *same* trade, they will infallibly carry it away from the Company.[2]

Further, Tucker added, a corporation will neglect minor branches, which a private individual would make pay, and further, it will never attempt to widen its market by cheapness, but will try to maximize profits by pushing up prices. Tucker, it is true, was largely concerned with trade; but the mechanism by which monopoly in trade inhibited free industrial growth was well known.[3]

The wealth of evidence was overwhelmingly in favour of these views, quite apart from the list of fifty-five joint-stock trading companies, quoted by the Abbé Morellet in 1769, which had been set up in various parts of Europe since 1600, 'and which, according to him, have all failed from mismanagement, notwithstanding they had exclusive privileges'.[4] Indeed, looking at the actual history of joint-stock enterprises, particularly those in mining and manufacturing industry, even from the less dogmatic point of view of the twentieth century rather than the antimercantilism of the eighteenth, such a conclusion is inevitable. These companies, no matter how well favoured by royal concessions, by monopolies or by technical innovation, came to grief almost without exception. The wonder was that there should be a body of men willing to invest in them in each new generation, rather than that the public should distrust their managers.

The causes of the disasters fall into several groups. In some cases companies were foredoomed to failure from the start, wasting too much of their capital, either by bribery or by letting it seep into the promoters' pockets instead of into productive purposes, or by copying the overelaborate and costly overheads of the existing large companies. It is worth noting that this tendency to invest in status, power or influence rather than in productive equipment is the bane of most industrializing countries at a similar stage of their development. In others capital was wasted by overestimating the likely production, sales or profits, especially in mining. Elsewhere costs could not be brought down to those of foreign products, or techniques could not be mastered, or the attempts to corner the market or create a home monopoly fell flat. In other cases, again, managers defrauded the proprietors, or disappeared. Thus, apart from the cases of deliberate fraud by the promoters (and the promoters themselves were often the managers), the causes of failure could usually be put down to faults in 'management' of a kind which it would be plausible to believe that men administering their own property would not commit; and, in contrast with the trading companies, the only units of productive manufacture generally successful as such were those subcontracted and in which, therefore, the 'managers' ' own property was at stake.

Some glances at the history of industrial companies of any size should prove instructive. Among the earliest the companies of the Mines Royal and of the Mineral and Battery Works, both formally established in 1568, and both setting up enterprises which were large by any standards, would appear at first sight to have begun in the most favourable circumstances: they had the use of technical innovation with the help of skilled foreign immigrants, a large capital and a legal monopoly. Yet, with the possible exception of the Tintern iron wire works, and an occasional satisfactory rent income from leasing out mines or works, both companies made enormous losses and were commercial failures. Letting the works to farm was said to be 'perhaps the best solution, as they had no one available who could

assume the position of managing director and control their manufacturing activities'.[1] The nature of the partial successes is significant,
and so is the fact that in the period of their consolidation, in the early
seventeenth century, they used most of their resources in attempts to
control their markets, by import and export restrictions and a
monopoly of pin- and wire-making, rather than by improving their
technical equipment.

Among the causes of failure must be reckoned technical difficulties and the inability to transplant efficiently Continental
methods;[2] overestimate of the yield of copper-mines and inability to
deal effectively with ore which was different in composition from
German ores; high costs due to other causes, such as transport or
extravagance; poor supervision; wasteful expenditure on the bribery
of courtiers; inability to raise enough capital, partly because early
estimates had been too low, and partly because many shareholders
were unable to meet their calls; frauds by managers and farmers; or
just 'mismanagement'. In the words of Moses S. Stringer, the
Mineral Master General of the combined companies, in 1712:

> their affairs were much obstructed and prejudiced by neglects,
> treachery, frauds and perjuries of their clerks and solicitors, and
> others employed by them, who omitted to call courts, and give
> due intelligence of many things relating to their concerns, which
> proved of very evil consequence to the interest of the society.[3]

Somehow, there was never a proper link established between the
adventurers in London and the scattered works in the provinces,[4]
and their history may aptly be said to 'illustrate the difficulties
experienced in the internal management of companies during this
early period'.[5] In the seventeenth century Sir Hugh Myddleton and
Thomas Bushell appear to have been successful in farming the
company's Cardiganshire silver-mines, but on their reversion to the
Company they again produced little, if any, profit to the shareholders.[6]

The contemporary attempt to create a salt-producing monopoly,
by a large-scale application of Continental methods, failed at least
as much because of the mutual jealousies of courtiers and merchants
as because of incompetence.[7] Saltmaking, however, was soon carried
on effectively by private adventure. The seventeenth-century salt
monopoly, investing a reputed sum of £14,000 in buying out existing
interests, was equally unsuccessful in 1636–9.[8]

The other sixteenth-century enterprise of any consequence was
the Mines Royal Company of Scotland, which succeeded in mining

and refining some gold, certainly from 1567 onwards. The company, however, was merely an appendage to a single entrepreneur, and the actual work was performed by subcontractors, so that no problems of management arose.

Many more industrial enterprises of a corporate structure and on a large scale were started in the seventeenth century. The projects arising directly from the gild organizations, like those of the Pewterers (1615–20), the Feltmakers (1612) and the Pinmakers (1616 and 1635–40), not to mention Alderman Cockayne's cloth export scheme of 1615, were all essentially schemes for regulating and monopolizing large-scale selling, while leaving production in its existing scattered units.[1] Yet it is significant that the Feltmakers, at least, were aware how far the success of their national marketing scheme depended on the skill and integrity of the managers of the proposed warehouse. All these projects failed, more or less disastrously. There were several diverse reasons for these failures, but among them were technical inefficiency, overcapitalization and the inability of the large organization to survive on a competitive basis. Many of the monopolists were 'not industrial managers, but pure financiers, and others mere swindlers'.[2]

Several companies were established in the second half of the century, particularly in Scotland, for productive enterprises. Despite their monopolistic privileges, very few lasted for more than a few years. Those which did, like the Glasgow soaperie of 1667, originally joined with a whale-fishing enterprise which soon lapsed, and the Leith Wool-card Manufactory of 1663, were really small-scale partnerships, like their parallel but less grandly named English enterprises, and many, in any case, did not survive the Union.

The York Buildings Company, founded in 1665, deserves separate mention. Originally founded as a water-supply company, it turned to broader speculation in 1719. It invested over £309,000 in large forfeited Scottish estates, which it attempted to administer indirectly, by leasing them to middlemen who were to remit the rents to London. Such a system, based partly on trust, was bound to fail, and a timber business, set up on a large scale, also suffered from mismanagement and extravagance and led to a loss of £28,000 in four years. The company then used its large resources to set up ironworks, saltworks, and glassworks and to mine for a large variety of minerals in Scotland,

> but all that the Company did was to introduce a few industries to a languid existence and fill the pockets of the Edinburgh lawyers by means of a rich crop of litigation.[3]

Where mineral ore was found, as in the case of the lead-mines, the results fell into the accepted pattern: first the company was involved in a large expenditure (some of it incurred with the object of raising share values in London) and then it made large losses. Finally, the mines were leased to an entrepreneur on the spot, Francis Grant, in 1737, who made them pay to benefit his own pocket, until the works were closed down in 1740.

It is now difficult to decide whether incompetent management or dishonesty was the more powerful cause of these sorry results. The later history of the company continued to be one of fraud, of losses by the company, together with the enrichment of the local agents in Scotland, out of what were in some cases well-paying estates. The winding-up Act was passed in 1777, but as rising land values produced much greater dividends than shareholders had had cause to expect, there was much further chicanery, and the final sharing-out was not completed until 1802, litigation continuing until 1824.[1]

The promotion mania of the 1690s, arising out of at least some genuine investment opportunities, brought forth a few companies intending to engage in mining and manufacturing, including lead- and copper-mining, iron-smelting, salt, glass, saltpetre and textile manufacture.[2] Some of these collapsed almost at once; others yielded small-scale productive units, well below the critical size at which management problems began, or they were acting as putters-out to pre-existing small-scale domestic workshops. Three, however, deserve special mention.

The English Copper Company, incorporated in 1691, set up works at Lower Redbrook in the Forest of Dean, and amalgamated with other works in 1720, to take some active part in the expansion of the industry in the eighteenth century and survive into the nineteenth.[3] This limited success was achieved essentially by subletting all direct management to active partners who were on the spot.

The so-called 'Quaker' or London Lead Company was even more successful. Formed in 1704–5 as an amalgamation of three concerns, a Company to smelt Lead with Sea Coal (1692), the Royal Mines Copper Company (1692) and the Ryton Company, the company was mining and smelting lead, over its long history, in Wales, Derbyshire, Ireland, Scotland, the Isle of Man and the North of England, and survived until 1905, showing satisfactory returns to its shareholders over most of this period. Its exceptional history will repay closer study.

At first there was little to mark it out from other enterprises. In 1692 the lead-smelting company, having taken over an existing

17

Bristol works, found the buying of ore and the smelting done ineffi-
ciently, 'the Bristol agent was accused of malpractices and bad
management, and after investigations was dismissed'. Again, in the
1730s it was stated,

> The Irish mines suffer under a weak manager who has allowed
> a Tippling House Keeper to get control and to give absurd
> wages for poor work. All improvements are opposed except in
> shotmaking.[1]

Early on, however, the company adopted a rule of regular inspection by district agents or by Court members who were experienced merchants or engineers. Four members of the Court, in
particular, 'travelled round all the mines, designed works, reported
on markets, processes, legal points, etc.' Although direct control was
loosened after the 1730s, when the original partners died or retired
and for a period management was less efficient,[2] there was a marked
recovery in 1792. All the workings were concentrated in the North
and came under the control of a single 'general agent' or secretary-
manager resident locally in Nenthead. Below him was a regular
hierarchy of district agents, 'mill agents', 'washing agents', and
'underground agents', all well trained and qualified, and all with
clearly defined limits of authority. With its carefully-thought-out
training and promotion programme, and its social welfare schemes
for workers coupled with an unusually tight discipline over them,
the company became one of the pioneers of modern management in
the nineteenth century.

Success thus depended on several factors. The company was
technically highly efficient, and took steps to see that it remained so.
It was also dominated by sober businessmen, intent on laying solid
industrial foundations, rather than by courtiers and speculators
hoping for quick profits.

> In mining practice, their contribution has been most marked in
> the insistence on long-date forward planning. At a time when
> mining was essentially an adventure, when most workings were
> confined to surface quarrying on the backs of the vein, we find
> the company at the outset of their work, planning long deep
> levels that will take from ten to twenty years to complete.[3]

Rational business attitude was thus important. One of the earliest
and most important ways in which this attitude showed itself,
however, was the careful way in which the management of very

large, scattered enterprises was planned and guided. In the attention to management problems, and in at least their partial solution, there is one important explanation of the company's exceptional progress.

The third example is, however, more typical. The Mine Adventurers of England were incorporated in 1698 to take over, as a going concern, Sir Carbery Price's silver mines in Cardiganshire and smelting works there and at Neath. From the outset the promoters of the company, led by Sir Humphrey Mackworth, revealed themselves to be more interested in share speculations than in production: they offered to the public not shares as such but lottery tickets for shares. The frauds, embezzlements and high-handed disregard of the shareholders' interests which followed are too numerous and complex to be traced in detail here. Suffice it to state that the company as a whole was quite unable to control the Mine Steward or 'Principal Manager', William Waller, a skilled northern mine engineer,[1] nor Sir Humphrey himself, the perpetual Deputy Governor, one of the most enterprising and ingenious engineers, lawyers and businessmen of his day, nor yet his secretary, William Shiers, and failed to make them work for the company's, rather than their own, interests.

> Alterations in such Management [it was said of Waller] (where it is difficult to find a skilful and Honest Man) are dangerous, all Misfortunes that should follow would be imputed by some to the Alteration; besides he had a considerable interest, and he gave great Assurance of Success.[2]

Hopes were absurdly raised by ludicrous calculations of possible returns from the mines,[3] and funds were squandered, not only by being shared out among the leading speculators, but also by careless management on the ground. It was only a quarrel between Mackworth and Waller in 1707 which brought some of the malpractices into the open, but the issue was never fully resolved, despite a House of Commons resolution of 1710 that Sir Humphrey, together with Shiers and Thomas Dykes, the Treasurer, had been guilty of 'many notorious and scandalous Frauds and indirect Practices',[4] and in 1720 he returned briefly to influence in the company. The Mine Adventurers illustrate the 'ruin of an industrial enterprise by mismanagement and dishonesty on the financial side',[5] and as a productive concern they remained of negligible consequence, though they survived to amalgamate with the older companies as the 'United Mines'.

The companies created in the eighteenth and even the early nineteenth centuries for industrial purposes did little to redeem the reputation of that type of organization. The Carron Company, established in 1759 in Scotland to work and smelt iron on a large scale by the latest techniques available, had the benefit of the direct supervision by some of its proprietors from the beginning, but suffered from 'over-expansion, faulty capitalization, and—most pernicious of all—divisions among its directors'.[1] It suffered still more from lack of adequate management. Under Gascoigne's draconian rule the company was put back on its feet, though the benefits accrued to himself rather than to other partners or the creditors. When he left, the company fell victim to a particularly able and unscrupulous family of managers, whose depredations have become classic.[2] The Albion Steam Corn Mill, built in 1784–6 for a partnership including Boulton and Watt, was another well-known example of a large firm ruined by the mismanagement of a salaried staff, though the proprietors included some of the most competent businessmen of the day. The British Plate Glass Co. of 1773 showed all the typical faults of waste and incompetence, though its performance improved after reorganization in 1792.[3] The short-lived Cornish Metal Company of 1785 could be compared most closely with the early Stuart monopolies of purchase and sale, rather than with the other contemporary companies, and it failed largely for commercial reasons. Nevertheless, the impossibility of maintaining adequate direction over so large an enterprise, and the incompetent detailed management, especially of warehouses, were noticeable features. It was, perhaps, not surprising that Boulton proposed for his Brass Company a manager who would pay his own workers, and carry his own risk, in return for a contract price.[4]

Even in the early nineteenth century we find companies such as the Basingstoke Canal Company ceasing to act as carrier in 1840 because it could 'in no way control' the expenses of navigation; 'it made their accounts voluminous and difficult, [and] obliged them to keep additional servants, upon whom also they were in a degree dependent'. The Thames and Severn Committee agreed, having

> long been aware of the disadvantages attending a large company, conducting so complicated and distant a concern, as the trade between London and the Ports on the River Severn . . . a large company being necessarily exposed to impositions, which individuals may avoid.[5]

The failures of the mining companies promoted in the boom of 1825 were due as much to fraud as to the mismanagement which was then associated with the indirect administration of corporate enter-

prise,[1] although in at least one case, that of the Arigna Iron and
Coal Co., situated in Ireland, the promoters promised to end a
period of inferior management under the former Company's Act,
by better management on incorporation, largely to be achieved by
going over from day work to piece work.[2]

Altogether, examples of dishonest, absconding or alcoholic
managers who did much damage to their firms abound in this
period;[3] and this experience reinforced the current theories that
self-interest was the only possible driving force in industry. There
were here two separate strands of economic doctrine: one looking
upon joint-stock companies as naturally seeking profit by monopoly
rather than by efficiency, and thus harming the public interest; and
the other stating that all large enterprises, indirectly administered,
invited fraud as well as lack of adequate interest or drive on the part
of merely salaried staff, and thus harming the owners. Both, however, led to identical practical conclusions.

Examples of these views could be found in all industries. In the
cotton industry it was significantly in the early nineteenth century
that those knowledgeable about cotton spinning decided that the
reason for the failure of Wyatt and Paul must have been the absence
of the partners from the works, and the control by a manager:
'disorder, negligence and mismanagement were the natural results
of the absence of the principal'.[4] In New Lanark, in the days of
David Dale, a co-operative journal alleged in 1826,[5] by reason of
the absence of the owner and the management by 'various servants',
'the population lived in idleness and poverty, in almost every kind
of crime; consequently in debt, out of health, and in misery'. In
1816 Sir Robert Peel was even more uncompromising:

> It is impossible [he alleged] for a mill at any distance to be
> managed, unless it is under the direction of a partner or a
> superintendent who has an interest in the success of the business.[6]

In the silk industry the tone of the questions and answers in the
following exchange before the Select Committee of 1831 are
significant:

> Q.: If a manufacturer leaves the management of his business
> entirely to a servant, do you think any business is likely to
> succeed in England in that way now?
> A. (Thomas Sawer): I know that it has succeeded.
> Q.: You mean formerly?
> A.: Yes.[7]

In coal-mining a textbook of 1708 set out to teach coal-owners how not to be cheated 'by their head servants, or such who imploy the poor Labourers or Miners in the Collieries', while as late as 1829 it could be alleged, even in the northern coal district, that accidents were more likely where inspection was left to under-managers.[1] Again, in the paper industry, it was stated in 1813 that

> the impossibility of the Proprietor's giving his constant and personal attention must operate greatly to the injury of the concern, or admitting it could be procured, the expense of others to effect the same must be greater.[2]

Finally, in the iron industry, where works tended to be large and distant from the towns, the tradition of the untrustworthiness of 'servants' was clear and long established. Ambrose Crowley, who had at one time rejected the offer of a Sussex furnace, on the grounds of having 'soe many workes of my owne that it is impossible for me to think of managing this', spent much of his great energies devising a system of management at long distance by means of a watertight code of laws: 'his letters indicate a profound lack of faith in the integrity and wisdom of individual managers'.[3] In 1790 Robert Lindsay wrote to his brother about their ironworks as follows:

> unless the Merchants bestow their whole time and attention to a manufacture of this kind, where there is so much competition, it never can be productive but to the proprietor of the estate;

and in 1796:

> The proprietor of these works by residing on the spot and being up to the business in all its subordinate detail may make a livelihood, but . . . it would never, I say, never, answer conducted by a Manager.[4]

In 1819 Darwin's ironworks at Elsecar was said to be 'suffering greatly thro' mismanagement, and want of personal attention in the Principals', and as late as 1860 William Crawshay II wrote to his son, from a lifetime of experience:

> I know what the Master's Eye is—nothing can go long without it and I dread the consequences of your longer continued inability to personally look after the large concern at Cyfarthfa.[5]

The sequel will show that, as a generalization, this sort of attitude was a serious libel on the newly rising profession of industrial managers. To some extent it was changing in the first quarter of the nineteenth century. The injunction of Edward Pease to George Stephenson, when ordering him to re-survey the Stockton-Darlington line, represents a much more positive approach: 'we wish thee to proceed in all thy levels, estimates and calculations with that care and economy which would influence thee if the whole of the work was thy own'.[1]

Nevertheless, up to the end of the eighteenth century at least, the opposite view predominated: management was a function of direct involvement by ownership, and if it had to be delegated either because of the absence of the principals or because of the size of the concern, then the business was courting trouble. This was a powerful argument against the enlargement of firms beyond the point at which an intermediate stratum of managers became necessary.

In the past this problem has habitually been confused in the literature with the problems of monopoly, since large companies, especially those with joint-stock and limited-liability privileges, tended to monopoly, and monopoly 'constantly tended to stifle enterprise'.[2] George Unwin, who saw economic development as the result of the struggle between the forces of darkness and of light, represented by monopoly and free competition respectively, went even further. Asking why so little was heard of economic activity in the seventeenth century, and why the industrial revolution did not occur a century earlier, he was convinced that

> The answer to both questions is the same. The triumph of honest enterprise was overshadowed by the feverish delusions of speculation and the selfish greed of monopoly.[3]

Today we would look for answers within a somewhat wider compass. We would look to the general conditions in which the 'selfish greed' of private competitive enterprise flourishes best; we would consider quantities of capital, size of markets, growth of population, attitudes of mind and legal restraints, among many others. Despite the belief of Nef that technical needs had in earlier centuries demanded firms of large size, we would today make the industrial revolution dependent, among other factors, on technological and scientific innovation which to some extent had a momentum and a logic of growth of its own.

Some real continuity of thought remains, however. In the centuries preceding the industrial revolution, firms engaged in production were unable to cope with the problem of size, essentially because they could not cope with the problems of management which it involves. After 1750 developments in marketing and in

23

technology made it imperative, if progress was to continue, that businesses should grow beyond the size which a single proprietor or a small group of partners could directly overlook. Firms *had* to cope, and they learnt to do so. This process of learning to manage large units, within a competitive, progressive environment and within a framework of economic motivation, is the subject-matter of the remainder of this book.

2/ Large-scale Enterprise on the Eve of the Industrial Revolution

Management of large industrial enterprises has many facets, and it has been argued above that previous experience had found partial solutions to some of them. Thus military organizations had developed techniques for the control of large numbers of men by the enforcement of discipline over several layers of authority; Government departments had learnt to administer large properties, though without having to show a competitive profit; and privileged overseas and other trade corporations had learnt to make use of accounts to present large numbers of economic facts in manageable form.

The most immediately relevant experience, however, was to be found among the many different large-scale industrial units which had been established by the early eighteenth century. They had this in common with the later firms of the industrial revolution, that they had to show a commercial success in a competitive environment, though they did not have to control numerous workers closely collaborating with much expensive capital equipment in a productive process. This chapter is devoted to an examination of the experience of these enterprises, and their relevance to the rise of industrial management. Many of the firms and the personnel concerned were, of course, among those which made the transition to the large-scale enterprises that typified the industrial revolution.

I

The earliest of these enterprises was the agricultural estate. The units were frequently very large indeed even before the middle of the eighteenth century, and formed by far the most important source of large individual incomes. This had been true, in the past, of most traditional societies. Typically, however, in those societies the unit of production is very small, consisting of a peasant family, and the large incomes arise out of rent payments, dues or services which have a legal-compulsory rather than an economic basis, and there is thus no problem of 'management'. Even where the *latifundium* type of estate had developed it was not normally 'managed' with purely economic incentives and for purely economic aims, nor was it much troubled by a progressive, changing technology. In eighteenth-century Britain, by contrast, there were numerous estates on which demesne farming, or the 'home farm', had developed into an important enterprise. More important still, under the influence of the much-vaunted achievements of the 'new husbandry', even the indirect administration of the whole estate had become a type of economic 'management' by influencing the actions of tenants as well as of ancillary rural enterprises, such as quarries or lime kilns.

None of this was strictly new. The direct or indirect administration of estates and of large farms for purposes of maximizing yields went back many centuries, and some accounts of such estates survive from Elizabethan days.[1] Moreover, the principles of running them had not changed between the sixteenth and the eighteenth centuries in this country,[2] and similar developments could be traced in the other major countries of Europe. By the middle of the eighteenth century there had been established, in Great Britain at least, some rules of administration and routines of management on the leading estates, and these showed many of the characteristics of the adolescent industrial firms.

There was much in common between a large coal-mine or an ironworks and an estate like that of Lord Dudley and Ward, which in 1701 named fifteen bailiffs and other agents in its rent roll, or the Norfolk estates, grossing £32,000 p.a. about 1800, or the for-feited estates administered by Greenwich Hospital, or perhaps the Cokes' of Norfolk estates, administered with striking efficiency by several generations of bailiffs, who standardized leases, laid down detailed instructions and spread the benefits of the experiments on the home farm amongst all the tenants.[3] The parallels were not lost on contemporaries, but before they are driven too far the differences should be emphasized.

Agricultural estates were rarely in direct competition with each other, either for markets or for factors of production. Moreover, the economy of the estate was at least as much a function of social status and social aspirations as of economic calculation, and the power of the squire or bailiff over the village had many undertones which, though they were not completely absent from the factory village of 1770, had certainly disappeared there by 1830. Finally, the landlords as ultimate beneficiaries of the estate economy enjoyed an easy control over the levers of political power which allowed them to use, as it were, extra-market means, such as the Private Enclosure Act, when the market threatened not to produce the right results for them.

In consequence the atmosphere within which the internal estate administration took place was different from that, for example, of the Manchester cotton spinner: as improvement was not undertaken for the sake of a direct competitive advantage, the mainspring of the capitalist economy was missing. One of the most striking aspects of this, and it is one touching the core of the subject of this book, was that estate agents exchanged experience much more freely, and management practices, considering the numbers and distances involved, spread much more quickly. While there were no textbooks whatever for industrial managers before 1830, other than purely technical works for coal-viewers, accountants and the like, the estate agent as a manager of his lord's affairs was aided by quite a number of far-ranging guide-books.[1] At the same time estates survived longer than industrial concerns in an unchanged form and routines were developed more easily.[2] While agricultural historians tend to stress the diversity among estate bailiffs and among their practices and status, the industrial historian is struck by their relative uniformity and firm traditions.

The typical agent was responsible for setting on farms, drawing up leases and tenancy agreements, seeing them observed, collecting rents, being the driving force behind the manorial court, if any, levying fines, 'riding the boundaries' in some districts, improving and supervising the home farm, keeping the estate accounts, including making payments to staffs, paying taxes, tithes and rates, watching poachers, and often supervising the household. When the master was away he might live in state in the house himself, and his responsibilities were correspondingly increased also during the minority of the master. Surviving instruction books not only stress the need to buy in the cheapest market and sell in the dearest but also enlarge on the less tangible psychological aspects of management. The superintendent on the Fitzwilliam estates was to

> endeavour, as much as possible, to promote the Comfort and Happiness of every industrious Person employed in the several Departments, by a fair and reasonable allowance of Wages, or Provisions, as the case may be, but by every possible means to prevent Idleness, Extravagance, Waste and Immorality,

and to act in every way as if the Earl were present himself.[3]

On the larger estates the agents might become, or be given the status of, minor squires in their own right; others had legal training, and the link with the legal profession was particularly close in Scotland.

> The nineteenth-century solicitor was well versed in financial matters. This is not surprising when considered against the history of estate management and arranging of loans by the legal profession from medieval times. By the eighteenth century such business activity was a major part of most Solicitors' operations.[1]

It was precisely because of the important share of estate administration handled by the legal profession in Scotland that accountancy itself became professionalized there long before it reached a similar stage south of the border.

More important, perhaps, was the fact that estate stewards were also, increasingly, men with much business acumen. Edward Hughes describes the competition for the post of estate steward for the Lords of the Manor of Gateshead in 1736, for which four well-qualified mathematical practitioners were considered, but which was ultimately given to a skilled farmer, who was a large tenant also. James Dodson, author of one of the most original textbooks of accountancy of his century, published in 1750, was at one time employed about the Earl of Macclesfield's estates. Bryan Donkin, F.R.S., one of the most inventive engineers of his day, was the son of an estate steward and coal-viewer in the North, and was trained as a steward on the estate of the Duke of Dorset. Again, the Holker estate was managed by a succession of eminent agronomists and able businessmen.[2] Conversely, John Perkins, senior executive of Thrale's brewery, would supervise the administration of Mrs. Thrale's agricultural estate.[3] In the eighteenth century,

> efficiency in administration was clearly of the first importance in so large and complex a business organisation as the great estate,[4]

and in the nineteenth century agents came increasingly to exercise not merely audit control but also management control over their farms, in the interest of efficiency.[5]

It was inevitable that a pushing and commercialized society should throw up agents who used their business ability and experience for their own as much as their employers' benefit. James Graham, for example, agent of the Earl of Cardigan, leased some land near Kirkstall, built up a series of mills and a goit, and leased them to industrialists, including the largest woollen manufacturer of all,

Benjamin Gott. William James, the railway enthusiast, was an estate agent, and so was John Blenkinsop, one of the most successful of locomotive pioneers. Best known of all were the two brothers, Thomas and John Gilbert, agents for the Earl of Gower and the Duke of Bridgewater, respectively, who not only developed their masters' estates, but were large-scale entrepreneurs in their own right. On a smaller scale, William Smith, civil engineer, pioneer geologist and land steward in Yorkshire, Isaac Bonne, agent of the Overton Hall Estate, Ashover, and one of the most active promoters of turnpikes and soughs in the county, and William and Thomas Barker, stewards to the Dukes of Devonshire and Rutland, respectively, and founders of a flourishing lead-mining and smelting business in 1729, also in Derbyshire, were typical of many more.[1]

Apart from the personal interest of the agents, however, many estate-owners developed large industrial enterprises themselves. The link was most direct in the case of mining, particularly coal-mining in the North and in Cumberland. There the estate agent became the chief mine manager, responsible not only for the conduct of the mine lessees, but also for the railways, bridges, staithes and other works which the mining companies might need. Many large estates, of course, administered their own mines, and among them were some of the most efficient, technically and managerially, as, for example, the Whitehaven collieries of the Lowther estates. South Yorkshire and North Derbyshire was another area in which some large estates developed substantial collieries, a few of which, like the Norfolk mines in the years 1780–1805, were at times worked direct for the owner by a skilled manager. In South Wales, again,

> in the eyes of the [landowners] there was no essential difference between winning their own coal, or smelting iron ore with charcoal made from their own woods, or working on a home farm.[2]

Even the sinking of capital was not new to them, as the better-run agricultural estates, at least, had also depended on much capital investment.[3]

Collieries were not the only large units to be managed by or for landowners. In some areas coal was found together with iron ore, and the estate developed its own ironworks, besides other enterprises such as tar-works. In Cornwall it might take a direct hand in tin- or copper-mining, and in Anglesey the copper-mining and smelting enterprises of Parys mountain were generally in the hands of the original landowners. A large complex of collieries, canals, timber plantations, boatyards and many other works were built up by the Duke of Bridgewater 'as an extension of the Worsley estates'.

In each case the estate agent, in the name of the landowner, was the superior of the industrial or mining manager.[1] The experience of the landed estate was therefore directly relevant, and its practice was enforced on its industry. Sometimes the influence was local and individual, but there were whole industries, such as coal-mining, which built their practices to a large extent on those of their direct forerunner, the agricultural estate.

II

While the agricultural estate might foreshadow some of the methods used later in the factories, the industrial 'domestic system' was often a more immediate ancestor. Many later factory-owners, especially in the textile trades, began as putting-out merchants and experienced the transformation in their own lifetimes and in their own firms. The line of historical evolution is tolerably clear. Just as at the end of the Middle Ages expanding markets and improved techniques, particularly the concentration of certain processes in large units such as blast furnaces or water-mills, had to be matched by the development of a merchanting or putting-out system out of the handicraft-gild system, so in the eighteenth century the success with which the merchant controllers of still largely domestic industrial processes expanded their markets set up the pressures which ultimately produced modern industrialism.

There is here, on the one hand, the link with the merchant and the mercantile community. By the middle of the century the merchant had been provided with a costly and routinized apprenticeship which could lead to high attainments, and he was usually also well supplied with capital and was not without political influence.[2] Many of his organizational and administrative ideas were worth copying, and became part of the fabric of factory organization. Benjamin Gott's remark, in 1828:

> I was brought up as a merchant, and became a manufacturer, rather from possessing capital than understanding the manufacture. I paid for the talents of others in the different branches of manufacture[3]

could have been made with equal justification by several others, including David Dale, each one of whose cotton mills was managed by an active, expert partner. At the same time there was also much direct transfer of talents and resources. Anthony Bacon, the Whitehaven merchant who became the founder of the South Wales mass-produced iron industry,[1] was no isolated phenomenon. The merchants' branch organization, their use of managers and their recognition of the importance of 'management', as well as their attention to profitability, had had their direct influence on industry since the sixteenth century, when the large German merchant houses transformed European mining and metallurgy; 'the methods of commerce were applied to industry', as one writer has put it.[2]

On the other hand, there was the less direct but more pervasive and more permanent influence of the putting-out system itself. It was a system of industry in which large-scale trade in manufactured goods, much of it overseas, was organized by merchant houses which disposed over much capital and considerable administrative and office staff, yet had to depend on the work performed in innumerable tiny domestic workshop units, unsupervised and unsupervisable. Such incompatibility was bound to set up tensions and to drive the merchants to seek new ways of production, imposing their own managerial achievements and practices on the productive sector.

The general methods of the putting-out system have often been described.[3] Apart from the West Riding woollen industry, 'the plan of giving out material and paying wages was characteristic of every other important industry in the eighteenth century'.[4] It was found not only in the textile industries but also in clothing, in the metal goods manufacture, such as nailing and cutlery, in the making of watches, straw hats, articles of wood and leather and many others, and as such survived in some cases into the twentieth century. The original basis of it was a primitive technique and a wide market; but the dynamic elements were the division of labour and the accumulation of capital which became possible on the basis of the system.

The sums of capital employed, largely in stocks of raw materials and finished goods, were large by any standards, and very much larger than anything employed in the early 'factory' industry in fixed equipment. While many West Country clothiers were said to be worth £40,000–£50,000, there were individuals or partnerships whose capital, like Benjamin Gott's, was in the range of £100,000–£200,000. Sums such as these represented a complex organization and employment running into hundreds, and in some cases into thousands.

In 1736 two brothers employed 600 looms and 3,000 persons in the Blackburn district; a little before 1750 a Warrington sail-cloth manufacturer employed 5,000 persons; in 1758 a small

31

group of Manchester check makers employed a great many of the weavers of Ashton, Oldham and Royton, and one spoke of employing 500 himself. The same state of things prevailed in other industries. In the Woollen district three families virtually controlled the trade of Rochdale and the surrounding valleys. Seven silk firms in Macclesfield in 1761 employed 2,470 persons in throwing alone.[1]

While these figures are obviously rounded upwards, and silk-throwing was a factory industry, such figures for putting-out employers could easily be matched from areas outside Lancashire and from later decades. Radcliffe, in 1801, employed 1,000 weavers in three counties and a Belfast firm was said to employ 600 looms; in 1812 at least fifteen employers giving evidence, representing hosiery, worsted, woollen, flannel, silk and cotton manufacture, blanket and smallware makers, employed 300 each or more: among them, James Kay of Bury, was said to be employing 2,500–3,000, and Thomas Cardwell, of Manchester, over 1,000. In 1769 a Warrington shoe-making firm employed 400–500 men, and a Glasgow firm 500 in 1773. One silk firm was said to employ 3,900 in 1825, and a West Country clothier 1,500 in 1833; John Foster employed 700 outweavers in 1836. In 1812 one buttonmaking 'dealer' employed 1,200 women and children, in 1802 an Aberdeen cotton manufacturer employed 3,000–4,000, and in 1831 we hear of a Coventry ribbon-weaver employing 900–1,000 persons, a Belper firm employing 400 silk and 2,500 cotton stocking frames, and a Somerset manufacturer employing 800, among others such.[2]

Clearly numbers like these needed a staff of agents and managers, as well as warehouse control, clerks and assistants, and brought their own problems of organization. Some merchants used middlemen trading virtually at their own risk and possibly with their own capital, such as 'foggers' in the Black Country or 'fustian masters' in Lancashire.[3] Others employed agents on commission, sometimes called 'undertakers', 'bagmen', or 'putters-out', who again took much of the ultimate employers' burdens on their own shoulders.[4] There were firms, however, which worked largely by paid agents or managers and therefore had much of the problems of the factories without their facilities for supervision.[5] The fact that the business operations, with outworkers as well as customers and other merchants, were conducted on the basis of a vast complex network of indebtedness, in which balances were cleared perhaps only once or twice a year, if ever, made any book-keeping or accountancy control even more difficult and hazardous.[6]

With the growth in the size of firms the achievement of control over production, particularly its speed, regularity and quality, as well as the prevention of embezzlement, became wellnigh impossible tasks within the framework of the putting-out system. Sometimes, as in the classic case of the West Country clothiers, noted by Arthur Young and Dean Tucker, the vast organization of outwork had become too ossified to accept changes in techniques or organization.[1] But wherever it was possible, factory organization began to be considered the lesser evil, despite its obvious drawbacks and even without the incentive of superior technique.

The attempts of masters to check the embezzlement of raw materials given out to domestic workers can be traced in the increasingly severe and explicit legislation of 1749, 1774, and 1777. The problem, significantly, appears to have assumed major proportions only in the third quarter of the century, though the system itself was centuries old. The Manchester manufacturers took common action in 1766, and in 1764 the worsted masters set up a prosecuting committee, appointing inspectors in 1773. Under the Worsted Act of 1777 a campaign of prosecutions was set in train by 'Worsted Committees' in Lancashire and Yorkshire, though it had but indifferent results. Similar action was taken by employers in the silk and waste industry, like the Strutts, and the problem was acute also in the nailing industry. It was particularly in the case of expensive raw material, such as the long-haired Spanish wool, that the potential losses by embezzlement were likely to outweigh any of the disadvantages of bringing all the workers under one roof, and led to concentration of this kind.[2]

> The principal Motive of those Clothiers who have weaving at home is to guard themselves from those Embezzlements which take place to an enormous extent in the Houses of the Weavers.[3]

More positively, the wish to control the rate of supply and its quality furnished another incentive to bring workers together into a central workshop or 'manufactory', directly under the master's eye. The Spencer ironmaster partnership had difficulty in selling their nails, as 'the supervision of outworkers supplied' was 'inadequate'. Peter Stubs, for the same reason, built nearby workshops for his formerly domestic file workers.[4] In textiles, it was said as late as 1840:

> The employer of domestic weavers can never tell within a fortnight or three weeks when every web sent out to the neighbouring

> villages will be returned . . . embezzlement of yarn . . . the risk of the work being taken out of the loom to be sold or pawned by a dishonest weaver . . . wrangling and disputes between the foreman and the men . . .[1]

Where the outworkers were part-timers, particularly adolescents and women, and where the merchants' agent was the local shopkeeper who was unwilling to incur unpopularity, the ultimate large-scale buyer could ensure neither uniform quality nor a regular supply.[2] While workers complained of the time-wasting disputes over quantities and payments, and the long waits at the warehouses, their masters, faced with the possibility that weavers might have work of five different masters in their homes, sighed for legal powers to compel men to complete their work.[3]

There was here also a powerful dynamic element at work, mentioned above, which should not be underrated. Part of the advantage of the putting-out system over the former handicraft methods had been the division of labour, and the specialization and the inventive talent which it encouraged,[4] but this process, once begun, set up its own pressure for further progress which demanded further concentration, perhaps in a central manufactory. There experiments could more easily be carried out, as the master disposed of relatively large resources; and improvements, once made, could be adopted on a large scale, until ultimately there was called forth the complex machinery and central motive power of the factory.[5]

Although not every major industry which was transformed during the Industrial Revolution went through the stage of putting-out and concentration in a central workshop-manufactory, there being some which developed directly out of handicraft conditions and others which were completely new, yet it has been tempting in the past to see this as a logical sequence in any scheme of consecutive stages of economic development. Certainly as far as organizational structure and the problems of internal management were concerned the earlier stages foreshadow, and in many cases closely parallel, the later. Historically, not only did one form arise out of the other, but there were many firms which went through the process of transformation from one stage into the next.

The penultimate stage, in which we can see the factory in embryo growing within the putting-out organization, was the combination of a central mill or workshop for some processes, with a penumbra of semi-independent outworkers for others. This form becomes typical in the last third of the eighteenth century, but is not limited to that period. At first, perhaps, only one subsidiary process is mechanized, like the fulling mill, which was, by then, of considerable antiquity, while the rest of the processes in the woollen industry remain manual; gradually mechanized methods spread, concentrating the industry increasingly in factories, until ultimately the whole industry is transformed. 'Mixed' industries or 'mixed' firms continue to exist over long periods, and in some cases, such as the making of cutlery at the end of a process beginning with blast furnaces and steelworks, full mechanization can hardly be said to be completed even today.

The process is clearest in the textile industries. In cotton the major inventions in spinning, carding and other subsidiary processes, as well as roller printing, were followed only after a generation by parallel changes in weaving; for most of our period centralized spinning mills were used to supply outworker hand weavers who increased in numbers from about 108,000 in 1788 to 240,000 in 1820 and remained at that level for some time. In Scotland the creation of the large spinning factory by the former linen putting-out merchant was particularly striking, James Finlay & Co. at one time employing 2,000 weavers and David Dale 300.[1] At New Lanark alone, in 1793, 324 persons were employed at domestic warping and weaving. Samuel Oldknow employed, in 1786, some 800 outworker spinners and weavers in Stockport and Anderton, while concentrating the finishing in his own warehouse, where he had twenty warping mills and fifty girls hand-finishing the muslin, besides controlling his own bleach and print works at Heaton.

At the beginning of the modern cotton industry we find much of the smallware manufacture concentrated in Manchester, and the bleaching and finishing processes, and sometimes even the weaving, carried out on the manufacturers' premises; Richard Arkwright supplemented the spinning work in his village mills by putting out the waste-picking into nearby cottages, while the Peels employed 6,800, in and out, in 1785. But there were traces of this 'mixed' system or 'semi-domestic, semi-factory framework'[2] even at the end of our period. J. & N. Philips employed, even in 1817, 300 looms (owned and hired out) at Tean, 120 in Cheadle, and fifty in Kingsley, before concentrating them all in their own mills; Adam & George Murray, of Manchester, in 1818, employed 919 workers 'in' and 300 'out'; Massey & Son, also of Manchester, employed 1,200 outweavers when they decided to build their own mill in 1824–5; and in 1833 John Bartholomew & Co., of Glasgow, employed 430 in two mills and 2,500 domestic weavers.[3]

In the silk industry the combination of silk-throwing mills with

35

large numbers of outweavers in a single large firm was common from the mid-eighteenth century onward. Henry Critchley, by 1818, had fifty of his 140–60 looms inside his Macclesfield factory, but even he admitted that those under his roof were only 'occasionally' under his supervision. Typically, in 1833, G. R. Ward, a Warminster silk-throwster, employed 300 workers 'in' and 300 'out'. The position was not dissimilar in the linen industry.[1] In lace-making, John Heathcote's factory in Tiverton employed, in 1833, 800–50 'in' and 1,500 workers 'out', Holyrood Mills of Chard employed 150–60 'in', 300 'out', and Wheatley & Riste of the same place, 500 and 200 respectively, and similar examples might be drawn from the framework knitting industry.[2]

Among textiles, it was, however, the woollen industry which kept its 'mixed' character longest. Partly the reasons were technical: while some processes were mechanized early, the basic spinning process remained manual for long, owing to the greater difficulty of dealing with the woollen than the cotton fibres. Partly, they were organizational: the industry, being old and firmly established, warded off innovation more successfully than cotton or silk,[3] and absorbed only those mechanized processes which would leave its basic domestic-merchanting structure intact.

The first phase of mechanization was represented in the West Riding by the scribbling mill which, like the fulling mill of old, could be set up by independent firms or by the manufacturers themselves on a co-operative basis, without disturbing the rest of the domestic structure of the industry. Elsewhere, particularly in the districts producing worsteds and fine-quality goods generally, other processes were centralized, such as sorting, scouring and combing, although there were as yet only managerial, and no technical advantages to be had from this. Typically, the spinning and weaving would still be done 'out', or domestically. There are a few examples of collecting the weavers in one shed, or even a series of connected cottages, as at Newark, in a method curiously foreshadowing the 'cottage factory' of Coventry of 1847–60,[4] but these were exceptions.

Towards the end of the century, technical inventions, such as the gig mill in 1784, and shearing frames from about 1800 on, tended to concentrate more and more of the work in central workshops; Benjamin Gott was dressing and finishing the products of large numbers of independent manufacturers in his own works even in the 1820s.[5] The real breakthrough, however, came with the adaptation of machine spinning to worsted and woollen yarns, from the early 1790s onwards. The typical 'mixed' works then came to be, for the next thirty years or so, a central mill, steam or water driven, containing preparatory, finishing and spinning departments, together with large numbers of domestic weavers.[1]

Significant examples, drawn from the Factories Commission of 1833, were the following:

	Factory Employment	*Out- Workers*	*Total*
Samuel Long, Wootton Underedge	230	*c.* 400	600–700
Wm. H. Sheppard, Frome	500	1,500	2,000
Wm. Hardisty, Shepton Mallet	500	100	600
Six large companies, Trowbridge	1,010	2,520	3,500
	–1,120	–2,720	–3,800

The last main stage was the introduction of the steam loom in the years 1815–35. Even towards the end of the period this was still relatively rare, and large weaving sheds full of hand looms were still to be found; but in some areas, and in the case of the carpet looms needing water power, the transformation had come early, and even led to firms with power looms but domestic hand or jenny spinners in this period—a reverse form of 'mix'. Among them were Pease's Darlington Worsted Mills, employing in the early nineteenth century 300 looms (power looms having been introduced there in 1796), 100 combers and 5,000 hand spinners, mostly in Scotland.[2]

The 'mixed' stage was less common in other industries in our period, but was not entirely unknown. Thus in nailing Ambrose Crowley was the first to combine large rolling mills and domestic nailmakers in one firm, but in the middle of the eighteenth century other such combinations could be found in the Midlands and elsewhere as well as later on in file-making. Few large firms existed in other industries at that time, but the Warmley Company, in its famous petition of 1767, in which it asked for powers to raise its capital from £200,000 to £400,000, with powers of incorporation, claimed 2,000 employees, of whom at least 1,200 were rural pinmakers.[3]

Of all the forerunners of the factory system the domestic system was organizationally the closest. It was of particular importance for our purposes because of the dynamic elements in its structure, which drew its firms, in a competitive environment, into the kind of progress which led, sometimes dramatically and sometimes imperceptibly, into the factory system.

37

III

The domestic system was, in its ideal type at least, the appropriate form of organization for small-scale production linked with large-scale mass markets. But as in the course of the eighteenth century the size of the typical productive unit in different industries began to grow to an extent which strained the managerial capacities of the employers of the day, one of the methods adopted was to sub-contract all or part of the work. The idea of subcontract was not new. It forms a link with an earlier period, and it was often resorted to in our period even without the incentive of unmanageable size. Further, it survived into the factory age, to become, if not a method of management, at least a method of evading management.

The entrepreneur who subcontracted out part of his activities could hope thereby to reduce not only his direct supervisory duties but also to share his risks, his capital and his technical knowledge with the subcontractor. Where, as was common, the latter was paid a fixed price per unit, the large manufacturer was saved all kinds of complicated cost calculations, and a measure of stability was introduced into his cost structure. The practice also encouraged specialization by subcontractors, who might ultimately branch off to supply others besides their original employing firm. Above all, when the incentive to work of both managers and workers was far less certain than today,

> the great advantage of this system . . . was that it supplied a 'self-acting stimulus', which dispensed with the necessity of incessant supervision of the managing-foreman by the employer.[1]

There were some disadvantages inherent in subcontracting. In mines or quarries, for example, permanent damage might be done to the property by men interested in short-run returns only; the cupidity of subcontractors often led to dissatisfaction and rioting; and it inhibited the development of either high-quality workmanship or high-quality management. Thus the London Lead Company, when it suspended its contracts with individual horsekeepers and began to draw its ore itself from face to bank in 1815–16, found not only that it could do the job more cheaply, but that it acquired the kind of knowledge in the process which enabled it to improve the layout of the mines. Yet many entrepreneurs clung to the system, rather than plunge into the unknown troubles of large-scale direct management.

Subcontract thus became another pre-capitalist method of industrial organization to survive into the age of mechanization. The parallel with the domestic system is evident, and it has been tempting to see this as an early stage, the 'adolescence of industrial society', or the 'transitional stage of factory organization where the shop was still distinguishable and direct supervision had not been completely introduced':

> during the period of transition which extended well into the nineteenth century, the recruitment and the management of labour was often left in the hands of masters, foremen, subcontractors, and others for reasons of technology and of organization. This delegation of all control over the workers to a variety of middlemen was not confined to the putting-out system, but prevailed in many industries in which the workers had already been gathered under one roof.[1]

Subcontract as such, however, does not itself form a 'stage', but may be compatible with different stages of development of industrial capitalism, according to technical and commercial needs and managerial competence. It survives, in many forms, into the factory age; in some industries it survives until today, and is not necessarily inefficient or anachronistic. It is, in fact, only the dogmatism of classical political economy as developed in the nineteenth century, which looked upon the capitalist-owner-entrepreneur, facing an individual, propertyless worker, as the 'normal', highest, finite form of organization, which has led us to ignore or minimize the importance of surviving systems of subcontract, group-contract or co-operation. Since some capitalist entrepreneurs had had to fight for a system in which they could keep all the decision-making, all the control, and all the surplus over the subsistence of the workers in their own hands, and had had to destroy earlier and more equable systems, such as the laws and organizations of free miners in the Stannaries, the Mendips, Derbyshire, the Forest of Dean, Alston Moor and similar areas in Scotland[2] in the process, it is not surprising that the political economists, establishing their victorious ideology, were only too eager to belittle or forget the achievements of the earlier organization. The present study, being concerned with the problems of large-scale direct management, will necessarily follow this bias and ignore other forms of organization also; but the extent of the survival of subcontract must be traced briefly here.

Until the Joint-Stock Companies Act of 1856 facilitated the creation of the type of concern in which owners and managers were neatly separated from each other, even some of the highest echelons of firms, namely the partners themselves, showed an untidy mixture of ownership, management, subcontract and co-operation. The charcoal iron industry, with its units necessarily scattered in quest of charcoal and water power, yet attempting to supply mass markets, was perhaps the best example of this delegation, or more correctly, dovetailing of functions. Here we find, in the period following the expansion of the 1690s, groups of interlocking partnerships, in which at least one partner acted as manager of each unit, yet used the links of the partnership to make sure of his supplies or his markets in vertical integration, while the groups as a whole controlled a sufficient number of furnaces and forges to smooth out the violent fluctuations in output from each, and guarantee its survival as a whole. In the conditions of the day, a centralized administration of these groups, some of which owned several scores of units (though no individual owner had interests in as many), would have been utterly impossible; but the complex system of actual delegation appeared to work, for in their heyday these groups completely dominated the English charcoal iron and later the early coke blast furnace industry. Two combinations in particular stand out: the Foley-Knight combine of works in the Midlands and North Midlands, Cheshire, the Forest of Dean, Shropshire and Wales; and the Spencer-Fell Group, centred on Yorkshire and North Derbyshire.[1] These two groups, in fact, had some links through William Cotton, and there were further, less direct links with the Coalbrookdale combine, with the Crowley Ironworks and the South Wales ironworks. These, in turn, used the delegation-subcontract method: the Coalbrookdale partners, for example, controlling at some time the Vale Royal Furnace, the Dolgyn Furnace, the Melingriffith plating mill, Horsehay and Ketley, while the leading South Wales works were linked, in the early years, by Isaac Wilkinson, himself a link with his sons' Midland and Welsh border works. The sons of Sampson Lloyd II formed a similar linked group, there were links among the Furness Ironmasters, and, among the newer works, the Carron Company sprouted subsidiaries which acted like subcontractors, including the Kinneil colliery at Bo'ness, developed by Roebuck, one of the partners, and the shipping company, developed by Gascoigne, another.[2]

Similar systems of delegation and subcontracting, rather than combination into a unitary form of enterprise, were found in other industries and firms at that time. Among the large firms alone, David Dale, the Scots cotton-spinning pioneer, created separate partnership, with separate managing partners, for each of his mills, while continuing his merchanting interests; Boulton & Watt took some part in the management of the Cornish mines which had paid them for their steam engines partly in shares; the Neath Abbey Iron Company and the Perran Foundry, set up in 1792, were linked by almost identical ownership, yet were separately managed; and the Midland glass industry in the eighteenth century was organized not very differently from the iron industry.[1]

One of the oldest methods was that evolved in the mining districts of Cornwall, Derbyshire and elsewhere and known as the 'cost-book' system. This enabled the owners, or 'adventurers', to take shares in many mines in what was a risky and uncertain industry, without necessarily owning much in each. It delegated the functions of management to some 'managerial personnel—managers, pursers, engineers and so forth',[2] and it made the interests of adjacent mines sufficiently interlocking to allow them to co-operate, by the same cost-book method, in the construction of soughs, and even of smelt mills and marketing operations.[3]

All these examples of the delegation of duties by owners were overshadowed in importance, in this period, by the practice of subcontract proper within the firms. Its best-known examples were to be found in coal-mining, and in other mines where the nature of the workings made such arrangements almost inevitable.

It is in the relatively small-scale mines of Staffordshire, subdivided by the pillar and stall system of working, that the subcontractor, the 'butty' and his partner, the 'doggey', flourished best. Ashton and Sykes long ago suggested that

> it is possible that the difficulty of supervising relatively large numbers of men, burrowing in many small pits, at a time before modern large-scale management had come into being, may be a partial explanation of the existence of the collective contract of the Midland and Welsh coalfields.[4]

Originally, miners probably took on contracts to work certain pits as groups of equals; by the later eighteenth century, however, the typical Midland butty was a capitalist employer, whose profits depended on reducing the men's wages below the bargain price he made with the coal-owner. In South Wales, in the mid-eighteenth century, the men were paid not on the coal raised but the coal sold, which yet further increased the opportunities for disagreements. In the North Wales coalfield it was usual for the

> manager to bargain with a few charter (or chalter) masters to work the whole pit. They were the only employees who received

their wages direct from the employer, and out of these earnings they hired and paid their own gangs of assistants and provided tools, timber and waggons.[1]

Practices varied, but commonly the owner sank the pits, again usually by subcontracting with a gang of workmen, and the subcontracting groups provided many of the other capital costs and the tools.

While the sinking of deeper pits, creating larger units with costly and complex equipment, including steam engines, generally led to direct control by the pit-owner instead of subcontracting, a stage reached on Tyneside by the mid-eighteenth century,[2] the development was not all in one direction. Towards the end of the eighteenth century a number of the largest collieries in the North-East were sublet, including the Lambton pits from 1784, the pits owned by the Tempest family, and others.[3] In their case, however, the pits were sublet as a whole, sometimes several pits together, to large capitalist combines which in themselves formed major enterprises. In South Wales also the tendency was for the subcontractor to grow in stature, until by the 1840s he might employ 100 men himself. In Scotland the Carron Company imported its own skilled miners from England, allowing them to recruit their own labourer assistants without making contact with the native serfs; by 1842 several of the company's pits were, in fact, worked by contractors.

In the Cornish tin- and copper-mines the traditional and normal form of organization was the contract bargain, made between a representative of the group of adventurers and groups of workers. Of the two main types, the 'tributers' took over a pitch after an auction, working as independent contractors at their own risk, and paying the adventurers a percentage of the proceeds of the ore sales; they were usually engaged in mining proper. The 'tut-workers' contracted to perform certain specified jobs, including sinking and other dead-work for certain specified sums. These contracts might run for two to three months before bargains were renewed or auctioned off again, and groups might vary in size up to twelve men or more. Some employed their own unskilled assistants, and while some were co-operative groups of co-evals, some tributers were employers on their own account, paying the gang members a fixed wage. Other middlemen would contract for stamping and ore crushing.[4]

This system spread also to other areas, including the Anglesey companies and Ireland, where Cornish 'captains' were employed as mining experts and brought their native methods with them.[5] Almost identical forms of subcontract, appropriate to this type of mining, were also found in the older lead districts, like Derbyshire, the Scottish Leadhills and the Cardiganshire silver and lead mines, in slate quarries, in the Lakeland copper-mines and elsewhere.[1]

The other main industry in which subcontract was widespread on a large scale was cotton spinning. Here, the method was not, however, to let the mill as a whole to a substantial group of skilled workers nor yet to an entrepreneur, but to put skilled spinners in charge of extensive machinery on the understanding that they paid and recruited their own child assistants, the 'scavengers' to clean the machines, and the 'piecers'. Originally the children thus employed were of the spinners' own family, or at least children known to them, and this corresponded to the family co-operation in the domestic textile processes. Cotton masters, indeed, continued for many years after to pay out wages on a family basis, even where the members of the family were scattered over several departments.[2] In the mills in large cities, like Manchester or Glasgow, the spinner-subcontractor soon became a stranger to the children. The system was open to many abuses, and the better employers abolished it as soon as they could be certain of being fully in control of the discipline of their own mills.[3] There was also some indirect employment of this kind in weaving sheds, among carders and slubbers, and in calico printing, though it was also declining there.[4]

The statistics worked out by Samuel Stanway from returns to the Factory Commission of 1833–4, which cover 225 mills in Lancashire, Cheshire and Derbyshire, employing about one-third of the total employment in British mills, show that almost exactly half of the 20,000 child workers investigated were still employed by other operatives, the other half being employed by the firm; among spinners alone, however, 8,136 operatives under the age of 18 were hired by other workers, and only 1,043 direct by the firm, there being no information for seventy-four others. Earlier on, in 1816, a count in twenty-four factories in the Preston area had shown that 799 children there were being paid by their masters, as against 1,168 by spinners and rovers.[5]

In the other textile branches domestic weavers commonly employed boy helpers and sometimes warpers and others out of their own earnings. In the largest mechanized woollen mill in existence, that of Benjamin Gott, it was found that as late as 1815 most of the weaving, even on the premises, was done by independent 'manufacturer' contractors who were not paid by the firm, but on the contrary paid Gott a commission for the use of the factory, 'on the cloth which they made to his order and which he bought from them'.[6]

At the firm's Armley mill (though not at the Bean Ing mill) the fuller was a subcontractor, employing his own labour. Carpet weavers also employed their own assistants:

> The master manufacturer has nothing to do with them [it was stated in 1833], except that if he know of any of them being a bad character, he would require them to be dismissed.[1]

Heathcote, developing his large lace mills within an old and tradition-bound industry, created the most astonishing mixture of direct and indirect employment in his Loughborough factory: while using foremen to supervise his own workers, he allowed each foreman to employ two or three machines, and hire his own labour for them, as a subcontractor.[2]

Other industries mostly fell somewhere between the two extremes of having a small number of substantial subcontractors, as in mining, or large numbers of skilled workers as subcontractors, each employing only a few child or unskilled assistants. In South Wales, for example,

> except in the copper smelting industry, where the technique of production did not easily lend itself to this system, by far the most common method of employing and supervising labour was by contracting out part of, or a whole step in, the process of production to one or more middlemen, who thus undertook the responsibility for its efficient functioning. These contracts varied considerably in importance. In the iron industry, where the system existed extensively, they might only employ a small number as did the limebreaker, coker or ore burner; or they might be skilled workmen with a few assistants, like the moulder or the collier. Sometimes groups of workmen undertook contracts, as did the mill workers in the iron industry; and finally, the contractor might be a small sub-capitalist, undertaking a large part, or the whole, of the process of production. All types were common. . . .[3]

The Dowlais ironworks as a whole were subcontracted to a managing partnership from 1765 to 1787, when the 'managers' gained control of the proprietors' shares. In blast furnaces, bridge stockers and stocktakers in the early years would be independent contractors employing gangs of men, women, boys and horses, and similar practices were common in rolling mills and brass works. In large tin mills the rollerman and the tinman were independent contractors, employing the labour force and thus sharing the control over virtually the whole works, the annealers being employed under a separate group contract. The Carron Company in 1786 offered Henry Cort the post of forge manager, to work as contractor at his own risk, employing his own labour, and while this plan fell through, a similar arrangement with John Raybould, as subcontractor for the nailmaking, actually did come into operation. At Crowley's iron-works the skilled nailers and toolmakers also employed their own assistants, and at Soho managers may have paid their own labour from the first; from about 1770 on, certainly, most Soho manu-factures, including that of the copying press, was subcontracted by the simple means of forming small partnerships to control each, with the manager of the shop as the active partner, and Matthew Boulton and perhaps one or two others as moneyed, sleeping partners, but all working in the same large factory.[1]

In the potteries subcontracting, e.g. by saggar-makers, has sur-vived into this century. Wedgwood employed in 1790, in the 'useful' department at Etruria, 150–60 workers, of whom seventeen were paid by the men; many children were employed by their parents. Small potters would subcontract their grinding to others. Again, in the 1790s Samuel Oldknow paid his colliers as well as his builders through gang leaders, and colliers, in any case, typically employed their own wives and children. It is clear that assembly industries, such as piano or coach manufacture, also devolved many of their tasks by subcontract.[2] Subcontract was perhaps even more common in industries which did not develop any large firms in that period, such as cutlery or framework knitting.

Building, which remained a small-scale industry in our period, and civil engineering, which was growing into a large-scale one, were the industries with subcontract *par excellence*. The building of the Admiralty in 1728, for example, involved a fairly large number of subcontractors, thirty-four of them being paid £57,584, an average of about £1,700 each.[3] The Duke of Bridgewater not only cut his canals and his tunnels into the Worsley mines by bargains with subcontracting 'companies' of workers but also let off the lime-burning on the estate and the brick kilns to 'companies' in similar bargains. Other canals were likewise built by subcontractors, and it was perhaps only to be expected that the Gas Light & Coke Company should sublet the laying of gas mains to contractors in its early years.[4] The Stockton and Darlington Railway Company thus had no hesitation in contracting out, in its turn, the building of the line, and it followed this up by subcontracting for its repair and upkeep for an annual retainer. The rolling-stock upkeep was also contracted for, but it took some time before it became clear that,

45

unlike the canal companies, the actual carrying trade could not be left to private enterprise but had to be organized by the company. As late as 1833 it let out its carrying trade on a subcontract basis to Timothy Hackworth, at 0.4*d.* a goods-mile.[1] By the time of the railway mania the practice had been established that

> when a railway contract has been taken, the principal contractor usually sub-divides the works, and lets them out to sub-contractors. On a long line of railway every cutting, bridge, tunnel, embankment or station is executed by one or more separate contractors. . . . The principal contractor, being responsible to the engineer for the faithful performance of the contract, would watch very closely the work done by sub-contractors, and see that it was executed in such a manner as to satisfy the requirements of the engineer, but he was not directly the employer of the workmen or the navvies.

The main subcontractors might employ 100–300 men each, but the workmen, in turn, might be divided into 'butty-gangs' of ten to thirteen men under a leader.[2]

So far, we have been concerned with the main activity of firms. Ancillary processes were even more easily subcontracted. Transport was an obvious field. In 1682 the Haddington Cloth Company contracted with one James Raeburn to undertake all its transportation for £14 p.a., and as a result was able to sell its own three horses. In coal-mining subcontracts for the carting of coal were found even in the larger and better-organized companies, such as the Worthington and Harrington pits or the Middleton Colliery in Leeds. On Tyneside the tenantry of the coal proprietors had to undertake carting duties as part of their leases, though the inefficiency of this method was increasingly felt in the larger mines in the course of the eighteenth century. At Ravensworth, for example, in 1728, 160 wagonmen were retained in anticipation of the season's needs.[3] It was this sort of expenditure which encouraged the early development of railways there.

In iron smelting much of the labour force consisted of charcoal-burners and carters, contracting independently with the company: a large part of the farming community in such areas as South Wales or Coalbrookdale was employed in carting duties at certain times of the year. When the coal-miners, iron-miners and lime-getters are included, the actual furnace staff formed only a small minority. Thus at Melyn-y-cwrt, in the first four decades of the eighteenth century, eleven were employed on the furnace, but total employment reached 100; in Furness 'for every dozen men, employed at furnaces and forges, many scores were affected by [transport, mining and charcoal-burning]'; and in a 'typical' contemporary Swedish furnace at Horndal the numbers were eighteen at the furnace and 170 farmers and tenants engaged in transport and other ancillary jobs.[1]

The slate quarries of North Wales hired farmers for transport well into the nineteenth century; the Gregory mine, the leading Derbyshire lead company in the eighteenth century, had besides its four 'companies' of miners, also coopers, builders, carpenters, blacksmiths and ten men carting coal, among its subcontractors. Similarly, the Quaker Lead Company contracted for its transport. In coppermining, the famous Ecton mines, in their heyday in the 1760s, employed many local farmers in carting, besides groups of women and children in sorting, etc. The Anglesey companies had, in the Christmas quarter of 1772, no fewer than forty-two different names on their books for payment for transport services, whilst by the early 1800s all the transport there was in the hands of one 'monopolist', William Hughes. His contracts with the two companies for carting amounted in 1825–7 to almost £3,000 a year.[2]

Subcontract of ancillary tasks was particularly prevalent in building, but was also found elsewhere. Thus the Lanchester Colliery, one of the Grand Allies' group, was found in 1784 to have subcontracted its supply of corves: the corver received $4\frac{1}{2}d.$ for every score of corves brought up, and in return was obliged to provide an adequate supply of usable corves. Samuel Whitbread, the brewer, subcontracted for his wheel repair and his cooperage in a like manner.[3]

It will be seen that in many cases subcontract was a survival from an earlier age, and it often staved off the necessity of tackling problems of large-scale management. However, this was by no means always the case. Some of the subcontractors, including the builders of canals, or the 'undertakers' for the deeper northern mines, were themselves firms large enough to have management problems of their own. In other cases the subcontractor became a specialist who might well outgrow in size and complexity his erstwhile 'parent' firm. While one form of subcontract declined with mechanization, others sprang up, and while some forms were conservative and inhibiting progress, others were centres of innovation. Subcontract was thus not a 'stage' of industrial development to be superseded in due course by a unitary factory-type organization, though in this period its general tendency was to allow entrepreneurs to escape the most urgent immediate problems of large-scale management.

IV

The large-scale industrial enterprises of the kind which could be found in Great Britain on the eve of the industrial revolution could be matched by concerns equally impressive in all the advanced countries on the Continent of Europe. Some of them were well run and were models of their kind, and from the vantage-point of the late eighteenth century it could be by no means clear that they would fail to advance into the next stage of the industrial revolution, parallel with industry in Britain. Did they have any lessons to offer to the British entrepreneurs grappling with their new problems?

Broadly speaking, Continental large-scale industry fell into three categories: the privileged manufacture, the centre of a putting-out industry, and the subcontract or group-contract type of concern, particularly in mining. There were, in addition, large units worked by unfree labour in Russia as well as in Western penitentiaries, workhouses and elsewhere.

The privileged manufacture was particularly notable in France, though it was copied by many other princes and governments. The greatest of these concerns were not only very large, but employed many of the finest artists and craftsmen of their day. As a result, they have often been described and we need deal with them here only briefly. Typically, this type of manufacture was either producing a luxury article for the Court and the nobility or was founded to introduce foreign techniques into the country, often with the help of foreign skilled workers. In either case there was an element of monopoly or privilege and an absence of any necessity of comparing costs competitively with other firms. What was often aimed at was technical excellence, either of the product, such as porcelain or furniture, or of the process, as copied from abroad or developed by home scientists. The pursuit of perfection is apt to play havoc with costs, and costs were in any case little regarded, because subsidies or other privileges would take care of deficits.

In many respects these 'manufactures' represented an important stage in industrial evolution. They greatly extended the division of labour and developed the 'central workshop' with its own type of discipline. They also advanced and spread new technology, and encouraged certain types of innovation. Yet it will be evident that their problems differed from those of the British entrepreneur. To some extent, the Continental companies recall the attitude of the Stuart privileged corporation, attempting to profit by controlling the market rather than by cheapening the product, and it is useful to remind ourselves that many of the manufactures in turn had been privileged merely to counteract the existing privileges of the gilds, which were still stifling enterprise and might have used their power to prevent the establishment of these concerns altogether. These companies also generally violated the contemporary canon of distrusting managers administering property which was not their own, and the results were commonly as unfavourable as those in Britain in similar circumstances.[1] Above all, however, most of them could assume that, for the buyer, price was no object: the buyers were looking for prestige goods, or (as in the case of arms) they were Government departments, or the firm had in any case a home monopoly. It was the absence of this strong price sensitivity, the absence of that competitive mass market which was such a decisive stimulus in the British industrial revolution, which makes the Continental example largely irrelevant.[2] The difference was clear at least to those Frenchmen who knew their Britain.

> This modest simplicity [wrote Saint-Fond on the occasion of a visit to a Newcastle glassworks in 1784] is of great advantage to the country; it encourages active and industrious men to embark in trade, who would otherwise be unwilling to form large establishments, being alarmed by the expenses which extensive works require, when constructed on a magnificent scale. It is a taste for pomp and grandeur which almost always ruins the manufactures of France, and prevents those new ones which we want from being established: men are afraid to involve themselves in ruinous expenses for mere warehouses and workshops.[3]

The typical large Continental firm, however, was not a centralized unit, but a comparatively small central workshop employing large numbers of outworkers. The putting-out system had, in many respects, developed further on the Continent than in Britain, and many of the royal and privileged 'manufactories' were of this type. They were to be found in all the major countries in the seventeenth and eighteenth centuries. In textiles the central workshop was responsible for preparatory and finishing processes and silk-throwing: but weaving, and much spinning, was put out to the villages, and similar arrangements dominated the metal, clothing and other industries.

Thus the numbers of employees often quoted were greatly inflated by outworkers, whose numbers, in turn, were often rounded up to suspiciously large figures. There can be no doubt, however, that some of these concerns were indeed very large employers. The

49

imperial woollen factory in Linz, reputed to employ in the 1770s some 26,000 workers, employed, in fact, about 750 weavers in the vicinity of the town, nearly 11,000 domestic spinners in the rest of Upper Austria, 10,000 in Bohemia and over 2,000 in Moravia, providing work for a whole countryside.[1] At about the same time a famous Orleans hosier employed 800 'in' and 1,600 'out', an Anvers sailmaker employed 642 workers (including weavers) 'in' and 6,000 part-time women spinners 'out', the Prussian 'Royal Warehouse' in Berlin, set up in 1740 to supply army cloth, employed up to 1,400 outworkers, and the royal carpet factory in Tournay employed in 1783, fifty-four weavers and 800 on preparatory work; by 1808 it employed 900 in its own workshops, and 4,500 hands altogether. Finally, the famous worsted factory at Calw employed 200 hands indoors, also 1,600 looms and a total of 9,000 hands altogether. Examples could be multiplied, but it is clear that there is here no factory system in embryo, and that the management problem was different: indeed, in many of the most famous examples the out-workers were not employed at all in any direct sense, but represented calculations of how many people were *set to work* by the activities of the central 'manufacturer'.[2]

Thirdly there were the mining enterprises, the earliest to grow to considerable size, and showing a great variety from State control to capitalist merchant control and co-operative miners' organization. By the eighteenth century much of the earlier glory had departed from the silver-mines and from other mineral centres. The old organization had survived, however, among the free miners, and employment in 'companies' was still to be found in some of the large units. The breakthrough into modern large-works conditions did not occur until the nineteenth century.[3]

Unfree factories, of the type established by Peter the Great, had least of all to teach English entrepreneurs, even had they been successful. It was doubtful if they were, even on their own premises: Telford, being employed to build the Gotha canal with a labour force consisting ultimately of 60,000 Swedish soldiers and seamen in 1809,[4] might legitimately have believed that a force of a tenth of that strength, but more skilled, better managed and provided with an economic incentive, would have completed the work more quickly. He certainly found himself in an environment in which all the normal assumptions of the private British employers he knew were irrelevant.

There were, among all these industrial concentrations, a mere handful which showed the independence, the progressive attitude to technology, and the competitiveness of the pioneer firms of the

British industrial revolution. The Anzin coal-mining company, employing 1,500 workers in 1756 and 4,000 in 1789, the Dollfuss calico-printing works, employing 800–900 on two sites in 1786, the Plauen calico-printing works, employing 1,620 in 1811 and the Chemnitz works employing 1,200 in 1788, the Le Creusot works, set up under British management and tapping its first furnace in 1785, when it employed 1,000 workers, and the French Royal Plate Glass Co., employing 1,200–1,400 in 1775, might be quoted as examples. The glass company in particular, building compact townships, almost like fortresses, and catering for all the needs of its workers, or Chaussade's blocks of houses for his ironworkers at Cosne-sur-Loire,[1] might have offered some experiences of value to British entrepreneurs. By and large, however, there was little for them to learn from the Continent in the field of industrial management.

V

If we define our terms closely enough, there could be no precedents for modern management problems before, say, 1750, if only because the whole economic environment, the attitude of labour, and even the legal framework were different. Nevertheless, there may be some value in examining in some detail the structure and problems of three particular firms, flourishing about 1700, partly because a good deal is known about them, and partly because they illuminate some aspects of the problems with which the later entrepreneur of the industrial revolution had to deal and because they pioneered some of the solutions. These firms are the New Mills of Haddingtonshire, the coal-mines and smeltworks of Sir Humphrey Mackworth at Neath, and the ironworks of Sir Ambrose Crowley at Swalwell and Winlaton on the River Derwent south of the Tyne.

The Haddington New Mills were among the more successful of the Government-sponsored Scottish manufactures before the Union.[2] While the company had no monopoly and laboured under some disadvantages, such as restrictive sales in the burghs and adverse foreign exchanges, it enjoyed a number of valuable privileges, including army contracts, the free import of Spanish wool, freedom from cloth duties, the exclusion of competing imports, and assistance in importing workmen from abroad. Further, it should be stressed that it had considerable legal powers over its workmen, who were virtually serfs, being unable to leave without the company's consent, yet could be expelled from Haddington if the company discharged them. The company, which maintained its own prison, could imprison its workers for insubordination or embezzlement of yarn, and had powers to fine its 'managers' (directors).

The concern had five supervisory staff, including two joint managers ('masters'), one for ordinary wool and one for Spanish wool. It depended on attracting highly paid skilled English workmen, who were to employ Scotsmen and teach them their trades. Opening in 1681, it ultimately provided work for over 700 hands in the complete series of processes from the wool to the finished dyed cloth. As long as English imports could be kept out, sales were no problem, as the proprietors were obliged to share in buying the output at cost plus one-sixth. There were also few problems of direct management, since all the spinners, framework knitters and weavers were outworkers. Yet great care was taken to create order in the warehouse and to develop a foolproof system of book-keeping for the wool and yarn given out. Labour was not only screened on employment, but watched and kept in discipline by condign punishment, and in good heart by an official piper and an annual 'Way-gouse' at Haddington Fair. Despite all these advantages and much thought given to management problems, the minutes show that control over the mills was always difficult and never complete.

Within a year the Board in Edinburgh demanded weekly accounts of all transactions, also 'what emergencies are of importance for us to know'. Good clerks were hard to come by: 'a letter being presented from James Marr', read the minutes of 25th April 1683, 'which very difficult to read ordered that he take more pains to write plainly'. Workmen, however, were the greater trouble. In June 1684 the company resolved to find out 'if we can establish a baillie for punishing our owne servants for transgressions', and if not, to present the Deputy Sheriff of East Lothian and his clerk with a suit of clothing and a pair of silk stockings each. In the long run, the main trouble was the fear that skilled men would leave or, worse still, set up in opposition on their own. In January 1682 it was decided to get '2 or 3 good shearmen such as are sober men that we need not fear the running away', but only three years later it was found that two of them

> hes wrought countrie work conterair to their contrack. . . . Mr. Robert B. to take with the masters advice ane effectuall course for the punishment which we think is to let us run into their debt ten or twelve pound sterling and then to take all the cloaths from them they have in dressing and thereafter take in all the work loomes from them and turn them off and setle their

prentices with others in the work who are to teach them at the shearboard as quickly as they can.

In the sequel, however, the company did not succeed in getting the better of these two men.

The minutes are full of fascinating further detail, which cannot be any further reproduced here. The overall picture, however, is fairly clear. It is one of a top-heavy structure, unable ever to control its staff and workmen satisfactorily, or even to train up a core of native skilled workers within the firm. It is constantly harassed by more mobile managers and skilled craftsmen and subcontractors who leave and undersell with apparent ease the more clumsy, and more expensive, large company. When English cloth was admitted into the country after the Union it was only a matter of time before English merchants employing more highly paid labour, but using the looser, more flexible domestic system, drove the company out of business. It began to wind itself up in 1711, and its property was dispersed in 1713.

Sir Humphrey Mackworth, a lawyer, an author on religious and economic subjects, for many years a Member of Parliament, and a man of an unusually enterprising disposition, became, with the help of his wife's dowry, one of the most colourful and successful projectors in the promotion boom of the 1690s.[1] His two main enterprises were a colliery at Neath and a copper-smelting house at Mellyngrythan, but with the foundation of the Mine Adventurer's Co. (see p. 19 above) the smelt works were transferred to them, and another one built on the Dovey, allowing boats to carry ore to Neath and coal to Aberdovey on the return journey. Sir Humphrey, who died in 1727, aged 70, was able to leave his family substantial industrial properties, especially the collieries, and later in the century his descendants developed copper-smelting plants as well, though in his lifetime he was mostly known for his speculative company flotations and his share speculations. His most fruitful innovating period as an industrialist occurred in the years 1695–1700, when he developed the industrial centre at Neath.

Technically, his coal-mine was far ahead of other Welsh collieries. Sinking 30–60 fathoms, the pits may have had an output of 30 chalders a day, or over 20,000 tons a year. A wooden railway was built from the coal face 1,200 yards underground to the water's edge, and a dock and canal completed at Neath to admit ships of 100 tons. For a time an attempt was made to use sails on the tramway, windmills were also erected, perhaps for pumping engines, and adits were dug to clear the workings of water. Apart from setting up new reverberatory copper-smelting furnaces, employing twenty-six workers, lead mills and silver mills, driven by two water-wheels, he also began making Stourbridge bricks.

Most interesting were his attempts to recruit and discipline his labour. One of the conditions of the grant of the coal lease by the town of Neath was that Sir Humphrey should introduce skilled labour from outside. He may not have been very successful in this, for at one time he accepted seventeen condemned criminals for the unpleasant underground work for five years as an alternative to their execution, and failed to prevent the escape of some of them. For the rest, there were detailed provisions for his work force. On the one hand, houses were built for a hundred of them, a schoolmaster was paid £30 a year to instruct the workers' children in 'catechism, and in Reading, Writing and Casting Accounts', they were given piece-work incentives, the criminals were promised advancement to 'master miners', and pensions for old age were instituted. On the other, most workmen were bound for fourteen years and a most severe set of rules and penalties regulated the men's lives. In the smelt house, for example, 'Swearing, cursing, quarelling, being drunk or neglecting divine service on Sunday', were fined one shilling. Absence for two hours was fined by a day's wage, absence for a day by a week's wage, the fines to form the sick fund. Disclosure of secrets, fraud or mismanagement were to be punished by a fine of £100—a sum not likely to be available to the ordinary workman.

Much of our knowledge of his works arises from a protracted dispute with the Mansell family, coal-owners at Briton Ferry and Swansea, who persuaded some local magistrates to harass Sir Humphrey by impressing his wagoners, causing the mines to stop and be flooded, by asking unreasonable coal rent for the Neath burgesses, by sending the immigrant workers out of the parish and by ripping up the rails as a nuisance. The hearings of 1705 seem to have ended in Mackworth's favour, but he was meanwhile involved in the disputes regarding the numerous Cardiganshire silver- and lead-mines (twenty-five mines and twenty-eight levels were named) which ultimately led to his exclusion from control of the Company of Mine Adventurers and his condemnation by Parliament.[1]

There can be no doubt that Mackworth was acutely conscious of management problems, both in his own works and in the larger enterprises of the Mine Adventurers. The larger company had an elaborate management structure and incentive payments for the managers, but Mackworth's own works at Neath was managed by a single individual, Thomas Hawkins, the 'Pay Steward', who described himself as 'gentleman' in the court hearings. As for the workers, Waller praised

> his prudent methods for reducing all his undertakings to a certainty, free from hazard, his copper men working by the ton, and his colliers by the weigh, at a certain price, which is constantly and punctually paid, whereby as no fraud can happen to himself, without a combination of all; so good encouragement is given to the workmen to be careful and industrious, for their own interest, as well as for their masters.[1]

Similarly, in the larger company, elaborate checks were designed in relation to the accounts, while capital provision was to be made easier by the establishment of an associated bank. As far as the foundation of the company was concerned, it is clear that part of the scheme, at least, was fraudulent, and as the cash ran out there were disputes among the managers and strikes and riots among the men; but even in his own works it would be hard to maintain that Sir Humphrey Mackworth had solved his managerial problems with complete success.

The ironworks of Ambrose Crowley are the best known of all, largely through the survival of the extraordinarily elaborate Book of Laws, with its many amendments and corrections in the original manuscript.[2] Crowley's was a large mixed works, consisting partly of rolling, plating and slitting mills, four steel furnaces and two large forges, relying on water power, and partly of innumerable small hand workers' shops for nail- and toolmakers, frying-pan makers, and others. Employment in the second quarter of the eighteenth century has been estimated at 800 in the works, perhaps 130 transport and outworkers and ancillary workers, and perhaps 150 more in London and elsewhere, a total of over 1,000 men, scattered over the central areas, ten warehouses and four company ships. While the firm used all the available mechanical aids,[3] it was technically not markedly superior to its numerous smaller competitors. The company's peculiar difficulties arose partly out of the sheer size of the works and partly out of the decision of Sir Ambrose to reside in London, where his mercantile activities were centred, and to administer from there in great detail an enterprise situated in County Durham.

> It was not so much the absolute scale of operations that mattered, as the transition of the industrial unit from one in which the familiar relations between master and servant held good into one in which the vast increase in the number of men employed created situations that were not amenable to the

traditional techniques of industrial control. In bringing together large numbers of workmen, and in attempting to serve a national rather than a local market, Crowley was groping in the dark.[1]

The result was the development of what one can only call a 'constitution', built up in the fifteen years or so following 1690, defining duties, compensations and penalties in the minutest detail.

Although Crowley was mostly dealing with skilled craftsmen used to outwork (those working the heavy equipment, the labourers, clerks and auxiliary workers forming a small minority), who could be expected to value their personal freedom and resent a factory-like discipline, the order created was logical and tight, at least on paper. Time was divided into ten-week periods called 'accounts', the tenth week, 'cypher week', being used to draw together the accounts of the rest of the period, and each week being numbered consecutively from the foundation of the firm, which can be worked back to be November 1685. The rest of the organization was also, as far as possible, made independent of the outside world. The firm provided a doctor, a clergyman, three schoolmasters and a poor relief, pension and funeral scheme, and by his instructions and exhortations Crowley attempted to dominate the spiritual life of his flock, and to make them into willing and obedient cogs in his machine. It was his express intention that their whole life, including even their sparse spare time (the normal working week being of eighty hours) should revolve round the task of making the works profitable.

The works were nominally managed by a Council, consisting of the departmental managers and some others, whose first task it was every Monday at 5 a.m. to read and obey the instructions in the weekly letter from London. Any one of the managers, who included the Ironkeeper, the Warekeeper, the Surveyor, the Toolkeeper, Toolmaker, Husbandman, Treasurer, Cashier, Broad Clerk and Clerk of the Mill, and others, might at any one time be the final local authority, as *primus inter pares*. To expedite matters, there was an executive, or 'Comptrol or Committee of Council', and several subcommittees, including the Committee for Leading (i.e. land transport), the Committee of Treasury, the Committee of Mill Affairs, and the Committee of Survey. There was also the 'Court of Arbitrators', consisting of the chaplain, usually two members appointed by Crowley, and one each by the nailers and oddwaremen, who administered the laws and penalties, the welfare schemes including the allocation of houses, and the insurance scheme, completely by-passing any local magistrates' courts. Finally, the Governors of the Poor administered the relief scheme, making fresh assessments in every ten-week period. In view of the large numbers of men involved, and the vast stocks of iron and of finished goods handled in so many places, including transhipment on the Tyne, three local warehouses, as well as tools in the hands of workers, not to mention houses and other fixed capital and the funds in the hands of the clerks, an enormous system of paper checks and controls was built up, much of it on printed forms and tied to a tight timetable. Each weekly report to London, for instance, had to contain at least fifteen specified returns (Law 57). A bell and a force of timekeepers checked the hours of attendance of workers and clerks alike.

Yet of at least equal importance with this written constitution, representing the aims of the owners, is the evidence we have from the wording of the laws themselves, and from other sources, about their effectiveness. At a time when so much economic legislation of Parliament remained a dead letter, and when the loyalty of all paid servants was suspect, it is not to be expected that things ran smoothly for Crowley. The evidence reveals, in fact, a constant stopping up of loopholes, of reaction to carelessness, idleness and embezzlement, the widespread use of informers, and a constant sense of despair about the efficiency of control on the part of Ambrose Crowley and his successors. In neither of the two main managerial problems, that of getting the maximum work out of the labour force and preventing any loss or theft of property, did the owners feel very confident of success. At the same time, the repeated revision of the laws, well into the nineteenth century, shows that they must nevertheless have remained the basis of working for well over a century. Perhaps the full flavour of Crowley's exasperation with inefficient or dishonest managers and workmen, and his attempts to curb the tyranny of managers over workmen, will be best conveyed by the following extracts from preambles, 'Laws' and 'Orders' of the Law Book:

> It hath always been the practice of wise and experienced masters at the settlement of any factory to lay such fundamentals for the members therof to be ruled by as might tend to the satisfaction of the one and the peace and tranquility of the other. My people at Winlaton had for some time suffered to very great degree by the ill qualities of some clerks and reckoning officers [hence they are to have] wholesome rules and orders for them to be governed as would make them quiet and easy among themselves and a happy and flourishing people amongst their neighbours (Law 49).

It hath by experience been found that where government or people leave the management of their business to any single person, that their interest suffereth for want of advice, their estate wasted for want of checks upon their managers, their business upon any change or death hath been put in great disorder (Law 83).

And whereas I have been grossly abused and much imposed by having labourers and others, when upon some extraordinary occasion employed, continued to pay though little or nothing to do but what ought to be done by the proper officer . . . (Law 44).

And whereas some workmen, out of a pettish fantasticall humour and without any reasonable cause, have made it a practice to be bringing in their stocks and threaten to be gone, it is ordered that when any workman, let it be who it will, shall in such a frantick humour throw up his stock or iron or tools, shall be judged a disturber of the peace of the work and shall be entered 'outlawed' (Law 64).

Whereas I have received great damages by reason of unskilfull negligent and corrupt surveyors . . .
[The Surveyor] must do all that in him lyes to give the workmen a ready and chearful dispatch, allways considering that their time is their bread and how grievous it is to them to be unnessarily delayed. Therefore, he must be as expeditious as he can in his surveys without causing the workmen to wait longer than they need, and must use no partiality in giving anyone undue preference, but must survey . . . without giving anyone just reason to complain.
In case of an order from me at London to put workmen upon ware they never made before or at least were never perfect at, in such cases the Surveyor may be sparing in his mulcting of them for faults committed really for want of skill.
[The Surveyor] must be prudent and cautious and allways have a great regard to what the workmen say, & especially in hearing their allegations and reasons where they are rationable, and where it is not very certain rather let 3 faults pass without a rebuke than find one where there is none for that will render his judgment weak in the workmen's sight, & lessen the authority his words ought to have over them (Law 45).

Whereas it hath been found by sundry I have imployed by the day have made no conscience in doing a day's work for a day's wages, nor have not had a due regard in doing their duty by labouring to do their utmost in the lawfull propagating my

interest and answer the end of their being paid. . . . On the
other hand, some have due regard for justice and will put forth
themselves to answer their agreement and the trust imposed in
them and will exceed their hours rather than the service shall
suffer (Order 103).

Whereas I have had great and grievous complaints of my workmen loseing much time for want of regular method and certain
time of reckoning and the legall demanding of the same, and
. . . considering that the workmen's time is their livelihood
and that they ought in justice to be speedily and cheefully
dispatcht . . . (Law 16).

Whereas I have considered the cruelty of my clerks to my workmen in not giving that attendance and dispatch they ought and
govern them with that rigor that few of them durst complain
of their aggrievances . . . (Order 105).

Ambrose Crowley died in 1713, and the business was ably carried
on by his son John, but he also died soon after, in 1728, aged 38.
John's widow, Theodosia, was in fairly effective control over the
period 1728–82, but his sons were in charge for brief periods only in
1739–55 before their early deaths, so that a salaried manager was
important even then. From 1782 onwards the business was in the
hands of the Millington family, descendants of the last of the highly
paid managers under the Crowleys. Despite a relative decline, the
firm survived as an industrial unit, in much of the original form,
until well into the second half of the nineteenth century.[1]
There are several common features in the history of these three
firms, to which one or two other contemporary companies, such as
the Quaker Lead Company, might be added. They are, on the one
hand, not truly unitary firms, but consist of several scattered mine
properties or of many outworkers operating with their own tools or
within their own four walls, and only loosely controlled. They were
each conscious of being pioneering, if not unique, in their size and
organization, and given the technical and market possibilities, it is
obvious that there was not room at that time for many such companies, either exploiting a semi-monopolistic position, as in Wales
or in Haddington, or capturing the huge naval contracts, as did
Ambrose Crowley. Above all, they were all troubled by the problem
of how to achieve effective control over their labour, and the
tendency for all of them was to invoke non-economic sanctions,
either by legal compulsion or discipline, or by dominating the
workers' whole lives inside their townships within the framework of

long-term 'bindings', a method which goes back to some large Renaissance firms, particularly on the Continent,[1] rather than to attempt to look forward to the relatively 'free' labour contract of the industrial revolution.

As it happens, no other comparably large or complex works were established until the second half of the century, with the onset of the industrial revolution, and so the break between the two types is all the more marked. Even without this break, however, it is clear that these large industrial companies, like the other forms of organization of earlier ages, such as subcontract or putting-out manufacture, could provide precedents only for certain aspects of the tasks which faced the entrepreneurs of the new factory industry. The task, in its totality, with its complex interrelationship of many different objectives in a flexible environment, had to be pioneered from the beginning within the framework of the British industrial revolution.

3/ The Course of Structural Change in Industry

Basically, the range of the problems of management was the same in all the industries that had to deal with them for the first time during the industrial revolution: labour recruitment and training, discipline, control over production, accountancy and accountability were the ingredients of a science which varied only in detailed application, not in principle, as between different sectors of the economy. This provides the justification for treating them all, in one book, as part of the same development.

Yet differences in detail mattered. Some industries developed earlier than others, and acted as pacemakers or models. Some developed in close geographical proximity and advanced as a group, while others were scattered and aware of their isolation. Again, technical problems differed, and so did the technical competence required of managers. Therefore, managerial personnel were very imperfectly mobile as between industries, and this included even accountants and clerks, precisely because their posts included an executive, managerial element for which experience was relevant for one industry only.

Lest the remainder of this book should slur unduly over these differences in tasks, timing and subject-matter, it is necessary to provide in this, the third introductory chapter, a brief account of the changes in structure of the main industries and the larger firms within them in this period. The industries to be described are limited to those which developed large-scale firms with management problems of the kind that we wish to study, and the only aspects of their history to be discussed will be the aspects relevant to these problems.

I

Among the earliest industries to be transformed, and among the most basic, was mining. Some mining, indeed, could be said to have become capitalistic very early,[1] and to have begun to grapple with organizational problems at a time when most of the rest of the industry was still at the handicraft stage. Thus, in many respects, mining became a model for other industries. In Great Britain, though not on the Continent, the most important developments occurred in coal-mining, which lay somewhere near the centre of the driving motor of the industrial revolution.

The British coalfields are scattered, and each has a distinct history of its own, but if we wish to trace the development of large-scale organization we must start in the North, with the field tapped by the Tyne and the Wear. Its proximity to water gave it its early monopoly of the London, the East Coast and some overseas trade, and happily situated as it was between the large-scale suppliers and the mass markets, that is to say, between the wealthy owners of great estates and the inclusive monopoly of the 'vend' in the North and the equally strict regulations in the South,[1] it was the earliest to develop large units and an advanced organization. These in turn helped it to preserve its monopoly even after the easy pits were worked out, and when deeper shafts and longer rail links became possible and profitable the local pits trained up the staff competent to manage large mines.

While the stories of the expenditure of £20,000–£30,000 by single prospectors in the seventeenth century may be exaggerated,[2] pits were large even by 1700. Some sixty pits in nineteen collieries on the Tyne were estimated to have produced 1 million tons a year,[3] and seventy-six men were killed by an explosion at Bensham colliery in 1710. In 1708 'J.C.', who had heard of a 'fire engine', could write regarding all those who developed a better method for draining mines,

> I dare assure such Artists, may have such Encouragement as
> would keep them their Coach and Six.[4]

The first Newcomen engine was, in fact, installed in 1715, and Raistrick identified a total of 137 in the coalfield by 1778, when the first Boulton & Watt engine was erected.[5] The largest of the older engines, at Walker pit, had a 74 in. cylinder, and had become a recognized stopping-place for all curious travellers and visitors.[6] There was, in 1769, one colliery with six engines, one with five and five with four engines each, in the northern field.

The 'Grand Alliance', consisting of the Ravensworth, Strathmore and Wortley families, had built up and buttressed their dominant position by buying up most of the leases for coal at a depth of less than 60 fathoms, in the belief that seams below that level were unworkable.[7] This belief had become increasingly untenable after 1750, and a new chapter in the history of the coal-field began about 1790 with the Wallsend pit, started in 1778 and working coal successfully from four shafts at 100 fathoms some twelve years later. Sinking to deeper levels opened up large new areas of the coalfield for the first time, particularly those lying east of the (Tyne) bridge. South Shields reached 140 fathoms in 1810, and by 1830 sinking was being extended from 200 to 300 fathoms.[1] Deeper pits requiring technical aids such as steam engines, metal tubbing and underground ventilation and haulage, increased not only the numbers employed by each enterprise but also its complexity and its cost. In 1787 Lord Ravensworth's Friar's Goose pit was reported to have cost £20,000 to sink. The cost of a steam engine was then put at £700–£3,000, tramways about £450 a mile, and a complete colliery sunk to 100 fathoms might cost anything from £15,000 to £40,000. By 1830 £70,000 had been spent on the sinking of a single pit.[2]

Both the increases in output and in cost were easily absorbed by rising demand within a monopolistic sellers' market. It was a profitable, progressive and booming industry. Large numbers of deep pits were sunk in the 1820s, at a time when local engineers and colliery-owners were developing, out of local colliery railways and locomotives, what was to become the greatest economic force of the nineteenth century. Among the new pits towards the end of our period were Gosforth colliery (1825-9), Wideopen colliery (1825-7), Waldridge colliery (1831), Pemberton Main (1826), South Hetton (1822) with its 8 miles of railway, Letch Pit colliery (1824) and St. Helens, Auckland, started by the proprietors of the Stockton and Darlington Railway Company in 1830.[3] In 1829, according to Buddle's oft-quoted calculation, there were £2–£2½ million of capital and 45,500 men employed in the coal trade of the Tyne and Wear, of whom 21,000 were actually in the collieries. Forty-one Tyneside collieries employed 12,000 men, or an *average* of 300 each, of whom 200 were underground. Much of the Wear coalfield was divided between only seven lessees or owners in 1831.

The typical northern mine was the property of either an active landowner or of a large capitalist partnership, employing highly skilled managers or 'viewers', who would also have to control the associated railways, staithes and port installations. The 'banksman', the kingpin of organization in the smaller pits, employing perhaps ten to twenty men with their families, and still to be found in several other areas by the end of the eighteenth century, had all but dis-appeared in the North even by the beginning, and the butty system had never had a firm hold. Significantly, the first large-scale modern pitmen's strike occurred in 1765, and it was from about the last third of the century onwards that the northern coal-mines could be said to have become large industrial units of a recognizably modern type.

The link between the North-East and the Cumberland field was always close. Although much smaller, the West Coast field was technically at least as advanced. The similar stimulus of an easy access to the sea and to a large, monopolistically controlled market in Ireland, together with an energetic group of large landowners, at Whitehaven (developed by the Lowthers), at Harrington and Workington (developed by the Curwens) and at Maryport (developed by the Senhouses)[1] called forth a similar expansion during the industrial revolution.

In 1688 one of Lowther's pits reached at least 17 fathoms, and output was 19,000 tons a year, reaching 38,000 tons in 1709.[2] After the 'Main Seam' was discovered at Whitehaven much greater depths were plumbed: by 1729, sinking went down to 80 fathoms and by 1790 to 150. The first Newcomen engine was installed there in 1715, and a hundred years later there were six. Among the technical achievements of the mine were the invention by the mine viewer, Carlisle Spedding, of the steel mill for safer underground lighting, the use of gunpowder for blasting in 1730, 'coursing the air' ventilation introduced by his son, James, about 1760, the driving of the workings under the sea, a series of hoists to bring up the coal and the offer of piped gas out of the pits for lighting the town, which Whitehaven refused. Of particular interest was the wooden tramway, begun about 1683, and laid direct to the staithes in the harbour, worked by gravity only, from Howgill, and another tramroad into the town from Whingill. In 1765 the pits were said to be worth £15,000 a year and by 1806 some £30,000. In 1813 there were 600 people employed and 1,000 horses, there were some 20 miles of underground railroads, and the company was linked with an ironworks. By 1842 the Lonsdale mines employed 1,300–1,400 workers.[3]

At the Workington collieries J. C. Curwen owned nine of the fourteen pits in 1794, Anthony Bacon's executors owning the others, and one shaft was being sunk to a depth of 84 fathoms. It was there that a Boulton & Watt engine was first used for winding coal in Cumberland, in 1789, and by 1790 there were eight or nine steam engines in use. In 1815, 400 persons were employed in the Workington mines and the Isabella pit, sunk in the years from 1808 to 1822, cost £80,000.

Elsewhere the development of large pits came later, and depended in each case on the size of the market. In order to grow beyond the stage of the small land-sale colliery, a concern had to be either very close to the large towns or groups of large ironworks or it had to wait for the development of canals and railways.

The Yorkshire-Nottinghamshire-Derbyshire coalfield, for example, for long an area of small pits near the outcrop, yet had a sufficient number of large estates with active landlords and other industrialists, using a stream of engineering experts from the North, to sink much capital into coal-mining as soon as the market allowed. Thus the Duke of Norfolk's pits near Sheffield were small, and provided for local consumption only, until the development by John Curr, an engineer trained in the North, who acted as the Duke's viewer in the 1780s and 1790s. In 1805, when the collieries were leased to a partnership, the capital and stock of tools was valued at £16,500 and the lease was £75,000: before its expiry, in 1819, the partners had to spend some £18,000 and the new partnership of 1820 spent £16,000 on the Manor pit before it was opened in 1823. In 1790 all the Sheffield collieries together could not have employed more than 200 men: by 1820 the Handsworth colliery alone employed 162 and the Manor pit 125.[1]

On the nearby Fitzwilliam estates, which developed their own collieries and ironworks, pits stayed small until about the turn of the century, when canals provided them and their associated ironworks with a wider market at last. By 1820 Fitzwilliam calculated that he had spent £122,000 in the past thirteen years in acquiring nine collieries, and while Elsecar, his largest, employed only 112 men as late as 1813, there were then several in the 200–300 range, not only on the Earl's estate, but on others in the South Yorkshire area, and they were growing rapidly.[2] It was, in fact, this rapid rate of expansion, which outgrew the experience of landowners and ironmasters and of their colliery managers, that made the area so notorious a field for mining disasters in this period.[3]

Other large estates included those of the Duke of Devonshire, the Earl of Effingham and Earl Manvers, and some of the gentry and lesser landowners were also capable of developing their own pits, or encouraging outside capitalists to do so. The Middleton colliery had the advantage of a monopoly of the Leeds market; employment there rose from seventy to eighty in 1773 to 230 in 1803 and 380 in 1820, falling again to 280 in 1830. In 1808 it had 1½ miles of double track, and a capital stock of £13,000, plus £5,000 for livestock, and the mine became one of the pioneers in the development of the locomotive.[1] Other collieries might develop early because of nearby ironworks, as at Staveley, Butterley or at Low Moor.[2] Typically, however, the mines remained small in this field before 1830,[3] although in 1810 Fairey counted fifty steam winding engines in collieries and metal mines in Derbyshire and Nottinghamshire alone.

In South Wales very little large-scale coal-mining developed until first a local market had been created by the ironworks, and then a world market by the canals and railways which the ironworks, in turn, promoted. In 1800–20 the typical colliery there had a capital of £7,500–£10,000 and was a subsidiary of an ironworks or a copperworks, being operated by small groups of subcontract miners.[4]

There were, however, a few larger pits. Mackworth's old collieries at Neath, sublet to the copper firm of Lockwood, Morris & Co., were reputed to have employed 300–400 men in 1767 and in 1786 replaced an older pumping engine by a Boulton & Watt model costing over £5,000. Their old rival, Lord Mansel of Margam, proprietor of the Briton Ferry collieries, sublet in 1749 the Llansamlet and Llanwerne pits to Chauncy Townsend, who became the largest coalmaster in the area, and was followed by John Smith, his son-in-law, and his grandsons, Henry and Charles Smith. By 1770, at John's death, £54,000 had been invested in the Llansamlet collieries. Townsend also sunk the Llanelly colliery, where he installed an early fire engine and built a canal.[5] The Blaenavon colliery sank £40,000 before it found coal. The Neath Abbey works also had a fairly large colliery by 1770, using a steam engine and a wagonway. In 1810 Edward Jones stated that he had spent £60,000 on the Risca colliery, and John Barnaby had invested over £30,000 in the Pontypool colliery.[6]

Some pits in North Wales were developed as early as those of the South of the Principality, and it was there that one of the first four recorded Newcomen engines was installed, in a Flint coal-mine, in 1714. Yet no large-scale units were created in the brief decades when the British industrial revolution seemed to take its lead from North Wales. Even the suspect optimism with which the 'Welsh Iron and Mining Co.' attempted to raise a capital of £1¼ million in the boom of 1825 could only refer to the existence, at Coed Talwryn, of two iron furnaces, six steam engines, forty shafts sunk, and 200 people employed altogether, for whom 100 houses had been built, and this does not sound like a major enterprise.[7]

The large unit occurs in other areas also, usually because of favourable market conditions, but it is the exception rather than the rule. In Scotland the Govan collieries, enjoying their favourable place in the Glasgow market, were valued at £30,000 in 1813: their total payroll, including carters, was only 137 in 1805.[1] The collieries associated with the Carron works were an artificial creation by English immigrant capitalists and miners: Bo'ness colliery had two Newcomen engines and experimented with Watt's prototype in 1765, and by the end of the century employed a maximum of 250 workers, including those above ground, producing 44,000 tons; the Grange Colliery, into which the Cadells, erstwhile founder partners of Carron, had sunk £12,000 in 1770–1800, employed only thirty.[2] The first Scottish atmospheric pumping engine was installed in 1720 in Elphinstone, Stirling, and the second at Edmonstone in 1725, while the Earl of Mar sent his manager into Newcastle as early as 1709 to improve his winding and pumping techniques. A Boulton & Watt engine was sold to Wanlockhead colliery in 1777. Yet the serfdom in the mines inhibited enterprise, and even in the early nineteenth century it was calculated that women bearers were cheaper than horses, and since they could be used in small, shallow pits only,[3] these remained typical until the expansion of the iron industry after 1830 called forth greater developments in coal.

In Lancashire the Worsley collieries stand out, capturing the Manchester market with the completion of the canal in 1761. Employing 100 colliers in 1777 and 331 workers underground in 1783, besides ancillary hands, they were part of a huge and unique industrial complex. By 1831 the underground system of canals was said to extend for 18 miles. The estate officers controlling all this did, indeed, become pioneers in many aspects of management.[4]

Staffordshire was the county of small mines *par excellence*, worked usually by subcontractors: even by the middle of the nineteenth century there were 400 collieries in the Black Country, employing each an average of £3,000 capital and sixty to seventy men and boys. Yet it was a Warwickshire colliery which was the first to use a Newcomen pump in 1712, and there were several collieries of medium size, like the Hawkesbury colliery at Bedworth, using three engines by 1774 in a shallow seam, and producing perhaps 50,000 tons a year. Towards the end of our period some of the larger ironworks began to develop large mining enterprises.[5]

Most exasperating of all was the experience of Irish collieries, which may be noted briefly for comparison. Because of the power of the landlords and the hope for subsidies, the few coal seams in the country tended to be worked on a large scale, yet they had an almost unbroken record of failure. The Arigna works in Connaught, employing 253 men, were in 1809 reported to have lost their owners £60,000. The manager, a Staffordshire man

> is apprehensive that the concern will never answer, partly on account of the difficulty he encounters in managing the working people, whom he describes as untractable, and given to laziness, intoxication, and quarelling at patterns and fairs. Besides the coal is of a bad quality.

It became subject to speculation, and in 1838 produced only 2,340 tons. The Leinster Collieries, it was reported in 1814,

> have been, and are, conducted in a faulty and expensive manner in almost every department. . . . The mines have hitherto been conducted on so rude and unscientific a system, that the ruin of those engaged in them has been almost inevitable.[1]

In 1844 Matthias Dunn, the northern coal-viewer, considered again Lord Wandesford's Leinster collieries, near Castle Comer.

> As the working was carried on without any rule by every small tenant [he wrote], not only a great deal of valuable coal was lost by the overrunning of it, but another large proportion stolen, or sold by the master colliers, who had the workings in their respective lands [?hands] without accounting.

In 1828 employment there was as follows:

```
1,000 colliers
  200 hurriers
  300 thrusters
  300 pullers at pit top
   70 scavengers
-----
1,870
```

For them, there were proprietors' staff:

```
 18 agents and clerks
  2 weighmen
 80 rangers and watchmen
 15 roadmen and labourers
---
115
```

But losses were made, coal was stolen from the bank, when it had become the proprietor's property, in spite of the expensive force of watchmen, and not even an English manager could introduce efficient working.[1] The enterprise, and its problems, reminds one of nothing so much as the privileged manufactures of eighteenth-century Europe.

In the British industrial revolution the collieries, it will be evident, had special problems of their own. They were geographically isolated, usually in rural surroundings, and their work force was regarded with disdain by the rest of the community, almost as a race apart.[2] In a period of rapid expansion, recruitment was therefore especially difficult. At the same time, particularly in the North, the rising demand forced coal-owners and lessees to dig deeper, and depth demanded technical competence, while large units became inescapable, with their large capital and their superior and skilled staffs of 'Stewards, Directors, Factors, Agents, Book-keepers, etc.'[3] Altogether, the coal-mines formed one of the most dynamic and fertile fields in the development of industrial management.

Large units developed among metal-mines also in this period. The tin-mines of Cornwall saw some early concentration encouraged by the compulsory deliveries to a handful of coinage towns, and by the fact that

> dependence on imported fuel meant that tin-smelting came under the control of merchants and shipowners with a fair amount of capital.[4]

The mines were owned by groups of adventurers on the 'cost-book' system, and work was divided among tributer and tut-worker gangs.[5] This system was also adopted by the adjacent copper-mines, which very quickly outdistanced the tin-mines in size and economic importance in the second half of the eighteenth century, and equally came to be dominated by large smelting interests. They may conveniently be treated together here.

The group contract work greatly reduced the load of management of large numbers of workers in difficult conditions: thus in 1786, Dolcoath mine had twenty-three groups of tut-workers and Cook's Kitchen had seventeen gangs of tut-workers and eleven sets of tributers. Yet because of the great depth of mining, the difficulties of pumping, and the high cost of coal, the Cornish tin- and copper-mines were difficult units to manage, and the 'pursers', or cashiers and accountants, the 'captains', or managers, and the engineers came to grow into one of the most skilled and competent groups of industrial managers in this period.

The first Newcomen engine was put up in Cornwall in 1720, and there may have been as many as sixty such engines about the mines when Ting Tang placed the first order for a Boulton & Watt steam engine in 1776, at a time when the prototype engine was only just running. Another one started pumping in 1777 at Wheal Busy, and before long over fifty engines were delivered, the first large market for them. Yet investment had been heavy even before the Soho partners appeared on the scene, and it was these high costs which induced local adventurers to brave the bitter jealousy of local engineers and turn in desperation to the Soho engine partnership. Thus, at the time, the Chacewater Company had sunk £50,000; North Downs, having been closed down, cost £60,000 to set to work again in 1784–6; and the Wheal Virgin Company, having lost £28,000 in ten months of unprosperous working, cost £35,000, and £10,000 a year thereafter, to keep at work.[1] Boulton & Watt's premiums for coal savings alone amounted to £76,000 by 1791 from Cornish mines, but with their engines the miners could venture deeper down. Up to the 1770s 90 fathoms was the maximum depth in Cornish tin-mines; in 1798 Dolcoath reached 138 fathoms, in 1808 it reached 228 fathoms, and in 1830 Tresaveal reached 320 fathoms. Cornish engine performances improved, and by 1829 fifty-three engines in the Duchy were listed by Joel Lean as having an average 'duty' of 41.7 million, the best reaching 100 million. A tramroad costing £16,000 was built by the mining interests from Dolcoath to Portreath and began to pay dividends in 1814, and two more systems were built in the 1820s, in the 'estern' and the St. Austell districts. A large system of underground drainage adits developed also, the largest of which, begun at Poldice in 1748, had reached a total of 30 miles, draining fifty mines, by 1819. At Penzance a mine had been driven under the sea and was drained by a steam engine.

The decline of Anglesey after 1800 and the discovery of the rich tin lode at Wheal Vor in 1812–14 gave further impetus to the mining companies.[2] In the boom of 1825 very large new sums of capital were subscribed. Output of tin rose from an annual average of 2,500–3,000 tons in 1750–85 to average well over 3,000 tons in the next ten years, and after a fall, to rise again to a maximum of over 5,000 tons in the 1820s. The yearly copper output of the Duchy rose more steadily from about 3,500 tons in the 1770s to 6,000 tons in the 1800s and 9,000 tons in the 1820s.[3]

Most of the investment consisted of current expenditure in sinking, which in the largest mines exceeded £10,000 a year each in the 1780s and 1790s. Thus fixed capital, in the books, as it appeared under the 'cost-book' system, was likely to be small, yet in 1799 at least seven companies had such capital of over £11,000 each. By contrast, Dolcoath alone distributed £37,000 in dividends among its shareholders in 1805. About 1790 the four largest mining companies, United Mines, Consolidated Mines with Wheal Virgin, Poldice, and North Downs, employed over 1,000 workers each, or a total of 6,000 hands, together with seventeen steam engines, in copper- and tin-mining.[1] By 1836, according to a more detailed count, there were thirty-six mines employing over 200 workers each, the largest five being

Consolidated and United Mines	3,198
Fowey Consols and Lanescot	1,680
Tresavean	1,354
Wheal Vor	1,174
East Wheal Crofty	1,004[2]

There was here something akin to the situation of the Tyneside collieries: a large group of concerns, separate yet interdependent as far as technique, technical personnel, and ownership were concerned, advancing on a broad front to meet a rising demand by deeper working, requiring larger and more complex units. Here, as in the northern coalfield, attempts were made to create a monopoly control over the national market.[3] Competition within the Duchy and the opportunities of copying piecemeal advances from each other created a specially fertile ground for the spread of new techniques, including techniques of management.

The other main copper-mining area, the Parys mountain on Anglesey, provides a strong contrast: two closely interrelated companies developing in isolation,[4] dominated by a single man, Thomas Williams, and owned by a small handful of partners. The easy accessibility of the ore made it a low-cost centre irrespective of efficiency, while it was parasitic on Cornish mining techniques and trained managers, as well as on smelting techniques and immigrant smelters from South Wales. Following the discovery of rich copper ores about 1768, the mines were largely exploited in opencast workings, and needed very little in the way of complex equipment, hence management and supervision were easier than in Cornwall, and the companies remained unadventurous, rejecting, for example, a railway to the port of Amlwch in 1825. In their heyday the two companies were very large. The improvements made in three years, 1785–8, at Mona Mine alone cost £61,000 and the annual dividends reached some £15,000, while the Parys mine was then of about twice that size. Amlwch harbour was built out and a township for workers run up, and the vast open workings, employing 1,200–1,500 men, attracted numerous visitors.[1] The company also owned several smelt works, mills and manufactures elsewhere, but after about 1800 a decline set in, which could be stemmed neither by the Vivian family, brought in as partners for a time in 1811–16, nor by Captain Treweek, the Cornish manager, though there was some revival in 1818–28. The mines went on, employing some 800–1,000 men each and relatively little capital, until the second half of the nineteenth century.

The third large copper-mining centre at Ecton, in Staffordshire, was even more short-lived. Reputedly rediscovered in 1739 by a passing Cornishman, it was developed by a group of Derbyshire miners, but after twenty-five years, in 1764, the lease was revoked by the Duke of Devonshire, who then worked the mine himself. Another spectacular concern, it consisted of a mountain of almost solid copper ore, producing in its heyday, from about 1770 onwards, up to 600 tons of copper a year, compared with 1,000 tons at Parys and 3,000–4,000 tons for the whole of Cornwall. The metal produced in the period 1776–1817 was worth £677,000. Drained by an adit at the level of the Manifold river, it was sunk 80 fathoms below that level by 1769, and 220 fathoms by 1802, the workings being kept clear with pumps and a Boulton & Watt engine dating from 1788, while scaffoldings and pipes allowed the caverns to be worked some 50 fathoms (300 feet) above the adit. There were underground rails, and from 1770 an associated smelt work was operated at Whiston. Employment, at its peak, amounted to about 1,000 men, women and children, supervised by 'proper overseers', and for this rather isolated community the Duke's estate provided a school and other social services.[2]

There were smaller copper deposits worked in other areas, including Scotland, Ireland, Middleton Tyas, Coniston and North Wales.[3] These works were all small, though some were linked with larger mining or smelting companies.

Lead-mining was not affected by the sudden large increases in demand, such as the sheathing of ships and brass making, which encouraged the expansion of copper-mining during the industrial revolution. Yet there were some large companies. The London (Quaker) Lead Company was set up in the foundation mania of the 1690s to exploit new techniques of coal smelting in a reverberatory furnace, and it was therefore always closely integrated with smelting plants and technically far advanced.[4] Consolidated between 1704 and 1710, it began mining at Gadlis in North Wales, where ultimately five Newcomen engines were installed, but in the course of the century it also spread to Derbyshire and at times had interests in Scotland (Wanlockhead and the Orkneys), Ireland, the Isle of Man and Bolton, Lancs. After the 1780s the company concentrated all its working in the Alston Moor and Teesdale area. Here, in an isolated district in which it formed virtually the only employer, the company greatly extended its close control over its workers' private lives and became a pioneer in providing welfare schemes, including housing, schooling and shopping facilities. In 1815–65 it employed an average of 865 miners, in addition to several hundred smelters, carters, boys, washers, estate hands and others, in several groups of mines in the neighbourhood. With its housing, its railways, the roads it had built itself and its smelting plant, the company's property represented a considerable investment.

In the rest of Derbyshire workings were relatively small, and owned by groups of adventurers in separate but related partnerships, as in Cornwall. Soughs and steam engines for drainage, for which a rent was paid by the mine adventurers, were similarly owned. The most successful was the Gregory mine, the rich vein of which was rediscovered in 1758. An atmospheric engine to pump water to the sough level was put in in 1768, and in 1779–81 a Boulton & Watt engine followed. Four groups of bargainers were employed, besides carters, craftsmen and ancillary workers, and in one year, 1772, a profit of £15,000 was cleared, the average output for the period 1758–83 being 1,511 tons of lead a year; but prosperity was short-lived, as the ore began to give out, and output declined despite further investment and digging to a depth of 150 fathoms. In the early nineteenth century a large proportion of the working mines came under the control of one group of owners, who also controlled their smeltworks, but none of their individual plants was very large.[1]

In Scotland the Leadhills deposits, under the Earl of Hopetoun's land, were worked by two companies over most of our period, down to 120 fathoms by 1800, employing about 500 men underground with perhaps a similar number engaged as ancillary workers. At Wanlockhead, on the Duke of Queensberry's land, there were several groups at work in the first half of the eighteenth century, including the Quaker Company; but from 1755 ownership fell into the hands of a single firm, Ronald Crawford, Meason & Co. The area was much troubled by water, and by 1827 there were five steam engines at work, of a combined total of 268 horsepower; it was stated in 1835 that £500,000 had been laid out in the past fifty years.[2] Elsewhere lead workings were smaller. In Wales, Sir Thomas

Bonsall was reputed to have made a profit of £40,000 in 1770–90 at Cwmystwyth; Lord Cawdor's mines in the Vale of Towy were reported to have employed about 400 men and the Marquis of Bute's Park Mine near Llantrisant about 500 in the 1770s. John Wilkinson also worked large lead deposits at Minera and Llyn-y-pandy about 1815. There were some smaller groups working in the North[1]

An industry which reacted to the stimulus of the expanding British economy in a way very similar to mining was slate quarrying. Closely parallel developments took place on several Welsh estates. Among the larger concerns, Richard Pennant was the first to buy out the right of his small slate-quarrying tenants on his Penrhyn estate in 1782, and develop a large unit employing 600–1,000 men, for whom a railway was built to the mouth of the River Cegin, a port developed and internal tramways built. Dinorwic was the next to be unified, in 1788, and, although marking time for a while, built its tramroad in 1824 and employed 600 quarrymen two years later. Cilgwyn, of similar size, was developed after 1800, and Port Madoc, built in 1821–4, with its railway completed in 1836, marked another large-scale enterprise at Ffestiniog. A similar but smaller development took place on the Duke of Devonshire's estate near Coniston. The boom of 1825, when several new companies were promoted, and Penrhyn quarrymen alone numbered 1,200, was a high point.[2] Although, again, work was subcontracted to groups of 'bargainers', the organization, and the capital investment in tramlines, harbours and new townships, presented many new managerial problems.

Finally, in this context, salt-mining might be mentioned. Although some firms had extensive workings in Cheshire, one pit extending to two acres in 1795, they do not compare with the largest coal or metal mines. In Scotland and on the north-east and north-west coasts, where salt was won from the sea, the industry was closely linked with the collieries. One saltworks in Cheshire was laid out in 1828–32 at a cost of £135,000.[3]

Mining as a whole, then, shows several common features. The opportunities of a rising demand were placed before most types of mines at about the same time. They were able, on the basis of the foundations laid in the first half of the eighteenth century, to meet them by more extensive and, above all, by deeper working, made possible by advances in engineering, which in turn was largely stimulated by mining. Rail transport, canals, docks, developed in one sector, in turn benefited and stimulated others. Mostly, labour was recruited from local communities which had traditionally worked the mines, but the exceptions were interesting and important. Nearly everywhere group 'bargains' relieved managers of some of their worst headaches at the beginning of our period. By 1830 the science and practice of management had advanced sufficiently not only to replace them in many cases by direct control but also to deal with units much larger than had been dreamed of in 1760.

II

The second main group of industries to develop large-scale enterprises in this period consisted of the metallurgical and associated engineering concerns. They were in many instances based on mining, and in the case of the iron industry, the most important in this group, the digging for iron ore remained small scale, and was generally a surface digging only, until it was taken over by large ironmaking companies.

Apart from the remains of the charcoal-iron industry which did not convert to coke smelting, but gradually closed down in the period 1750–1830,[1] two main groups of ironworks may be distinguished. The first consisted of the survivals from the charcoal age which adapted themselves, and by a process of vertical integration, so typical for the industry, acquired both the rolling mills, wiremills and other later stages of production, as well as, in many cases, their own ore-fields and coal-mines. The other works were essentially the children of the coal-and-iron age, greatly furthered by Cort's puddling process which allowed even inferior British ores to be refined into merchant or bar iron on a mass-production basis.

In the days of charcoal smelting the typical organization was a combine of works in associated ownership, but physically and geographically separated and therefore separately managed.[2] Some of these units represented substantial capital sums, but rarely as many as a hundred workers, and many of these were scattered as charcoal burners or farmer-carters.[3] When coke smelting began to spread outwards from Coalbrookdale about the middle of the century the fortunate close proximity of coal and iron ore in so many parts of the British Isles allowed horizontal and vertical growth to proceed in one works complex, to create very large units. At first, indeed, the larger works seemed to continue to consist of quite separate blast furnaces, forges, rolling mills and so on, which were placed in the same vicinity, perhaps along a river which provided the power, or a canal which provided the means of transport, but had not been consciously planned as a unit. The Darby's Coalbrookdale works

75

and the Walkers' combine along the River Don, were of this type.
Coalbrookdale's capital rose to £96,000 in 1798, and its capital
valuation, together with the associated Horsehay works, was
£125,000 in 1830. It had, in the last third of the eighteenth century, some 20 miles of internal railways in use and there was the
canal and the famous inclined plane, and in 1785 it had sixteen
fire engines, eight furnaces, and nine forges, while the associated
Ketley Ironworks were valued at £138,000 in 1793; they were
closed down in 1816. Employment, including mines, was set at
nearly 1,000 as early as 1776 and 'over 1,000' in 1800. Joshua
Walker's, opened in the 1740s, employed some 500 men in 1769 and
by the turn of the century had become the largest ironworks in the
North of England, with its own collieries and iron mines, making
pig iron in three blast furnaces, bar iron, steel, tinplate and many
other products. As the local ore began to give out, the firm closed
down its Rotherham plant from 1822 onwards, but meanwhile the
partners developed large ironworks at Gospel Oak, where in 1824
they employed 700 men in the works and 1,300 in the mines, with
seven steam engines of a total of 350 h.p., in two blast furnaces,
rolling and slitting mills, a foundry, and tinplate mills.[1] The Carron
Ironworks was another huge combine, founded on a large scale in
1759–60, employing 800 people in 1765 and some 2,000 in 1792,
in a works consisting of five blast furnaces, three cupolas, fifteen air
furnaces, rolling and slitting mills, boring mills and a gun foundry,
besides associated mines, nailmaking shops, a canal and shipping.
The capital, originally £12,000, was raised to £150,000 in 1773, and
concrete assets as early as 1769 amounted to £90,000. In 1842
employment still stood at 1,349, besides miners in associated
collieries.[2]

In the 1790s, when the spread of puddling had further encouraged
integrated coal-iron works, producing not only pig and bar iron,
but also rod and wire, castings, or even steam engines and other
engineering products, the 'typical' size began to grow to 200–300
workers, rising in some areas, like Shropshire, to 700 workers each.[3]
Some combines were much larger. Samuel Fereday of Bradley enter-
tained 1,500 of his workmen on the occasion of Waterloo—though
he went out of business soon after. The Smiths of Chesterfield, with
works at Brampton, Duckmanton, Calow and at Manchester,
employed 1,200, and had an output of 2,600 tons of pig alone, but
they wound up their firm in 1833. Neighbouring Butterley employed
about 1,500 men, besides twenty-six steam engines, in 1825, with a
capacity of 5,000 tons a year, and Low Moor and Bowling, both

near Bradford, employed about 1,500 each in 1815. At a time when Anthony Hill estimated that it took an investment of £100,000 to create a capacity of 100 tons 'manufactured' (presumably bar) iron a week, William Foster at Stourbridge, in 1821, used eight steam engines to produce 200–300 tons of pig iron, plates and bars weekly, and William Hanbury Sparrow, with seven blast furnaces at Bilston and one at Lane End, produced 300 tons of pig and 200 tons of bar a week.[1] Among the most advanced, technically, were the works of John Wilkinson, his father and his brother, scattered over Broseley, Bradley, Hadley, Brymbo, and Bersham, but most of these were derelict by 1830. At Ruabon, the British Iron Company took over in 1825 and spent £140,000, employing 1,400 workers by 1842.[2]

Most breathtaking of all was the rise of the iron industry in South Wales. There the favourable juxtaposition of coal and iron, the cheap leases and the easy provision of canals and tramways to the ports encouraged sufficient capital and enterprise from Wales as well as England to exploit the new puddling process, and build up most rapidly the giant concern which for a time put the rest of the country in the shade. At the centre of the field, developed by the commercial genius of Anthony Bacon and the technical ability of Isaac Wilkinson in the 1760s,[3] stood the four works of Merthyr Tydfil: Cyfarthfa (Crawshay), Dowlais (Guest), Penydarren (Homfray) and Plymouth (Hill). Cyfarthfa employed 1,000 men by 1804, 1,500 perhaps by 1812, 5,000 by 1830. Its furnaces numbered three in 1796 and nine in 1830, together with four in the associated Hirwain works, while average capacity of a furnace had increased from 20–30 tons a week to over 60 tons. In 1799 its famous water-wheel, the largest in the country, measuring 50 ft. in height and having two smaller wheels either side of it, was built at a cost of £4,000, but by 1830 the works also had eight steam engines and 450 horses, three forges, a foundry, eight rolling mills and a boring mill. At that time Dowlais had twelve furnaces, together with twenty-six fineries, six mills, and employed (including the coal mines) also around 5,000. Plymouth (including Duffryn) had seven furnaces with a labour force of 2,000 and Penydarren had five. Works such as Nantyglo, with its seven furnaces, and Abersychan, Aberdare, Abernant, Bute, Sirhowy and Ebbw Vale, with their six furnaces each, would be considered giants in any other part of the country, and so would Tredegar and Blaenafon, with five each. The Welsh works remained large by comparison with the rest of the country, matching their pig-iron capacity with puddling plant. Tinplate mills, however, remained relatively small.[4]

Capital investments have been estimated as follows:

1816 Blaenafon	£250,000 in real capital
1820 Cyfarthfa and Hirwain	£400,000
1817 Tredegar	£100,000
1817 Penydarren	£100,000
1820–1 Ebbw Vale	£62,000

By 1830 the actual output of South Wales, 277,600 tons, represented 42 per cent of the British output.[1] However, growth had been general, and while, in 1815, a firm with an output of 5,000 tons a year had been considered exceptionally large, by 1830 Scrivenor enumerated forty-seven such firms, and several more whose *capacity* easily exceeded that figure. Of these, fifteen had an *actual* output exceeding 10,000 tons, twelve of them in Wales.[2]

Some ironworks, notably Neath Abbey, Carron, Gospel Oak and Coalbrookdale, had their own casting and engineering departments. The engineering industry, however, had other roots also, particularly among millwrights and civil engineers, as well as instrument makers and others, and began in this period to develop a recognizably independent existence of its own. It included not only some of the most influential pioneers of the industrial revolution, but it also gave birth to some of the most acute problems of management, and some of the most interesting attempts to solve them. The firm of Boulton & Watt, sole designers and manufacturers of the steam engine with the patent separate condenser for the period of 1775–1800, stood at the centre of this development. It did so for several reasons. For one thing, the Watt engine was the culmination of a development of mining pumps which had represented the most advanced form of engineering in the period immediately preceding.[3] For another, the rotary power which began to be exploited by the Soho partnership in the 1780s itself called forth further machine-making, first in the form of stationary machinery and secondly in the form of the locomotive. Thirdly, the hitherto unnecessary precision with which Watt's engine had to be finished was the basis of the next big forward sweep in engineering in the period 1800–30. Finally, the genius of the partners of the Soho firm, and the inescapable needs of a firm making a composite commodity with the help of a wide variety of skilled labour, required Soho itself to become a pioneer, perhaps the pioneer, of many different advanced management practices, and it so happens that the firm also left a magnificent collection of records behind it, which has been well preserved and has provided the material for the only major study of management practice in this period, to which all who work in this field are much indebted.[1] This pre-eminence of Soho is not greatly affected by the recent evidence that a flourishing steam-engine-building industry existed outside Soho, even in the years of the patent.[2]

The Soho engine partnership developed out of Boulton's 'toy' manufactory, itself advanced for its time. At first it intended to produce designs only for others to build, but it soon took to producing some of the most difficult components itself, such as nozzles and valves, for sale to customers. Even these may well have been produced by subcontract 'undertakers'.[3] As the end of the patent period approached, however, the firm decided to become a large-scale producer of complete steam engines, and erected in 1795 the 'Soho Foundry' for this purpose. It was carefully planned from the start, mainly by Matthew Robinson Boulton and James Watt Junior, the new generation of partners, and became an astonishingly fertile pioneer of scientific management practices. Among its outstanding innovations were careful and most elaborate costing, planning of the flow of production and of products, standardization of components and processes, and subdivision of labour among the many skills, some of which the firm itself had introduced and developed.[4] The foundry was well equipped with steam engines and other aids, and £30,000 had been invested in it by 1797, a sum which had doubled by 1830. Employment was given as about 100 men in 1821, and 251 in 1831.[5]

With the ending of the patent, steam-engine makers multiplied and some grew to considerable size. Other main types of engineering works were concerned with textile-machinery making and locomotive building, while in London a number of highly competent firms developed which built many different types of machines and machine tools for various industries, greatly advancing the accuracy of work and the idea of mass production within engineering.

Some of the great engineers of the day had started in the millwrights' shop:

> The millwright of [Brindley's days] felled his own timber; forged his own . . . iron; could erect a foundry complete with windmill or waterwheel, races and sluices, gearing and shafting; and often he made the machinery as well. Brindley even constructed steam engines; at first with home-made barrel-stove cylinder, brick boiler and cast-iron fire box.[6]

This tradition survived and some of the most famous, most productive and most inventive works remained very small indeed.

Henry Maudslay's, in London, which carried out the vast naval contract of blockmaking machinery to make 130,000 blocks by 1806, the first real mass-production engineering in Britain, arising out of the ideas of Sir Samuel Bentham, the Taylors, and Marc I. Brunel,[1] and which at the same time trained many of the great engineers of the next generation, employed only eighty men. Bramah's, the senior firm in London, had only 100 in 1824–5, Galloway about the same number, William Fairbairn sixty to seventy, most others, as Napier's, in London, or the Hazeldine Foundry at Bridgnorth, rather fewer.[2]

In the textile areas many of the large mills had risen to success by building their own machinery in the first instance, and they were weaned away from this practice only gradually in the 1820s. McConnell & Kennedy, Robert Owen and Henry Houldsworth were only the greatest names among those who had done so in the cotton trade, while Marshall's, the Leeds flax spinners, considered in 1825 setting up their own machine shop to employ about seventy men, or about the size of a large independent maker. Among the sizeable firms which nevertheless developed in the textile areas, Fenton, Murray's 'Round Foundry' in Leeds, employing 160 in 1802, T. C. Herves in Manchester, employing 140–50 in 1824, and the largest Manchester firms Bateman & Sharrett and Peel, Williams & Co., perhaps reaching 200 each at about that time, stand out.[3]

Among the engineering works in the North which developed the locomotive in the period 1804–25, even the largest, the Forth Street works of Robert Stephenson & Co., at Newcastle, which had built twenty locomotives in 1825–30 and another twenty-five in 1830–1, or perhaps more than the rest of the world put together, could hardly have had as many as 100 employees by 1830.[4] By 1838, indeed, it employed 400, and the growth in size among other engineering firms in the 1830s was startling; but before that date it is difficult to speak of large-scale enterprise at all, though in the nature of things even a staff of 100 may set grave managerial problems in this particular assembly industry.

In other metal industries workshop conditions remained the rule, and the few large-scale enterprises are exceptional. Among them, by far the most interesting in its scale, organization and equpiment was the Soho factory of Boulton & Fothergill. Although it became the Mecca of innumerable pilgrims, many of whom have left their descriptions in writing,[5] and although the firm's surviving records are among the best we have from the eighteenth century, it is nevertheless not quite clear how the works were, in fact, managed internally.

Boulton's original idea in transferring from the typical innumerable separate workshops of the Birmingham 'toy' trade to the single factory complex in what was then open heath country at Soho was linked only partially with the idea of technical advance. It is true that Soho had its own central motive power which drove all the little lathes, drills and polishers within the works, in the form of a water-wheel, the inadequacy of which was one of the reasons for taking an interest in Watt's improved steam engine; but in the main Boulton sought the sort of organizational advantages which were summarized so brilliantly by Adam Smith as the 'division of labour', illustrated by a pin factory. Boulton's works, and very soon others in Birmingham which copied him and the larger works of John Taylor, used the large scale of production first to divide and subdivide the work, secondly to replace the thus simplified tasks by primitive machinery, such as stamps and dies or lathes, and thirdly to make full use of skilled artists and designers of the kind which the smaller firms could not afford at all. The innumerable different articles, in steel, silver, plated metal, bronze, ormolu, tortoiseshell, enamelled, japanned and painted ware, the buttons, buckles, clocks and tools, each had their own rooms, their own specialists and their own responsible foremen. Although it is not clear whether these foremen were supervisors or subcontractors, it is likely, judging from the large proportion of the labour force of 600–700 assembled by 1762 who were women and children, that some sub-employment went on, together with much lowering of skills and of wage costs. The most important branches, such as buttonmaking and the production of the copying press invented by James Watt, as well as the engine patent of Watt, and Boulton's improved mint, were conducted by separate partnerships within the single range of buildings.

By 1770 some £10,000 had been invested in the factory, and such capital investments as large buildings, including some dwellings within the factory complex, and some machinery were of a kind which the ordinary Birmingham merchant did not have to provide. Large sales, therefore, were vital, and in exact parallel with Adam Smith's dictum that the division of labour depended on the extent of the market, 'the reduction of costs and the sale of the product stood in so intimate relation to one another as to be little more than the two sides of a single process'.[1] The difficulty lay in the fact that, in an industry in which outwork and the independence of workmen was traditional, and was to remain traditional for another century or more, Soho alone from its earliest days . . . combined, in a factory, all classes of workmen engaged in the manufacture of its various products; and in the owner of this factory was vested the technical as well as the entire economic control over his employees.[1]

It is likely that the other large industrialists in Birmingham at the time, such as John Taylor, who employed 500 hands in 1755, and Henry Clay, reputed to employ 300 workers, were controlling domestic workshops only, rather than large-scale industrial enterprises.[2] By 1815 one gun-barrel maker was reported to have employed 300 men and Thomas Messenger, brass founder, about the same number, while by about 1830 William Fox employed 250 men in wire drawing and wire working, another firm employed 1,000, indoors and out, in pinmaking, and a third, about 300 in pinmaking. Ledsam's button factory employed 318, John Turner, another, employed 130–50 plus 350 outworkers, and William Walter Jenkins, brass founder, about 250.[3]

The leading firms outside Birmingham were probably staffed largely by outworkers. Thus William Whitehouse of West Bromwich, ironmonger, employed his 1,200–1,500 nailers largely as outworkers, and so, for that matter, did the nailing department of the Carron works. Sheffield manufacturers employed very few men directly, even if they had large warehouses for goods from many workmen. Messrs. Ryton & Walton, of Wolverhampton, employing over 600 in 1810, may have employed them indoors, but Peter Stubs's file workers, the Warmley Company's pinmakers, and the Warrington pinmakers, were likely to have been fairly independent outworkers.[4]

Among the remaining metal trades a typical tinplating mill might cost £10,000–£15,000 at the end of our period, but would not employ as many workers as the giant works enumerated elsewhere. Lead-smelting had some very large units, though these were either associated with mines, as in the case of the Quaker Lead Company, or with lead warehouses, as in the case of Walker, Parker & Co. It was in the copper-smelting industry and the related brassworks that some of the largest firms and some of the most interesting managerial experiences were developed.

The early development of large capitalistic enterprises in the copper industry had several causes. There were the technical factors, including the need for expensive capital equipment, and the economies made possible by combining copper-smelting, brass-making, and some specialized final goods manufacture, such as wire-, pin- and nailmaking, casting, sheet rolling, or the making of kettles. At the same time, the geographical concentration of copper-mining and zinc-mining on the one hand, and the concentrated market, particularly in London and Birmingham, on the other, allowed these firms to assume a mercantile role and carry heavy stocks, to bring these two large markets into contact with each other.

Growth began in the foundation mania of the 1690s, and was in part based on the new reverberatory smelting furnaces. By 1720 the English Copper Company (1691), at Lower Redbrook, the Upper Redbrook works, the Bristol Brass Wire Company (1702), the Temple Brass Mills, near Maidenhead, the Cheadle Company, set up by Thomas Patten, who began smelting about 1717 or 1719, and the associated Warrington Company had been established. For the remainder of the century much of the concentration and the creation of large companies continued in the two main existing regions, the Bristol area and the Lancashire-Cheshire-North Wales belt. The Warmley Company of Gloucestershire, set up by William Champion in 1746 and employing 2,000 workers, including outworkers, in 1767, passed into the hands of the Bristol company, but was discontinued from about 1809 onwards. Roe & Co., which began smelting in 1758, enjoyed the riches of the Anglesey mines for a time and later sank £40,000 into mining in Ireland. It maintained, at one time or another, smeltworks at Macclesfield, Holywell, Liverpool and Swansea, but went out of production about 1811. Largest of all was the combine headed by Thomas Williams, who maintained smeltworks not only at the Mona and Parys mines' property at Amlwch but also the Ravenhead works, the Holywell works, Upper Bank works in Swansea, Temple Mills, and the Penclawdd works, as well as, through the Mona Mine Company, the Stanley works at St. Helens, the Middle Bank works in Swansea, and the Greenfield works.

Birmingham manufacturers, being among the largest consumers of brass, entered the industry with the Birmingham Brass Company in 1781, the Birmingham Mining and Manufacturing Company in 1790, and the Rose Copper Company in 1793. In the nineteenth century the weight of the industry increasingly shifted to Swansea, to the coal, where by 1830 five-sevenths of the British smelting capacity was located. Control also came to be increasingly exercised by mercantile and coal-owning interests, particularly the Vivian family (Penclawdd, 1800, and Hafod works, 1810), Grenfell and Williams (arising out of the Anglesea combine, Upper Bank works, 1803) and Nevill & Co. (at Swansea in 1794, Llanelly in 1804).

Employment in a typical smelting mill was not large, being rarely above 100 in 1750 or 200 in 1830, but most companies had several plants, besides rolling mills, coal-mines and other associated property. Capital, however, could be substantial, though partly it consisted of stocks of copper.[1] Some estimates are tabulated below:[2]

	Year	Capital £000	Year	Capital £000
English Copper Co.	1720	105	1750	150
Lockwood Morris & Co. (Swansea)	1745	20		
Roe & Co.	1760	15		
Warmley Co.	1767	200		
Mines Royal	1767	150		
Cheadle Co.	1780	30	1804	106
Birmingham Metal Co.	1781	20		
Birmingham M. & M. Co.	1790	50		
Rose Copper Co.	1793	100		
Anglesea Combine	1799	800		
Keysbury Brass Mills	1809	320		
Vivian & Co.	1840	400–500		
Foster Williams & Co.	1840	400–500		

III

There were few large firms in shipbuilding and building, nor were these industries much affected by the industrial revolution, at least before 1830. Ships continued to be built of timber and propelled by wind, and although naval blockmaking, and the copper sheathing of warships and some merchantmen had led to transformations in ancillary industries, the shipyards were scarcely changed.

The largest units in the shipbuilding industry were the naval dockyards,[3] and these, with their discipline compounded of civil service and armed service practices, and the absence of any direct profit motive, fit badly into our concept of 'management'. Private yards remained small, particularly in the outports, and were scarcely more than of workshop size, even by 1830. Some London yards were larger, but only the Blackwall yard was of any significant size: valued at £8,000 in 1779 and at £81,000 in 1819, it employed some 600 workers in its various branches by 1830. The other main assembly industry, coachmaking, may also have had one or two firms employing over 200 workers each, made up of many crafts in many quite separate departments. The largest London piano factory, Broadwood's, employed, similarly, 'several hundred' on one site, and 150 on another in 1843, but again these were divided into many separate crafts and departments. Nevertheless, for some purposes, such as buying and storing components, these had to be treated as single large establishments, with their own special management problems.[1]

In building, the small craftsman firm predominated. The time-honoured method of contracting was for one craftsman to make himself responsible for the job, subcontracting the various specialist jobs to others, and for these roles to be frequently reversed.

As long as contracts remained relatively small there was no in-centive for the most enterprising among any craft to move over per-manently to contracting. Even the large architect-designed country houses of the period were built in this way, and there was

> general agreement among seventeenth and eighteenth-century architectural writers that to put all the work into the hands of a single 'undertaker' was to court disaster.[2]

An essentially similar subdivision, which also limited the size of any given enterprise, was maintained in the Office of Works and Buildings.

Two developments stimulated the emergence of permanent con-tractors in our period. The first was wartime building by the Govern-ment, particularly of barracks. There were only some six contractors, and one of them, Alexander Copland, was paid over £1,300,000 for his contracts in 1796–1806. At one contract alone, that on the Isle of Wight, he had 700 men employed, and

> he explained . . . that he was able to manage such large opera-tions successfully because he had 'able foremen' who were accustomed to carry out large works at a rapid rate.[3]

The other was the building, in the Metropolis, of substantial office and warehouse blocks, and above all of estates of dwellings, which were large enough to allow, not necessarily any new technical apparatus, but all the advantages of better organization of the type stressed by Adam Smith and which we have already observed in works such as those of Matthew Boulton. Thomas Cubitt was the greatest of these new 'master builders', who, unlike those of the eighteenth century, maintained a permanent large establishment of craftsmen. By guaranteeing employment he could hold the best craftsmen, he could employ them most economically, and he could give 'permanent employment for the foremen and clerks upon whom the efficiency of such an enterprise must have depended'.[4] When he dissolved his partnership with his younger brothers in 1827, Thomas, going into estate development, employed 1,000 men permanently, while William employed another 700 on speculative building. Another, somewhat earlier firm, Thomas Burton, employed up to 235 men, and others were growing to that size.[1]

There was, in effect, a third type of large-scale enterprise, typified by the Liverpool 'master-labourers' who might, about 1825, have 200–300 Irish labourers on their books to be hired out by the day for excavation work, etc., to builders.[2] This, however, is best considered as an example of civil engineering. The new roads, canals, docks and railroads did, in fact, represent by far the largest concentrations of capital in this period, and their building, not unnaturally, led to the growth of some complex enterprises in the civil engineering and contracting industries.

The building of turnpike roads could normally be managed by small gangs of labourers under some barely skilled supervision, though in a few cases these ran into three figures. Thus J. L. McAdam, claiming to spend £12,000–£15,000 a year for the Bristol Turnpike Trust in 1823, included £4,833 on labour, which must have represented at least a hundred men.[3] Telford, on all his Highland road building together, may have employed as many as 3,200, and some 500 on the Holyhead road in 1816.

Drainage and navigation schemes were normally larger. Even the seventeenth-century drainage of the Fens might employ as many as 600 labourers,[4] supervised directly by the 'engineer'. The early navigations, such as the Aire and Calder, begun in 1698, tended to employ large numbers of small contractors, with minimal supervision. The eighteenth century saw a marked rise in the status and the skill required by the engineer, who would plan the enterprise and then act for the navigation company as his clients, keeping the builders to their contracts. The typical size of contractors' gangs also increased, as did the experience of their gang-masters and contractors. While running repairs as well as the management of the finished enterprise might be farmed out to smaller private venturers, by the early nineteenth century the whole of a major work might be undertaken by a single firm of contractors.[5] Enterprises such as the building of the Thames tunnel, begun in 1802, the various docks in London and the docks and harbour works in the outports, and the bridges over the Thames, the Severn, Tyne and other rivers, as well as over the Menai Straits, among others, had their own difficulties of management and supervision. Plymouth breakwater, built towards the end of the Napoleonic Wars by Rennie, could not find a contractor, and had to be let out in small labour contracts, the Government finding the plant and the materials.[1]

It is possible to view many of these activities as prologues and by-products of canal-building,[2] the most important single civil engineering industry in our period. It was the canal-builders, and Thomas Telford in particular, who first called into being the large contracting firm, responsible, resourceful, and pioneering its own managerial solutions,

> who brought their methods of business to a new standard, whether on the side of skill or on that of honesty.[3]

Their problems should not be underrated.

> If it is possible to find contractors, solvent and capable to take on a general contract [a French engineer had written in 1729],[4] one will do well to deal with them. But it is rare to encounter men of strong enough character to take on a burden as heavy as that of a general contract. For, the haste with which these works are usually undertaken, and their long duration, often reduce the contractor to a state of nervous exhaustion . . . if the job is somewhat heavy, and if it is awarded to poor or ignorant men, they will take it on rashly at any price, in the hope of making some profit in one way or another . . . the workers, being poorly paid, will desert, and will only turn up in small numbers. All this will give the engineers plenty of headaches.

Contractors learnt but slowly in the course of the century to avoid these and other pitfalls. It was only at the very end of the century that

> Telford introduced or elaborated the system of monthly payments; of the retention of definite sums as guarantee of satisfactory workmanship and punctual completion; of a period of maintenance during which the contractor is responsible for the state of the new work. . . . [In order to have competent and contented contractors, he] always endeavoured to use one or other of the small group of contractors that he had trained to his ways, selecting them individually, each for the class of work for which he was best suited.[5]

This division of functions between the company's engineer, or his deputy, and the contractor shifted most of the burdens of management on to the latter. While, even in 1769–73, James Watt, as engineer-surveyor to the Monkland canal, had all the tiresome details of workers' bargains, pay and discipline to see to, with little help:

> I have above 150 men at work [he wrote in 1770], & only one
> overseer under me, beside the undertakers, who are mere tyros
> and require constant watching;[1]

and while James Brindley, building the Bridgewater canals under
John Gilbert's supervision, may have had to be 'land-surveyor,
carpenter, mason, brickmaker, boatbuilder, paymaster and engineer'
all in one,[2] and William Reynolds, building the Ketley canal in 1788,
had to be 'head and subschemer, Engineer and Director',[3] by the
time of the canal mania of the early 1790s, i.e. by Telford's time, a
certain managerial structure had crystallized out. It began with the
large schemes which were not the property of a single man or firm,
like those of the Duke of Bridgewater or the Coalbrookdale combine,
but were drawn up as companies, including leading landowners,
agents and industrialists, on the model of the Trent-Mersey (Grand
Trunk) committee of 1766[4] which prepared to spend a sum of
£300,000 on the building. Contractors undertook work by the foot
or yard, and when the work grew beyond a certain size they subcontracted in turn to gangs on a similar basis, while supplying them
with 'engines', such as cranes, steam engines or windmills. Some, like
William Hazeldine, the ironwork contractor for Telford, began with
a foundry at Ruabon, but ended as owner of a blast furnace at
Callcot and of the Bridgnorth engine works.[5] It was perhaps a sign
of a transitional period that in the building of the Cromford canal
in 1789–92, the contractors absconded after a quarrel, leaving
Benjamin Outram, the engineer, to complete it with direct labour.

Brindley's canal employed some 600 men, and so did the Grand
Trunk works, as well as the Harecastle tunnel and other fair-sized
canals of that time. At the end of our period, however, Telford's
last canal, the Birmingham and Liverpool Junction, employed as
many as 1,600 on the northern section under John Wilson in 1827,
600 on the southern section under the same contractor from 1830,
while another contractor had begun on the middle section in 1829.[6]
Labour was generally either footloose and undisciplined, or local
and inexperienced, and thus set its own problems.[7]

These methods were taken over by the railway builders, of whom
more details have survived, and who grew to much larger size,
though mostly after 1830 only. The engineer's position as the designer of the work, its controller during the building, and the arbiter
of the sufficiency of the work of the contractors, was greatly
strengthened, possibly because of the other tradition, that of building 'Newcastle' wagonways, which were usually directly under the
viewer's or engineer's control.[8] At the same time contractors became

more competent and devised new ways of subdividing and subcontracting their responsibilities down to the lowly 'ganger' and his
gang.[1] In the later days of Brassey, when a single main contractor
would undertake a large line or stretch of a line, the subcontractors
themselves might employ up to 300 men each, but in the early days
engineers were much troubled by the builders' incompetence and
by having to undertake too much themselves.[2]

The Liverpool-Manchester line was built by about 600 men
divided into three sub-engineers' groups of 200 each, but the major
lines were soon to count their employment in as many thousands.[3]
The system, as developed out of the older canal and navigation
contracts, required the following numbers of managers and foremen, according to the statistics for 1st May 1848:[4]

Employment on lines not yet open:

Secretaries, managers	195
Treasurers, clerks, storekeepers	1,384
Engineers, draughtsmen, surveyors	737
Inspectors, superintendents, foremen	2,701
Workmen	182,963
Miscellaneous	197
	188,177

Finally, this period also saw the development of a new type of
public utility, the gas companies. The Soho works were first lit by
gas to celebrate the peace of Amiens in 1802, but within ten years
the chartered 'Gas Light and Coke Company' had been formed with
a capital of £200,000, experimenting vigorously to solve the
problems of practical application, and within a further ten years
several other large companies were in operation and others in process of formation. By 1822, for example, the Westminster station,
the initial cost of which had been £150,000, had 57 miles of gas
mains and fifteen gasometers, and London as a whole had 200 miles
of mains.[5] In this field not merely the managerial problems but the
very technicalities of the industry had to be learnt as the companies
grew.

IV

As in every discussion of the industrial revolution, here also the
experience of the cotton industry must play a central part, for not
only were the cotton mills among the earliest and most numerous

concerns which grew to a size in which managerial problems became important, but it also so happens that some of the entrepreneurs, managers and outside observers of this industry were among the most self-conscious and articulate regarding this problem. Yet in some respects this industry throws less light on our problems than do some of the others. This is precisely because large firms here were so numerous, so geographically concentrated and so quickly developed, that organization and management techniques could be copied without thinking, so that despite their relatively early appearance there were relatively few pioneers among the cotton entrepreneurs. Again, a cotton mill was so closely circumscribed by its standard machinery, and there was so much less scope for individual design, skill or new solutions to new problems, by 1830, at least, as compared with the other leading industries of mining and engineering, that little originality in internal layout was required from any but a handful of leaders, and 'no more than one or two men were required to manage a cotton mill' unless it were of exceptional size. Among those, of course, we shall find some of the true pioneers, the true epitomes, of the industrial revolution. It was here, also, that some of the worst failures occurred, the well-known abuses in the early cotton mills being 'evidence that the factory system soon outgrew the administrative technique which was being developed to cope with it'.[1]

The pioneer firms were built along the swift streams of Derbyshire, Nottinghamshire, North Wales and some of the less accessible parts of Scotland, but the industry was quickly localized around two centres, Manchester and Glasgow, the former being the leading one. The minor centres, such as the West Riding, the Furness district, North Wales, South Wales, the Belfast and Dublin areas, and the older centres of calico printing around London, which as late as 1805 contained twelve works in Surrey alone, employing 3,000 people or an average of 250 per firm, declined soon after 1800.[2]

In the bustling, expanding cotton towns competition was tough. It was easy to rise to the top, starting from nothing, borrowing funds and renting premises, but it was also easy to drop out of the race again. Technical changes followed so quickly on the heels of each other that the man who failed to innovate was at once unable to compete.

> The men who did establish themselves were raised by their own efforts—commencing in a very humble way, and pushing their advance by a series of unceasing exertions, having a very limited capital to begin with, or even none at all save that of their own

labour . . . the celerity with which some of these individuals
accumulated wealth in the early times of steam spinning and
weaving are proofs—if any such were wanting—that they were
men of quick views, great energy of character, and possessing no
small share of sagacity; and were by these means able to avail
themselves to the utmost of the golden advantages, which were
presented to their grasp, from 1790 to 1817, a time when they
supplied the whole universe with the products of manufacture.
. . . [These] men . . . had a practical acquaintance with
machinery, and . . . laboured themselves, assiduously and
diligently, [showing] that rapidity of action and quickness of
calculation, which were essentially necessary [to] keep pace
with the daily improvements projected and carried out around
[them].[1]

It was an environment encouraging ruthlessness, not only towards
one's competitors, but also towards one's employees, many of whom
consisted of women and children, and towards the fair face of the
countryside defiled by the builders of the cotton towns. The few
individuals among the cottonmasters who stand out as having a
social conscience regarding their communities were favoured by
cheap power, by cheap labour, or by being in the fine spinning
trade, in which profits were much higher and conditions of survival
easier, or by a combination of these factors.

The mills of Richard Arkwright and his partners grew to fair
size in the 1770s; and after a brief setback following the riot of 1779,
in which his Birkacre mill was destroyed, the numbers of mills
multiplied, especially when Arkwright's patent was declared void
in 1785. By 1788 there were at least 142 water-driven mills in Great
Britain, including forty-nine in Lancashire and Cheshire, thirty-
nine in Derbyshire and Nottinghamshire, and nineteen in Scotland;
and by 1796 Glasgow had thirty-nine water-mills and thirty large
calico-printing works.[2] Even in this early, water-twist phase of the
industry there were some giant works, particularly in Scotland,
where New Lanark with its 1,300–1,400 indoor and 300 outdoor
workers led the field, while several other famous mills, including
Catrine, Ballindaloch, Deanston, Stanley, Spinningdale and
Blantyre, mostly founded in the mid-eighties, employed 500–800
each, and some were soon to employ 1,000 or more.[3] In England
also Oldknow's Mellor, the Gregs' Styal or the groups of works
developed by the Peels in Bury and elsewhere, based on their calico-
printing shops, reached similar size.[4]

In the second phase, based increasingly on steam power, introduced in the mid-eighties, and on the power-mule, larger works

grew up in the cities also. About the turn of the century Atkinson's mill in Manchester employed some 1,500 under one roof, Phillips & Lee around 1,000, and John Horrocks was reputed to have been worth £150,000 at his death in 1804.[1] In 1798 Monteith began to operate power looms on a large scale at Pollockshaws, outside Glasgow, and within the following ten years or so increasing numbers followed his example.[2]

Expansion continued in the new century, and although some of the leading firms changed places, some of the largest, indeed, going to the wall, the representative firm became ever larger, and after 1815 it was increasingly a mixed spinning and weaving firm. The blue books of 1816 and 1818 permit us to describe a fair cross-section of the industry at the end of the war. At that time New Lanark employed 1,600, James Finlay & Co. an average of 500 in each of three mills in neighbouring counties, and Monteith, Bogle & Co. some 4,000, including outworkers. Forty-one Glasgow mills averaged 244 workers each. In England, Horrocks, Miller & Co. employed 700 spinners in four mills, but 'a whole countryside of weavers', some 7,000 all told; at Garstang, Fielding's print works had become the largest in England. The Strutts at Belper and Milford employed 1,494 in 1815 and 1,613 in 1818, while in Manchester itself, in 1818, McConnell & Kennedy, and Adam & George Murray employed about 1,200 each, Thomas Houldsworth 777 hands, Birley & Hornby 1,028, Phillips & Lee 937, Peter Marsland 644, Thomas Marriott 649, William Mitchell 540, the Ancoats Cotton Twist Co. 612, and the Pendleton Cotton Mills 531. There were several others in the 400–500 workers range. In 1812, 118 mills in Manchester and district averaged 210 workers each, and in 1816, according to one calculation, forty-three mills averaged 300, while according to another seventy mills averaged 330. Large mills outside this area included the Arkwrights' Cromford mills, employing 727, and the Holywell Twist Co. with 840. In Great Britain as a whole there were at least fifty-eight mills of over 200 workers, including twenty of over 400 and ten of over 600.[3]

There are further statistics available for about 1825, when some new large works had come to the fore, including James Dunlop (Glasgow, 500 hands), Joshua Milne (Oldham, 900–1,000), Joseph Horsefield (Manchester, 500–600) and the Darley Abbey Mills with 500–600 workers.[4] The best statistics, however, are those for 1832–3, the result of the two major factory inquiries.[5]

By the early 1830s the average of the Manchester mills had risen from about 300 to about 400 workers each; some thirty mills

employed over 500 and another forty-six employed 200–499 workers.[1]
There were seven firms in the Manchester area alone employing
over 1,000 workers each (not counting supervisory staff):

Birley & Kirk	1,692	Manchester and Dukinfield
Ormrod & Hardcastle	1,576	Bolton
McConnell & Co.	1,545	Manchester
E. & W. Bolling	1,356	Bolton
Thomas Houldsworth	1,201	Manchester
Joseph Horsefield	1,183	Hyde
Thomas Ashton	1,149	Hyde

In addition, Samuel Greg employed some 1,400–1,500 in five
separate locations.[2] Some of these, it will be seen, were recent additions to the list of giants. No similar calculations were made for
Scotland, and the average was probably lower, as there were
numerous mills in the 200–500 range. The relative decline of
Scotland was also evident from the fact that there were now no
concerns with over 1,000 workers, with the possible exception of
William Graham, reputed to employ 1,000–2,000 in Glasgow mills,[3]
and the largest mills were still the early water-mills of the 1780s:

Walker & Co.	930	New Lanark
Buchanan & Co.	920	Stanley
Finlay & Co.	776	Ballindaloch
Finlay & Co.	869	Catrine
Finlay & Co.	700	Deanston
Henry Monteith	800	Blantyre

Most of these had now added steam power as well as power weaving.

The extraordinary expansion in the output per worker, particularly in spinning, which accompanied this growth, was achieved
largely by constant improvement as well as enlargement of the
capital equipment. Water-wheels were replaced by steam machinery,
mules became more complex and began to be professionally built,
and the same applied to machinery for carding, roving and other
ancillary processes. While at the beginning of this period investment
in fixed equipment and stocks would cost £10 per worker, by 1830
this had risen to about £100, or £15 million for an estimated labour
force of 160,000 in spinning and weaving. Investment in a 'typical'
mill of the 1830 period would therefore cost some £20,000–£50,000,[4]
though many of the existing mills had cost rather less to build, and
much of the equipment had been put in by the firms' own mechanics
rather than bought out from specialist makers.

The technical innovations which had turned the cotton industry into a factory industry reached the woollen and worsted districts about a generation later, the first spinning mills being set up in the 1790s, and the power loom and power mill not until the very end of the period. Further, there were large areas, particularly in the West Country, which did not take easily to machine methods and concentration in factories, and in which the large firms continued to the end of our period to consist of a few centralized, powered workshops linked with large numbers of outworkers. Consequently the woollen and worsted industries did not reach the degree of concentration and capitalization of cotton by 1830. In other respects, however, there were great similarities, factories being spread out, in the early phases, along the streams for power, and later concentrated in the towns, and employment being largely for women and children, especially in the spinning sections.[1]

Benjamin Gott, whose works were to become among the largest and most mechanized, set up his Bean Ing Mill in 1792. Built on the outskirts of Leeds round the water power, but otherwise most up to date, it employed 744 indoors in 1813, 1,019 in 1819 and 1,120 in 1829, at Bean Ing, plus 300–400 in the other mills, but for most of this period only the scribbling, fulling and jenny spinning were mechanized; power weaving, shearing and mule spinning were introduced towards the end of the period.[2] By 1833 there were only ten other woollen factories in Yorkshire with over 200 workers, the largest being T. W. Stansfield (Leeds, 610), James Akroyd (Halifax, 550), John Wood (Bradford, 527), and Pim, Nevins & Son (Leeds, 552). For the West Country it is not easy to establish comparable figures, as outworkers were often included, and the area ran counter to the usual practice, by having many of the weavers working indoors, on power looms and carpet looms, while many of the spinners continued to work domestically. The following, however, seem to be examples of figures for inworkers only, in most cases some outworkers being additionally employed: Matravers & Overbury (Westbury, 500–550), Wm. H. Sheppard (Frome, 500), Wm. Hardisty (Shepton Mallet, 500), Edward Cooper (Trowbridge, 400–500), J. W. Partridge (Stroud, 500), and in other parts of the country, Wilson & Co. (Bannockburn, 500) and Clark's Market Harborough carpet factory, employing 600. Pease's Darlington worsted mills had employed 400 indoors and several thousand out at the beginning of the century, but were burnt down in 1817. While the average employment in West Country mills had been about 110 in 1816, it had probably grown somewhat by 1833, but could hardly have exceeded

200; by 1838, in a more complete list, it was fifty to seventy. In the West Riding in 1833, there were 204 worsted mills, using 159 steam engines of 3,186 horsepower and 102 water-wheels of 873 horsepower, and employing 16,742 hands, or an average of eighty per mill; in Lancashire, the eight mills employed an average of 130 each. Woollen mills were, on average, smaller still.[1]

By comparison, the linen industry appeared to consist of scattered units. Although much of it could be found in two regions, Yorkshire and north-eastern Scotland, the individual works were more isolated from each other and thus did not form the compact groups among which mutual copying was easy. Technically, flax proved even more difficult to deal with by machine spinning than wool, and the industry was much smaller and advanced less rapidly, until it broke into the European market towards the end of this period. Though first tried out about 1787, machine spinning did not develop on any scale until it was taken up by John Marshall, whose firm became by far the largest concern. Beginning with a merchanting business inherited from his father in 1787, he opened his first mill in Holbeck, in 1791, and began building his branch plant in Shrewsbury in 1796. By about 1815 he employed some 700 in the Leeds mill and over 400 in Shrewsbury, and had made a fortune of £400,000; by 1831 the Leeds mill employed 1,039 and in 1833 about 1,317, the Shrewsbury figures being about 400–500 then. There were other works of considerable size in Leeds, including Messrs. Benyon, former partners of Marshall, employing 611, Messrs. Hives Atkinson, other former partners, employing 554, and Titley, Tathams & Walker, 447.[2]

The Belfast industry did not get beyond the stage of a central workshop with many outworkers in this period,[3] though Messrs. Boomar & Co. employed 600 in two mills in flax and cotton spinning in 1833; but the Scottish centres, and Aberdeen in particular, developed some large units. Leys, Masson & Co. employed 544 in 1816 and 1,152 in 1833, and among others, in 1833, Mill, Cruden & Co. of the same district employed 500, T. A. Mulholland some 660, and there were several others employing well over 200 each. Altogether, in 1833, 352 flax mills were enumerated, employing 33,862 hands, or an average of just over 100 each.[4]

In silk, although weaving remained domestic even longer than elsewhere, the preparation of the yarn, known as silk 'throwing', became a factory industry earlier than any other, beginning with the erection of Thomas Lombe's silk mill on an island in Derby in 1717. The mill, a marvel of ingenuity in the eyes of contemporaries, was copied quickly,[1] and silk mills became concentrated in a few centres, in Coventry, East Anglia, Macclesfield and Stockport. They employed, proportionately, far more children, and far younger children, than other mills. In 1765 John Sherrard, silk-throwster, employed 1,500 hands in four areas, Spragg, Hopkins & White, 800, John Graham 500, John Powell 400, but it is not certain whether all of these were, in fact, employed indoors. In Stockport, a little later, four mills employed 1,000 workers between them, and Philip Clowes, of Macclesfield, had employed 720 in 1761. By 1833 the typical factory employed 200–300 women and children, and some were considerably larger. Grout, Baylis & Co., with works in London, Yarmouth, Norwich, Bungay, Millinghall and Bockingham Bramhill, who had employed 3,900 in 1825, were still employing 2,700 in 1833, a large proportion of them indoors; S. Pearson & Bros. of Macclesfield, employed 800 (of whom 600 were under 15), and in the Manchester-Congleton-Macclesfield area there were eleven firms employing over 200 each, with an average of 460. Finally, Jonas Brook & Bros. of Meltham Mills, spinning cotton and silk, employed 623. In Norfolk, four silk factories employed an average of 568 each, and the average over the whole country was 128.[2]

Hosiery knitting and lace manufacture were the last major textile trades to remain organized on the 'domestic' system. Even here, however, technical inventions were made, including the ribbed hose by Strutt. John Heathcote's bobbin-net machine patented in 1808 and 1809, led to the establishment of a large factory, first at Loughborough, and then at Tiverton, where by 1833, he employed about 800 workers under his roof and 1,500 outworkers. Another firm to expand quickly on the basis of machine lace-making was Wheatley & Riste, of Chard, employing 500 in the factory and 200 out. Other large employers continued to lighten their burdens of management by superimposing their new stocking frames on the old subcontract system: they included I. & R. Morley, who provided work for 2,700 frames about 1840, and Heard & Hurst, who provided work for 2,000.[3]

V

Finally, there were some industries which perhaps played a lesser part in the national transformation of the economy as such, yet included a handful of interesting pioneering firms which influenced the development of industrial management. The varied firms which were coming to be thought of under the common heading of the 'chemical industry' and were largely concentrated in two areas, the Midlands and Scotland, formed one such group. Its members may not have been very large in this period, but they were not without consequence. Among them we might include Roebuck & Garbett's sulphuric acid manufactory, transferred from Birmingham to Prestonpans in 1748 and employing fifty men there, and James Keir's Tipton chemical works, concentrating largely on alkali and soap production from about 1782 on, whose 'organisation and running showed features of considerable technical and human significance'.[1] In Scotland, Charles Tennant, who discovered the use of chloride of lime as a bleaching powder about 1794, began production at the St. Rollox works in 1797. By 1825 the works consumed some 30,000 tons of coal yearly, by 1830 it covered 10 acres and by about 1840 it was said to employ 1,000 workers. Another partner in the venture was Charles Macintosh, F.R.S., whose father had employed 500 operatives in mass-producing boots and shoes, a man interested in cotton spinning, and the inventor, in 1822, of a process of waterproofing by using naphtha, a formerly useless by-product of the tar that was accumulating outside the gas plants. Tar-making itself was a process developed by another Scotsman, Lord Dundonald, and led to the establishment of some works of considerable size on the coalfields from 1792 onwards.[2]

A related industry was brewing, where the technical and economic advantages of size had led to the establishment of exceptionally large units among the London porter brewers in the eighteenth century. Campbell lists them, together with ship carpenters (i.e. shipbuilders), distillers, potters, soap-boilers and sugar-bakers, among the manufacturing trades of London requiring the largest quantities of initial capital:

> the Business of a Brewer requires a large Stock of Ready Money to set up with, and the Profits returned are proportionally considerable.[3]

This was an exceptionally capital-intensive industry, since the transformation was largely chemical and required heat rather than manipulation, while the handling was minimized by using the force of gravity. Nevertheless, by the end of the century the largest breweries employed up to 100 workmen each, together with an almost equal number of horses, as well as steam engines; the capital tied up in the leading half-dozen firms reached £200,000 by the 1790s, and up to four times that amount by 1830, though about half of this would be represented by investment in tied houses.[1] Distilleries did not reach quite the same size, yet before 1788 the Kilbagie distillery in Scotland produced 3,000 tons of spirits a year and fed 7,000 black cattle and 2,000 swine on its refuse. It employed 300 people and 'buildings and utensils' cost over £40,000. There were several others of similar size. Sugar refineries and soap-boiling houses were, however, distinctly smaller.[2]

By contrast, there was only a single really large grain milling enterprise, the famous Albion Mill, built by Rennie in London for a partnership in which Boulton and Watt played a leading role, largely with the object of popularizing the use of their steam engines to drive rotary machinery. Its history is too well known to need repetition here. Before it was burnt down, in mysterious circumstances, in 1791, it had threatened to replace a considerable proportion of the small millers around London, and had employed a capital of £106,000 and a staff approaching seventy-five men.[3]

The potteries were also helped by chemical and physical discoveries, but their drastic transformation from an industry of small, workshop-like units, a 'peasant industry',[4] to large complex organizations with national, and in some cases international, markets was caused more by organizational than by technical changes. It was above all the genius of Josiah Wedgwood which transformed a provincial backwater into one of the leading growth points of the industrial revolution, by-passing and overtaking the several fine porcelain works which had been established, in London and elsewhere, in the first half of the century on the Continental pattern to cater for a narrow luxury demand.

The familiarity of the potters with machinery in wind- or water-driven flint grinding mills, and with pumping equipment in the associated mines, led to the early adoption of Boulton & Watt engines in Staffordshire. Wedgwood installed his first in 1782, and had a second before the first Lancashire cotton mill had ordered one. There were four in his works by 1800. The potters were also among the first to encourage the building of canals, being dependent on this means of transport for their bulky and fragile but cheap goods. Wedgwood's firm, established in the factory village of 'Etruria' in 1768–9 along the canal that was to link it with the rest of the world, together with a Chelsea enamelling and finishing branch, was a pioneer of new techniques, such as the use of the pyrometer, the mixing of new clays and glazes and the use of lathes. Josiah Wedgwood also pioneered methods of internal management, sales by showrooms in London, Dublin and Bath, and internationally effective advertising, and introduced art into a major mass-production industry.[1]

By 1770 Wedgwood had 150 men employed at Etruria, besides numbers of others on 'useful ware' in Burslem and on enamelling work in Chelsea. By 1790 there were 160 in the useful branch, and 110 in the ornamental, organized by a far-reaching division of labour. At first the steam engine concentrated the preparatory processes round the grinding mills. Soon after it was also applied to wheels for throwers and turners, who were freed from other tasks by subdivision of the workforce. The 'jolley' for pressed ware was attended by women and printing simplified the application of painted decoration to pottery. In the design, however, as well as in much of the painting, craftsmen of a high order still continued to be employed, and helped to create the national and international reputation on the basis of which the mass production of goods then became possible. By about 1810 the 'net worth' of Wedgwood's company was put at £35,000, though Josiah I was reputed to have left £½ million at his death. In 1812 the firm employed 478 wage-earners, while another one, Robert Hamilton, reported reducing its labour force from 400 to 210, and in 1816 Wedgwood's numbers had fallen to 387. By 1833, however, the firm had been overtaken by several other potters, as follows:

Enoch Wood, Burslem	1,000	employees
Pratt, Fenton	700	,,
Thomas Minton, Stoke	c. 700	,,
Josiah Spode, Stoke	c. 700	,,
Hicks, Meigh & Co., Shelton	600	,,
R. Stevenson, Cobridge	600	,,
J. Ridgway, Shelton	500	,,

besides several others in the 300–400 range. Although there was still much subcontract, particularly by skilled workers, these firms required much capital and considerable production organization.[2] Elsewhere potteries were smaller. The Derby factory, in the 1770s, employed but seventy, and many of these were children; the Rockingham pottery employed 270 in 1826, on a capital of £15,000–£20,000; the Herculaneum pottery in Liverpool was valued at £5,500 in 1816, excluding the value of the cottages.[3]

Great Britain had developed into one of the leading European glassmaking countries in the course of the seventeenth century. Carried on in relatively small units, with fuel problems not dissimilar from those of the iron industry, the industry developed a structure of family interrelationship akin to that of the latter, especially in the Midlands. Towards the end of the eighteenth century larger works in Birmingham and Dudley began to replace the older and smaller units of the Stourbridge area. In 1774 it was said that a plate-glass furnace would cost £3,500 and would take six years to build: the British Plate Glass Co., established in 1773 with a capital of £40,000, took, in fact, three years. It had indifferent success at first, and was re-incorporated in 1798 at a valuation of about £105,000. In 1795 it employed 300–400 men and a steam engine for grinding and polishing which was said to have saved the labour of 160 men. A second St. Helens 'Crown Glass' works, set up in 1826, and managed by W. Pilkington in 1830, was valued at about £20,000 at that time. The numerous glassworks in the Newcastle area were all much smaller.[1] By 1841, however, William Chance, then the largest crown-glass maker in the country, was employing some 700 workers in Stourbridge, Cookson Bros. at South Shields and Newcastle employed 462, and Ridley Bros., Newcastle, 379.[2]

Finally, papermaking has sometimes been considered to be an industry which became subject to a capitalistic form of organization in this period. Machines and steam power were, indeed, expensive, and there is record of at least one projector who organized a joint-stock company with a capital of £71,000 in 1800–1. This firm, however, lost its money, and the typical mill cost £4,000–£5,000, the largest costing no more than £15,000 in our period, and while there were a few firms which might have approached a labour force of 200, it was unlikely that more than one or two exceeded it.[3]

VI

The foregoing sections are not intended to be comprehensive histories of the different industries in the period under review. On the contrary, they are meant to concentrate exclusively on the features which have a bearing on the development of industrial management, omitting others that have no such connection, and they are intended to show, further, the great differences between industries. In the chapters following we shall necessarily have occasion to refer to problems, for example of recruitment, training, or disciplining labour, or of capital accounting, as if these were uniform and generalized over the whole field of industry. Many of them were general and developed general solutions of their own, but any impression of uniformity should have been dispelled by the present chapter. Among the major relevant differences in the process of industrialization were those relating to speed and timing, to location and concentration, to the degree of technical change, to the type of industry, to the type of structure of firms and industry, to the type of labour employed, and to the form of control.

Some industries, as, for example, porter brewing and coalmining, began to show problems of size well before 1750; an important group of industries passed their threshold in the 1780s, including cotton spinning, bar-iron making and engineering; others, like gas plants, did not develop until the early years of the new century, and others still, like linen and woollen weaving, did not begin to be transformed until the very end of our period. Similarly, the speed of development varied markedly: hand cotton spinning, with minor exceptions, was wiped out almost at once; flax spinning survived machine competition much better. Handloom weaving and framework knitting dragged on interminably in face of a new machine method of operation.

Secondly, there were great differences in location. Mining and early metallurgy were largely rural industries; later metallurgy, engineering and textiles were urban. The degree of social control available to, or forced upon, the manufacturer and his managers might differ widely as between these two groups. More important still was the difference between isolated firms, typical for the engineering industry, for example, and clusters of them such as were found in coal-mining or cotton spinning. From the point of view of this study, this is one of the cardinal distinctions, involving the degree to which entrepreneurs had to pioneer their own management techniques, or were able to pick up the habits current in their neighbourhood. It might also vitally affect the pressure placed on them to find ancillary or complementary industries, and their ability to meet that pressure.

Perhaps the most obvious of the changes which, in the aggregate, form the industrial revolution are the changes in technique, the technical inventions and innovations. They, too, were anything but universal. In some cases, as in textile spinning, in printing or in steam-engine making, entrepreneurs were dealing with mechanical devices completely different in nature from the equipment they replaced; in others, as in iron puddling and in some engineering processes, there were substantial changes in techniques, which yet merely replaced earlier, recognizably similar, though less 'efficient', methods; in the chemical industry and in coke smelting, there was the discovery of possible chemical reactions which had just not been known at all before; and in other industries still, as in civil engineering and mining, it was possible by new methods of calculation and measurement to register achievements on a scale which had been quite unthinkable as long as work had progressed merely by rule of thumb and by unsystematic experience. Over and against these 'technical' changes, however, there were improvements in organization rather than technique or productive equipment, involving better layout of factory space, division of labour, design of the product with the process of production in mind, interchangeability of parts, control of raw material stocking and supply, and so on. This difference in principle between technical and organizational changes was one of the major determinants of managerial problems.

Fourthly, there were, then as now, the important distinctions between the problems of 'process' industries and those of assembly industries, each with their various subgroups. Most of the industries concerned, in fact, belonged to the former group, as, indeed, the production of final customers' goods was frequently the last to be mechanized and in many fields was still carried on by hand at the end of our period. Building and civil engineering, producing unique products on unique sites, had their own problems again, and so had the genuine multi-product firms, like Soho with its metal goods and ornaments, steam engines, copying presses and complete mint installations.

The structure of the industry is also important. In some, as in coal-mines or in some textile mills, managers were dealing with large single units; elsewhere, as in some lead-mining, and in most of the ironworks, firms were 'large' only because they contained many linked yet in many ways quite independent small units, each of which could almost be managed as if it belonged to a separate owner. The latter had a strong incentive to integrate backward, as in the Welsh ironworks, for example, which owned their own coal-mines and ore-fields, or to integrate forward, like the iron-masters who employed their own nailers. Others, again, developed ancillary enterprises, like machine-building shops, transport departments, or farms.

The nature of the labour force and the changes in its composition again form distinctive characteristics which will be stressed repeatedly in the sequel. Some employers dealt essentially with skilled craftsmen of the traditional, apprenticed type, like papermakers or masons, or with men of new apprenticed skills, like engineers or ironfounders. Others employed men of experience if not 'skill' in the accepted sense, like coal-miners or blast-furnace workers, and others used large numbers of unskilled labourers, as in civil engineering. The textile mills employed women and children, and silk-throwing mills largely very young children, while building and civil engineering employed what was often a temporary labour force, unattached to any firm. Again, some labour was local and some was largely immigrant, as in South Wales, and while most of it became settled, civil engineering continued to deal with a nomadic specialist force supported by local part-timers.

Finally, there were firms, for example in non-ferrous mineral-mining, which were traditionally companies or large, impersonal partnerships; in other industries a small number of active partner-owners was typical, and others still, like the potteries, were traditionally one-man businesses. The tasks, and the status, of the management hierarchy would differ in each of these.

The list is not exhaustive. It is, however, long enough to emphasize the danger of treating all industries as if they belonged to a single process called the 'industrial revolution'. These dangers are real and should be in the mind of the reader as they have been in that of the author. Yet, it is hoped, the evidence of the chapters which are to follow shows that there was a common thread running through that process of economic transformation, and that there is some value and purpose in treating all management problems of that period as if they had a unity—a unity, moreover, which transcends national borders and embraces the industrialization processes of other countries and other centuries also.

4/ The Managers

In the industrial revolution the typical entrepreneur was his own manager. Yet, as firms grew larger and required salaried staff, and as the second or third generation of owners retired from active control, the problem of management became increasingly a problem of personnel: the numbers and the skill of the managers. The concept of a 'manager', not very clear even today, had no fixed meaning at the time, nor had related terms such as 'supervisor' or 'superintendent', while the structure of larger firms was more idiosyncratic than in the twentieth century. Nevertheless, by concentrating on the centre of the range, on the manager of a large works, below the active proprietors but above the foremen or clerks, we may catch a glimpse of the essence of the new skills required and the methods by which they were created or by-passed.

This chapter will examine the training, origins, status and payment of the industrial 'manager' in this period.

I

The early and mid-Victorian age, when higher technical studies of all kinds and the education of the poor were indeed neglected, fostered the myth that the eighteenth century was a dark age in popular or technical education. The excellent work by Hans and by Webb[1] and the large number of recent studies on the Nonconformist academies and the training of the professions have made it evident that there was, in fact, a rich variety of education as well as a wide range of standards, including the very highest, available to broad sections of the population in the later eighteenth and early nineteenth centuries. The number of genuinely self-taught geniuses was remarkably small, in spite of the large space they occupy in the literature. It is also difficult to resist the conclusion that the important changes in educational provision which did occur to meet the new commercial and industrial demands prove the system to have been responsive, and that more changes would have been made had they been felt necessary. Although very few completed the whole journey from rags to riches, society was at least as open to the talents, in the

industrial-commercial sphere, as it has been at any time since.[1]
Here is the testimony of a hostile source in 1818:

> First, then, as to the employers: with very few exceptions, they
> are a set of men who have sprung from the cotton-shop without
> education or address, except so much as they have acquired by
> their intercourse with the little world of merchants at the
> exchange at Manchester. They bring up their families at the
> most costly schools, determined to give their offspring a double
> portion of what they were so deficient in themselves.[2]

In considering the formal educational provisions of the time, it
should be remembered that entry to the universities could take
place at the age of 14, and that preparation for even the most highly
organized professions ended at a comparatively early age, though
practical pupilage might take several additional years. The sheer
quantity of knowledge to be absorbed, and the number of books
available on any given subject, were incomparably smaller than
today. As a result, the *savants* of the day were well versed in many
fields and easily switched subjects in their teaching,[3] while the
students preparing for the different professions, the law, medicine or
divinity, or for none, were given a largely identical curriculum,
except at the highest stages and in the practical part of the training.
The incipient struggle between the arts and the sciences (or rather,
between the classics and modern education) was not, therefore,
dealing with exclusive specialization, and it was possible to learn
the ancient languages and still absorb all there was to know of
science. At the same time, scientific subjects were in flux, but
communication had not yet adapted to this, so that the discoveries
of some teachers in such subjects as medicine, chemistry or physics
might stay unknown to other learned institutions for a generation.
Above all, educational institutions overlapped to a degree difficult
to grasp now, and some private tuition, taken before boarding
school and academy, might well be above the standards of the
universities. 'Standards', in fact, more correctly applied to individual teachers or schools than to types of school, academy or
university.

At the lowest level, the village school, attended by the children
of the poorer classes, of yeoman farmers and skilled craftsmen,
varied between very wide limits; the Scottish parish schools maintained more uniform standards, although even here there were many
underprivileged parishes.[4] There were villages with adequate schools
in England and Wales, and others had at least one devoted

individual,[1] often perhaps following quite an ordinary non-scholarly occupation, but yet delighting in learning and in opening the eyes of talented boys in the neighbourhood. William Edwards, the Welsh bridge-builder, George Stephenson, Joseph Bramah, Richard Arkwright, J. B. Neilson, Josiah Wedgwood, Jedediah Strutt, Richard Trevithick, John Kennedy, James McConnell, Samuel Garbett, Matthew Murray, Richard Roberts, John Heathcoat, John Gilbert, John U. Rastrick and Timothy Hackworth are only some of the illustrious names among the makers of the industrial revolution who had the village school as the main, or sole, basis of their formal education. In virtually every case formal education was followed by apprenticeship to some local craftsman, and it was such skilled men in the building and metal trades in particular, as well as in commerce, who 'enhanced the potential wealth of entrepreneurial ability'[2] and formed an important reservoir of managerial personnel, as well as a driving force of technical progress.

In the northern counties especially, elementary education was widely available. There the bequests of pious post-Reformation school founders[3] had not been ravaged as much as in the South by the greed of the intervening centuries, perhaps because of the close example of Scotland, or because yeoman democracy held out longer, or perhaps because, as in all fringe areas less favoured than the richer metropolitan centre, education was held in higher esteem. Thus the North-West was said to have supplied in this period 'a continuous stream of emigrants who filled the counting-houses in London or found a corner in the Church or the lower ranks of the public service'. 'By 1796', according to Tom Rumney, writing from London, 'the north of England had "become quite a manufactory for Bankers' and Merchants' clerks".' From Northumberland, John Grey said of his village school that 'several youths' had been sent 'as bailiffs and stewards to different parts of the United Kingdom . . . whose fitness for such situations was mainly attributable to the instruction obtained there'.[4] Such judgements confirm what the breathtaking advances in technology and organization surely proved by themselves, that it could by no means be taken for granted that

> the headlong advance of industrial activity . . . had far out-distanced the growth of those educational facilities upon which trained leadership and a disciplined labour force ultimately depend.

If a particular

industry had to turn for its managers to men schooled only in the craft which they practised and lacking both the rudimentary general training and the discipline which formal education of the most elementary kind would have afforded,[1]

this merely reflected an unusual backwardness and narrow-minded attitude of its leaders, in this case, Black Country mine-owners—and illustrates once again the uneven tempo of the industrial revolution.

While elementary education could take some of the early strain, it was to the 'secondary' schools and colleges that the leaders and managers of the revolutions in industry and transport looked for a parallel revolution in education. Thus the new economy and the new society served to pull apart and widen the gap between the education of the middle and working classes, just as they served to polarize their wealth, their status and their political power.

As in so many other fields of management, the foundations of this new education were laid by the merchants of the first half of the eighteenth century. They had not been alone in attacking the classical learning and the grammar schools and old public schools at which it was taught. Attacks were made also on grounds of religion against Anglican exclusiveness, and against the practices of concentrating on the needs of the clergy and neglecting those of the other professions, as well as of ignoring the demands of gentlemen for such subjects as politics, belles-lettres and modern languages. Some schools had stopped teaching altogether, their funds being consumed by sinecurists or corrupt corporations; and others, defying their charters, taught fee-paying scholars only. But it was the merchants, including those important forerunners of later industrialists, the putting-out masters, who felt the greatest urgency to demand new curricula, and possessed the largest means to establish them.[2]

The older institutions had provided, in addition to the basic classical education (grammar, Latin, Greek and ancient history and philosophy), the background teaching for the three main types of graduates: clergymen, doctors and lawyers. The new learning demanded two additional broad groups of subjects, though the division between them was by no means clear-cut: there were the 'commercial' subjects, including modern languages (significantly called, in many prospectuses, 'commercial languages'), book-keeping, shorthand, commercial law and practices of the chief countries, including their taxation systems, political economy, commercial calculations, geography and navigation. Secondly, there were the scientific and technological subjects, including mathematics, pure and applied, physics, chemistry, anatomy, botany and zoology, engineering and surveying, and astronomy. In addition, some other subject groups were developed, including military and naval studies on the one hand and subjects for young gentlemen, such as fencing, dancing, 'polite literature' and history on the other, but these were of no interest to capitalist entrepreneurs, except as additional battering-rams to break down the walls of the citadels of the classics.

The grandiose schemes of Defoe, who proposed a University of London (though admittedly without any great changes from the curricula of the existing universities), and of Postlethwayt, who demanded a mercantile college for London, are well known;[1] but lesser schemers were active also. Parents wishing for a mercantile career were easily converted to the view that more useful knowledge was acquired in practical work on a job, in the merchants' counting house or as supercargo on journeys abroad than at existing colleges and universities, even though apprenticeship fees to the better merchants were much higher than the school fees at the better schools.

> A Youth designed for . . . any Mercantile Branch, has no occasion for spending his time at the University, or for a critical knowledge of the Dead Languages. . . . At present, private Boarding Schools, called Academies, are preferred to the Public Seminaries, and, perhaps, not without a great deal of reason.

For after sevens years' schooling,

> whatever progress they have made in *Greek* and *Latin*, it is certain they often know no more of their Mother Tongue (except the mere sound) than if they had been born in *Japan* or the Cape of *Good Hope*.

Seven years of

> cramming a Boy's Head full of a Dead Language, of useless words, and incoherent terms, satiates his memory and confounds his judgment.

These sentiments of Campbell, printed in his careers guide of 1747, clearly represented a widespread attitude in commercial London.[2]

With the rise of large-scale industry the leading industrialists developed an outlook necessarily as broad as that of the leading merchants, and the mercantile views on education came to be shared by the captains of industry. Thus William Reynolds deplored the lack of interest in physics in 1777:

> I look upon it to be a good deal owing to the faults of Education
> —children are too often taught to construe a Latin book & write
> a good hand without ever being acquainted with the most useful
> truths of Natural philosophy which are far better suited to their
> capacities and far more agreeable to their inclinations than
> droning for years over a Latin Accidence which is often the case
> —the knowledge of things is too much disregarded while that
> of words is too much attended to and which is the most useful
> as well as agreeable every one will readily determine.[1]

Dr. Erasmus Darwin, Wedgwood informed his partner, Bentley, in 1779,

> said he thought it a very idle waste of time for any boys intended
> for trade to learn Latin, as they seldom learnt it to any tolerable
> degree of perfection or retained what they learnt. Besides they
> did not want it, and the time would be much better bestowed
> in making themselves perfect in French and accounts. He
> advises me not to send (my sons) again to Bolton but to teach
> them what we can at home and then send them to some French
> academy, unless we can get a french prisoner, or some such
> opportunity of teaching them the french language here.

Wedgwood himself agreed that if grammar was required it had
better be studied in English, and while he conceded the arguments
of the Latinists, that Latin enabled one to derive the origins of
words and helped in polite conversation,

> this is learning a *thousand* things to make use of *one*. . . . Seven
> years is a large portion of life . . . that time must be employ'd
> in education, which should be devoted to learning a business, I
> mean from about 14 to 20, whilst fine habits of gentlemanly
> learning would dispose against the drudgery of business.[2]

He did, in fact, have his children taught at home, finding not only
a prisoner to teach French but also some of the leading scientists of
the age, including (Sir) John Leslie, Dr. Erasmus Darwin and
Alexander Chisholm to teach science, whilst he himself introduced
his boys to his experiments and, no doubt, to his habits of business.
    These were some of the men standing at the centre of the scientific
and cultural as well as industrial revolution of the age, 'and it was
not least the need to provide education for their own families which
first prompted and kept alive an interest in educational ideas and

methods'.[1] Similar examples of the new, utilitarian attitude to education could be found in other leading centres of industry, such as Nottingham, Newcastle, Leeds, Glasgow, and Bristol.

> Surely a person of your liberal spirit [wrote Dr. Beddoes, the former Oxford don dismissed for his Radicalism, and now tutoring the Lambton boys in Bristol, to John Wilkinson, one of their guardians] cannot suppose that to spend much of the best years of a young man on Hexameters and Pentameters, Alcaics & Sapphics is the proper sphere for the human understanding. I would have these boys good classics . . . but they should surely be taught those sciences which are almost the principal hinges on which the world turns.[2]

Again, the industrialists were not alone in their attacks, but merely joined their own powerful forces to those of others. One important force was Puritanism, gaining influence with the rising wealth and consequently social position of certain groups of Nonconformists, particularly the Quakers and the Calvinists. In clear antithesis to the ideals of Lord Chesterfield, the world of the Friends was spiritual and vocational in aim:

> It was not cultural in the sense that interests could be pursued for their private and personal intimations of pleasure and enrichment . . . these things in which one had personal pleasure or elation because they were beautiful or because they deepened human understanding, or because they enriched emotional experience or gave intellectual satisfaction, were not to be taught.

The emphasis was

> actual and moral . . . It creates an atmosphere in which the vocational subjects are paramount.[3]

As for the Calvinists, the link between their beliefs and the educational needs of the industrial revolution is well illustrated by the following words of Doddridge, perhaps the leading teacher within the Nonconformist academies, addressed to a tradesman:

> It is in the capacity of a *Tradesman*, that you are to serve your Family and Country, tho' I would not have so fine a genius entirely discouraged from entertaining itself with the refined pleasures of a Student; yet it would be Imprudence to yourself, and an Injury to the World, to spend so much time in your Closet, as to neglect your Warehouse; and to be so much taken

up with the volumes of Philosophy or History, Poetry or even
Divinity, as to forget to look into your Books of Accounts. . . .
Let us remember that we are to place our Point of Life . . . in
a care to do that *well*, which Providence hath assigned us, as
our peculiar Business.[1]

The other, and perhaps even stronger, influence was the Utilitarian philosophy.[2]

There had been [it was said in 1810][3] from about 1780, a
diffusion of knowledge among the body of the people the like of
which had never been known. There had been an astonishing
multiplication of elementary books, summaries, abstracts,
tables, museums, exhibitions and collections, all to provide
information at a glance . . . To be a person of good education,
therefore, meant keeping up with a multiplicity of subjects . . .
Even to 'pass current in the informed circles of society' meant
knowing something of political economy, chemistry, mineralogy,
geology and etymology . . . (art and literature) . . . over and
above some little knowledge of trade and agriculture; with a
reasonable acquaintance with what is called the philosophy of
politics . . . The middle order of Society, composed of merchants, merchant-shopkeepers, bankers, stockbrokers, cashiers,
tax-collectors, doctors, lawyers, manufacturers, certain yeomen,
mine-owners, scholars, school-teachers, some craftsmen and
ministers of religion clamoured for education. They developed
the new disciplines that were taking shape and which were to
change the pattern of learning. Without altogether despising
the educational routines of Oxford and Cambridge, they
aspired to found new institutions for those children who were
destined to the pursuits of art, trade and commerce, in which
not Latin and Greek (almost useless in these avocations) should
be taught, but the national language, which has generally been
neglected, together with all those branches of knowledge, which,
if not absolutely necessary, are always useful and agreeable.

The fact that new subjects became respectable in this period
was the result largely of the needs of those playing a leading part in
the industrial revolution, aided by the new professions themselves.[4]
The main impetus, the leadership, and the funds necessarily came
from the proprietors rather than the managers of industry with
which this chapter is largely concerned, but the two, in this context,
are inseparable. Managers were often the relations or friends of the
owners of their own or other firms, or were themselves future owners.
The education of the two groups overlapped over nearly the whole

range—except, indeed, where the arrived *nouveau riche* sent his sons to the great public schools to make aristocratic friends, his income being assured by the family wealth.[1]

The new influence worked through the whole range of secondary and higher education, old and new.[2] It was to be found in private tutors' studies, in the grammar schools, the great public schools and other boarding schools, the academies, and the universities. It was also found among the many new institutions for adult education, the public lectures, the societies, and the mechanics' institutes.

Domestic tuition was spreading from the landed classes of the top rank to the middle classes. In Wedgwood's establishment three of his own children, a nephew and two of his clerks' children were taught Latin, writing and accounting by three of his employees; a French prisoner taught French and drawing; while several other academic subjects, physical exercises and character building were also included.[3] It was certainly one of the best known, but not the only one. The tutors in this period of the 'domestic experiment'[4] included such leading scientists as Joseph Priestley, Colin Milne, Charles Hutton and John Bonnycastle. This type of education had, however, obvious drawbacks, and had to be supplemented by more formal institutions. If it created 'intellectual, religious and social precocity, an early maturity and adult standing',[5] and allowed in consequence an earlier start of practical training in the management of firms, then this by its very nature would apply to the sons of proprietors rather than to those who still had to rise into the managerial class.

More widespread, and more significant, were the private schools kept, usually by clergymen, for boarders and others. They were operating at many different levels, but at their best they provided a good general education and reacted most sensitively to the demand for modern, commercial or scientific subjects.[6] Joshua Field was at such a boarding school from the age of 7 to the age of 16 when his training was considered good enough to qualify him for the responsible and, as it proved, pioneering post of draughtsman to Sir Samuel Bentham, about to introduce mass production into naval blockmaking. George Stephenson, regretting his own lack of education, sent his son Robert to such a school in Newcastle. Samuel Whitbread found his schooling (and £300 paid for his apprenticeship to a brewer) sufficient for one of the most successful industrial careers in the eighteenth century. Matthew Boulton acquired at the Rev. John Hanstead's private school not only sufficient knowledge for worldly success, but also an abiding interest in and appreciation of scientific and cultural progress. Edward Pease returned aged 14, after three years of boarding school with Joseph Tatham, sen., of Leeds, 'well educated in English, with a very fair knowledge of Latin, proficiency in French, and able to draw and paint a little'. Again, Strutt sent his second son, George, to Thomas Astley, Unitarian minister at Chesterfield in 1775.

Some of these schoolmasters took up management themselves. John Kelsall was perhaps a less successful example of such recruitment, but there were others like John Buddle, sen., later manager of Wallsend, the largest colliery on Tyneside; John Griffiths, master of the first school for Baptist ministers at Trosnant, who later became a tinplate manager for Capel Hanbury and took over the Caerleon Ironworks with Samuel Watkins; James Stirling, F.R.S., Science Master at Little Tower Street Academy, later a manager of mines in Lanarkshire; and Joseph Dawson, alumnus of Daventry Academy and Glasgow University, minister, schoolmaster and scientist, who became an active partner and manager in the Low Moor Ironworks. Others, like Simeon Shaw, produced widely read scientific textbooks.[1]

Schooling might cost from £12 to £20 a year, including the boarding, and would thus be within the means of the trading and industrial employing classes. Typical charges were as follows, for 1778:

	£	s.	d.
Reading, English, Latin and Greek		5	0 a quarter
Accounts or Writing and Accounts		10	0 a quarter
Navigation	1	1	0 a quarter
Shorthand		10	6 a quarter
Writing or Reading and Writing		7	6 a quarter
Book-keeping	1	1	0 a quarter
Gauging	1	1	0 a quarter
Boarding and Washing, per week		4	3[2]

Some of these schools were successful enough to employ assistant masters, others achieved continuity. The Nonconformist minorities also set up permanent foundations, and from the 1820s parents of many types of background combined to found the so-called 'proprietary schools'. Offering modern or mixed modern and classical subjects, many of these were a significant response to the needs of industry and commerce. At the same time, many Scottish grammar schools taught not only the Latin necessary for admission to the Scottish universities but also achieved standards in mathematics and other subjects which fitted their alumni for the highest technical and commercial posts. Even some of the English grammar schools widened their curricula to include the new learning.

There was clearly some efficient teaching in Scotland at Dunbar High School for John Rennie, at Greenock Grammar School for James Watt, at Edinburgh High School for James Nasmyth or at Glasgow Grammar School for Charles Macintosh. Similarly, the results speak well for the Penketh Quaker School which trained Abraham Darby's children, the Pickwick Quaker School (Richard Reynolds) or the Newton-in-Slaidburn Quaker School (George Birkbeck). Among English grammar schools, Bingley G.S. trained Benjamin Gott and Leeds G.S. John Smeaton. If the basis laid there was adequate for men of this stature, it was certainly adequate for the humdrum industrial manager.

The degree of adaptation of the English grammar school to the demands of the new industrialism in this period has, indeed, often been underrated. In the great commercial and industrial centres the merchant classes were often powerful enough to convert classical teaching (or total neglect) into practical courses. In London, Christ's Hospital was the outstanding example. Other important centres were Manchester, Hull and Newcastle.[1] Borough control allowed schools in Congleton, Chorlton and Middleton to introduce subjects like writing, arithmetic, accounting, French and geography; elsewhere, the curriculum could be changed by Private Act, as at Macclesfield (1774), Bolton (1784), Haydon Bridge (1785) or Wigan (1812). By 1818 it was estimated that of 500 grammar schools nominally tied to their classical and Anglican traditions, 120 with 10,000 pupils, taught 'every variety' of subject, and fifty-six (4,000 pupils) taught English subjects only. Eighty allowed the parents to choose between English and classical studies. As an example of a newer foundation, Dr. Pickering's Free School in Gateshead may be quoted, which was set up in 1701 to teach Latin, Greek, writing, 'casting up accounts' (arithmetic) and navigation.[2]

In addition to the private school and the partly reformed grammar school, the eighteenth century developed its own distinctive contribution to education, the academy. At its lowest, it might be the part-time venture of the master in some narrow specialism; at its highest, as at Warrington, it was an institution of some permanence which employed several teachers pursuing the teaching and the advancement of their subject at a level which could stand comparison with the leading contemporary universities.

From the beginning of the century onward the better of them, even if run by one or two owner-masters only, provided tuition of value for merchants and tradesmen, and later also for sailors and industrialists. Hans distinguished five main 'streams' of subjects among them: classical, naval, military, commercial and technical. Some academies, indeed, included four or all five of these streams: Tower Street, Islington, Soho, York, Lancaster, Bristol and Wapping. Most of them had one or two streams, but the range of subjects within each was very wide. These institutions grew in number very rapidly after 1750, and by the end of the century there were perhaps 200 of them. The teaching was greatly superior to that of the public and grammar school, being often individual, and occasionally part-time, in the authentic 'sandwich' type of course for vocational training.[1]

Little Tower Street, for example, which included such well-known scientists as Thomas Watts, Benjamin Worster and James Stirling among its staff, made it its claim to attention in 1727 that 'from this Academy Noblemen, gentlemen and Merchants may be always likely to be supplied with stewards, clerks or book-keepers duly qualified and capable to give security for their fidelity'. In 1750 it advertised that

> those who would be formed for the Counting House learn to write strong and free,—to compute with ease, expedition and demonstration [?]—to enter Mercantile Transactions by double entry—to know the use of all the books kept by Merchants with their different methods—to draw all forms of business—the nature of foreign exchanges and the proper style for correspondence.

There was relatively little new in Postlethwayt's scheme for a mercantile college.[2]

Other academies in London taught subjects like mensuration, navigation, shipbuilding and architecture, as well as chemistry and physics.[3] In the industrial provinces also the emphasis shifted in the second half of the century towards subjects of use to industrialists, besides those necessary for the counting house. Thus Dr. Henry Clarke, combining for a time the teaching at his Salford Academy with a post at the Manchester 'New College of Arts and Sciences', the successor of Warrington Academy, before he removed to Liverpool to open his 'Mathematical Academy' there, taught not only commercial subjects, but (with his brother) modern languages, surveying, and natural and experimental philosophy (i.e. physics and chemistry). Leonard and Thomas Burrow, at their Manchester Academy, taught in the 1750s among other things arithmetic 'with an application of it to all the useful purposes of life and branches of trade. Book-keeping, mensuration, etc.' Charles Hutton, originally a miner, then a village schoolmaster, taught at the Mathematics School at Newcastle upon Tyne between 1760 and 1773, before becoming Professor of Mathematics at Woolwich Military Academy; its subjects included writing, arithmetic, merchants' accounts ('or the true Italian method of Book-keeping'), algebra, geometry ('elemental and practical'), mensuration, trigonometry, projection of the sphere, conic sections, mechanics, statics and hydrostatics, doctrine of fluxions, etc., 'together with their various applications in Navigation, Surveying, Altimetry and Longimetry, Gunnery, Dialling, Gauging, Geography, Astronomy, etc.' In Durham, Thomas Wright, the scientist, taught in the 1730s mathematics and navigation to sailors. At the end of the century C. F. Accum, one of the scientific pioneers of the age, maintained a school at which the fees approached those of the ancient universities. Dr. Beddoes, at his 'Pneumatic Institution' in Bristol, taught not only the classics, but also 'Mathematics, algebra, botany, physics, French and . . . Moral Relations, which seems to have been a form of elementary economics'. Simpson's Academy, near Greta Bridge, Yorkshire, taught besides English, Latin and Greek, also 'arithmetic, Merchants' Accounts and the most useful branches of the Mathematics' as well as French. Samuel Catlow, at Mansfield, included commercial accounts, French, geography, mathematics, natural philosophy and moral and religious principles. Finally, at Inverness Academy, established by subscription in 1790, the Rector and the four tutors taught English, Latin, Greek, arithmetic, book-keeping, geometry and mensuration, geography, navigation, naval, civil and military architecture, practical gunnery, perspective and drawing.

At the same time, most of the authors of textbooks of accountancy in the period 1650–1820, whose large number is itself significant, were writing masters or teachers of accounting in academies and schools of this kind. These include John Clark, James Dodson, Charles Snell and Richard Hayes of London, Richard Dafforne of Northampton, Robert Goodacre of Nottingham, and James Morrison 'Accountant and Master of the Mercantile Academy, Glasgow'. By 1765, it was stated that 'Book-keeping . . . is now introduced and taught in all our Academies which qualify youth for Business'.[1]

From this type of academy the 'Nonconformist academy' was distinguished by more than its obvious religious interests. It was clearly an attempt to parallel the universities, by maintaining similar standards, and by making preparation for the ministry the core of its teaching, with training for the two other professions, medicine and the law, as its main branches. The students, on the whole, were older than in the other academies, the subject choices less frivolous, and the tutors in all the main subjects were divines. Yet the two types of academies had much in common. Both were essentially vocational in objective; both were created to fill gaps left by the educational provisions of the Establishment; and both were being carried along the tidal wave of the new demand for education set up by the commercial and industrial classes. With teachers like Dr. Doddridge, Joseph Priestley and John Dalton, the Nonconformist academies stood, together with the Scottish universities, at the centre of the great awakening of the human mind to scientific and humanist discovery; but in this advance the spadework of teachers elsewhere, including the private academies, should not be forgotten or belittled.

In their earliest phase, following the Test Acts, the Nonconformist academies were small and itinerant religious seminaries, depending on a single teacher. With the growth of religious toleration under the Hanoverians the academies became more firmly established and more balanced, and included some of the modern disciplines demanded by the commercial classes, who began to send their sons there even if they were not destined for the ministry or the other professions; the aptness of their courses is demonstrated by the numbers even of Anglican young men who attended them.[1] This second phase was dominated by Philip Doddridge at Northampton Academy in 1729–51. Thus at Newington Green, at the turn of the seventeenth century, Defoe claimed to have learned five languages, as well as mathematics, natural philosophy, logic, geography, history and politics, while at Hoxton, which boasted three distinguished Fellows of the Royal Society on its staff in the middle of the century, the subjects included logic, geography, algebra, trigonometry, geometry, natural philosophy and various branches of applied mathematics, like navigation and astronomy. In the final phase, dominated by Warrington Academy (1757–83), the modern subjects seemed to take precedence over the traditional training, at least as measured by the numbers of students. Thus at Warrington, where there were courses in modern languages, including English literature, geography, commerce, political economy, book-keeping, drawing and designing, and, under Priestley's guidance, history and politics, as well as anatomy, chemistry, physics and mathematics, it appears that of 393 students only fifty-nine entered a clerical career and a further forty-three went into the other two professions, medicine and the law, while at least 114, and probably as many as 200, went into commerce and industry. Similarly, at Exeter Academy under Samuel Merivale, six out of ninety-three students entered the law, four the Church, nine medicine, twenty-four commerce and thirteen were 'esquires'.[1]

The examinations at Carmarthen in 1817 included, apart from classical and theological subjects, also physics and chemistry, geometry, trigonometry, conic sections, mensuration, land surveying and algebra. At Manchester Academy again (1786–1803), Dr. Barnes lectured not only on divinity but also on the 'history and Principles of Commerce, the Commercial Laws and Regulations of Different States, and Commercial Ethics, including the nature of Oaths, Contracts and Commutative Justice', while the students were to get their science at the College of Arts and Sciences, and later had John Dalton as science tutor. Small wonder that only about twenty of the 142 students passing through became divines, or that the Rev. Lewis Lloyd, pupil and tutor there, later became partner in a banking firm.[2] Of course, the academies were not exclusively commercial: the teaching of divinity still went on, and was to become predominant again in the nineteenth century, particularly as the political Radicalism of the students had frightened the authorities, while thinkers like Priestley stressed the need to educate the gentry, and the cultured classes generally;[3] but the commercial-technical education was there. Among the leading industrialists of the age, John and William Wilkinson, Joseph Whitworth, John Wedgwood, Samuel Galton, jun., and Thomas Bentley were educated at these academies: their education must have stood lesser pupils also in good stead. At the same time they helped to create the closely knit groups of mutual attachment, and the knowledge of each other's ability as well as creditworthiness, which was so desirable in a period of 'uninstitutionalized finance'.[4]

Formally, the degree-awarding institutions, the universities of England and Scotland, stood at the top of the educational ladder. The role of the Scottish universities in the advancement of pure and applied science to industry has been too often described to need repetition here, but the English universities were not entirely without merit in this field either. In the first half of the century both Oxford and Cambridge taught some science, though it never became an integral part of a degree course, and it decayed in the second half of the eighteenth century and in the beginning of the nineteenth. Again, although it was not necessary for undergraduates to acquire any useful knowledge, some of the seminal minds of the age were not actively prevented from doing so. Hans calculated that 34 per cent of all English pioneers of science in the eighteenth century were educated at the two English universities, and if medicine and technology, which were not taught there, were deducted, the proportion rose as high as 80 per cent of the total of 380 scientists listed, including thirty-four chemists, 180 physicists, 122 mathematicians and astronomers and forty-four archaeologists and historians. The proportion of farmers, traders or industrialists, however, was much smaller. Among the subjects taught, mathematics and chemistry were of greatest potential benefit to industrialists.[1] By the end of our period, the foundation of University College, London, with its strong scientific bias, as well as the reform (or foundation, respectively) of the East India College and the naval and military colleges were other overt signs of the pressures on this form of education.

Besides the formal institutions of learning, there were other means of instruction developed in this period which could be of direct benefit to those who were to manage commerce and industry. Travel abroad had been a recognized way of finishing the education of young noblemen, some of whom studied in foreign academies such subjects as modern languages, geography and mathematics, and it has been stated that 'the gradual modernization of the school curriculum was largely due to this practice of the nobility'.[2] The young Duke of Bridgewater, in his stay in France, not only inspected the canal du Midi, but also attended a course on 'experimental philosophy' at Lyons. Fothergill, Boulton's partner, had been apprenticed on the Continent and spoke French and German, James Watt, jun., and Matthew Robinson Boulton, the sons of the founders of the Soho firm, both spent several years of study on the Continent to perfect their French and German and take courses in science, Lawson was sent from Soho to Sweden to learn Swedish and German in order to sell steam engines to the mines there, Francis Garbett studied commerce and technology in Sweden and elsewhere, and John Henry Vivian, one of the pioneers of the copper industry, was sent to Germany to study metallurgy. Again, I. K. Brunel completed his education at French academies.[3] All these men were key figures in the industrial revolution, and the influence of Continental technical knowledge on British developments (apart from such less direct influences as the Leyden Medical School earlier in the century and the perusal of Continental scientific journals)[4] was thus not negligible. Nevertheless, the practice was not widespread; British engineers, for example, owed little to Continental example, of which they were often completely ignorant.[1] While this insularity might lead to some waste of effort and might retard some sectional progress, it could not be said to have held up economic and scientific advance.

The itinerant public science lecturer might rely for his audience on 'polite' society who came to watch the spectacle of chemical or physical experiments, or to broaden their culture, but he occasionally sowed seeds of knowledge among future industrialists and their managers. Dr. John Theophilus Desaguliers, lecturing in the first half of the century, had several important successors in the second half, who combined such activity with resident teaching, the writing of textbooks or industrial management. Among them were Adam Walker, John Dalton and John Banks, Warltire and Dr. Warwick.[2] Count Rumford's Royal Institution, established in 1799, represented the transformation of such public lecture courses into permanence, and was followed by others, such as the London (1805), the Philomathic (1807) and the Russell Institutions (1808), while Sir John Sloane started a vigorous training course when he became Professor of Architecture at the Royal Academy in 1806. By contrast, the famous literary and philosophical societies, beginning with the greatest of all, the Lunar Society of Birmingham in 1768, and being followed soon after in Manchester, Edinburgh (the Royal Society), Newcastle, Bath, Exeter, Northampton, Plymouth, Glasgow, Derby, Bristol and Liverpool, included mostly established manufacturers and professional men, and did not, therefore, directly affect the schooling of managers.[3] Indirectly, however, the Manchester Society was responsible for setting up the New College of Arts and Sciences in 1783, and the Newcastle Society for regular lectures on science from 1803 onwards.

Parallel with this movement a second stream of adult scientific education was directed towards the skilled artisan. Some of its origins go back to the middle of the eighteenth century. In Glasgow, Dr. Anderson had lectured to large classes of working men on science in his lifetime, and by his will founded an institution which gave the opportunity to several hundreds to listen to some of the best science lecturers of the age, Birkbeck, Garnett and Ure, every year. Picked up in Edinburgh, where it led to the foundation of the School of Arts in 1821, this idea received much wider propagation by the creation, in 1824, of the London Mechanics' Institute. There had, of course, been other local forerunners, including the Birmingham 'Brotherly Society' of 1796, and the lecture courses of others, like Clarke in Salford, James in Newcastle and Nicholson in London.[4]

The mechanics' institute, it has often been noted, quickly became swamped by the demands of white-collar workers and lost the support of the artisans. 'It was observed, particularly in Manchester, that a large proportion of the members were clerks, warehousemen, small tradesmen and shopkeepers.'[1] It was often from precisely these classes that managers were recruited. James Nasmyth was a product of the Edinburgh School of Arts, while J. B. Neilson acquired his knowledge at the Andersonian Institution—a debt he repaid by establishing workmen's reading rooms and classes at the Glasgow Gas Works.[2] Charles Dupin, travelling in Britain in 1816–18, 'was escorted round the chief manufactories of Glasgow by Dr. Ure, and noted that a great number of these concerns were directed by the doctor's pupils'.[3] This claim, which had been preceded by a similar claim for the pupils of Anderson himself, was later extended by Dr. Ure, who boasted that his students were 'spread over the Kingdom as proprietors and managers of factories', and it has been upheld by other evidence, not merely for Glasgow, but for the Manchester Mechanics' Institute also. Nor were these the sole instances: a Leeds weaver, for example, qualified himself not only to become a tutor at the institute in drawing and mathematics but ultimately rose to be a manager and partner in the famous engineering firm of Fenton, Murray.[4]

The education available to potential managers was thus extensive and varied, and it was flexible, in the sense of reacting well to the demands of industry, though there were some weaknesses, and there were large underprivileged sections of society for whom any education was out of reach. The social and economic power of the mercantile and manufacturing community had successfully superimposed on the existing unsuitable educational structure a system of education geared to its own needs.[5] This conclusion would in any case be borne out by the eventual success of the country's economic progress and the many different strata from which managers were actually drawn. The main specific weakness was the widespread ignorance of pure science and of the achievements of the Continent, but this did no more than hold up sectional progress, or create small pockets of waste.

The education we have traced, however, dealt only with commercial, or scientific-technological matters. The greatest failure of all, the failure to deal adequately, or even sensibly in terms of long-term low cost, with labour, was paralleled by the complete absence of any science or teaching on the subject of labour management, apart from some *a priori* reasoning of the philosophers and political economists.

We cannot, therefore, do more than note it at this point, and leave it to be treated elsewhere in this book.[1]

II

Since formal management training was so rare as to be negligible, and since formal education ended at an early age, managers, typically, were trained by practical work in the firms.[2] In this they were not essentially different from the professional men of the day, like physicians, architects and attorneys.[3] In the nature of the case, managers' training was less formalized or standardized than theirs, but the amount of deliberate training given in the larger and more progressive firms should not be underrated. As ever, there was a considerable difference between the pioneers, ploughing a lone furrow, and those in groups large enough to develop a body of knowledge, particularly of technical knowledge required for management, which could be codified and handed on as such. 'Economic Development, like other social changes, occurs in nodes. . . . Development requires that clusters of people who have developed a stake in the new nourish the new.'[4]

The larger ironworks, such as Coalbrookdale, Dowlais, or John Wilkinson's concerns, trained not only the partners' sons as future managing partners but also others, and progressive works in general became the schools, not only of technologies, but of management techniques.[5] Towards the end of our period, indeed, there was the realization, among some at least, that for managing an ironworks technical competence was the least important, since the right sort of man would soon achieve it:

> character, capacity and technical knowledge . . . are the three essentials, and I have placed them in the order of their importance . . . In the choice of your subordinates the same general principles would be observed. Character is the first requisite, cleverness and skill in his craft the second.[6]

Among the engineers, Matthew Boulton himself was brought up from an early age in his father's works, and in turn he and James Watt sent their sons to other progressive firms, as well as training them in their own. Thus, James Watt, jun., was sent to Bersham 'to study practical book-keeping, geometry and algebra in his leisure hours; and three hours a day he works in the carpenter's shop'. He and the young M. R. Boulton were then allowed to cut their teeth on the management of the small copying-press firm.[7] The two of them were 'travelled linguists, trained in business and of higher attainments generally than persons who were carrying on engineering works elsewhere'[1]. Soho also helped to train, among others, the younger Josiah Wedgwood and the son of John Gilbert, the Duke of Bridgewater's agent (himself trained in business by the elder Boulton), who urged the firm to 'keep my son employed in those studies you think most proper for him: writing and accounts you must not neglect'. Several other engineering works performed a similar function[2] and so did the leading collieries, though mostly the training was technical only.

> There is scarce a Viewer or Engineer of Notice in either Tine or Wear [William Brown wrote to Carlisle Spedding on 10 July 1751] but has been solissting me to take a trip with me to see . . . your works.[3]

In copper- and lead-mining and smelting the same practices prevailed: the school for managers maintained by the Quaker Lead Company has been mentioned above. Conversely, James Treweek, manager of the Mona copper-mine and smelting firm, complained in 1833:

> we are here completely shut up in a corner and no one leaves home for any time to see or make any enquiry of the improvements of the day.[4]

In brewing there were few management apprentices, hence

> those who intend to set up in the Business have either been acquainted with it, by being Son or Relation to some man in the trade, or take their chance by dependence on the skill and Honesty of the Clerks and Servants.

In the potteries also, typically, only sons and relations were trained up as managers. In the older textile trades the training of managers within the industry had become almost routine. An advertisement of 1765, referring to the London silk industry, read as follows:

> middle-aged sober person to superintend a large manufactory both in the silk and woollen branches. He must be a man of general knowledge in the trade [possibly have some capital to invest], ready with his pen and can understand figures as well, and if master of the French language will be a recommendation, and his having been acquainted with different branches of the hosiery business.

Benjamin Gott's woollen firm, deriving directly from a merchanting house, also took its managerial training seriously, inside the works.[1]

Only in upstart cotton was growth so rapid that managerial posts greatly outran the supply of trained personnel, and the more able workmen were quickly promoted to superior positions. In the early days, it is true, Archibald Buchanan was trained by Arkwright in the techniques of spinning and of factory management before returning to Scotland to set up one of the largest spinning firms there; David Dale sent 'instructed people' to manage his Highland mills; and Jedediah Strutt's sons were trained in the works from a tender age;[2] but soon, it was said,

> the demand for hands necessarily led to the employment of all male relatives of the master manufacturers, at a very early age. His own sons were invested with a considerable authority— taken from school to superintend certain portions of the mills. . . . The same remark holds good with reference to others—his relations.[3]

Robert Owen, in his mule factory, learnt as he went along:

> I looked very wisely at the men in their different departments, although I really knew nothing. By intensely observing every-thing, I maintained order and regularity throughout the establishment, which proceeded under such circumstances much better than I had anticipated.[4]

Elsewhere, men of little education or training came to the fore, as long as they could keep order and discipline in the works; in the 1790s,

> to judge by advertisements, the manager of a factory was often an illiterate workman who received little more than the other hands, and who was attracted by the position of authority and the power of employment for his wife and children.[5]

Even in the 1820s and 1830s the youthfulness of many of the managers of the largest mills was striking.[6]

In cotton spinning the exceptionally rapid transition to automatic machinery transferred the skill largely from the spinner to the designer of frames and mules, and thus reduced the technical train-ing and competence required by managers and overseers. It should be noted that these factors, which were not always present in other industries, were interdependent: the rapid expansion of the machine-spinning industry, based on striking cost reductions, needed both elastic markets to react to these lower costs, and a type of machine which could be worked, and supervised, by personnel whose training would not hold up the expansion of their numbers.

All fast-growing industries had to recruit some managers from the ranks, a method which would at least guarantee some technical knowledge, and almost certainly led to the selection of men of character who could keep discipline. Examples for this may easily be added from the civil engineering, pottery, engineering, iron, lead, coal-mining and silk industries. In Cornish mining, the mine captains

> have generally been brought up as miners, and [have] attained their station by their stability and good conduct.[1]

The process of selection has been described with great clarity for the railway-contracting industry in the mid-nineteenth century:

> The principal contractor for the undertaking, by paying frequent visits of inspection, has opportunities of becoming acquainted with every sub-agent in his employ. He observes the progress made on his section. He can test his capability of dealing with every kind of engineering difficulty, by . . . putting him in charge of work in districts totally dissimilar in their physical character and resources . . . and yet . . . the supervision of the agent, having the general charge, will prevent the mistakes of a subordinate from producing very serious consequences. Thus, with the lapse of time, and without any grave risk of loss, the contractor may form an opinion as to who are his most trustworthy sub-agents, and can select principal agents from their number with confidence.[2]

The alternative route of promotion within the firm was *via* the counting house. Examples of these rises are almost as numerous as those from the shop floor. The *forte* of such men would be their business and financial acumen, and their relationship of trust to the employer, leaving technical know-how to be acquired later, as the less important consideration. In some cases, to be sure, the promoted 'clerk' or 'cashier' may in his years of service, like David Mushet, or (Dr.) Thomas Clarke,[3] have picked up a good deal of technological knowledge, while in other cases, as in the charcoal-iron industry or in silk-throwing, 'clerk' was simply the common title of the manager[4] (pointing, perhaps, to an earlier tendency to let book-keeping take precedence over technology). There were also a few industries in which the technical production knowledge required was negligible.

Examples of such promotions can be found among lead smelters, tin platers, flax spinners and iron and steel makers, grain millers, cotton spinners, woollen spinners, and civil and railway engineers. Even in the collieries, where technical professionalism had gone farthest, it was alleged in the 1820s that cashiers had often the duty of inspecting the works.[1] But there were firms in which the line could not be crossed: James Watt, looking for a clerk for the engine partnership in 1780, confessed sadly that

> Mr. Pearson (the cashier) does not understand our business and Playfair (the engineer) does not understand book-keeping nor method.[2]

III

Since managerial ability was not, and perhaps could not be, isolated from sheer technical competence and know-how during the industrial revolution, no account of managerial training would be complete without reference to technical training and professionalism. While the level of technology to be absorbed differed greatly as between industries,[3] technical know-how necessarily involved a considerable range of managerial techniques appropriate to the respective industries.

Some of the older professions which threw up a number of industrial managers in this period have been mentioned already. These included the large body of landed estate agents,[4] now provided with textbooks, a professional etiquette, and some fairly well-recognized salary scales; attorneys; architects;[5] and clerks and accountants, whose training and ethic were developed almost exclusively in merchants' counting houses. By the end of our period the titles of textbooks available for the training of accountants ran well into three figures, though virtually nothing was written specifically for industrial offices. In some industrial firms, as at Walkers', there might be a rise

> or regular progression from the making of a tally, and marking of a cask, to posting in the ledger in the counting-house,[6]

but typically the training, particularly for the senior posts, took place in merchants' offices,[7] or occasionally in banks:

> I consider such a person [as a principal bank clerk] as a very valuable acquisition to your works [Watt, who was normally hard to please, wrote to Boulton in 1774], and think you need not hesitate to give him such terms as will make him yours.[8]

Perhaps the single most important group of professionals with managerial functions was the body of coal-viewers, spreading outwards from the Tyne and Wear in the course of the eighteenth and early nineteenth centuries. In the northern collieries professionalism was encouraged not only by the large quantity of capital involved and the large number of independent units developing in close proximity, creating a market for skill and a comparison of achievement, but also by the element of danger, which, as in the parallel case of masters at sea, placed many lives in the trust of the professional competence of the viewer. What emerges most clearly from their biographies, produced with such loving care to the tune of over a hundred by Matthias Dunn, is not only their family connections and the way in which their careers interlock in a limited number of large mining companies, but their awareness of each other, the creation of an applied science by piecemeal improvements quickly adopted and further improved by others, and an ethos which produced a ranking among them according to ability, originality, honesty and personal courage underground.[1] There were also the 'schools' of men proudly acknowledging the training of such viewers as William Brown and Carlisle Spedding (mid-eighteenth century), Thomas Barnes and John Buddle, sen. (end of eighteenth century) and Ralph Dodds and John Buddle, jun. (at the beginning of the nineteenth century).

The viewers began as the agents of landowners, subordinate to the estate stewards and appointed to check the work of lessees and prevent them from despoiling the property during tenancy;[2] but before long they were acting as managers for both lessees and for owners working their mines direct, and some had become owners in their own right. As consultants, they might be called in to judge the work of other viewers, necessarily with reference to some commonly accepted standard. By the nineteenth century this group had become the source not only of mining engineers and managers, carrying their accumulated knowledge into other areas,[3] but also a fountain-head of managerial and engineering talent in the engineering industry generally, and above all, it had become the ancestry of the giant race of railway builders.

Basically, the viewer's skill was technical; but inevitably he incorporated into his professional training and skill managerial functions of all kinds:

> The general direction of a large colliery, as to the scale and disposition of its workings, and also with regard to whatever

requires a profound theoretical as well as complete practical, knowledge of obtaining the coal economically and safely, is in the North confided to persons called viewers. The *viewer* being not only a person of education, but who is presumed to have the best information and largest experience as to all matters connected with mining, he is consulted professionally by the coal-owners; and in the degree that he is found to possess judgement and integrity, his services are often retained by several independent concerns.[1]

Hidden in this summary valid for 1835 are the non-technical responsibilities of the viewer. He had to make contracts for coal and for wayleave, to set on workmen, and to settle their piece rates: it is significant that the miners' union in 1825 addressed John Buddle with their grievances and demanded a meeting between miners and viewers, and not owners. The viewer was also responsible for land sales and for the shipment of coal, including the maintenance of the staithes, for book-keeping and for stock-keeping.[2] At the same time, he was the most skilled builder and user of Newcomen engines in the eighteenth century, the most advanced engineer and innovator of rail systems and works connected with them, including tunnels and bridges, and it was within the viewers' profession that the men arose who put improved Watt engines on wheels and developed the locomotive. In the printed viewers' textbooks, of which a significant number existed, technical, managerial, disciplinary and accountancy techniques were variously stressed. Thomas Fenwick, indeed, was the author not only of a book on underground surveying but also of others on mechanical engineering and on the physical sciences.[3] Some districts, notably Staffordshire and Yorkshire, developed their mines without such skilled supervision, so that, in the words of an official report of 1851, 'there was much waste of time and money in the working of the mines, and . . . sheer ignorance often led to the loss of life';[4] but it was the coal-mines which saw the creation of the first true professional class of skilled managers.

Very similar, though much smaller in extent and ultimate importance, was the development in the copper- and tin-mines of Cornwall, and in the lead-mines of Derbyshire and the North. Again, the technician-managers, called 'captains' in Cornwall, may have developed from the needs of landlords or adventurers with interests in many mines for independent checks on their property;[5] but by the latter half of the eighteenth century they had become managers and consultants, and a very few, from family connexions [wrote a hostile authority], and their influence consequent on being Captains of extensive mines, have on certain occasions been called in at the onset and progress of new undertakings, as inspecting and consulting agents,

not only in Cornwall but all over the country.[1] Managerial functions, such as setting on men, keeping discipline and supervising sales, were included in their expertise also, though it was true that they had far less abstract knowledge and formal education and a less-developed professional code than the coal-viewers. The accounting was left to another set of officials, the pursers, and while some captains, like Richard Trevithick, became fine engineers themselves, the costly and controversial installation of pumping machinery, particularly during the era of the Boulton and Watt patent, called forth a separate group of extremely gifted and widely-sought-after engineers, including the Hornblowers, Jonathan, sen. and jun., Josiah and Jabez, Edward Bull, John Nancarrow, Arthur Woolf, Davies Giddy (Gilbert) and many others.

The profession of civil engineers was the culmination of a separate line of evolution, called forth by an original need for technical competence, and developing in the course of the eighteenth century and the first quarter of the nineteenth a code of ethics and conduct and a range of managerial functions.[2] The builders of fen-drainage systems, of river navigations, canals, docks, tramroads, dams and mills, had sufficient technology in common to form a single body, each member of which could normally undertake any of these works. Like the coal-viewers, the most gifted of them, including Sorocold, Smeaton, Brindley and Telford, collected 'schools' of disciples, imitators and assistants around them, who developed knowledge, absorbed the ideas of the gentleman scientists of the day, and created an applied science.[3] Early in the century, in the absence of other expertise, they were forced to undertake not only the technical surveys, but the estimates, the contracts with suppliers, workmen and landowners, the accounts and the disciplining and supervision of the work force. John Hadley's contract with the Aire and Calder Navigation Company in 1699 provided for his 'Contriving, Attending, Supervising and Directing the work and workmen to be employed for the said undertaking'.[4] Under Smeaton, the status of the consulting engineer was raised and clarified. James Watt, for example, who hated the supervision part of the work when he eked out his living as an instrument-maker in Glasgow by survey and engineering work, explained to Dr. Small in 1772:

Why, therefore, shall I continue a slave to hateful employment when I can otherwise by surveys and consultations, make nearly as much money with half the labour and I realy [*sic*] think with double the credit. . . . What I can promise to perform is to make an accurate survey and a faithful report of anything in the engineer way, to direct the course of canals, to lay out the ground and to measure the cube yards cut, to assist in bargaining for the price of work, to direct how it ought to be executed, and to give an opinion of the execution of the Managers from time to time. But I can on no account have anything to do with workmen, cash or workmen's accounts, nor would I chuse to be bound up to one object that I could not occasionally serve such friends as might employ me for smaller matters.[1]

Yet even in this division of functions the consulting engineer was left with a wide range of non-technical, managerial duties.

By the 1770s civil engineers, rather like architects,[2] could insist on their independent consultancy status much more clearly, because of the nature of the work which involved only short-term engagements during the building, in contrast with the permanent employment in the mines. Those of any standing were supervising several works at the same time, while one or more junior men, called 'resident engineers', deputized for them at each separate contract. Still lowlier officials, perhaps with no technical skill at all, remained as 'engineers' after the work was completed. At the same time, 'the distinction between consultant and contractor was by 1771 reasonably clear',[3] though some engineers, like Telford, formed long-term associations with subcontractors whom they had themselves trained up.

As in the case of the mines, there was by about 1790 a sufficient body of knowledge to allow one engineer, or a panel of them, to judge the work of others: thus Telford's design for a single-span bridge over the Thames in 1802 was submitted to James Watt, John Rennie, Professor Hutton of Woolwich, Professors Playfair and Robison of Edinburgh, William Jessop, John Southern and Dr. Maskelyne—a galaxy of talent to which there can have been few equals anywhere, and which perhaps explains the diversity of opinion offered.[4] Similarly, the ill-starred Gloucester-Berkeley ship canal, designed by Mylne, was reported on at different times by Jessop, Whitworth, Telford, Walker, Hodgkinson and Rennie, and the London Bridge Waterworks were the subject of reports 'by some of the most eminent surveyors of the time: Brindley, Smeaton, Yeoman, Mylne and Wooler'.[5] The personal and professional links between the leading engineers were indeed close, and techniques pioneered by one were quickly copied and adopted by the others, while lessons from his mistakes were equally quickly learnt.

In the shifting relationship between clients, contractors and engineers, status and clear limitations of function and authority were particularly important to the civil engineer, and at times he had to fight for his position. As Smeaton once complained,

> Not only are all the inferior departments ambitious to become practical engineers, but even members of the Committee have a propensity that way too—by which means, all becoming masters, and he who ought to be so being deprived of authority, it is easy to figure the confusion that must follow.[1]

It is perhaps for this reason that the civil engineers were the first to form a professional organization. The Society of Civil Engineers, founded by Smeaton in 1771, was largely a dining club, and after its break-up in 1792, the re-formed 'Smeatonian Society' of 1793 became too exclusive to carry much weight, though some of the leading lights in the profession belonged to it. In 1818, however, a handful of younger engineers met as a separate society, largely for instruction. The decision of Telford to become their President in 1820 quickly improved the fortunes of the 'Society of Civil Engineers' and a Royal Charter was granted to it in 1828.[2] Significantly, what the members stressed in their letter of invitation to Telford was the importance of securing a higher status for engineers, and the need to become a profession, with recognized training and a code of behaviour, as well as the hope to increase knowledge: on Telford's advice, their main activity became the reading of practical papers to each other. Along these lines success came quickly; but in the process the management functions were pushed into the background, increasingly left to clients or subcontractors. For a crucial period, however, the genius and experience of civil engineers were responsible for some of the most interesting developments in the genesis of modern management practice.

Out of eighteenth-century mining and civil engineering developed two further professions of some interest for our period, the mechanical engineers and the railway engineers. The limits of the first group were difficult to draw. Watt, the Rennies, Brindley and Smeaton, for example, were eminent civil *and* mechanical engineers. Yet with the development of the steam engine and with the growth of precision engineering, particularly in London, a separate profession was clearly beginning to grow up about the turn of the century. Again, the training was not formal but took place in the 'schools' of practical work in the leading and pioneering firms. Thus Coalbrookdale trained the succession of engineers who managed the foundry of that name in Liverpool; Soho trained Peter Ewart, William Murdock, John Rennie and Samuel Clegg, among others; Maudslay, himself the beneficiary of the 'school' of Bramah and of the innovations of Samuel Bentham and the elder Brunel, trained Richard Roberts, Samuel Seaward, David Napier, William Muir, James Nasmyth, Joseph Whitworth, Arthur Woolf and John Clement. Similarly, the 'Round Foundry' at Leeds was the school of a generation of brilliant mechanical and railway engineers, while David Napier, on the Clyde from 1815 onwards trained up a quiverful of future owners of Clyde shipyards.[1] Although in each case technical skill and competence were the primary consideration, and this was a field in which the quality of the product might allow the price to cover up any shortcomings in internal management, yet in view of the fact that the pupils quickly established large, flourishing works, employing often hundreds of men, they must have adopted some of the successful management as well as engineering techniques of their masters. At a lower level, Patterson's Edinburgh foundry was in 1820 said to have a good set of foremen, for

> the men were for the most part promoted to their foremanship from the ranks, and had been brought up in the workshop from their boyhood.[2]

Among the early railway engineers the balance was very much the other way. Overwhelmed by demand for work on a scale which greatly outran the resources of trained or skilled staff, the coal-viewers and mining and civil engineers who built up the first English railway network had to be their own surveyors, engineers and managers. The Stephensons, father and son, with their own locomotive works, their surveying partnership, their numerous simultaneous railway contracts, their railway owning and before long also colliery proprietorship, epitomize the way in which these new men rose to their opportunities. Among them, Ralph and Isaac Dodds, Nicholas Wood, Timothy Hackworth, John Dixon, Joseph Locke, William Allcard, George Overton, John Blenkinsop, William Hedley, the Rennies, William Jessop, William Brunton and William Chapman contributed largely their engineering skill, but others such as William Losh, William James, John Stevenson and Tommy Harding, were prized for their organizing skill as contractors and promoters.[3] The development of a profession of railway engineers after 1830, however, falls outside the scope of this study.

132

Outside these fields of engineering in the widest sense, the managerial profession was still in its embryonic stage. There were traces of it in the iron industry, among road surveyors trained by J. L. MacAdam, among gasworks engineers trained by Samuel Clegg, among potters, who rejected, however, Wedgwood's scheme of 1775 of establishing an experimental works for the use of the whole industry, and in the large porter breweries:

> By [the end of the eighteenth century] the standardised staff positions common to all the great breweries show how institutionalised, almost how professionally bureaucratic, their organisation had become.[1]

Elsewhere there was even less sign of a managerial class.

The absence of a strongly professional group among cotton mills may be particularly surprising at first sight, since the number of large units, and their geographical concentration, would have led one to expect an early development here. Towards the end of our period there were signs of the appearance of works managers, at least.

> There are . . . many mill managers, perfectly fitted by judgment, knowledge and integrity, to second the sound commercial views of the millowner, and to advance the business with a profitable career. These practical men form the soul of our factory system.[2]

Yet these were clearly considered very subordinate, and it was not, in fact, until 1835 that the first guide-book on cotton-factory management, including technical and managerial advice, was published.[3]

One thing which is common to most of the industries in which managers were slow to make an appearance, is the absence of any complex technology beyond the accumulated practical experience in the works. In some industries, in addition, there were so few large units that professional managers felt as individuals, rather than as members of a class. In others, particularly in the textiles, there was a continuing tendency for the owners to be their own managers, with the help only of overseer-foremen.

IV

The most important question which must be asked is whether the numbers of managers supplied by these methods of training, formal and practical, were adequate to the needs of the economy of the day. Would industry have expanded more rapidly, or with less waste, if more trained or potential organizers and technicians had been available at reasonable rates of pay, or if they had been better trained? Or was there, on the contrary, a waste of talent?

Of course, at times of sudden expansion, as after a war, after a major technical breakthrough or after the ending or breaking of a patent, there would be acute local shortages. Arkwright, in 1772, could not find anyone to manage his spinning for him: a young man he found had a good handwriting,

> but has all to learn. I am afraid no one man will know all that I should Expect the[y] might [*sic*].[1]

Twenty years later, during the first great expansion of the machine-spinning industry, Drinkwater, opening his large steam-driven mill in Manchester, was in 'difficulty, for the processes involved were new, and it was not easy to find a man with the necessary technical knowledge to replace Mr. Lee'.[2]

In the iron industry Ambrose Crowley was short of managerial talent in 1710, largely because there was no other works quite like his; but even in 1759, during the Seven Years' War, a gun foundry could grind to a standstill because the foundry manager could not be replaced, and in the 1790s and even later, ironworks which depended on salaried managers rather than managing partners were rarely out of trouble. On the closure of Bersham Ironworks in 1796 the managers were snapped up at once; in 1821 William Crawshay, jun., looked after four works and was in danger of neglecting them all; and even in 1833 the Smiths of Chesterfield had to close down their works because of inadequate managerial staff.[3] James Watt was stated to have been 'overburdened with detail' and to have had 'excessive difficulty in finding intelligent managing clerks', and even in 1799 James Watt, jun., wrote anxiously to the younger Boulton that 'Little or nothing will be done until (William Murdock) returns'. The Albion Mill failure could also largely be ascribed to the lack of a good manager.[4] The shortage of engineers during the canal manias could only be overcome by pluralism among qualified men and the multiplication of incompetent 'resident engineers'. Wedgwood was grossly overworked, and the St. Helens Crown Glass Company clearly overloaded its new manager in 1827.[5] Similarly, among railways,

> one of the first difficulties of the early lines was to find suitable officers; and, since civil life offered few opportunities of obtaining the necessary experience, the Army was drawn upon heavily

for men capable of controlling a large staff and executing detailed large-scale plans. Hence the predominance of military titles among early British railway managers.[1]

These examples may, however, all be considered non-representative, even among the rapid-growth industries. There might well be several special periods of local shortage without any necessary long-term unbalance. Could, then, a direct examination of numbers be undertaken, to judge their adequacy in the light of modern practice?

Unfortunately, a direct comparison is impossible, even where data exist, since in so many works it was the partner-owners who acted as managers. As far as the lower echelons of foremen and overseers were concerned, the impression is that their numbers were adequate and recruiting was easy: in fact, status and pay were only little, if at all, above those of skilled men. In the cotton industry, by the end of our period, the average ratio of overseers to workers among 151 firms was about 1:28 (though this average hides the surprising variation of 1:84 for mules, and 1:14 for throstles); in silk-throwing and weaving, it was 1:29; at Bean Ing, the largest mechanized woollen firm, it improved to 1:45 in 1830, having been as high as 1:68 in 1813, and at Wood's Bradford mill, the other large unit, it was about 1:35.[2] These ratios do not seem unreasonable, bearing in mind the widespread subcontract system of employment. In mining, such usable figures as exist suggest a very much higher ratio for overmen, a ratio which nevertheless, in view of subcontract, group contract and pieceworking, seems adequate. Individual works of which details survive, like the Albion Mill and the Etruria pottery, also seem to have been adequately staffed, and while in the dockyards the ratio of foremen and quartermen to the total work force fluctuated around 1:27–30 in the eighteenth century, the construction work of the Grand Junction Canal in 1810–11, employing an estimated 200 labourers, had four superintendents of workmen, besides a surveyor and an accountant: but it also employed seven subcontractors. In the same way, the slightly later statistics of 1848, showing that the 188,000 men engaged on railway construction had only 1.4 per cent of inspectors, supervisors and foremen, or, say, 1:71, are likely to exclude the subcontractors and the gang-leaders of the contractors.[3]

It is when we come to the managers proper, 'middle management' and upwards, that figures are missing or unhelpful. First impressions are that, like clerical staff, managerial staff was very small in relation to the size of firms. At the same time there is no indication that, by and large, firms were conscious of a shortage. The situation appears to have borne a remarkable resemblance to that of Puerto Rico in the 1920s:

> The fear of delegating authority helped to prevent the rise of a middle management group. Managers could not be found by advertising in the newspapers or consulting an agency. Sales managers or chief accountants had to be trained from the ranks, and unless they were relatives, the senior partner was unlikely to consult with them on policy . . . In general, the situation tended towards undermanagement, a failure to recognise that a higher productivity might come from more careful planning and supervision.[1]

The most fruitful line of approach would seem to be to investigate the social status of managers and its change. A continuing low status might be an indirect indication that there was no unmet demand. The actual history which, to anticipate, shows a rising status of managers in this period would, at least, be consistent with a rising demand for managerial talent pressing on a somewhat inelastic supply and a gradual realization of the potential benefits of adequate management.

V

In dealing with the status of managers within their works and in society in general, it may be advisable to remove first the complication of the status of 'clerks'; for clerks, unlike the remainder of managerial personnel, appear at first sight to have suffered a serious decline in their standing over the course of the century ending in 1830. In part this view is based on an illusion, since 'clerks' was often the title of executive managers in the eighteenth-century firms, but had become that of routine clerical workers by the end of the period. In part, however, there is some truth in the view that more widespread literacy[2] reduced the scarcity value of the trained clerk.

Early in the eighteenth century it was possible for the son of Sir William Claytor, Bart., though burdened with the Christian name of Clarvaux, to become a merchant's clerk (his older brothers joining the army and navy, respectively). Sir Daniel Gooch's father was described as 'a reduced gentleman, who came from the North of England with the Homfrays, as an accountant'. Even early in the next century the Penydarren office contained Mr. Maskew, an 'Irish gentleman of refined intellect and punctilious manner', whose pet subject was the question of the authorship of 'Junius': it has, indeed, been alleged that since incompetence can be hidden more easily in administration than on the shop floor, the office becomes the last refuge of nepotism in industrializing countries.[1] Maudslay's chief cashier was the brother of Dr. Thomas Young, the natural philosopher, while in 1779, James Watt wrote to his partner, Matthew Boulton,

> Dr. Black has wrote to his brother to apply to us and has advised him to accept of the office of Clerk to the engine business how small soever the salary may be.[2]

In the early, relatively small office there was a necessarily close personal relationship between the partners and the clerks.

> Thomas Broadbent died November 9th aged 63. He has been above 30 years in the counting house; not a very brilliant man, but faithful and inoffensive. George Clark died November 15th aged 61. He has been above 30 years clerk at the Navigation Warehouse—

so runs the entry in the Walkers' otherwise most laconic annual statement for 1790. Another one of their clerks, Ebenezer Elliott, father of the Corn Law Rhymer, later became proprietor of a foundry for which he had worked. At the dissolution of the works, annuities totalling £380 a year were to be granted to the clerks from the date of their discharge.[3] Matthew Boulton left several of his clerks substantial sums, ranging from £20 to £200, at his death (his banker left two of the Soho clerks £500 each) and gave them considerable independence during his lifetime; his overseas trade required a number of educated clerks fluent in foreign languages, as did that of Wedgwood and of Benjamin Gott. Even William Crawshay agreed that Matthew Wayne, the accountant, had merited his 'douceur' of £50 in 1814.[4] This close contact might, however, have its drawbacks: Watt was prepared to employ John Southern as his draughtsman and clerk in 1782,

> provided he gives bond to give up music, otherwise I am sure he will do no good, it being the source of idleness,[5]

though it should be added that Southern did not give up his music, and nevertheless stayed with the firm all his life, was made a partner, and became one of the leading theoretical and practical mechanical engineers of his age.

While there were some breweries employing thirty to forty clerks who dealt with the large numbers of outstanding debts by publicans, the typical office, even of large firms, contained only one or two clerks in the early days of the industrial revolution, and developed a book-keeping system but slowly:

> I apprehend a good book-keeper would form a regular set of Books for our Journals [Wedgwood wrote in 1776]; it would give me a great deal of satisfaction to have it done. The expense would be nothing to the pleasure and satisfaction I apprehend it would give us both, and I believe Mr. Smith [the clerk] would be as well pleased as either of us.[1]

After the turn of the century, however, larger and better-staffed offices, particularly in Government, finance and commerce, though less so in industry, lowered the status of clerks, and made them more dispensable, more exchangeable, and less treasured.

> You are I am sure aware [R. Scott wrote to George Newton from London in 1811], as every intelligent man must be . . . from the innumerable failures in the mercantile world that the Metropolice [*sic*] swarms with clerks of every description,

and despite his connections he found it most difficult to secure a post for Newton's son. He was echoed by George Smith, who stated that in the slack trade conditions of 1833 there was no shortage of clerks and book-keepers in Manchester:

> If any person should make an advertisement for one, he would have very many applications I know.
> 'A moderate education,' he was asked, 'qualifies a man for that situation, does it not?'—'Yes.'[2]

These were the men who were soon to crowd the mechanics' institutes and to appear in surprisingly large numbers in the first occupational census of 1851.[3]

The multiplication, and consequent loss of status of the 'clerk', was not, however, paralleled by the fate of the manager: on the contrary, the expanding clerical and accounting staff in the counting houses pointed to the growing complexity and size, and growing problems of administration, of industrial firms. Perhaps the most tangible proof of the rise in the status of managers is the course taken by their typical salaries.

It need hardly be stressed that managerial salaries do not lend themselves easily to generalization. This is not because of lack of

data: on the contrary, the number of salary scales among the surviving records is embarrassingly large. It is rather that, as today,
there were no generally accepted standards of payment. The reasons
for the imperfections in the managerial labour market were not very
dissimilar from those of today: secrecy and ignorance of conditions
and payments elsewhere (showing itself especially clearly when
applicants for a post were asked to state the salaries they required);
the differences in the work performed and the responsibilities
carried; non-pecuniary considerations, which in the eighteenth
century included generally a house, coal, candles and possibly
grazing for a cow or the use of a horse, and might also include
expense allowances, opportunities for by-employments or contracting, and the chances of a partnership. When to these are added local
differences in the cost of living, obligations in many posts of paying
clerical assistants out of the salary or opportunities by gaining from
their apprenticeship premiums, differences in training and skill
required, security of tenure and pensions, it will be clear why no
easily recognized 'standard' managerial salary emerges from the
figures.

Nevertheless, some definite broad conclusions can be drawn, and
they are not without significance for our main theme. First, there
was the acceptance in the early decades of the industrial revolution
of the older tradition of paying the largest differential, not according
to the job or indeed any economic criteria, but according to the
social class from which the occupant came or was expected to come,
and the gradual erosion of this principle after the 1790s in favour of
payment for the job, not the man. Secondly, salaries proved to be
very sticky downwards, and any rise, from whatever cause, whether
it be a general shortage of managerial talent, as in Manchester in
the years after 1785, or a specific shortage, as of competent engineers
during canal manias, or whether it be a wartime price rise, tended to
become permanent, and after the disappearance of whatever caused
it represented a real rise in incomes. Thirdly, this rise was not merely
the adventitious result of a temporary and fortunate price or income
inflation, but was strengthened, and perhaps ultimately caused, by
a parallel real increase in the economic value of industrial managers,
either because their firms grew in size, or their jobs in complexity,
because second-generation owners left more responsibility to their
managers or gave them less chance of a partnership, or simply
because in the successful firms which became large enough to
require managers total profits rose while real wages did not and the
managers succeeded in extracting a share of the growing surplus.

139

Of course, all the factors mentioned here were subtly interrelated. The large salary difference by class distinction can be exemplified in the public services, of which the Office of Works and the Admiralty Dockyards offer the nearest parallels to industrial firms. In the Office of Works in the first quarter of the century the Comptroller (Vanbrugh) drew a salary of £158 p.a., which several additions for perquisites and sinecures raised to well over £700 by 1726; the Surveyor or chief officer (Christopher Wren) drew a salary of £320, raised to about £500 in practice. There were half a dozen other headquarters officers drawing over £200 a year each, and several of the 'clerks' in charge of individual palaces or works made up their salaries of £40–£60 a year by expense allowances which in some cases exceeded £100. These were largely status payments. By contrast, the 'master craftsmen' and clerks who were actually in charge of the work had salaries of around £25–£50, though some of them added to their incomes substantially by 'outside' contracting. The dockyards, on the other hand (as distinct from the Admiralty Office in London), had no such overheads. Chatham, as an example, in 1700 paid its six chief officers £200 each, three others £100, and the 'Bos'n of the Yard' £80. The Purveyor, all other master craftsmen and foremen were paid around £50: these salaries remained unchanged in 1790, except that the Purveyor's salary had been raised to £100.[1]

This should be compared with the typical contemporary salary for managing a large ironworks, coal-mine or textile mill (small ones were normally managed by the owner), of around £30–£60, averaging perhaps £40 a year. Such a sum would also represent a reasonable clerical stipend, or double the salary of a schoolmaster. These levels of payments had changed little since the price inflation of Elizabethan days and were to remain typical in the private sector until the 1760s. Significantly higher salaries than these usually had some distinctive features. Some were paid to the chief officers of large public companies, very much akin, in Adam Smith's mind at least, to the public service. Thus in the 1660s the two chief officers of the amalgamated Mines Royal in Wales received £100 plus one twenty-fourth of the profits each; William Waller was paid £200 a year to manage Sir Carbery Pryce's silver-mines in 1690 and £250 a year a little later by the Mine Adventurers; £100 a year was paid to the two chief managers of the Haddington New Cloth company at about the same time, and the London Lead Company also paid a similar salary to its chief officers.[2] Similar or even higher salaries might be paid to stewards on large estates, who would have a status of substantial squires in their communities. Even here, however, such salaries as John Gilbert's on the Duke of Bridgewater's estate (£300 in 1762, plus additions), Ralph Caudwell at Holkham (£500 in 1759) and Ralph Ellison at Ravensworth (£400 in 1729) were exceptionally high: Caudwell, indeed, was trustee of the estate, and Ellison a relation of the owner.[1] Thirdly, such salaries might be paid to owner-managers, and would thus include a profit element. Otherwise, only the rarest individuals in the most successful enterprises would command salaries at such levels. John Hanmer, the able chief (London) officer of Ambrose Crowley's firm, received on the death of the proprietor in 1713, and again in 1728, £450 a year —a sum kept for his successor also; but the actual managers in the North do not appear to have been paid more than £100–£150 each. Again, Carlisle Spedding, the brilliant mining engineer who had built up the Lowther coal-mines at Whitehaven to yield fantastic profits, was given £150 p.a. in 1755, but did not live long to enjoy this salary, as he was killed in an explosion within the year. His son and successor was paid £100.[2] High salaries were also paid to the chief clerks of the London porter brewers, even before 1750, and to men who had to be induced to emigrate to Scotland.

To put these figures in perspective, it should be noted that clerks' and book-keepers' salaries were little above the wage of skilled men, say £15–£30 a year, as were foremen's wages: in the mines, for example, it was common to give the overmen and the banksmen a few shillings a week over and above their miners' wage. Also, salaries were higher in London, and below the average in distant areas like Cornwall or Wales. At the same time, the profits which might arise from even a small mine or ironworks were very high compared with the manager's salary, and might run into hundreds, even thousands of pounds on a labour force of twenty or thirty. Clearly, up to about 1760 managerial talent (with some significant exceptions) was held in little regard, unless it was accompanied by ownership or by high social status.

A slow but significant rise in salaries began in the 1760s and continued to the 1790s. Rises in the cost of living played little or no part in this, the causes being a compound of the growing status of managers in certain industries and acute temporary shortages in the supply of managerial talent at times of rapid industrial expansion. The increases in salary were therefore irregularly spaced both in time and as between industries, though the general trend was unmistakable.

Thus a comparison of about a dozen managerial posts on the

Worsley estate and canal between about 1780 and 1791–3 showed a general rise of at least 50–100 per cent (with a more rapid rise in the inflationary years thereafter), which was in part a reflection of the growth in the size and income of the enterprise, and partly of the general improvement in the status of managers.[1] Similar reasons, as well as the fact that some of them were managing partners, secured such salaries as the £330 a year paid to James Watt on his arrival at Soho, the £500 a year to Wyatt, and £315 a year to the master miller at the Albion mill, the £250 up to £1,000 paid to the chief clerks of large breweries and the £500 upwards to the manager of a glass works, the £360 to Strutt's agent at Derby, the £300, soon raised to £400 and £500, paid to Robert Owen in Drinkwater's mill, or the £300, rising to £500 in 1791, paid to Joseph Stainton as clerk to the Carron Company.[2] As examples of the effects of temporary shortages, the salaries of engineers in charge of canal or other large civil engineering works rose sharply in the 'mania' building years: every experienced engineer could then secure employment by several companies simultaneously, being paid by each at a rate which would have formerly represented full-time employment, or he insisted on being paid a retaining salary by a single firm which was correspondingly larger. Thus the typical salaries of the first half of the century, £1–£3 a week (even the great Smeaton, in mid-century, only taking two guineas a day), turned into rates of £200–£300 per annum for Brindley for *each* of the half-dozen canals he surveyed about 1770, and in the mania of 1793–4 a relatively untried Telford received £500 a year gross at Ellesmere, an even younger James Potter received £500 a year at the Harecastle tunnel, Robert Mylne was paid £350, plus expenses, for part-time supervision of the Gloucester-Berkeley Canal, and William Jessop £350 for building the Cromford Canal (1789–92), devoting one-third of his time to it. Even junior assistant (resident) engineers were paid £200 a year. Lower down the scale, experienced clerks and accountants, draughtsmen and works managers, were paid £100–£200 in the larger and more successful firms.

Again, however, these salaries were not universal. In some outlying areas, like South Wales, or the mining districts of Cornwall and Derbyshire, and even in the cotton water-mills, the salaries of managers and mine captains and engineers were lower, £50–£100 being a typical salary for responsible positions, most clerical salaries without executive responsibilities lying around the lower limit. On the whole, therefore, salaries had doubled between about 1750 and 1793, all types of managers proceeding roughly in step, though certain scarce skills, like those of canal-builders, rose more than in proportion. Since prices had barely changed, this represented a substantial rise in real incomes.

In the years of war, inflation was added to the other upward pressures, and the rise in typical managerial salaries was accelerated. Yet in the postwar depression salaries hardly fell at all and many continued to rise. There was thus an appreciable gain carried forward into the next period of money rate rises in the 1830s.

The top managers could now reach £1,000 a year and managing partners £2,000 or more. Robert Owen began with £1,000 a year in 1800; William Crawshay I had £1,000 in 1813, £2,000 in 1823; Edmund Darby and Richard Denman, about 1800, had £500 each at Coalbrookdale; Robert Stagg, general agent of the London Lead Company, had risen from £500 a year to £1,000 in 1817; William Taitt, at Dowlais, received £1,000, and this was the figure also virtually reached by Southern, James Watt's right-hand man in 1802. Murdock was paid over £500, and Soho paid similar salaries to one or two more men, like Lawson and J. Woodward, the London agent. The Gas Light and Coke Company paid its secretary and its engineer £500 a year on its establishment in 1812, soon rising to £700, while Carron paid Joseph Dawson £1,000 a year in 1825, and Henry Stainton, £2,000. R. H. Bradshaw, managing the Worsley enterprises after the Duke's death, received a starting salary of £2,000 in 1803, while Fawcett, managing partner of the 'Coalbrookdale Foundry' in Liverpool, was paid a salary of £1,000 a year in 1821. Similar salaries, after like increases, were now paid to the leading estate agents, and among engineers Marc Brunel was paid £1,000 a year by the Thames Tunnel Company, and the Stockton and Darlington Company engaged George Stephenson as engineer in 1822 at £600 a year (gross), the engineer and his son forming a surveying partnership two years later, in which the joint salary was to be £1,500 before any profits were declared.[1] At the Royal Mint, apart from the Solicitor, who was paid £1,200 plus expenses, there were five officers receiving £500 a year or more and several others at £250–£400.[2] Among managers in the £400–£500 group could be found such men as Richard Hill of the Plymouth Ironworks in 1803, William McAdam, manager of the Muirkirk Tar Works, J. L. McAdam, as General Surveyor of Bristol's roads in 1816, the two managers of Marshall's Shrewsbury flax mill and his other chief officers in the 1820s, R. J. Neville, the 'principal agent' of his family's copper works, John Bateman, manager of the Lowther Collieries in 1800, and James Neilson, at the Glasgow Gas Company in the

1820s. The salary of the manager of the Herculaneum Pottery was raised from £150 a year in 1806 to £300 in 1813, £450 in 1817, and £500 in 1819.[1]

Many, if not most, of these men were partners in their firms, though their salaries as quoted were paid before profits on shares were distributed. The more typical salaries would run from £100 to £250, with an upward tendency throughout this period, in all but the very largest firms. Similarly, from about 1820 onwards, the surveying fees of canal and railroad engineers rose to two guineas a day, and one guinea for their assistants.[2] In other words, salaries had doubled again since the early 1790s. The figures may be summarized as follows:[3]

ANNUAL SALARIES

	Top managers and managing partners, largest firms	'Typical managers'	Book-keepers, cashiers, clerks, with some supervising powers
	£	£	£
1690–1750	200–500	30– 60	15– 30
1750–1790	300–1,000	50–100	40– 60
1790–1830	500–2,000	100–250	50–100

By this time there had also developed a sizeable class of under-managers, foremen and overlookers. Again, generalization is hazardous, as conditions, jobs and payments varied so much, but the class distinction between under-managers, paid low managerial salaries, and foremen, paid manual wages with a little plussage, was too large to be fortuitous. Thus, where the standard wage itself was low, as in the textile mills, 'overlookers' were paid low wages also, often at rates no higher than, or even lower than, those of skilled craftsmen in the same works; as in the case of the managers, this was not a capricious result, but accurately represented the low skill and low qualifications required for the job. Typical figures are presented below, and could be matched in, e.g., civil engineering, or in small coal-mines where artisans also habitually received higher pay than foremen of labourers.

By contrast, in the Anglesey copper-mines, while James Treweek, the general manager, received £200–£250 a year in the period 1820–30, the under-managers (mine captains) received £63–£93, and the subordinate managers of the smelting works received £125–£150 a year, and these salaries should be compared with well under 15s. a week for the miners. Similarly, at the Lowther collieries about 1800, while the viewers might gross £300 a year, the overmen might get £90–£170. In these cases the foremen and overmen were promoted from skilled workers who required some technical knowledge or carried much responsibility underground. Their pay was of a very different order of magnitude from that of ordinary wage-earners.

WEEKLY WAGES

	Overlookers, etc.		Mechanics, artisans	Other male workers
Styal cotton, 1790	12s.	–15s.	12s.–25s.	9s.–11s. 9d.
Hyde cotton, 1824	24s.	–30s.	30s.	24s.–30s.
Cotton, averages, 1833	22s. 5d.	–29s. 3d.	—	—
Silk, averages, 1833	15s. 10d.–19s. 6d.		—	—
Cotton, 1831	16s.	–18s.	18s.–22s.	8s.–15s.
Cotton carding, 1831	14s.	–16s.	13s.–15s.	—
Cotton spinning, 1831	13s. 3½d.		12s.–14s.	—
Bradford worsted, 1833	20s.	–40s.	—	15s.–27s. 4d.
Clitheroe calico printing, 1833	15s.	–20s.	—	25s.–60s.
Stockport cotton, 1833	35s.		—	20s.–50s.
Manchester silk, 1831	18s.	–28s.	—	12s.–16s.

Perhaps the most interesting trend to emerge from these figures is the reduction in the differential between managing partners and salaried managers. It matched the social change from the mid-eighteenth century, when these two groups were divided by a large gap, to the 1830s, when they were broadly overlapping. And this, in turn, was associated with the strikingly high upward mobility of managers into proprietorship and partnership.

To begin with, the practice of recruiting the management personnel from among the families of the partners was the rule rather than the exception. Brothers, sons, nephews or sons-in-law who were brought up in the industry and the locality, and could be trusted to act in the family interest, were clearly preferable to outside talent, and they had the additional advantage that they secured the business for the family in the next generation.

To be fair, there were among the kinship appointees some of the outstanding, most original and most successful managers of their age. They include James Watt, jun., and Matthew Robinson Boulton, sons of the two founders of the Soho steam-engine firm, Charles Gascoigne, son-in-law of Samuel Garbett, the strong man of the Carron Company, John Smith of Deanston, nephew of Archibald Buchanan, the founder of the famous cotton firm, the sons of Arkwright, the Strutts and Samuel Oldknow, Michael Hughes, younger brother of the Rev. Edward Hughes, and manager of the Anglesey copper companies' extensive smeltworks, the sons and grandsons of the powerful Crawshay 'Dynasty', the descendants of John Guest, Tom Byerley, Josiah Wedgwood's nephew, besides Wedgwood's own offspring, John and William Wilkinson, John Marshall's sons, the Walker Brothers of Masbro', the brothers and relations of John Horrocks, and the brothers Houldsworth and their relations in the early cotton trade. Among the ironmasters it was family relationships which allowed widely separated productive units to be combined in syndicates and managed in a co-ordinated manner, by having one member of the kinship group in charge at each furnace or forge, and apart from the numerous descendants of Abraham Darby over several generations, and the Lloyd and Fell family groups, the Quaker ironmaster families generally, together with their interests in merchanting and related trades, guaranteed markets and supplies and provided 'virtually . . . vertical integration on a large scale'. An examination of the brewing industry led to the conclusion that

> Kinship . . . must be regarded as one of the most fundamental considerations in the study of entrepreneurship in industry in the eighteenth century. Cousinhood can give the clue to much success.[1]

There is, in fact, hardly an example of a major firm in this period in which management posts were not at one time found for members of the family, often prior to being admitted as partners, creating the family dynasties' of modern typology.[2]

Conversely, at the beginning of the period, the lack of family members able to manage the firm, would pose the cruel dilemma of either selling out or entrusting one's fortunes to a stranger:

> The assigned reason for selling [the Madeley Wood Ironworks] [Watt wrote to Boulton in 1794] is that many of the company are females, who do not find it convenient to carry on such extensive concerns.[3]

Within the next generation or so, however, the trustworthiness of managers and their professional standing had risen sufficiently to make their appointment less agonizing. Indeed, the replacement of nepotism by merit became one of the more significant aspects of the growing rationalization of industry.

As second and third-generation owners came to depend increasingly on salaried staff, and firms grew too large to be managed solely by one's kin, the figure of the trusty manager became more familiar. Working side by side, perhaps on the same level, with members of the family, he came to approach them in social standing. Others commanded personal recognition by sheer ability. By 1830 one author complained of the cotton industry that

> interest and influence, not merit are the only means by which these situations are obtained.[1]

Sixty years earlier such a complaint could hardly have hoped for much sympathy.

In absolute terms, there was a great variety in the status of managers in different industries and in different parts of the country at any one time. Among the lowliest, colliery banksmen and managers were generally considered greatly inferior to estate agents (whose status, in turn, might vary widely), and similar conditions applied in copper- and zinc-mines. Some managers were semi-literate and were viewed with barely concealed contempt or condescension. The reference for Watson, Lord Ribblesdale's agent at the Maltham Moor zinc-mines, read that his employers had

> always found him faithful in his small trust. His general character is, a laborious, sober, honest man,

while the reference for William Morgan, manager of large coppersmelt mills, stated that he was

> a very sober active little man. . . . He does not pretend to be a thorough book-keeper but he understand[s] arithmetic very well.[2]

'I am a more able man with my pick than my pen,' confessed Captain Lemin, one of the managers of the Mona Copper Mine in 1824, and Michael Hughes, looking for a copper-works manager, had, in fact, written in 1804:

> if he is a fine gentleman and foppish in the bargain, he is out of the question . . . for I never will give my consent to have a *Gentleman* Agent at any Copper works in which I am concerned.[3]

Again, at Cyfarthfa, in times of stress in 1822, the salaries of all agents were cut by 20 per cent with the brutal alternative of dismissal. Similarly, Taitt at Dowlais showed little consideration for his managers in 1794:

> if any of the keepers, *no matter who he is,* neglect their work and will not attend to it after being remonstrated with, you ought to exercise the authority you have to discharge him, taking care at the same time to have another ready.

In the Sheffield steel industry, indeed, owners were said to

> leave the direction of actual operations to simple workmen. It is the latter who are the true metallurgists of Yorkshire.[1]

At the other extreme, among the top ranks of firms and managers, we can find examples of very different treatment.

> In March died John Rhodes, one of our Clerks, and Principal manager at the Holmes Mill, etc., where he had presided many years. We are under great obligation to his ingenuity and industry, and we have certainly lost a valuable servant.[2]

It is perhaps not without significance that at Dowlais, J. J. Guest's 'confidential clerk' of six years' standing resigned at the very suggestion of having his salary cut, as he could not bear 'servitude'.[3] Clerks and managers might be given houses, entertainments allowances and other perquisites, and in return, as in the case of the Quaker Lead Company, security of up to £1,000 might be demanded from them on appointment. Some managers, of course, were related to, or married into, owners' families (not necessarily of their own works). At Marshall's, in the 1820s, where it was the policy to retain only staff of the highest calibre,

> a chief traveller, chief clerk or principal mechanic would be hired on a seven-year contract and might receive as much as £400 a year in the 1820s, twenty times more than the average worker.[4]

At a lower level, the manager of the Leadhills Co. in the 1790s was Archibald Stirling, the mathematician; William Playfair, one-time draughtsman at Soho was a land agent, banker, statistician, inventor and most prolific political author; John Condie, manager of the Blair Ironworks, improved both Neilson's hot blast and Nasmyth's steam hammer; whilst a man like Isaac Bonne, manager of the Gregory Mine sough in Derbyshire, was also an estate agent, secretary to two turnpike trusts and a grocer. At a higher level, Marc Brunel, the engineer, 'moved freely in good society and was able, despite financial vicissitudes, to give his son an excellent education and training';[1] Edward Banks became the first engineering contractor to be knighted since Sir Hugh Myddleton; whilst Thomas Gilbert, land agent to the Earl of Gower, was one of the most influential members of Parliament of his day and a key figure in Poor Law reforms. At the associated Bridgewater estate his brother, John Gilbert, the agent, was also part-owner of a colliery, a lead and grate polish factory, a haulage business and salt-mine, and on the death of the 'Canal Duke' the agent was in effect put in charge of the whole enterprise and permitted to occupy Worsley New Hall.

More significant than a study of the extremes at any one time, are the clear signs of the rise in status in this period. Men like Brindley in the Bridgewater enterprise, or Southern, Lawson and Murdock in Soho, were able to rise from barely literate craftsmen to become the leading managers and engineers of their day. In Cornwall, a professional and far superior type of mine 'manager' crystallized out of the former 'captains' and 'pursers' in the early decades of the nineteenth century. Perhaps too much should not be read into the experience of Robert Owen, from whom, as manager, a prospective partnership was withheld in favour of Oldknow, a factory-owner and possible son-in-law, and who yet, within a few years, himself married the daughter of a large merchant-manufacturer and became a wealthy manufacturer himself; but firms like Boulton's which were

> besieged with requests to take in as apprentices, boys of wealthy and noble families

helped to raise the status of industrial employment.[2] Of course, in this rapidly changing and turbulent age there were times when society had not yet fully taken account of the new importance and standards to be accorded to the men who designed and ran the new enterprises.

> What changes one sees! [exclaimed George Stephenson, surveying the Liverpool-Manchester railway line] this day in the highest life, and the next in a cottage—one day turtle soup and champagne, and the next bread and milk or anything that one can catch.

Of the five managers in the Bean Ing mills, one figured as

'gentleman' in the local directory of 1817, two as 'woollen manufacturers', and one as plain 'overlooker'.[1]

The factor which contributed most to this relative rise was undoubtedly the frequency with which managers, often of lowly
origins, succeeded in entering the ranks of owners, and thence perhaps even more exalted ranks, both within their own firms and in
rival concerns. Such movement was likely to make their talents
scarce and thereby increase their value; it was likely to induce more
able and more ambitious men to enter the career of industrial
management, and, not least, it created within a short time a class
of factory-owners and others of power and influence, who could not
despise, but, on the contrary, were bound to regard with respect an
occupation which they themselves once held.

The tracing of the process of the rise of the salaried manager to
the ranks of the industrial capitalists must be seen against a background of the adaptation of society to both these new classes, and
the common interest of both to rise within it. If the manager had his
way to make, so, in most cases, had the entrepreneur himself, and
the ladders which the latter erected for himself, such as the creation
of schools to train his sons, and the clamour for political power,
were bound to benefit the former at the same time. As the manager
rose frequently to become a partner, and the boundaries between the
two groups tended to be blurred, new ones were being created,
between them and the men they had left behind them at one end of
the scale, and on the other between them and the small number of
extremely successful entrepreneurs who aspired to the ranks of the
landed nobility and gentry.

The partnership system, inflexible though it was in many respects,
was admirably suited to offer scope to the capable manager. For
while it allowed the collaboration of members of a family, all of
whom might be actively engaged in the business, it also allowed
capitalists who were not familiar with the business, or who did not
even live in the industrial area, to entrust their funds to a manager
who would be paid only a small salary, but would receive, after
interest had been paid on all share capital, a share of the dividends
much larger than his own negligible holding would entitle him to,
as a reward for his managerial work as well as a guarantee to his
moneyed partners that his own fortunes were intimately bound up
with theirs. The firm of Newton Chambers provides an illustration
of this process, which was typical of most developing industrial
firms. In that firm the division of partnership capital and of profits
in 1799, 1802 and 1817 was as follows:[2]

	1799		1802		1817	
	Capital £	Share of profits	Capital £	Share of profits	Capital £	Share of profits
Active (managing) partners:						
G. Newton	1,577	$\frac{1}{4}$	1,740	$\frac{1}{5}$	16,360	$\frac{1}{3}$
T. Chambers	688	$\frac{1}{4}$	931	$\frac{1}{5}$	14,852	$\frac{1}{3}$
Sleeping partners:						
H. Longden	6,247	$\frac{1}{2}$	7,215	$\frac{2}{5}$	—	—
R. & T. Scott	—	—	4,746	$\frac{1}{5}$	19,878	$\frac{1}{3}$
	8,492		14,663		51,090	

Bearing in mind that the capital was accumulated largely by ploughing back profits, which had been credited in the proportions shown, the process is clear. The manager could become a partner with a minimum of capital, and his disproportionately large share of the profits in a successful firm would allow him quickly to build up his nominal capital holdings and enter the ranks of moneyed capitalists, perhaps buying out his former sleeping partners and going into partnership anew with a fresh generation of capable, but poor, managers. This was the path followed by many of the most successful industrialists of their day. Others accumulated funds more slowly, by savings out of salaries only, or by private speculations or by-employment, and others still made the transition by the time-honoured method of marrying into their employers' families. There was also the traditional reward for the faithful servant who would be invited into the partnership after many years of successful salaried service, as were William Murdock and John Southern in the Soho firm in 1810. At times a partnership might be expected almost as of right; when the Walker Brothers refused to extend a partnership to John Crawshaw, jun., the Crawshaws, father and son (who were related to the owners by marriage), were reported to have left in a huff, 'and neither father nor son appeared again in the works as managers'.[1] By contrast, the method so common in mercantile circles, of buying an apprentice just out of his time into a partnership with a substantial payment by the boy's father, was so rare in industry as to be almost unknown.

In a society as open to the talents as was industrial England in that period, the successful manager had no need to stay with his own firm, if promotion was not forthcoming. Others might offer him a partnership, or he could find a moneyed partner and set up with a minimum capital holding himself. While this process helped to spread technical and managerial innovation,[1] it also had its share in raising the status and prospect of the managerial class.

This was the path trodden by many of the men who figure in some of the best-known success stories during the industrial revolution. In cotton spinning there was George A. Lee, clerk and then manager for Drinkwater, who was invited into a partnership by Sir George Philips of Salford, to form one of the leading firms in the industry; his successor at Drinkwater's, Robert Owen, similarly emerged, after several changes, as a partner of an even more famous firm, the New Lanark Mills. Again, Samuel Slater, Strutt's overseer at Belper, emigrated to the U.S.A. to become the 'father of the American cotton industry'.[2] Among ironmakers, Francis Homfrey and his sons came originally from the Brosely ironworks, Peter Price, trained at Coalbrookdale and foreman at Carron, became a partner in the Perran Foundry in Cornwall and the Neath Abbey Works, and Isaac Wilkinson became independent after being foreman at the Little Clifton furnace. Longridge, the managing clerk of George Stephenson's surveying partnership, was a partner in the Bedlington Ironworks. Other, lesser-known examples abound in the iron industry, and while the Walkers' Ironworks were sold off mainly to the former managers in 1815-30, the Falkirk Iron Works were in fact founded by a group of foremen and workers from Carron.

Similar promotions were open to the managers in the engineering industry, where technical competence and know-how played a particularly important part. Gilbert Gilpin, at one time clerk at Brosely, Henry Maudslay, once Bramah's foreman, Matthew Murray, and indeed several of his own foremen and managers, the great George Stephenson himself, and on a smaller scale, Isaac Dodds, builder of locomotives, all made their managerial posts the jumping-off grounds for ownership of important works. In the pottery industry also skill stood at a high premium and Josiah Spode as well as Thomas Minton rose from the ranks of skilled men to found porcelain works of world renown, while lesser managers could find partners for setting up on their own quite easily. Similar conditions created similar opportunities for managers in glassmaking, brewing, tinplating, the chemical industry and copper and zinc smelting. Examples are also known of managers who became their own masters in flax spinning, in coal-mining, and in other industries.

Men who failed as independent entrepreneurs might still be sought after as managers, and this helped further to blur the distinction in status between the two. Thus the first manager of the Stanley Copper Company was Alexander Chorley, the near-bankrupt proprietor of a slitting mill and a nailing business; William Greatbatch, Wedgwood's manager, had had a pottery of his own, but had been ruined; George Abernethy, the Dowlais foundry manager, had had his own foundry in Aberdeen which had failed; and when Earl Fitzwilliam took over the ownership of the famous Swinton pottery the former owner reverted, in practice, to the status of manager.

Finally, an interesting sidelight is thrown on the growing acceptance of industrial management as a worth-while career by the tendency of managers to perpetuate their office in their own children or other relations, and to found, in a surprisingly large number of cases, 'dynasties' of managers, as well as filling the inferior managerial and clerical posts in their firms with their own relations. In some cases this was little more than eighteenth-century nepotism, but in rapidly growing firms each new generation of managers was administering, in fact, a larger property, and the retention of control by the family represented a rise which might satisfy even ambitious men. Both tendencies worked towards a professionalization of management and its recognition as a well-defined occupation, worthy of a man's efforts.

In the South Wales iron industry John Guest, brought in to manage Dowlais, introduced two of his brothers to the works, and while his own son became his direct successor his nephews filled the posts of 'moulders, master refiners, forge clerks, etc. as the works expanded'.[1] This family eventually took over control, but elsewhere in Merthyr Tydfil families of managers remained managers and engineers for several generations, like the Kirkhouse family in Cyfarthfa, the Martin family at Penydarren and the Evans family at Dowlais.

In mining enterprises control was often initially in the hands of estate stewards, who had also begun to form their own dynasties and from whom the mining industry learnt the practice of inheriting managerial posts. Thus on the Lowther estate, where the Speddings, father and eldest son, were the principal estate agents, Carlisle Spedding, fourth son, was made the mine manager, and when he was killed by an accident in 1755 he in turn, was followed by his son, James Spedding. In the Derbyshire lead district in a slightly different succession of posts the Barkers' mining and smelting firm was founded in 1729 by William Barker, steward of the Duke of Devonshire, then continued by his son in partnership with Thomas Barker, steward of the Duke of Rutland, before being handed on to the next generation of the family.

In deep coal-mining sons of viewers who had technical training and experience had telling advantages. The chronicles record John Buddle, father and son, John Watson, father and son, James Ramshaw, father and son, Simon and Peter Donnison, Edward, John and Thomas Smith, as well as the men succeeded by brothers or nephews, such as Ralph and John Allison, George and John Johnson, John, Ralph and Thomas Dodds, James and Thomas Easton—the list could be greatly prolonged: in all these cases the advantages of nepotism were combined with those of skill, standing and reliability, to create 'dynasties' of viewers. Similar combinations of nepotism, skill and experience favoured the engineering managers. The sons of Telford's assistants, John Gibb, John Mitchell, John Wilson and Matthew Davidson all inherited their fathers' trusted posts; John Dixon, co-surveyor of the Stockton-Darlington line, was the grandson of a well-known surveyor; the Clegram family gradually filled most engineering and clerical posts on the Berkeley-Gloucester canal; William Jessop, brought up by Smeaton, in whose service his father had died, introduced his own two sons, Josias and William, to the profession; J. L. MacAdam's sons dominated road engineering in the 1820s, just as Welsh canal-building in the 1790s had been dominated by Thomas Dadford, father and son, and by Thomas Sheasby and his two sons; George Leather, the early railway engineer, was the son of a leading canal and navigation engineer, and George Stephenson found many important posts for members of his family; J. B. Neilson was the son of the works engineer of Dr. John Roebuck's Bo'ness colliery. As one biographer put it, in the case of I. K. Brunel:

> [he] benefited greatly at the outset of his career from the lustre which his father had already given to the name of Brunel and from the help, the example and the experience of the distinguished friends whom his father had made in society and in the engineering profession.[1]

Where mining and ironmaking concerns developed into large corporations with something of the impersonal relationships of the modern joint-stock company, the establishment of dynasties of managers in their interstices was relatively easy. The method by which the related families of the Staintons, Dawsons and MacLarens occupied all the important managerial posts in the Carron Company from 1786 onwards, and in the process defrauded the remaining shareholders, formed the basis of one of the major industrial scandals of the nineteenth century; but even where the shareholders remained firmly in control, as in the Quaker Lead Company, we find Robert Stagg, chief agent in the North, succeeded in 1808 at his death by his son Joseph and at the latter's death next year by his other son Robert, who was in turn succeeded by his son. A careful investigation of the steel industry in the second half of the nineteenth century has shown the growth there of 'bureaucratic dynasties':

> the father, having worked his way up within the firm, was able to ease his son's career within the same firm . . . Two generations of the same family, whose role was primarily managerial rather than proprietory, have controlled some companies,[1]

and since then the withering away of shareholder control in large concerns has led to further developments in this field. The impersonal company was rare in the industrial revolution, but the few which did exist made an exceptionally large contribution to the creation of a managerial class.

In isolated areas, opened up only with the help of immigrant skilled labour, the manager would of necessity be able to fill many of the leading posts with his own family and thus perpetuate his control, for it was perhaps only his influence which induced the work force to migrate in the first place. Such was the case among the Homfrays and Guests in South Wales, and among the foundry and furnace managers who helped to set up the Carron Company. In the Mona Mine Company in Anglesey, 'Captain' Treweek, the skilled Cornish miner who became the successful manager of the firm, found two of his 'captains' from among his own family, J. H. Treweek, a brother, and Job, a cousin, and later placed his sons in agents' and clerical jobs under his control. Rees, the smelter, and Webster, the assayer, were equally successful in providing for succession by their own sons. In this critical period of expansion in copper-mining and smelting, managerial dynasties, based on skill which was often at least as much managerial as technical, were particularly important: thus the Vivians, a family of Cornish mine captains who for a time had a share of the Anglesey mining ventures, ultimately came to dominate the Swansea smelting industry; Richard Trevithick, the famous engineer and captain, followed his father and father-in-law, both well-known mining managers; and at the Ravenhead smeltworks, Joseph Harris, the first manager, ensured that his sons were placed in managerial posts.

In industries in which the owners were less dependent on the professional skill of the managers, examples of managerial dynasties are rarer, but by no means unknown. Greatbatch, Wedgwood's manager, filled many important posts at Etruria with his family; at Gott's mills, Joseph, John and Charles Hopps dominated the head office for fifty years; the Shrewsbury flax mills were filled with William Whitwell's relations in leading posts after 1806, and the New Wire Company at Cheadle showed a surprising number of Brindleys in responsible positions in the 1790s and 1800s.

There were even some managerial families which spread across an area of an industry, holding comparable posts in different firms. The two Gilbert brothers, administering the vast estates of Earl Gower and the Duke of Bridgewater respectively at the critical period of mining expansion and canal-building, might be exceptional in their own sphere, but there were some comparable families in industry: thus George Cranage, the inventive foreman at Coalbrookdale, boasted a brother in a similar position in the Bridgnorth Forge, acquired by his firm in 1760. Perhaps the most remarkable was the Vaughan family, descendants of Joseph Vaughan, associated with Monmouth furnace, who died in 1788, aged 89. One of his sons, Thomas, was manager of Pentyrch Ironworks from 1789 on, his son, in turn, being under-manager; another, Joseph, managed Melingriffith; a third, John, managed Machen; and there was a William Vaughan, perhaps a fourth, managing Caerphilly Furnace at the same time. Other members of the family were associated with other ironworks, including one agent at Dowlais, and it was a scion of this family who moved to Witton Park in 1825, where he later joined Bolckow in founding one of the leading steelworks of the nineteenth century.

VI

Industrial managers, like industrial entrepreneurs from whom they are hard to distinguish in this period, formed one of the most dynamic social groups of their age, responsible for initiating many of its decisive changes. Generalizations and conclusions about their origins, training and about the standing of their profession are therefore likely to have to ignore many exceptions and to do much violence to the evidence. Yet some conclusions of validity do emerge from our cursory survey.

At the beginning of the industrial revolution the educational system, already under pressure from the mercantile interests and from other quarters, proved remarkably flexible and capable of providing a large minority of the population, including the promising boys of almost all classes, with sufficient formal background education and some specialist training to fill clerical, technical and managerial positions in the growing industrial firms. In the early years, about the middle of the eighteenth century, such educational facilities as existed were sufficiently varied, and the subjects taught were often taught at such low levels of attainment, as to allow promising boys from the lower classes to compete with middle-class boys without too great a handicap, and this was the period at which social mobility within industrial firms was extremely high. In the course of the next two or three generations educational differentiation contributed its share to the growing class barriers in industry,[1] as schools and colleges for middle-class and professional children improved and were turned more purposefully to train captains of industry and commerce, while schools for the poor deteriorated in curriculum and in quality.

At the same time there were other forces at work to isolate and develop a separate managerial class which, though it could not be called a 'profession' in the accepted sense, yet had many of its attributes, including the development of a code of behaviour and a body of knowledge. The social differentiation downwards became much more pronounced than that upwards, towards the capitalist owner, and, in fact, the line between the manager, the managing partner and the moneyed partner was increasingly difficult to draw, as mobility between these categories remained high and helped to determine the status of the manager himself.[2] The status of the entrepreneur, which the manager was aspiring to share, was rapidly rising in Britain, in contrast with France and Italy, where, it is alleged, 'industrial management, in comparison with other elites, has gained neither respect nor power'. Whether it is true, as Harbison and Myers believe, that in these countries 'industrialization has been retarded partially because of the inability to develop an effective managerial elite', or whether we should share the views of Gerschenkron and possibly Redlich, that

> the adverse social attitudes towards entepreneurs and entrepreneurship do not emerge as a retarding force upon the economic development of European countries in the nineteenth century,[3]

it seems certain that in Britain ambitious men could without qualms make a managerial career, with a partnership at the end of it, their target.

While the growing size of the typical up-to-date firm required more managers and perhaps new echelons of managers at different levels, giving some of them much greater responsibilities than had been possible before, and while at the same time owners, being richer and farther away from the foundation date of the firm, became more inclined to leave power to the managers, this demand for managerial talent was met by a supply which was constantly diminished by the recruitment of managers to the ranks of owners. It would be wrong to imply that there were many places at which the shortage of capable managers was felt acutely, for it was one of the characteristics of an industrializing society, still groping its way to a new equilibrium in the factories and the mines, that it did not realize easily how under-managed it was. Yet at certain specific points entrepreneurs might be consciously aware of a shortage of qualified staff, and wherever a manager's post as such had been firmly established, whether it was based on technological or managerial competence or on both, its growing esteem pointed to a growing importance within its industry.

A common body of knowledge and a code of behaviour, as far as they existed, were valid only for each industry separately, and hardly for an industrial managers' class as such. The case of T. Pearce, whose father was a manager of lead-mines at Llynypandu, and who became the clerk and manager for John Wilkinson at Bradley and then at Hadley, is most exceptional: where son follows father in the profession it is within the same industry, usually within the same region. The training, of course, is still largely technical, concerned with materials, processes, practices or legal obligations, arising out of specific industries only. The 'codes' are likewise specific to an industry, such as the responsibility for safety, or the safeguarding of a landlord's permanent interest in a coal-mine, or the production of the most efficient currently available design in engineering. Apart from the natural growth of one industry and of one type of management out of another, as railway-building grew out of colliery-viewing and engineering, there is no crossing of industrial boundaries.

In technology regional boundaries were being broken down for the first time during the course of the industrial revolution to create national technologies as a first step in their codification and their intermeshing with the discoveries of pure science, themselves about to burst their national boundaries to become supra-national. By contrast, industrial management had not even attained the dignity of a subject worthy of investigation or improvement. Managers might be judged by their character, ability, trustworthiness and their technical-industrial competence, which in some cases had developed to a stage where it had become codified, standardized and testable. They were not judged for their abilities simply as managers, and there was thus virtually nothing to link the groups of managements across the boundaries of their industries. There were well-defined groups of managers in many industries: there was, by 1830, as yet hardly a managerial profession as such.

5/ The Adaptation of the Labour Force

In many respects the rational and methodical management of labour was the central management problem in the industrial revolution, requiring the fiercest wrench from the past. Yet, whatever the actual difficulties of practising managers, it was as little discussed in a scientific spirit as any of the other aspects of management. It was held, by those who thought about these matters at all, that there was nothing new to be learnt, since workshop masters had had to control labour in the past (though the numbers involved were small); and generals had commanded larger numbers (though they had greater powers of discipline, and did not have to show a commercial profit). In any case, success or failure to control a group of this kind could be attributed to 'character' and to individual idiosyncrasy, and did not become subject to generalization.

Thus the pioneers of the industrial revolution were forced to lay the foundations of the practices of labour management themselves, involving a subject as complex, novel and full of pitfalls as the other applied sciences they had to master, without the full realization that they were, in fact, experimenting or innovating at all. Problems were met and solved *ad hoc*, and only a tiny minority of masters could bring the experience of others, or even a consistent set of principles, to their aid. And while we can hazard a guess as to how many of the survivors were successful, like Robert Owen, largely because they mastered this aspect of the tasks of management, we shall probably remain for ever ignorant of the number of those who failed because they did not.

I

Most of the firms growing to any size in the early stages of industrialization had a problem even anterior to that of controlling their labour: they had to recruit it first. There were here two distinct, though clearly overlapping difficulties; the aversion of workers to entering the new large enterprises with their unaccustomed rules and discipline and the shortage of skilled and reliable labour.

The worker who left the background of his domestic workshop or peasant holding for the factory entered a new culture as well as a new sense of direction. It was not only that 'the new economic order needed . . . part humans: soulless, depersonalised, disembodied, who could become members, or little wheels rather, of a complex mechanism'. It was also that men who were non-accumulative, non-acquisitive, accustomed to work for subsistence, not for maximization of income,[1] had to be made obedient to the cash stimulus, and obedient in such a way as to react precisely to the stimuli provided.

The very recruitment to the uncongenial work was difficult, and it was made worse by the deliberate or accidental modelling of many works on workhouses and prisons, a fact well known to the working population. Even if they began work, there was no guarantee that the new hands would stay. 'Labourers from agriculture or domestic industry do not at first take kindly to the monotony of factory life; and the pioneering employer not infrequently finds his most serious obstacle in the problem of building up a stable supply of efficient and willing labour.' Many workers were 'transient, marginal and deviant', or were described as 'volatile'. It was noted that there were few early manufactures in the seaport towns, as the population was too unsteady, and Samuel Greg, jun., complained most of the 'restless and migratory spirit' of the factory population. Thus it was not necessarily the better labourer but the stable one who was worth the most to the manufacturer: often, indeed, the skilled apprenticed man was at a discount, because of the working habits acquired before entering a factory.[2] Roebuck and Garbett left Birmingham for Prestonpans among other causes in order to escape the independence of the local workers for the 'obedient turn of the Scots', while Henry Houldsworth found hand spinners to have such irregular habits that the introduction of machine spinning in Glasgow 'rendered it desirable to get a new set of hands as soon as possible'.[3]

Elsewhere in Scotland even the children found the discipline irksome: when the Catrine cotton mills were opened, one of the managers admitted, 'the children were all newcomers, and were very much beat at first before they could be taught their business'. At other mills, 'on the first introduction of the business, the people were found very ill-disposed to submit to the long confinement and regular industry that is required from them'. The highlander, it was said, 'never sits at ease at a loom; it is like putting a deer in the plough'.[4]

In turn, the personal inclinations and group mores of such old-established industrial workers as handloom weavers and framework knitters were opposed to factory discipline.

> I found the utmost distaste [one hosier reported] on the part of
> the men, to any regular hours or regular habits. . . . The men
> themselves were considerably dissatisfied, because they could
> not go in and out as they pleased, and have what holidays they
> pleased, and go on just as they had been used to do; and were
> subject, during after-hours, to the ill-natured observations of
> other workmen, to such an extent as completely to disgust them
> with the whole system, and I was obliged to break it up.[1]

It would be difficult to imagine a more powerful form of social
pressure than that indicated by the last sentence, though the men
did not have to change their trade or their equipment, but merely
changed its setting. In fact, 'as long as there was some measure of
freedom of choice between cottage and factory the workman preferred the cottage'.[2]

The reasons for the 'attractions of cottage industry',[3] or rather
the repulsion of factory industry, were many and varied and they
were not all economic. There was more to overcome than the change
of employment or the new rhythm of work: there was a whole new
culture to be absorbed and an old one to be traduced and spurned,[4]
there were new surroundings, often in a different part of the country,
new relations with employers and new uncertainties of livelihood,
new friends and neighbours, new marriage patterns and behaviour
patterns of children and adults within the family and without.

Small wonder that the problem was often seen in moral terms.
The men of Saddleworth, threatened with the harbingers of the
new factory system in 1806, resolved:

> that the domestic system is highly favourable to the cultivation
> of paternal, filial and fraternal affections, the sources of domestic
> happiness, and the generation of good moral and civil habits,
> the sources of public tranquillity; that the factory system tends
> to the prevention of these affections and habits, and leads youth
> sooner into the stronger temptations.[5]

This resolution, it should be stressed, and many others like it passed
in Yorkshire, represents not the harking back to a mythical golden
age, but the defence of *existing* social relationships. While the danger
to public morals represented by the factories may have been
exaggerated, then and later, the resolution shows fully the fear and
suspicion of change.

Coupled with the tenacious attachment to the existing culture
and the fear of the unknown, there was the fear of the known, for
there were few areas of the country in which the modern industries,

particularly the textiles, if carried on in large buildings, were not associated with prisons, workhouses and orphanages. This connection is usually underrated, particularly by those historians who assume that the new works recruited free labour only.

If recruitment to the factories had been entirely voluntary, nothing would have been more inept than this early association, but clearly it was not. The thoughts of the early entrepreneurs, looking for docile labour of a new kind, turned easily to unfree labour, both here and on the Continent.[1] Nor were the complementary efforts to turn poorhouses into workhouse-manufactories entirely unconnected, for the aims to see idle men punished and educated to work, and to lower the poor rates, were aims of the employing classes everywhere.[2] Not only Sir Humphrey Mackworth about 1700 but other Welsh coalmasters a century later were employing numbers of ex-criminals and of wanted men, for lack of any free labour.[3]

Some workhouse-manufactories were started at the end of the seventeenth century, including Bristol in 1697 and Exeter in 1698–1701, but the main impetus came from the Act of 1723, which rapidly led to the building of at least sixty such workhouses in the provinces and fifty in London. Not all of these were successful, though some went on for many years before they were defeated by lack of skilled management, by embezzlement, or by machine-spinning competition: Shrewsbury, for example, had a famed municipal workshop in a large building, working competitively, and Attleborough made profits which whetted the appetites of other parishes. These enterprises were to be found not only in the old textile areas, such as Suffolk, Norfolk and the West Country, but also, more significantly, in the new textile centres, like Manchester, where a new building was begun in 1730, Liverpool, where the 'House of Industry' cost £8,000, and Nottingham, where the Borough leased land to each of the three town parishes in 1726 for the erection of workhouses.

Following Gilbert's pamphlet of 1764, which advocated the extension of the East Anglian method of grouped parishes, and the schemes of Fielding, Sir Richard Lloyd and the Earl of Hillsborough, the Act of 1782 led to further attempts to set paupers to industrial work.[4] At the end of the century the 'working school' movement caused the foundation of at least fourteen schools in England in which the children spun flax and wool, knitted stockings and made shoes or pins. This idea was further supported by Pitt's abortive Bill of 1796, which was to have created 'schools of industry', to put pauper children to work on textiles and leather in the workhouses, and by the Poor Law Committee of the House of Commons in 1817.[1] Houses of Correction and Bridewells also found employment for men and women in textile and other industries, in conditions not dissimilar from those in the early manufactories, as, for example, in the Bridewells of Wymondham, Norwich City, Ipswich County, Beccles County, Warwick County, Lincoln City, Devizes County, Preston County, Manchester and York Castle.

The association of the idea of the factory with unfree labour was also fostered in other ways. Thus in Northern Ireland the cotton industry took its origin in the attempt to employ usefully the children in the Belfast Charitable Society's Institution, and Greg's obtained not only their pauper apprentices but even some of their 'free' labour from the Cheshire overseers. Elsewhere pauper children were handed over to outside contractors running private enterprises. In the Lake District, it has been noted,

> in some instances there may have been little difference between the workhouse and a sort of factory. Kirkby Stephen workhouse, bought for £1,500 about 1816, had been a cotton mill; and in 1827 part of it was leased to a Manchester manufacturer who employed many of the paupers, with others, in the production of silk and cotton goods.[2]

In Scotland, significantly, factories were referred to as 'public Work', showing the mental association with workhouses, and migration to factory districts was likened to transportation. While Telford used gangs of prisoners to help in his canal-building work in Scotland, serfdom was only just being abolished in Scottish coal-mines and saltworks.

The most widespread cause of the association of the new large-scale industry with unfree labour, however, was the massive employment of pauper apprentices in private industry. Some of them were found in the metal industries, in such new works as Soho and Carron, and others were sent to small masters or to sea, as formerly; but the significant employment from the point of view of publicity was in textiles, mainly, though not exclusively, in cotton.

These pauper apprentices were not employed because they were cheap: on the contrary, most of the larger masters who made the comparison (it is highly doubtful if any of the smaller ones ever did) found them, like James McConnell,

> more expensive than paid labour . . . and troublesome, inconvenient . . . and objectionable in almost every point of view.

To say nothing of the expense of providing buildings for their reception [Henry McConnell explained in 1833], and of being at more expence with their maintenance than their labour would be worth, we should be under the necessity of keeping them, when from their bad conduct, or bad work, or bad health, it would be our interest to dismiss them; or when from bad times, or accidents of machinery, or turnouts, etc., we should be compelled to work short time, or entirely stop our works.[1]

Greg of Quarry Bank, Styal, found the cost of his apprentices to be, in all, 3s. 6d. a week in 1790, rising to 5s. in 1822 and 1830, or more expensive than free labour; even Samuel Oldknow, whose apprentices cost him 4s. a week each in 1798, when free labour averaged 4s. 8d. a week, but whose cost rose to 6s. a week in 1804,[2] found any possible saving more than outweighed by the extra trouble and risk.

Apprentices were taken on because otherwise the mills would have been without sufficient labour, or at least without sufficient child labour in relation to the number of adults. For, whatever might have been the conditions in the 1830s, when the second generation of factory workers had grown up[3] and parents were only too eager for their children to be accepted into the mills, in the beginning the pauper children represented the only type of labour which in many areas could be driven into them, and even then it was usually by force and in ignorance of conditions in the North rather than by opportunism. Blincoe records that the complaint of a child to his mother who alerted the parish officers led to great improvements in the mill in which he worked, while in Exeter only the threat of cutting off their own dole forced the paupers to agree to the employment of their children in the mills. Sir Robert Peel the elder himself has put on record his horror at the conditions of the near 1,000 children in his family mills before he persuaded Parliament to pass the Act of 1802; the few magistrates who did carry out inspections under this Act were equally critical of conditions in such dread places as Litton mill, later to be made famous by Robert Blincoe.[4] The thrill of horror felt by present-day readers at the treatment, the hours of work and nightwork, the conditions of life which were then considered fit for pauper children, were shared by many contemporaries: the factory agitation in the years to 1819 was no idle whim, and the children were not 'free' workers in any normally accepted sense.

Parish apprentices were scattered unevenly over the countryside, and were rarely found in town mills. Peel, the largest employer, had up to 1,000 at one time, and David Dale had nearly 500 at New Lanark. Few others exceeded 100 each; nevertheless, their work was well known, and the association of factory labour with pauper compulsion was strong in people's minds. It helped to maintain and reinforce the feeling of aversion to factory work on the part of the potential working population.

The comment, in the face of this hatred, that 'there was no strong desire on the part of the workers themselves to congregate in large establishments' is an understatement to the point of travesty. When its author goes on to say, rightly, that 'it was only under the impact of powerful forces, attractive and repellent, that the English labourer or craftsman was transformed into a factory hand',[1] it should be remembered that these 'forces' were much more varied than those normally considered by the economist.

The main repellent forces, such as enclosures in England or the Highland clearances, are largely outside the field of this book; but while it is true that the attractive forces included higher money wages, by themselves these would have been utterly inadequate. Measured against changes of such magnitude, the economist's normal assumptions, of fixed parameters of social customs and a permanent supply of labour willing to work in large establishments and reacting marginally to wages and conditions, are untenable. To judge that factory work could not have been too hateful, since the workers 'chose . . . the conditions which the reformers condemned', and factories which reduced hours lost their labour, and that 'in modern times the workers had to be induced by substantial gains, probably in the form of a greater yearly income or wage or more continuous employment',[2] to work in factories, forgets the compulsive elements of that inducement on desperately unwilling labour, and runs counter the large evidence which all points to the fact that continuous employment was precisely one of the most hated aspects of factory work.[3]

Thus the paradox of the eighteenth century, the lack of employment opportunities, as seen from the point of view of the displaced peasant or the hand worker, existing simultaneously with a labour shortage, as seen by the rising large employer, is in part explained by the fact that the worker was averse to taking up the *type* of employment offered, and the employer was unwilling to tolerate the habits of work which the men seeking work desired. It is also partly explained by the shortage of labour trained in old and new types of skill.

Any expansion of industry is likely to come up against bottlenecks of skilled labour; the British industrial revolution represents a particularly unbalanced expansion, interrupted by major wars and their special demands for labour,[1] and as such its problems were exceptionally acute. The easiest to solve, relatively, was the simple shortage of men of traditional skills of whom larger numbers than hitherto were required. Typical here were the coal-mines, where the expansion in the early years of the eighteenth and again of the nineteenth century drove up hiring premiums to as much as twelve and eighteen guineas on the Tyne and Wear, before labourers 'who had hitherto never thought of pit work' were brought in and depressed wages again.[2] This kind of shortage could normally be dealt with by a rising and fairly flexible supply from redundant village and handicrafts labour,[3] as well as from workhouses, orphanages and prisons, and it was by reference to this type of problem that the often-noted fortunate balance between specific labour shortages, solved by inventions, and by additional supplies of labour, could be said to have existed.

The real problems were those faced by the innovators, who needed large concentrations of craftsmen of a type which had hitherto worked scattered in small workshops; who wanted new skills, often created or developed in the works of the innovators themselves; or who required workpeople willing to suffer the new factory routine.

Of the first type was the shortage of masons in early canal works:

> Finding that Masons were very scarce and not as ready to enter with us as might be expected—Agreed . . . to give it out that we shou'd keep a Number of Hands During the Winter,

Smeaton noted in 1760. Another instance was Wedgwood's voracious appetite for painters, and his inability to meet it fully.[4] Ambrose Crowley set up his works in the North rather than in the Midlands, for there 'the cuntry is verry poore and populous soe workmen must of necessity increase'.

More significant was the second type, the shortage of men with new skills, be they foremen or highly trained craftsmen. The pool of such key men was very small, and the absence of a single man could hold up a major works: thus the Calder Iron Works could not meet Peter Stubs's order on one occasion, as their tilter was down with a fever, and there was not a competent tilter in the whole of Scotland to replace him; Fenton and Murray, the leading Yorkshire engineering firm and one of the main rivals of Boulton & Watt, lost the one moulder who could cast nozzles in green sand, and therefore had to switch to dry sand; while the Soho partnership itself, looking for a millwright to build the Albion Mill, had to ask Professor Robison of Edinburgh to send them a good pupil, and having secured John Rennie in this way, employed him for most of their general millwork henceforward.[1]

As for ordinary engineers and erectors, the Soho firm was in perpetual straits for them as soon as its sales of steam-engine designs began to mount:

> You ask for men but I do not see that we can send you any without stopping the works here [Watt wrote to Boulton from Soho in 1786].
> As to men [he had written to Wilson in Cornwall a year earlier], we are entirely deficient in that article even for the works we have in hand . . . we must see if we can get some hands from another works which we are constantly in quest of but there is so much machinery going forward all over the nation that it is difficult to get any that are worth hiring.
> You may as well write to us for a waggonload of gold as to ask us for men to erect and repair engines, we have not one to repair our own,

Boulton confirmed in 1791,[2] and in 1795 James Watt, jun., echoed these words to his father:

> It is impossible we can part with any of our own people, so far from it, we are using every endeavour to get more hands and more hands we must have, for orders appear likely to increase beyond calculation.

When Bersham ironworks was closed, Soho snapped up some of its best people, but Boulton failed to attract away any copper workers from Temple Mills, Maidenhead, when these changed hands in 1788.[3]

The ironmasters of South Wales were so conscious of the shortage of labour that they dare not blow out their furnaces in slack times, for 'the men once lost would be with difficulty regained'. Wedgwood was similarly afraid of losing his men to rival firms in slack times. Marc I. Brunel was held up in the production of his blocks for the navy because of the shortage of skilled mechanics, while textile-machinery makers were scarce not only in the early days of Arkwright, but continued to be rare and overworked as long as the primary expansion period lasted in the cotton industry.[4] The Mona Mine Company could recruit neither smelters nor enginemen in North Wales, and had much trouble finding them in the south of the

Principality, while another copper-rolling mills put up in 1805 manned its works by poaching the erector workmen.

Poaching and defences against it became troublesome but necessary activities in all the expanding and innovating industries. Soho lost many of its skilled workers and attempted to entice away Murray and Fenton's men in turn. Roebuck and Garbett lost their men in Prestonpans to rival firms. Samuel Crompton lost his workers as fast as he trained them. In South Wales poaching was a constant source of friction. Crawshay accused Bailey of this malpractice, Taitt accused Homfray and Homfray accused Dowlais. 'I can hardly think that thou wouldst be the means of enticing T.D. from these works', Peter Price wrote more in sorrow than in anger to J. Guest in 1801, but it appeared more than likely that he was.[1] Elsewhere, local firms made agreements not to poach each others' workers: such agreements existed, with varying success, in the Nottingham-shire-Derbyshire water spinning industry, among the West Cumberland coalowners, and even between the Berkeley and Gloucester and the Herefordshire and Gloucester Canal companies.

The distinction between poaching and normal recruitment was a fine one, but the latter usually referred to recruitment of workers who had a generally recognized and apprenticed skill, as distinct from one learnt and developed within an innovating rival firm. Much of both went on, and formed a major cause of that migration of craftsmen which served at that period both to diffuse skills and local practices, and to turn the country into a single labour market for skilled men. Such men were attracted from the backward regions to be trained up in the latest techniques or in new trades in the most advanced, and then dispersed again to bring the practices of the rest of the country up to date.

The role of Soho as such a centre of craft training and fertilization in engineering, an industry which may be said to have been created within its walls, was as important as its better-known role as an academy of engineering employers and professional men. Typically, a large proportion of its own top engineers and draughtsmen came from Scotland, whose poverty and schooling provided her young men with an education and an ambition far superior to the normal run of Englishmen, Welshmen and Irish. But expansion meant recruiting elsewhere, too.

> I want a few very good workmen at Soho [Boulton wrote to Thomas Wilson in Cornwall, in 1788], such as good smiths and good turners. . . . Pray consult Mr. Murdock to find me some steady men.

And some weeks later:

> If you have any worthy honest men that are very good workers,
> who can forge, file, turn and fit mathematically true send them
> to me upon the lowest terms you can agree for 3 years & if they
> deserve more they shall not complain of me.

Three years later he sent agents and letters to Liverpool and
Manchester to recruit watch- and toolmakers who might be trained
up to Soho needs, only to find that most of them had gone into the
cotton-machinery trade. The opening of the Soho Foundry and the
beginning of engine manufacturing in 1796 caused the recruitment
of a 'proper regiment of founders'. This was the time when Soho
advertised widely for 'Moulders, Turners, Smiths' in the Birmingham, Shrewsbury and Chester papers, and took on some pauper
apprentices from Bedfordshire and some skilled men from Wilkinson's closed Bersham works. There was much active recruiting in
the years following. At the same time, Soho lost many of its men to
others both at home and abroad: a letter from the Roosevelts at
the Schuylers' Mine in New Jersey acknowledged that Soho
workmen and Soho equipment had built it all.[1]

The Carron works, it has often been noted, imported all its
original skilled labour, including the nailmakers, from the main
English centres and from Sweden. In turn, at least twelve skilled
men went with Gascoigne from there to Russia. South Wales recruited widely in England, Homfrey bringing in skilled ironworkers
both from Yorkshire and from Stourbridge to start up his works in
Merthyr Tydfil. Others recruited from Scotland, or from neighbouring ironworks:

> I should be obliged if you could help us to a good Melting
> Master Finer . . . as our present one is too refractory and
> troublesome to keep. I am thinking as Mr. Crawshay has of
> late contracted his make, may be a good time to get a good
> civilized man,

Thomas Vaughan of Pentyrch wrote to Robert Thompson at
Dowlais in 1794.[2] William Spencer, in 1744, looked for a finer in
Cheshire or Staffordshire; Robert Lindsay, in 1790, drew on many
areas to fill his Haigh ironworks. Ambrose Crowley recruited some
skilled men from Liège, and attracted others from the ironworking
districts by newspaper advertisements and recruiting agents. In
general, whenever an ironmaster moved, he 'took his skilled workers
with him, and such movements are recorded to Furness from

Cheshire, Ireland and South Wales; from Shropshire to Scotland and South Wales, and from Staffordshire to South Wales'. Many of these new centres of ironmaking took 'Shropshiremen to teach their 50 years' experience in the new technique'.[1]

In coal-mining mobility also helped to spread new methods.

> There is 9 or 10 Men run away from our place [William Brown wrote from Tyneside to Carlisle Spedding in Cumberland in 1750], and I hear some of them is with you.

In 1755, by contrast, he heard from another leading mining agent, John Burrell at Bo'ness:

> In this my last jaunt to the West I was not idle in procuring pitmen both for you and me. Those who have families I propose to take and the Yonkers who have nothing to care for but themselves I send to you. It is the colliers about Glasgow I have the most dependence upon as they seem to be or at least soon will be in a staggering condition.

And a year later Brown wrote to him

> I have got plenty of pitmen this year especially Scotchmen many of which has been in this country 2 or 3 years and has as one man com'd to me this time and are realy fine workmen has nothing less than 14 or 15 come since Martinmas last.[2]

Normal mobility between Scotland and England was slight before the end of serfdom in the Scots mines. But Irish immigrants did enter both Scottish and Cumberland coal-mines, and occasionally, as in the case of Carron's mines, it was possible to safeguard English miners from being bound. During the rapid expansion of employment in the mines after 1800 most areas went to the established districts for their skilled men. The Duke of Bridgewater, for example, recruited men from Newcastle, Whitehaven, Workington, Wales and Shropshire; North Wales from Northumberland; Warwickshire and Staffordshire from Shropshire; Ireland from England; and South Wales from Shropshire. In turn, the chief coal centres, while providing the skill for much of the rest of the country, also attracted labour from outside when in need. During the 1832 coal strike on Tyneside 'the northern coaches were crowded with the adventurers, and the stage waggons were piled with their bedding and boxes. Many walked from Staffordshire and Yorkshire, and others hired vehicles'. However, typically, the men recruited over long distances remained footloose: of forty-three miners leaving Whingill colliery in 1810–11, nineteen were Irish, nineteen from Newcastle, two Scots, and one each from Wales, Lancashire and Alston Moor, not one being native.[1]

In the non-ferrous metal industries Derbyshire miners were not only opening out coal- and iron-mines, but also some of the new copper areas. South Wales recruited its copper-smelters in Cornwall, and Anglesey brought smelters from South Wales and miners from Cornwall, 300 of whom 'had been chiefly drawn to the works by the Cornish system of bidding'. Other Cornishmen went into the Shropshire coal and ironworks, while the eighteenth-century copper and brass industry benefited by foreign immigration.[2]

The skills required by the new large civil engineering works, such as canals, were not as obvious, and mostly did not develop into apprenticed crafts, particularly as the rate of expansion in the recruitment was, during the building boom, much too fast for any such practice. Men with experience were eagerly sought, and other recruits were brought in from Ireland, too old to qualify for a craft, from Scotland and from agriculture, particularly in the fen areas, where they had experience in digging drains. Once played in together, groups of navvies would be recruited together: thus John Davidson brought with him to the Great Caledonian Canal a gang of Welshmen who had helped him to build Pont Cysyllte; the builders of the Sankey navigation and the Worsley canal at times 'exchanged' gangs to help each other out, and the Duke of Bridgewater recruited forty men from Hartshill in 1772, where probably the tunnel had just been completed.

Other new or growing industries had similar problems of recruitment and of moving and re-training existing labour. Wedgwood periodically scoured the country for painters and other craftsmen; Peter Stubs's sons, setting up in pinmaking at Warrington, recruited skilled workers from Gloucester, the main English centre, and from Ireland; Portmadoc, the slate centre, attracted immigrants from Ireland and Cornwall; and Clegg, beginning the manufacture of gas in London, brought with him skilled men from Manchester with their families.

Recruiting to the textile factories was geared chiefly to overcome the third type of problem: the shortage of labour willing to work regular hours and endure factory discipline. The unfree labour, noted already, did not, in most cases, amount to more than one-third of the labour force, and usually much less: free labour also had to be recruited and adapted.

In Scotland, since 'all the regularly trained Scots peasantry disdained the idea of working early and late, day after day, within cotton mills', and 'it was most difficult to induce any sober, well-doing family to leave their home to go into cotton mills as then conducted', the founders of mills had to employ the scum of the cities, or snatch at people in distress, like David Dale, who heard of the shipwreck of 200 emigrants from Skye and hastened to offer them employment at New Lanark.[1] Others were then recruited more regularly from those suffering agricultural distress in Ireland or who were driven out by Highland clearances, and this is where a large part of the early Scots millworkers came from: Glasgow masters, indeed, preferred the Irish, who were docile and willing to take starvation wages on first arrival.[2]

In those early days,

> a few persons professing knowledge of the art were occasionally got from Glasgow, and some from England; but these were generally of loose and wandering habits, and seldom remained long in the establishment. The more respectable part of the surrounding inhabitants were at first averse to seek employment in the works, as they considered it disreputable to be employed in what they called a 'public work'.
> Such was the general dislike of that occupation at the time [according to Robert Owen], that, with a few exceptions, only persons destitute of friends, employment and character were found willing to try the experiment.[3]

In other parts of the country, too, the original work force came not from skilled textile workers, but, as far as female labour was concerned,

> largely from agriculturists unsettled by the agrarian revolution, from domestic servants, the unskilled of all trades and parish paupers.
> Factory work in the early period might almost, indeed, be described as casual employment for unskilled labour.[4]

In the villages, as Joseph Nicholson reported from Bessbrook, in Ireland, women refused to work in the factories at 8*d.* a day, whilst 'in their own houses [they] are satisfied with fourpence or fivepence'. In the towns labour was easier to obtain: Manchester never had a real labour shortage, and in Glasgow at least one enterprising Scot made a living by enticing town workers into the outlying villages.[5] The work was not hard to learn, but the critical task was to condition men to the idea of it, to break down their opposition, and to 'commit' them as full-time workers.

Commitment [according to W. E. Moore] involves both the performance of appropriate actions and the acceptance of the normative system that provides the rules and rationale. Whether such commitment can be achieved in a single generation is debatable . . . Labour surpluses can lead managers and scholars alike to minimize the importance of commitment. But the uncommitted worker is likely to quit or perform minimally, and to require much supervision. These probabilities have economic costs as well as implications for the long run viability of industrialization measures.[1]

Once commitment was achieved the undoubted higher wages in the mills attracted nearby textile labour, such as linen workers in Lanarkshire and Renfrewshire, silk workers in Stockport, and hand weavers and spinners in many parts of Lancashire. The long-distance recruitment of the earlier years, when the Irish moved into Scotland, the Scots into Lancashire, and the English into North Wales, continued to some extent. Of the 318 workers in Richard Jackson's cotton mill in Carlisle, 206 came from Cumberland, thirty-four from Ireland, fifty-two from Scotland, and twenty-six from Wales and elsewhere.[2] All the early mills necessarily employed their own carpenters and mechanics and built their own machines, but the problems of their recruitment were more akin to those of other skilled crafts, noted above.

II

Once he was employed in one of the large modern works the new recruit had to be trained in the ways of his employer. 'In developing areas . . . considerable managerial effort must be devoted to actual education rather than to giving orders or enforcing discipline.'[3] There were many aspects of this training, but few of them were crystallized out into general maxims. Training was, again, a matter largely of individual trial and error.

There was, in the first place, the training in traditional skills, such as those of apprenticed crafts or of coal-miners. The latter, however, depended partly on the experience of the routine of a large-scale establishment, in the larger mines at least. This, then, became the second type of training: the adaptation to factory routine and discipline. There was, further, the training in entirely new skills, either in new trades, as in the chemical industry, or in trades changed out of recognition by a novel division of labour. Finally, there was the growing need for literacy and the ability to absorb formal book learning.

Central within the technological progress of the industrial revolution was the development of the skills in engineering. This sprang from the experience of Boulton & Watt, for although the older Newcomen engine also required much technical skill, Watt's improved engine demanded a degree of accuracy hitherto unknown. Smeaton, the doyen of engineers, while he admired Watt's improvements, had declared them impracticable, as there were no workmen accurate enough to build them, and Watt admitted to him as late as 1778 that 'we have yet found exceeding few of them—partly owing to the inaccuracy with which they have been used to proceed, and partly to their prejudices against anything new'.[1]

There were here at least three distinct problems: the absolute shortage of men with likely skills, such as millwrights and instrument-makers; the need to transform their traditional skills into the new work of engineering; and the need to teach them the accuracy, the types of measurement and the method of work appropriate to the new engineering industry.

Boulton had no doubt that he could develop this as easily as he had transformed the traditional toy trade:

> We could engage and instruct some excellent workmen [he promised Watt in an early letter], who . . . could execute the invention 20 per cent cheaper than it would be otherwise executed, and with as great a difference in accuracy as there is between a blacksmith and a mathematical instrument maker.[2]

But he was too optimistic. It might have been possible to use the institution of the seven-year apprenticeship, or to build on the experience of Newcomen-engine making, carried on with 'primitive tools, and with labour which had to be trained in the use of unfamiliar material and devices'.[3] But the expansion went on too rapidly for that. Hence, Watt complained to Boulton in 1780,

> We are still much plagued with the boring & squaring the Rolls and our axles are very ill forged. . . . Soho people have no accuracy . . . the people at Soho do not gett forward. . . . I never go out but I am provoked by some gross inaccuracy or blundering.

Nor was the supply of craftsmen in the areas where the engines were actually built and erected any easier to expand, even in Cornwall which, at the time, boasted an exceptionally large complement of experienced engineers:

> The smith's work at Wh. Virgin [Watt wrote in the same year] including Boylers, will require 40 pair of smiths, which are not

to be found in all this country [Cornwall]; for in all the mines where we are concerned I find a scarcity of these animals. We must have more men [he wrote in 1786], and these we can only have by the slow process of breeding them.[1]

Thus, much more slowly than Boulton had allowed, a team of skilled mechanics was built up by formal seven-year apprenticeships; by accepting pauper apprentices; and by recruiting people with related skills which could be adapted. Just as, in the years before the association with Watt, Boulton's works had become a 'seminary of artists for drawing and modelling', 'perfected . . . in both design and modelling in a school of their own within the walls of Soho', so, in the days of the engineering partnership, 'the training under Boulton's own eye produced the well-known "Soho workmen", whose services were sought directly and indirectly wherever their fame has spread.' Only Soho workmen had, and knew how to use, the 'Soho slide rule'; and apprenticeship there was a recommendation to any firm in the trade.[2] As these men took their skill and knowledge elsewhere, other firms in turn became training centres for engineering craftsmen, like Fenton and Murray's Round Foundry in Leeds, or Maudslay's in London, and the new skills were spread further by the 'itinerant engineer and mechanic' of the early nineteenth century.[3]

Similarly, it was experience under such men as George Stephenson and Timothy Hackworth in the steam-engine and railway workshops of the obscure collieries in the North-East which trained up the first set of locomotive-builders, engineers and drivers to serve the whole country, just as it was a handful of specialist engineers in Manchester who developed and trained skills in cotton-machinery making that not even the best engineers of London or Glasgow could imitate.[4] This specialist engineering, like the steam-engine making, spread outwards to other centres by the migration of skilled men.

The process of spreading innovations by the medium of recruiting men from firms which used the latest methods, also worked in iron-making. Coalbrookdale was the training-ground for the men who brought the new methods to Carron or to the Perran Foundry and the Neath Abbey Company. In turn, Carron became a 'school of ingenious moulders and founders', teaching and spreading the methods of Smeaton and Gascoigne, and South Wales became the training-ground of puddlers. Just as, in an earlier period, Bodfari forge, in North Wales, had imported a Midland hammerman to teach the local forgemen to draw out with coal, so the newer iron firms, like Wilkinson's and the Walkers of Masbro', absorbed their coke-smelting knowledge from immigrant craftsmen and passed it on to others in the same manner.[1] Needless to stress, this method had its teething troubles. '*Do not push the puddling with new men who will spoil iron and cause loss*', William Crawshay enjoined on his works manager as late as 1813, emphasizing his fear by underlining.[2] Carron, with all its training, had to resort to unskilled labour when sudden demands for cast pipes overwhelmed the foundry, and the same was true of other works.

In coal-mining the problem was particularly acute in periods of rapid expansion, when normal methods of training could not keep up with the demand. In South Wales, for example, only 20–30 per cent of the labour was skilled, and the running of the collieries depended on a handful of overmen and on experienced cutters, who were made responsible not only for their own work, but for supervising and training large numbers of unskilled assistants and ancillary workers. Elsewhere, it was the men from Shropshire and Tyneside who introduced new skills and methods. In lead-mining, the London (Quaker) Lead Company could use these methods of training internally, and its smelters and agents were sent to the branches which had reached the greatest efficiency in any given trade: thus the Eggleston smelt mills became the firm's 'smelters' school' and Nanthead the 'training ground for miners and surveyors'.[3] In copper-smelting Swansea learnt by recruiting from Cornwall and Anglesey by recruiting from Swansea.

The Gas Light and Coke Company, in its early days, 'being the pioneer undertaking . . . could not call upon any experienced "district" men, but had to recruit and train its staff as it went along, often from unpromising material'. In the chemical industry Roebuck and Garbett found it impossible to prevent their workmen from absconding, both in Birmingham and Prestonpans, and teaching their secrets to others. In large-scale brewing, also, 'a migration of skills necessarily involved a migration of individuals'.[4] The same applied to civil engineering: sixty of the 600 men building the Liverpool and Manchester Railway came from Durham and Northumberland. Farther north, Telford, on completing the Caledonian Canal in 1822, in which, in course of eighteen years, 3,200 men had been taught the use of tools, observed that 'these undertakings may be regarded in the light of a working academy from which eight hundred men have annually gone forth improved workers'. He thought they had brought Scotland forward by a century.[5] In the Potteries Wedgwood, who had himself devised many new tools, the division of labour to make the best use of them,

177

and new materials and methods of treating them, had also to train his own workers.[1]

Finally, even in the cotton industry, some of the new skills were absorbed from those who had developed and first learnt them. In 1783, when two immigrant Scotsmen tried to find work in Arkwright's Manchester mill,

> Arkwright had so many applications from people anxious to enter his employment that he could do nothing for the Scotch emigrants.

In those days, indeed,

> many who had been employed by Arkwright, left his service, pretending to a knowledge of the business which they did not possess; and those men were eagerly sought after by new adventurers in the manufacture in both Kingdoms.[2]

Walshman, an early partner of Arkwright, used his influence to send some of his workers to be taught in Cromford, when he set up his own cotton mill in Keighley in 1780; Gordon, Barron & Co., an early firm to lease the Arkwright patent, received with their licence the offer to train some of their men in the Derbyshire works; Thomas Slater, the founder of the American cotton-spinning industry, learnt his trade at the Strutts's mill. To be sure, apart from such traditional crafts as calico printing, there was no formal apprenticeship involved in the textile mills. Children learnt the trade by watching others from an early age. Instead of physical strength or manual skill and accuracy, what was required was mostly 'watching, checking, serving machinery', but this work also needed training and adaptation.[3]

Two further aspects of these methods of training up skilled labour for the new works must be noted. First, this form of practical training on the job, and the haphazard acquisition of knowledge from the most advanced works as the fountainheads of the new methods, not only trained the skilled men, but often also the foremen and managers of the day. Thus in the ironworks and the rolling mills the normal progression was from cold-roll boy up the ladder of the roller team to head rollerman and ultimately foreman and manager, and the same applied to hammers and tinplate works. In Patterson's Edinburgh foundry, in 1820, it was stated that the foremen were men promoted 'from the ranks, and . . . brought up in the workshops from their boyhood'. John Marshall also stressed that their training was on the job only, and promotion by efficiency at work in their flax mill.

Even in the coal-mines it was said that

> the colliers . . . have almost uniformly been the servants of
> capitalists between whom and the actual labourers there have
> existed several gradations of rank . . . the duties of the upper-
> most of which, however, bear very lightly, if at all, on the real
> independence of the lowest—the latter indeed rising meri-
> toriously from the bottom to the top of the scale.[1]

Even if such optimistic statements did not entirely correspond with
the facts, in coal-mines or anywhere else, they had some significance.

Secondly, some of the new 'skills' were merely the result of a
successful subdivision of work. In several industries the importance
of the division of labour as a driving force in the early stages of
industrialization, by providing increased output and furthering
innovating ideas, was fully as great as Adam Smith, and William
Petty before him, believed. Boulton and Fothergill at Soho, and
Wedgwood at Etruria, obtained virtually all their advantages in
production from a skilful use of the division of labour, and this also
applies to others of the more successful metal firms in the Midlands
and to some extent to the engineering industry, particularly the
textile-machinery making section, as a whole.

Finally, some of the new employments also made demands on the
more formal educational accomplishments of reading and writing,
as well as elementary arithmetic and geometry. A few of the larger
and more isolated works, such as New Lanark and John Marshall's,
evolved their own schooling provision, but generally education of
this kind was considered a matter for public authorities or philan-
thropy, rather than a by-product of industrial employment.

Provision for the formal education of the bulk of the urban poor
was utterly inadequate in the early years of industrialization. The
Charity Schools had become the resort of the 'respectable' poor or
even the lower middle classes, and in any case much of their initial
impetus had left them, and for the really poor little was done until
the rise of the Sunday Schools. In effect, while there was provision
for the outstanding individual from the lower classes, schooling for
the rest had become lamentable. Bright lads of the poorer classes
like Telford or George Stephenson seemed to find it easier to obtain
rudiments of education within the older environment of the village[2]
than within the towns.

Towards the end of the century, however, several new developments opened up much-improved provisions for working-class
education and the express needs of the new employees were not

without influence on these. The growing hold of Methodism over the mining areas, the Corresponding Societies and other political interests, as well as the Sunday Schools and Schools of Industry, all in their different ways contributed to the spread of literacy which was carried into the nineteenth century, to be further enhanced by such employers as chose to follow the educational clauses of the Apprentices Act of 1802. In the next two decades the two rival school societies, the Adult Schools, and the further political activities, embodied in such associations as Hampden Clubs, Secular Sunday Schools and the Political Protestants, as well as Cobbett's writings, encouraged and rewarded literacy. The figures derived from numerous small censuses between about 1815 and 1835, showing that at least two-thirds even of the factory proletariat could read, are likely to be correct, or perhaps even conservative, though ability to read was not synonymous with ability to read fluently. The estimates for ability to write, reaching sometimes such high proportions as 40 per cent or 50 per cent, however, seem greatly exaggerated; one-third would be a generous estimate, though invariably the proportions would be higher for the North of England and for Scotland than for the South with the possible exception of Cornwall.[1]

In the early stages of factory industry literacy seems scarcely to have been necessary, though some firms appear certainly to have made great efforts to achieve it. Printed notices were rare and workers could draw their wages, or even use the truck shop and its paper money, with the help of experience, memory and the practice of group contracts and group and family payments, while being unable to sign their names. The growth in the complexity of factory organization and in such objectives as safety in mines, did, however, increase the importance of literacy after 1815. The engineering crafts, or those of head melters, furnacemen and rollers working to specifications, required an ability to read and to understand drawings as well as some scientific understanding. 'For the mode of managing my business', Alexander Galloway, the engineer, declared, 'by drawings and written descriptions, a man is not of much use to me unless he can read and write.'[2] In view of the small share taken by the drawing office or the laboratory, and the large responsibility borne by the skilled man, compared with modern practice, reliable training for the craftsman *élite* was soon found vital, and was quickly provided.

In the 1790s began the lectures to artisans in the Andersonian Institution in Glasgow, the Brotherly Society in Birmingham and (from 1789 to 1800) the lectures by Peter Nicholson in Soho; in Manchester the earlier College of Arts and Sciences (1780) partly met a similar need. After the war a second wave of foundations, heralded by Timothy Claxton's Mechanical Institution in London (1817–20), and spreading to Edinburgh, where the famous School of Arts was launched in 1821, to Greenock, Liverpool and Sheffield, culminated in the establishment of the Mechanics' Institute in London. The astonishing spread of this idea across the country, particularly into industrial regions, was paralleled by the works of the Society for the Diffusion of Useful Knowledge. The relative ease of the creation of these institutions and their flexibility point to the fact that few of the demands of employers for formal training, at any rate in the second generation of factory workers, went unsupplied, so that, by and large, modern industry obtained the formal training that it thought it needed.

III

If this kind of formal education began to receive some attention towards the end of our period, no frontal attack could be made on the more difficult educational problem, the creation of work discipline. Masters might believe that in England,

> in practice, the workers were managed by a reliance upon the traditions of craftsmanship and of the master-servant relationship.

But,

> however important these traditions were for industrialization, they were not always compatible with the requirements of industrial production.

What was needed was regularity and steady intensity in place of irregular spurts of work; accuracy and standardization in place of individual design; and care of equipment and material in place of pride in one's tools.[1]

None of this came easily to the new workforce. Attendance was irregular, and the complaint of Edward Cave, in the very earliest days of industrialization, was later echoed by many others: 'I have not half my people come to work today, and I have no great fascination in the prospect I have to put myself in the power of such people.'[2] Cotton spinners would stay away without notice and send for their wages at the end of the week, and one of the most enlightened firms, McConnell and Kennedy, regularly replaced spinners who had not turned up within two or three hours of starting-time on Mondays, on the reasonable presumption that they had left the firm: their average labour turnover was twenty a week, i.e. about 100 per cent a year.

Matters were worse in a place like Dowlais, reputed to employ many runaways and criminals, or among northern mining companies which could not guarantee continuous work: 'The major part of these two companies are as bad fellows as the worst of your pitmen baring their outside is not so black,' one exasperated manager complained, after they had left the district without paying their debts.[1] Elsewhere, ironworks labourers, copper- and tin-miners and engineering labourers deserted to bring in the harvest, or might return to agriculture for good if work was slack.

'St. Monday' and feast days, common traditions in domestic industry, were persistent problems. The weavers were used to 'play frequently all day on Monday, and the greater part of Tuesday, and work very late on Thursday night, and frequently all night on Friday'. Spinners, even as late as 1800, would be missing from the factories on Mondays and Tuesdays, and 'when they did return, they would sometimes work desperately, night and day, to clear off their tavern score, and get more money to spend in dissipation', as a hostile critic observed.[2] In South Wales it was estimated as late as the 1840s that the workers lost one week in five, and that in the fortnight after the monthly pay day only two-thirds of the time was being worked.

As for the regular feasts,

> our men will go to the Wakes [Josiah Wedgwood complained in 1772], if they were sure to go to the D . . . l the next. I have not spared them in threats and I would have thrash'd them right heartily if I could.

Again, in 1776,

> Our men have been at play 4 days this week, it being Burslem Wakes. I have rough'd & smoothed them over, & promised them a long Xmass, but I know it is all in vain, for Wakes must be observed though the World was to end with them.

Soho was beset by the same troubles.[3]

Employers themselves, groping their way towards a new impersonal discipline, looked backwards sporadically to make use of feasts and holidays, typical of the old order, in cementing personal relationships and breaking the monotony of the working year. Thus John Kelsall noted in 1725 that Charles Lloyd was 'abroad this day with the workmen, etc, coursing', and about the same time the famous Derby silk mill had an annual feast and dancing at Michaelmas, financed by contributions of the curious visitors in the course of the year. The Arkwrights and the Strutts, standing on the watershed between the old and the new, had feasts in Cromford in 1776, when 500 workers and their children took part, and annual balls at Cromford and Belper as late as 1781, whilst in 1772 the Hockley factory had an outing, led by the 'head workman' clad in white cotton, to gather nuts and be regaled to a plentiful supper afterwards.[1]

Other examples from industries in their early transitional stages include Matthew Boulton's feast for 700 when his son came of age, Wedgwood's feast for 120 when he moved into Etruria, Heathcoats' outing for 2,300 from Tiverton, and the repast provided by the Herculaneum Pottery at the opening of its Liverpool warehouse in 1813. Conversely, the Amlwch miners organized an ox-roast in honour of the chief proprietor, the Marquis of Anglesea, when he passed through the island on his way to take up the Lord-Lieutenancy of Ireland. Six hundred workmen sat down to a roasted ox and plenty of liquor at the Duke of Bridgewater's expense to celebrate the opening of the canal at Runcorn, and feasts were usual thereafter at the opening of canals and railways, but within a generation it was the shareholders that were being feasted, not the workers, whose relationship with the employers had by then taken on an entirely different character. Communal feasts, as part of the old pattern of leisure activities, were to be throttled together with other relics of an older morality.

Once at work it was necessary to break down the impulses of the workers, and to introduce the notion of 'time-thrift'. The factory meant economy of time, and, in the Webbs' phrase, 'enforced asceticism'. Bad timekeeping was punished by severe fines, and it was common in mills such as Oldknow's or Braids' to lock the gates of the factory, even of the workrooms, excluding those who were only a minute or two late. 'Whatever else the domestic system was, however intermittent and sweated its labour, it did allow a man a degree of personal liberty to indulge himself, a command over his time, which he was not to enjoy again.'[2]

By contrast, in the factories, pioneers like Arkwright had the greatest difficulty 'in training human beings to renounce their desultory habits of work, and identify themselves with the unvarying regularity of the complex automaton'. He 'had to train his workpeople to a precision and assiduity altogether unknown before, against which their listless and restive habits rose in continued rebellion', and it was his great achievement 'to devise and administer a successful code of factory diligence'. 'Impatient of the slovenly habits of workpeople, he urged on their labours with a precision and vigilance unknown before.' The reasons for the difference were clear to manufacturers: 'When a mantua maker chooses to rise from her seat and take the fresh air, her seam goes a little back, that is all; there are no other hands waiting on her', but 'in cotton mills all the machinery is going on, which they must attend to'. It was 'machinery [which] ultimately forced the worker to accept the discipline of the factory'.[1]

Regular hours and application had to be combined with a new kind of order in the works. Wedgwood, for example, had to fight the old pottery traditions when introducing 'the punctuality, the constant attendance, the fixed hours, the scrupulous standards of care and cleanliness, the avoidance of waste, the ban on drinking'. Similarly, James Watt had to struggle to introduce cleanliness into the Albion Mills.

Finally, 'Discipline . . . was to produce the goods on time. It was also to prevent the workmen from stealing raw materials, putting in shoddy, or otherwise getting the better of their employers.' It allowed the employer to maintain a high quality of output, as in the case of John Taylor and Matthew Boulton in Birmingham, and of Samuel Oldknow at Stockport.[2]

Works rules, formalized, impersonal and occasionally printed, were symbolic of the new industrial relationships. Many rules dealt with disciplinary matters only, but quite a few laid down the organization of the firm itself.

> So strict are the instructions [it was said of John Marshall's flax mills in 1821] that if an overseer of a room be found talking to any person in the mill during working hours he is dismissed immediately—two or more overseers are employed in each room, if one be found a yard out of his ground he is discharged . . . everyone, manager, overseers, mechanics, oilers, spreaders, spinners and reelers, have their particular duty pointed out to them, and if they transgress, they are instantly turned off as unfit for their situation.[3]

In a Haslingden mill, about 1830, one rule read:

> Any person found from the usual place of work, except for necessary purposes, or talking with anyone out of their own Ally [*sic*], will be fined 2*d*. for each offence.

While the domestic system had implied some measure of control, 'it was . . . an essentially new thing for the capitalist to be a disciplinarian'. 'The capitalist employer became a supervisor of every detail of the work: without any change in the general character of the wage contract, the employer acquired new powers which were of great social significance.'[1] The concept of industrial discipline was new, and called for as much innovation as the technical inventions of the age.

Child work immeasurably increased the complexities of the problem. It had, as such, been common enough before, but the earlier work pattern had been based on the direct control of children and youths, in small numbers, by their parents or guardians. The new mass employment removed the incentive of learning a craft, alienated the children by its monotony, and did this just at the moment when it undermined the authority of the family, and of the father in particular. It thus had to rely often on the unhappy method of indirect employment by untrained people whose incentive for driving the children was their own piece-rate payment.

In the predominantly youthful population of the time the proportion of young workers was high. In the Cumberland mines, for example, children started work at the ages of 5 to 7, and as late as 1842, 200–250 of the 1,300–1,400 workers in the Lonsdale mines were under 18. At Alloa collieries 103 boys and girls of under 7 were employed in 1780. In the light metal trades the proportion was higher still. Josiah Wedgwood, in 1816, had 30 per cent of his employees under 18, 3.3 per cent under 10 years of age. The greatest problems, however, were encountered in the textile mills.

The silk mills were dependent almost exclusively on child labour, and there the children started particularly young, at the ages of 6 or 7, compared with 9 or 10 in the cotton mills. Typically from two-thirds to three-quarters of the hands were under 18, but in some large mills the proportion was much higher; at Tootal's for example, 78 per cent of the workers were under 16. Adults were thus in a small minority.

In the cotton industry the proportion of children and adolescents under 18 was around 40–45 per cent. In some large firms the proportions were higher: thus Horrocks, Miller and Co. in 1816 had a labour force of whom 13 per cent were under 10 years of age, and 60 per cent between 10 and 18, a total of 73 per cent. The proportion of children under 10 was mostly much smaller than this, but in water mills employing large numbers of apprentices it might be greater: in New Lanark, under David Dale in 1793, 18 per cent of the labour force was 9 years old or younger.

In the flax and the woollen and worsted industries the proportions of workers under 18 were rather higher than in cotton, being around 50 per cent. Again individual large works show much higher figures. In John Marshall's Water Lane Mill in 1831, for example, 49.2 per cent were under 15, and 83.8 per cent altogether under 21. Further, in all the textile branches the children were largely concentrated in certain sections, such as silk-throwing and cotton-spinning. In such departments the difficulties of maintaining discipline were greatest.

These, then, were the problems of factory discipline facing the entrepreneurs in the early years of industrialization. Their methods of overcoming them may be grouped under three headings: the proverbial stick, the proverbial carrot, and, thirdly, the attempt to create a new ethos of work order and obedience.

Little new in the way of the 'stick', or deterrent, was discovered by the early factory-masters. Unsatisfactory work was punished by corporal punishment, by fines or by dismissal. Beatings clearly belonged to the older, personal relationships and were common with apprentices, against whom few other sanctions were possible, but they survived because of the large-scale employment of children. Since the beating of children became one of the main complaints against factory-owners and a major point at issue before the various Factory Commissions, the large amount of evidence available is not entirely trustworthy, but the picture is fairly clear in outline.

Some prominent factory-owners, like Benjamin Gott, Robert Owen and John Marshall, prohibited it outright, though the odd cuff for inattention was probably inevitable in any children's employment. More serious beatings were neither very widespread nor very effective. Robert Blincoe's sadistic master was untypical, and large employers frowned on beatings, though they might turn a blind eye on the overlookers' actions. 'We beat only the lesser, up to thirteen or fourteen . . . we use a strap,' stated Samuel Miller, manager of Wilson's mill in Nottingham, one of the few to admit to this to the Factory Commission. 'I prefer fining to beating, if it answers . . . [but] fining does not answer. It does not keep the boys at their work.' The most honest evidence, however, and the most significant, came from John Bolling, a cotton-master. He could not stop his spinners beating the children, he stated,

> for children require correction now and then, and the difficulty is to keep it from being excessive. . . . It never can be in the

interest of the master that the children should be beaten. The other day there were three children run away; the mother of one of them brought him back and asked us to beat him; that I could not permit; she asked us to take him again: at last I consented, and then she beat him.[1]

Dismissal and the threat of dismissal were, in fact, the main deterrent instruments of enforcing discipline in the factories. At times of labour shortage they were ineffective, but when a buyers' market in labour returned a sigh of relief went through the ranks of the employers at the restoration of their power. Many abolished the apprenticeship system in order to gain it, and without it others were unable to keep any control whatsoever. Where there were no competing mill employers, as at Shrewsbury in the case of Marshall and Benyon's flax mills, it was a most effective threat.

In industries where skill and experience were at a premium, however, dismissals were resorted to only most reluctantly. At Soho, Watt lost his temper quickly with engineers who made mistakes and demanded their discharge, but Boulton quietly moved them elsewhere until the storm had blown over. Similarly, John Kelsall, being accused of leniency at his Welsh ironworks, defended himself in his diary with the excuse that 'being strangers in the Country and divers necessities upon us at times', he did well to keep his labour together at all.[2]

Fines formed the third type of sanctions used, and were common both in industries employing skilled men and in those employing mostly women and children. They figure prominently in all the sets of rules surviving, and appear to have been the most usual reaction to minor transgressions. Where the employer pocketed the fine there was an additional inducement to levy it freely, and in some cases, as in the deductions and penalties for sending small coal or stones up in the corves from the coal face, these became a major source of abuse and grievance.

Their general level was high and was meant to hurt. Typically, they were levied at 6*d.* to 2*s.* for ordinary offences or, say, two hours' to a day's wages. Wedgwood fined 2*s.* 6*d.* for throwing things or for leaving fires burning overnight, and that was also the penalty for being absent on Monday mornings in the Worsley mines. At Fernley's Stockport mill swearing, singing or being drunk were punished by a fine of 5*s.* and so was stealing coal at Merthyr. Miners were fined even more heavily: average weekly deductions were alleged to be as high as 1*s.* or 2*s.* out of a wage of 13*s.*

Deterrence as a method of industrial discipline should, strictly, also include the actions taken against workers' organizations, but as these are well known, they need only be noted briefly here. The law could usually be assumed to be at the service of the employer, and was called into action for two types of offence, breaches of contract and trade-union organization and rioting. Workmen's combinations were widely treated in employers' circles as criminal offences, even before the law made them explicitly such, and in turn the legal disabilities turned trade disputes easily towards violence, particularly before the 1790s. In the Scottish mines serfdom was only just being eradicated, and in the North-East the one-year contract, coupled with the character note, could be used also to impose conditions akin to serfdom; opposition, including the inevitable rioting, was met by transportation and the death penalty not only in the mines but even in such advanced centres as Etruria as late as 1783.

Where their powers permitted, employers met organization with immediate dismissal; 'any hands forming conspiracies or unlawful combinations will be discharged without notice', read one rule as late as 1833.[1] More widespread, however, was the use of blacklists against those who had aroused the employer's disfavour. Little was heard of them, even in contemporary complaints by workmen, but their importance should not be underrated: as more evidence is becoming available, it is increasingly obvious that they were a most important prop of that reign of terror which in so many works did duty for factory discipline.

By comparison with these commonly used examples of the 'stick' more subtle or more finely graded deterrents were so rare as to be curious rather than significant. John Wood, the Bradford spinner, made the child guilty of a fault hold up a card with his offence written on it; for more serious offences this punishment was increased to walking up and down with the card, then to having to tell everyone in the room, and, as the highest stage, confessing to workers in other rooms. Witts and Rodick, the Essex silk-mill owners, made their errant children wear degrading dress. It is worthy of note that these measures presuppose a general agreement with the factory code on the part of the other workmen which today few would take for granted.

Employers showed as little inventiveness in the use of the carrot as they did in the use of the stick. For a generation which drove its children to labour in the mills for twelve to fourteen hours a day positive incentives must indeed have been hard to devise and, for the child workers at least, were used even less than for adults. Much better, as in the case of at least one flax mill, to give them snuff to keep them awake in the evenings. The extent of the predominance of the deterrent over the incentive in the case of the factory children is brought out in the returns of the 1833 Factory Commission, in replies to item 57 of the questionnaire sent out: 'What are the means taken to enforce obedience on the part of the children employed in your works?' In the following tabulation the number of answers does not quite tally with the number of factories who sent replies,[1] as doubtful, meaningless and obviously formal answers, e.g. 'scolding', 'persuasion', 'kind words', have been omitted, while some firms gave more than one reply. Bearing in mind that most respondents were merely concerned to deny that they beat their children, and that many replied with the method they thought they ought to use, rather than the one actually in use, the following proportion may appear even more surprising:

NUMBER OF FIRMS USING DIFFERENT MEANS TO ENFORCE
OBEDIENCE AMONG FACTORY CHILDREN, 1833[2]

Negative		*Positive*	
Dismissal	353	Kindness	2
Threat of dismissal	48	Promotion, or higher wages	9
Fines, deductions	101	Reward or premium	23
Corporal punishment	55[3]		
Complaint to parents	13		
Confined to mill	2		
Degrading dress, badge	3		
Totals	575		34

The contrast is surely too strong to be fortuitous, especially since the bias was all the other way.

For adults there were two positive methods which formed the stock-in-trade of management in this period. One was subcontract, the transference of responsibility for making the workers industrious, to overseers, butty-men, group leaders, first hands and other subcontractors of various types. But this solution, which raises, in any case, questions of its own,[4] was not a method of creating factory discipline but of evading it. The discipline was to be the older form of that of the supervisor of a small face-to-face group, maintained by someone who usually worked himself or was in direct daily contact with the workers.

The other method was some variant of payments by results. This provided the cash nexus symbolic for the new age. It was also a natural derivation from the methods used in earlier periods in such skilled and predominantly male trades as iron-smelting, mining, pottery or the production of metal goods. In 1833, of 67,819 cotton-mill workers in 225 mills, 47.1 per cent were on piecework and 43.7 per cent were paid datally, the method of payment for the remainder being unknown. Labourers, children and others under the direct supervision of a skilled pieceworker, and some highly skilled trades in short supply, such as engineers and building crafts-men, did, however, remain on fixed datal pay.

In many enterprises the 'discovery' of payment by results was greeted as an innovation of major significance, and at times the change-over does seem to have led to marked improvements in productivity. Piecework was said to have transformed the character of northern lead-mining in 1688 and of copper-smelting at Neath some years later; Benjamin Gott spread piece payment from the overlooker to all men at Bean Ing and noted that 'the men consequently feel that they are as much interested as he and cease to look upon him as their master'.[1] In Soho the near-bankruptcy of 1773 was diagnosed to have been caused partly by the lax super-vision of the datal workers in the button and related trades, and Scale, the manager, proposed universal piecework, though it was only the establishment of the Soho Foundry in 1796 under the senior partners' sons, with their newer and tighter management structure, which permitted the general change-over to piecework among the engineers.

Many of the older systems of payment by results, as in copper- or tin-mines, or in sinking colliery shafts, consisted of group piece-work, in which the cohesion and ethos of the group was added to the incentive payment as such to create work discipline. The newly introduced systems, however, were typically aimed at individual effort. As such, they were less effective, unless they were made as sharply graded as that of Blincoe's overlooker, who was sacked if he produced less than the norm, and received a bonus if he produced more, and they were often badly constructed, particularly for times of rapid technological change. There were many examples of the usual problems of this type of payment, such as speed-up and rate-cutting, loss of quality, and friction over interpretation and de-ductions.

Nevertheless, it represented a major change and forward step in the employer's attitude towards labour, not only because it used cash as such but more specifically because it marked the end of the belief in Sombart's principle of 'subsistence',[2] the belief, in other words, that workers were looking for a fixed minimum income, and the beginning of the notion by 1750 that the workers' efforts were elastic with respect to income over a wide range. There may have been some employers and some philosophers who had emancipated themselves from the eighteenth-century view that the hands worked the better the less they were paid;[1] but the slow breakdown of this dogma forms one of the most significant developments in the field of labour management in the industrial revolution.

The rise of the belief in the efficacy of incentive piece payments coincided with a decline of the belief in the efficacy of long-term contracts. These contracts were largely a survival of the pre-industrial age, adopted by many employers even during the industrial revolution at times of acute shortages of labour. In the north-eastern coalfield the one-year binding had become almost universal since the beginning of the eighteenth century, and it had spread to salters, keelmen, file-workers and others. Ambrose Crowley bound his men for six months, Arkwright for three months, Soho for three to five years, some potteries for seven years, some cotton mills for five and up to twenty-one years, and the Prestonpans chemical works for twenty-one years. But any hope that these indentures would ensure discipline and hard work was usually disappointed, and the system was generally abandoned as a disciplinary method, though it might be continued for other reasons.

A few employers evolved incentive schemes with a considerable degree of sophistication. In their simplest form overseers bribed children to work on for fourteen or fifteen hours and to forgo their meal intervals, and John Wood paid them a bonus of 1*d.* weekly if they worked well, but hung a notice of shame on them if they did not.[2] At Backbarrow mill apprentices received a 'bounty' of 6*d.* or 1*s.*, to be withdrawn if offences were committed, and in silk mills articles of clothing were given to the children as prizes for good work; at one silk mill, employing 300 children aged 9 or less, a prize of bacon and three score of potatoes was given to the hardest-working boy, and a doll to the hardest-working girl, and their output then became the norm for the rest. Richard Arkwright, in his early years, also gave prizes to the best workers.

Later on these bonuses were made conditional on a longer period of satisfactory work, or were modified in other ways. In the early 1800s the Strutts introduced 'quarterly gift money'—one-sixth of wages being held back over three months, and paid out at the end only after deductions for misconduct. At John Marshall's the best department received a bonus each quarter, amounting to £10 for the overlooker and a week's wage for the hands, and some Dowlais men, at least, also received a bonus of £2 every quarter, conditional upon satisfactory performance. At the Whitehaven collieries the bonus to the foremen was annual and was tied to net profits: when these exceeded £30,000 the salary of the two viewers was nearly doubled, from £152 to £300, and those of the overmen raised in almost like proportion from a range of £52–£82 to a range of £90–£170—a particularly effective and cheap means of inducing industry. In other coal-mines the ladder of promotion to overmen was used effectively as an incentive. It was left to Charles Babbage to work out in 1833 a more detailed analysis of the effect of monetary incentives on work, and to stress the importance of norms, of specific awards for exceeding them, and of accurate calculations of costs, of savings and of payments for them. But this remained on paper only, and another half-century was to elapse before incentive schemes began to be made integral with general efficiency schemes.

Compared with the ubiquity of financial rewards, other direct incentives were rare and localized, though they were highly significant. Wedgwood at times appealed directly to his workers, in at least one case writing a pamphlet for them in which he stressed their common interests. Samuel Greg, jun., attempted to create a settled community spirit at Bollington. Arkwright gave distinguishing dresses to the best workers of both sexes and John Marshall fixed a card on each machine, showing its output. Best known of all were the 'silent monitors' of Robert Owen. He awarded four types of mark for the past day's work to each superintendent, and each of them, in turn, judged all his workers; the mark was then translated into the colours black-blue-yellow-white, in ascending order of merit, painted on the four sides of a piece of wood mounted over the machine, and turned outward according to the worker's performance. These daily marks were entered in a book as a permanent record, to be periodically inspected by Robert Owen himself.

IV

It may be asked why these methods, which were successful among all the leading manufacturers named, were not copied as widely as the technological innovations. The reasons may have been ignorance on the part of other masters, disbelief or a (partly justified) suspicion that the enlightened employers would have been successful with or without such methods, enjoying advantages of techniques, size or a well-established market; but to limit the reasons to these would be to ignore one of the most decisive social facts of the age.

An approach like Owen's ran counter to the accepted beliefs and ideology of the employing class, which saw its own rise to wealth and power as due to merit, and the workman's subordinate position as due to his failings. He remained a workman, living at subsistence wages, because he was less well endowed with the essential qualities of industry, ambition, sobriety and thrift. As long as this was so, he could hardly be expected to rise to the baits of moral appeals or co-operation. Therefore, one would have to begin by indoctrinating him with the bourgeois values which he lacked, and this, essentially, was the third method used by employers.

The qualities of character which employers admired have, since Weber's day, been to some extent associated with the Protestant ethic.[1] To impart these qualities, with the one addition of obedience, to the working classes could not but appear a formidable task. That it should have been attempted at all might seem to us incredible, unless we remember the background of the times which included the need to educate the first generation of factory workers to a new factory discipline, the widespread belief in human perfectibility, and the common assumption, by the employer, of functions which are today provided by the public authorities, like public safety, road-building or education.[2] The preoccupation with the character and morals of the working classes, which became a marked feature of the early stages of industrialization, was thus less irrational than it might appear today.

Some aspects of this are well known and easily understandable: it was believed that firms laying stress on morals, and employing foremen who 'suppress anything bad', would get the pick of the labour.[3] Almost everywhere churches, chapels and Sunday schools were supported by employers, both to encourage moral education in its more usual sense, and to inculcate obedience. The Board of the British Plate Glass Company, discussing the salary of its manager in 1815, resolved that 'the moral order and regularity of the small community belonging to the works must be seen to enable the Committee to form a just estimate of the Superintendent's merits'. The Quaker Lead Company, lauded for its social conscience, never dismissed anyone except those guilty of 'tippling, fighting, night-rambling, mischief and other disreputable conduct, or evidence of a thankless and discontented disposition'.[4] Those dismissed were never taken on again and in effect, in those isolated mining villages, were forced to starve or to emigrate.

The question of drink does, perhaps, show the link between morals and efficiency most clearly. Drunkenness was the only cause of dismissal operating at New Lanark; it was equally seriously regarded by the Quaker Lead Co., by Marshall's of Leeds, and by other model employers. It was, indeed, a perennial problem especially among skilled men, who were paid enough to be able to afford it, and who were scarce enough not to be sacked too easily. At Boulton & Watt's it affected some of their best engineers, and at one strike at Soho negotiations had to be suspended for a day, as the men were all drunk. Carron suffered similarly, and Kelsall, in Wales, found some of his ironworkers in 1729 off work, 'committed to the stocks for being drunk and abusive'. Wedgwood was much troubled by it, and so were the Manchester millowners, as is evident from Robert Owen's well-known account of his interview with Drinkwater. Later, indeed, it was claimed that Manchester mill workers were healthier and better workers than men in other occupations, as the factory left them no time for drink and debauchery. Where it was within his powers as controller of a factory town the entrepreneur could restrict the sale of liquor. Owen made it a monopoly of his own shop, entered all purchases of liquor in a book, and used the profits to pay for his school; neither the controllers of Deanston nor those of Blantyre permitted any public house to open in their villages. Lord Penrhyn, also, enforced the same ban in his model village, and in 1831 J. J. Guest reaffirmed that no one in his employ would be allowed to keep a public house or a beershop, though his reasons for this were not merely the sobriety and industry of the workforce, but also the prevention of truck.

The attack on drink could be seen as part of an attack on much else of the existing village culture. 'Traditional social habits and customs seldom fitted into the new pattern of industrial life, and they had therefore to be discredited as hindrances to progress.'[1] Two campaigns here deserve special mention.

The first was the campaign against leisure on Saturdays and Sundays, as, no doubt, examples of immoral idleness. 'The children are during the weekdays generally employed,' the Bishop of Chester had declared solemnly in 1785, 'and on Sunday are apt to be idle, mischievous and vitious.' This was not easily tolerated. Thus Deanston had a superintendent of streets to keep them clear of immorality, children and drink. Charles Wilkins of Tiverton formed an 'Association for the Promotion of Order' in 1832 to round up the children and drive them to school on Sundays. All the hands at Strutt's and Arkwright's under 20 had to attend school for four hours on Saturday afternoons and on Sundays to 'keep them out of mischief'. Horrocks' employed a man 'for many years, to see that the children do not loiter about the streets on Sundays'. At Dowlais the chapel Sunday-school teachers asked J. J. Guest in 1818 to order his employees to attend, otherwise there was the danger that they might spend the Sabbath 'rambling and playing'.[1] Even Owen expressed similar sentiments: 'If children [under 10] are not to be instructed, they had better be employed in any occupation that should keep them out of mischief,' he urged.[2]

The second was the prohibition of bad language. At the beginning of the eighteenth century Crowley's 'Clerk for the Poor' was to correct lying, swearing, 'and suchlike horrid crimes'; while at the same time Sir Humphrey Mackworth, at Neath, fined 'Swearing, Cursing, Quarrelling, being Drunk, or neglecting Divine Service on Sunday, one shilling', and the Quaker Lead Company, at Gadlis, also prohibited swearing in 1708. Later this became quite regular whenever rules were made: at Darley Abbey, in 1795 the fine was 9d. or 1s.; at Mellor, 1s.; at Nenthead, 6d.; at Galloway's, where 'obscene and vulgar language' was prohibited, the men themselves levied the fines. At Marshall and Benyon's also, according to Rule 4 of 1785, a jury of seven was to judge the offence of striking, abusing or harming another workman.

Again, the rules of Thomas Fernley, jun., Stockport, cotton mills, stated: 'While at work . . . behaviour must be commendable avoiding all shouting, loud talk, whistling, calling foul names, all mean and vulgar language, and every kind of indecency.' Swearing, singing, or being drunk was fined 5s.; overlookers allowing drink in the mills were fined 10s. 6d. Gott's, Sheepshanks and other large works in the West Riding had similar rules.[3]

This preoccupation might seem to today's observer to be both impertinent and irrelevant to the worker's performance, but in fact it was critical. The worker's own ethics were such that he was not normally susceptible to the kind of inducements which his employer could provide within the new work conditions. Ambitions to rise above his own idea of a 'subsistence' income by dint of hard work were foreign to him. He had to be made ambitious and 'respectable', either by costly provisions of material goods, like the famous gardening plots for miners praised by Arthur Young, or the loans for houses granted by Dowlais to its privileged workers,[4] or by the cheaper means of changing his attitude, often falsely called his 'character'. For unless the workmen *wished* to become 'respectable' in the current sense, none of the other incentives would bite.

Also, as it was said in the 1830s,

195

> A man who has no care for the morrow, and who lives for the passing moment, cannot bring his mind to indulge the severe discipline, and to make the patient and toilsome exertions which are required to form a good mechanic.

Such opprobrious terms as 'idle' or 'dissolute' should be taken to mean strictly that the worker was indifferent to the employer's deterrents and incentives. According to contemporaries, 'it was the irrationality of the poor, quite as much as their irreligion, that was distressing. They took no thought of the morrow. . . . The workers were by nature indolent, improvident, and self-indulgent.'[1]

The code of ethics on which employers concentrated was thus rather limited. It was left to the Evangelical Movement and to other forces outside industry to develop out of the needs of the bourgeoisie a momentum of its own, and to direct and absorb the spiritual energy of the working classes which was largely left untouched by the new work discipline. It was Dean Tucker who had discovered that 'the motives to industry, frugality and sobriety are all subverted to this one consideration, viz.: that they shall always be chained to the same oar, and never be but journeymen'. The resulting distortions of the Puritan Ethic, and such interesting accompanying phenomena as the examples of the Messianic Sectarianism, the chiliasm of despair, of that period have been recently described with great insight by E. P. Thompson. David Riesman before him had noted that in this period 'evangelistic religion' had joined with the 'tradition-directed' outlook of the first generation of factory workers to ensure the acceptance of bourgeois values and of otherwise intolerable work conditions. Riesman was acute enough to notice that, although 'there was much talk of the need for discipline, sobriety and integrity', employers were more preoccupied with the administration of things than the administration of men: 'the human mood of the work force was not yet felt to be a problem', and 'even in large and bureaucratized organizations people's attention was focused more on products (whether these were goods, decisions, reports or discoveries makes little difference) and less on the human element'.[2] The human element was merely to be manipulated as if it were an inert piece of machinery. In this sense, by treating human beings as means rather than ends, the essence of Christianity was denied and subverted by the new moralists.

In fact, the maintenance of control over their workers may not have been as easy to employers as Riesman suggests, at least in Great Britain. They could, it is true, rely on professionals to drive home the new morality. As far as their own influence went, however, warnings against greed, selfishness, materialism or pride seldom played a large part, sexual morals rarely became an important issue to the factory disciplinarians (as distinct from outside moralists) and, by and large, they did not mind which God was worshipped, as long as the worshipper was under the influence of some respectable clergyman. The conclusion cannot be avoided that, with some honourable exceptions, the drive to raise the level of respectability and morality among the working classes was not undertaken for their own sakes, but primarily, or even exclusively, as an aspect of building up a new factory discipline.

V

In their attempts to prevent 'Idleness, Extravagance, Waste and Immorality',[1] employers were necessarily dealing with the workers both inside the factory and outside it. The efforts to reform the whole man were, therefore, particularly marked in factory towns and villages in which the total environment was under the control of a single employer. Here some of the main developments of the industrial revolution were epitomized: these settlements were founded by the industrialist, their whole *raison d'être* his quest for profit, their politics and laws in his pocket, the quality of their life under his whim, their ultimate aims in his image.

At their best they were, or could have become, models of social progress, the creations of men with a conscience and some social idealism, vehicles for transferring at least some of the benefits of industrial invention and work to the mass of the working population. Such was Robert Owen's New Lanark. But others were typified by the owner who oppressed Robert Blincoe and his fellow apprentices, or the masters of the mills at Backbarrow and Penworthen who obtained notoriety by turning their apprentices loose in a period of slack trade, to beg their way into their home parishes.

For our purposes, we have to see them not in terms of social conscience but in terms of managerial necessity. Smelser, in his recent perceptive study of the cotton industry, was driven to the conclusion that, great though the outward difference was between the flogging masters and the model community-builders, 'from the standpoint of control of labour, both types of factory management display a concern with the enforcement of discipline'. The much-publicized evils of the factory system, concluded another historian, 'were symptoms of managerial inefficiency and inadequate capital resources rather than the inevitable concomitant of factory employment'. The manufacturer who found himself in charge of such a venture had, like Kirk Booth of the Lowell Company, 'to be its town planner, its architect, its engineer, its agent in charge of production, and the leading citizen of the new community'.[1] The pressure on management and the structure of the factory villages are ultimately connected with each other.

The large-scale entrepreneur of the day began with very limited managerial, clerical or administrative staff: he wrote his own letters, visited his own customers, and belaboured his men with his own walking-stick. Yet his range of responsibilities was much wider than that of today's entrepreneur, who is concerned almost exclusively with the activities inside the factory, with buying, producing and selling. In the early years of industrialization many outside services now taken for granted or dealt with by the single action of paying taxes, had to be provided by the large manufacturer himself.

Among the most important were those creating the 'infrastructure' of an industrial economy. There were, first of all, the costly means of transport. The large collieries on the Tyne and Wear, it is well known, provided their own rail systems from the seventeenth century onwards; by 1725 one line was 5 miles long, and within a generation some local lines reached lengths of 8–10 miles. Collieries at Whitehaven, Leeds, Sheffield and South Wales had tram rail systems of similar length. Some ironworks were similarly placed: the first iron rail system was built out within Coalbrookdale, and the Merthyr tramroad system maintained by the local ironmasters extended to 40 miles, and by 1831, it was reputed, to 120 miles. Extensive tramways were also laid by North Wales quarry-owners and Cornish mine adventurers.[2]

In the canal era the Duke of Bridgewater's agent had to supervise the building of the premier canal as part of his duties of running the Worsley collieries, besides managing an extensive agricultural estate, draining marshes, dovetailing a tree-planting programme and generally supervising the erratic innovating genius of Brindley. Many other coalowners found canals indispensable and had to build them; elsewhere the canals and docks built by Wedgwood, by the Carron works, by Soho, the Merthyr Tydfil ironworks, John Wilkinson at Brymbo, Foster's at Stourbridge, the Horsley ironworks and by Samuel Oldknow have long since become standard examples in the textbooks. Other entrepreneurs, again, had to build ports and harbours. This includes the major coal magnates in West Cumberland, the Lowthers, the Curwens and the Stenhouses, as well as the Anglesey copper-mining companies, which had to create the harbour of Amlwch; they, indeed, also owned much shipping, as did Carron and the builders of the Menai bridge. In northern collieries the 'staithman' became an important executive.[1] Others, again, built roads: Arkwright's small mill at Bakewell spent £1,000 on roadmaking, besides the personal contributions of the owners to the county's turnpike system. The Quaker Lead Co. also built its own, besides contributing to wider schemes. Many companies had to undertake large schemes of water engineering to obtain power.

Other enterprises had to go in for large-scale farming mainly for the sake of food for workers, fodder for the horses (the works transport), pit props or timber for fuel. Ambrose Crowley devoted much energy to his works farm, and examples in the period 1770–1830 may be found in a wide range of industries represented by Plymouth and Cyfarthfa ironworks, Litton mill, Coalbrookdale, Greg's at Styal, Oldknow at Mellor, the Backbarrow Company, the Swinton pottery, the Cheadle New Wire Company, Woolaton pits, the Quaker Lead Company, Darley Abbey cotton mills, and the Parys Mine Company. The early textile mills, again, had to be their own engineers. Thus the New Lanark machine shop cost annually £8,000, employing eighty-seven men, and the works at Deanston and at Bean Ing were scarcely less extensive: 'It was almost impossible for anyone to begin spinning on any considerable scale with the new machinery without first making it'.[2] Heathcoat's, removing to an engineering backwater at Tiverton, had an engineering branch which soon acquired its own reputation, building agricultural machinery; and firms in other industries had their machine-building and repair shops also. Civil engineers and canal-builders, as well as ordinary firms building their own premises like Wedgwood at Etruria, or Coalbrookdale, would also often develop their own brick and tile works; others pioneered fireproof building methods.

Finally, the early entrepreneurs frequently had to arrange for their security. It was not only in the barbarian Highlands that troops had to be provided in the absence of reliable local police, or in the mining areas where it was said that there were 'strong, healthy and resolute men, setting the law at defiance, no officer dared to execute a warrant against them'.[3] The introduction of new machinery such as cotton frames, gig mills or power looms, could cause riots, and so could ordinary strikes and food shortages. Some managers were then turned into military officers on top of their other duties.

All these, however, were tasks which might face the men managing factories and mines anywhere in Britain. Those who set up in isolated villages and created, in effect, company towns and villages, had many additional duties.

The first and most obvious need was to provide houses. In Scotland, in particular, the decision to establish a large works in the open country was taken to be synonymous with the need for new housing: Adam Bogle, managing the Blantyre mills, calculated simply that the working of double shifts would involve Monteith, Bogle & Co. in an expenditure of £15,000–£20,000 on new houses. In England the position was not very dissimilar. The north-eastern collieries, for example, provided cottages ('hovels') for their men, who would vacate them when changing their employment, and each mining village was simply a group of pits, with its attached colliers' houses. Cottages entered into normal capital costs, and were included in the standard yearly miners' bond. Cumberland, as always, followed the Tyneside practice closely.

A list of large works providing their own attached cottage estates or a controlling share of them reads like a roll-call of the giants of the industrial revolution. Among English cotton mills there were Hyde, Newton, Dukinfield, Cromford, Milford, Belper, Bakewell, Mellor, Stalybridge, Cressbrook, Backbarrow, Darley Abbey, Styal and Bollington, the Peel's settlements at Bury and the Horrocks's at Preston; in Scotland, New Lanark, Deanston, Catrine, Blantyre, the Stanley Mills; and in Belfast, Springfield. Among ironworks there were Carron, Ebbw Vale, Cwmavon, Dowlais, Plymouth, Nantyglo, Ketley, Butterley (Golden Valley and Ironville) and the Walkers of Masbro'. There was Benjamin Gott's in the woollen trade, and the Worsley complex of enterprises. In the copper industry the Warmley Co., Charles Roe's and Morriston; in lead, Nenthead, Carrigill, Middleton and Leadhills. There was Melingriffith in the tinplate trade, Tremadoc and Portmadoc in slate, and Etruria in pottery.

In a few cases workers were housed in one large tenement. Boulton put his workers in the top floor of the wings of the first block at Soho. At Paisley, John Orr housed thirty-five families in one building. At Neath, Sir James Morris's 'Castellated lofty mansion of a collegiate appearance, with an interior quadrangle, containing dwellings for forty families, all colliers, excepting one tailor and one shoemaker, who are considered as useful appendages to the fraternity',[1] had a higher reputation than Henry Houldsworth's block at Anderston, Glasgow, of which even Dr. Ure could find nothing better to say than that it was very healthy after ventilation had been put in.

At Merthyr Tydfil, a company town in many respects, though dominated by four iron companies rather than one, Crawshay, having monopolized all the likely building land round his works, leased it out to others, with disastrous results for the health and amenities of the area. Richard Hill, at neighbouring Plymouth, being too poor to build workers' cottages himself, had them built by a Bristol merchant who found the speculation most profitable.

By contrast, city firms might own a few houses for key workers at best, and if small firms provided a row or two of cottages, these had no further social significance. According to the returns of the Factory Commission of 1833, of 881 large firms,

>   299 gave no details
>   414 made no housing provisions
> and 168 provided some houses.

But of these the majority provided a few only.

The management of the housing property gave the villages their character and was usually symbolic of the employers' attitude to his workmen in general. Robert Owen began by building a second storey on to the New Lanark houses, having the dung-heaps cleared, and organizing a permanent cleansing service. Finlay's at Deanston offered prizes for the best-kept houses, and at least fourteen other works in Scotland reported in 1833 special incentives, or company services, in cleaning and whitewashing their cottage property. Thomas Ashton's stone-built houses at Hyde, having at least four rooms, with pantry, a small backyard and a privy, were 'an object of wonder and admiration',[1] and Samuel Greg paid special attention to housing in his model settlement at Bollington.

At such exceptional firms as David Rattray's flax mills in Perthshire workers lived rent free; elsewhere rent was deducted from pay. The works management, rather than a special housing manager, thus looked after the settlement and housing could be turned into a tool of discipline. In the coalfields evictions were used to defeat strikes, but even as routine policy the Worsley mines explicitly reserved the best houses for the best workers and withdrew them when their discipline or obedience showed signs of falling off. At Dowlais housing was used to create a privileged group of workmen who would provide some stability for the township and the ironworks.[2]

In addition, the houses had, of course, to be made to pay, and this was not difficult when cottages cost about £50 to build, rising from about £40–£45 in the 1770s to £60 during the war inflation, while rents were 2s. to 3s. a week, and certain. With yields thus well over 10 per cent, housing accounts chalked up regular profits in most firms.

Schools were traditional in Scottish parishes, and even the less enlightened owners of flax mills round Aberdeen and Dundee, and of cotton mills round Glasgow and Paisley, provided at least school-rooms and often the teaching also. In England and Wales school provision was rarer. It was again largely confined to the entre-preneurs who were also community-builders.

In the textile areas schooling was particularly important, since the pupils were not the workers' children but the 'hands' themselves. Everywhere, however, it was partly subsidized and partly paid for by the children themselves. In many villages much thought and effort went into the organization of the day and evening schools, and some were dovetailed with working hours and came under works discipline. Sunday schools had a far more important part to play, being largely designed to inculcate current middle-class morals and obedience, but they were widespread in the cities as well as in the factory villages.

Dissenters among the community-builders, like the Strutts, Newton Chambers or the Gregs, built chapels, others built churches, and Quakers, like Darby's, joined with many of their staff in regular religious meetings. At one extreme, Robert Owen provided out of his own pocket for a number of different sects, with none of whose teachings he agreed. At the other, Richard Crawshay laid it down that he

> wishes every Man to worship God in his own way, but is no friend to new fanatick secretarys. The two Establishments of Church and Presbytery afford choice enough for Humble Men to find their own way to God, Grace and Holy Spirit.[1]

In some industries, as in the Cornish tin-mines, in the dockyards, and in some South Wales ironworks, medical assistance was commonly provided by a 2*d.* weekly deduction from wages. Else-where, 1½*d.*, 1*d.* or even ½*d.* a week might be deducted, and White-haven miners paid £20 a year to a surgeon in the mid-eighteenth century 'for cureing burnt men'. At least as often firms paid surgeons direct, either by retainer or whenever they were called in. Ap-prentices, in particular, usually had regular attention.

This service was usually accompanied by the support of sick clubs and by pensions. Sick clubs were largely financed by the men themselves, but in numerous cases the employer, by virtue of a small or contingent contribution, had absolute control over the management of the fund, directly or indirectly, and used it as a means of disciplinary control, in combination with a system of fines and rewards. Among the best-known works schemes was that of Matthew Boulton, which was copied widely, though it led to much dissatisfaction in Soho because of its autocratic government, and Curwen's, established in 1786 at Workington and Harrington, which received much attention, as he proposed its extension to the whole country, in place of the Poor Law, in 1816. In some firms membership was compulsory and deductions were made from wages.

Some of these funds made death grants also and other firms paid pensions. Provision varied widely, from the derisory sum of £12 a year set aside by the Strutts for compensation to accident victims at a time when there were 200 a year, to the average total of £8 a week paid out, year after year, by the Mona Mine Co. to widows of men killed at work, to injured men, and to retired agents.

Among all the social measures taken in factory villages, truck shops have perhaps received the largest amount of attention. In our present context, however, they require a new interpretation; for truck shops were not only, like workers' cottages, sources of welcome petty profiteering: they also added yet further to the sheer burdens of management.

Not all company shops were predatory. Clearly the occasional purchase of grain wholesale, to be sold at cost price or less in times of harvest failure, was to benefit the company only in as far as it benefited the workers, and such deliveries are known to have been made by Coalbrookdale, the Quaker Lead Co., David Dale, the Anglesey mines, the Lambton collieries, the Tehidy estate, Tredegar and Sir Watkin Wynne's collieries.

Where truck shops were meant to be profitable, or at least to pay their way, they often strained the limited managerial capacity available. They created permanent ill will, disputes and occasional riots, such as those caused by the truck shops at Dowlais and Penydarren in 1800. Of the notorious shop at Dowlais, opened in 1800, the senior partner wrote in 1803: 'Tis a pity that our shop-keeping has been so very much less profitable than our neighbours. Mr. Lewis and myself have made up our minds that we will not have anything to do with shopkeeping other than receiving a good rent for it.' Hence the shop was let, but the tenant, despite the trouble taken to suppress competition for his sake, had paid neither rent nor interest on the stock advanced after five years, and had to be sold up. A manager was then put in, and was paid a salary plus a share of the profits, but there were further difficulties. At neighbouring Cyfarthfa, likewise, William Crawshay ordered: 'I must desire that neither Butter, Cheese, Flour, Tallow or *aught else* may be bo't for money', as it locked up his precious capital.[1]

Deductions from wages for tools, etc., could also be most troublesome. Thus the Mona Mine Co. had to deduct, at each pay day (once every two months), separate items for powder, candles, German steel, blister steel, waste of iron, shovels, mats, copper wire, smiths' cost, carpenters' bill, drawing, week's club, cartage and sieve rims: and of the 100 workers due for payment on 31 December 1825, for example, only thirty-nine had credit balances left; the rest were in debt which had to be carried over to the next period. Also, it should not be forgotten that competitors who did not engage in truck got away with paying lower wages, and that indebtedness worked both ways: while it tied the worker to his master, it also, in effect, forced the firm to continue to employ the worker.

The link between the works and the truck shop was often the substitution of shop notes for cash in wage payments. This was another expedient which could be turned to good account, as Samuel Oldknow found, but it was not an unmixed blessing, and could be more trouble than it was worth: 'Issue no more Promissory Notes under £100 at any date whatever,' ordered William Crawshay in 1816. 'It is not anyway honourable and respectable to issue small Notes'—nor do they compensate for the trouble they cause. Similarly, his neighbour Taitt asserted in 1813: 'We are not Bankers and do not wish to extend our circulation beyond our own payments', and he noted with glee that Anthony Hill's notes in adjacent Penydarren never stayed out for more than £1,000 at a time. The work involved was, indeed, considerable. The Cyfarthfa balance sheet for 1813 noted over £7,300 outstanding on the £1, 1 guinea and £5 note account; while the printer's bill for Dowlais on 9 February 1822 included the following notes:

```
5,500 at £1
5,000    £1. 1. 0.
3,000    £1. 10. 0.
2,000    £5. 0. 0.
  500    £10.
```

besides 770 bills of exchange. Soho managed its own bank for years.[2]

In addition to all this, employers also had to make themselves responsible for the exercise of civil power within the communities they had created. This was especially so where a landed upper class was lacking, as in the West Cumberland or South Wales. Thus the police power in Merthyr Tydfil was merely an extension of the ironmasters' own long arms. In 1799 brandy dealers and trade unionists alike were dealt with by Homfray or Crawshay, the two ironmaster-magistrates. There was no doubt as to the outcome of the hearings, nor were the magistrates accused of impartiality. In 1793, Homfray had promised 'never to sign a licence for any Workman belonging to the Ironworks without an application being made by their Masters', while in 1799 workmen who withdrew from the Volunteers were punished by being summarily dismissed by Guest. Twenty years later travelling troupes of actors still found it necessary to ask the employers' permission before opening in Merthyr. Small wonder that William Crawshay, sen., bitterly opposed the notion of a resident magistrate for the town in 1828: 'You resident Ironmasters sh'd be the Justices and keep the Power in your own hands, your stipendiary man may turn against you, . . . it would not at all surprize me when once seated in Place he would annoy instead of serve the Iron masters. . . .' However, he need not have worried: Mr. Bruce, the man chosen, was a 'most proper gentleman'.[1]

In Whitehaven the Lowthers were kings. The first Earl of Lonsdale, losing a case over subsidence in 1791, simply decided to close all the town's collieries, and was only persuaded to reopen them on a guarantee of indemnity in future cases, by 2,560 petitioners. His manager, John Bateman, found the local coroner in 1803 as dangerous as Crawshay had thought the stipendiary, because he had dared to hold an inquest on a woman killed in a mine accident,

> *a thing never practiced here in my memory,* such enquiry being supposed only calculated to frighten the ignorant and discourage them from going into the Pits; on this account the workmen were always forbid to even talk about any accidents which happened in the Pits; your Lordship can judge better than me how far it may be proper to *check this new practice.*[2]

Colliers lived in isolated and easily tyrannized communities, but textile manufacturers also cherished the power which the factory towns gave them. Richard Arkwright, jun., reflected that in a large town he could not have the control over his workers which he had in Cromford, and G. A. Lee allowed that village millowners 'command the population, and those who live in manufacturing towns are in some degree commanded by the customs of the population'.[3]

The extent of that control may be illustrated by Catrine, a typical cotton village: of a population of 2,716 in 1832,

> 1,304 were women and children at home
> 853 worked in the Company Mills,
> 759 worked elsewhere, but of these 194 were

employed in ancillary textile occupations. The proportions were similar in 1817 and 1819. Thus well over half of the earnings of the village came directly from the mill. In some villages, as in New Lanark, the proportion approached 100 per cent.

Nothing strikes so modern a note in the social provisions of the factory villages as the attempts to provide continuous employment. 'There are two objects you wish to gain,' Treweek, the Mona Mine manager wrote to Sanderson, Lord Uxbridge's agent, 'the first is to make the Mine yield a profit, the second is if possible to employ all the men', and he went to great trouble to find them employment. Similarly, William Crawshay commanded in 1817, 'Do not even hold out reduction of the men, employ them if they behave quietly. . . . Bad and ruinous as the trade now is, we must lose rather than starve the labourer.'[1] Yet, of these two places, Cyfarthfa was noted for its persecution of unionists, and at Amlwch, in 1813, it was reported that with the decline in employment 'many families have fled, and their cottages are now falling to ruin, but there is still a much more numerous population than can be tolerably supported by the mines, and numbers are consequently left in a miserable state of destitution'.[2] The provision of continuous employment for members of their workers' families, it is clear from the example of Samuel Oldknow, was a necessity, not a philanthropic luxury, for otherwise the families could not have been kept alive on the starvation wage paid by the mill to women and children.

If we add to this economic and political power of the employer his power over education, housing and the like, it will be clear why management of a factory or mine might come to mean government of a whole community.

VI

It will be evident that, no matter how detached the entrepreneur community-builder was from his workers as persons, and how crude his notion of worker psychology and motivation, the very fact of having to cater for a broad range of their needs forced on him some modicum of understanding of the humanity of his 'hands'. Even though the typical village factory-owner did not deliberately seek to become a provider of public services, but rather was forced against his will into non-industrial activities by his circumstances, his resulting experience made it easier for him than for the town employer to get an inkling of the complexities of social and industrial psychology.

The difference was, perhaps, only marginal, and it was only towards the end of our period, about 1830, that common humanity began to combine with self-interest among the larger or more honourable employers to induce them to think of labour administration in terms other than crude force, punishment or monetary reward. In this they were helped very little from the outside. There was no doctrine, and no expression of the need for a doctrine. The earliest writings of advice on management, which began to appear about that time, were as banal as the worst of the books on similar topics still are today.[1] Even those employers who acquired some useful experience in the management of labour did not, with the single exception of Robert Owen, think it worth while to communicate their findings to the rest of the country. Like the rest of 'management', labour administration was not even an embryonic science.

Perhaps, in the pioneer country of industrialization, it was inevitable that many years of experience should precede any attempt at generalization and theorizing. But there is more to it than this; for the time which elapsed before industrial psychology began to treat the workers as fully human was much too long to be accounted for merely by the wait for experience. Besides, the measures like Factory Acts and trade union rules, introduced from the outside to force employers to work with, rather than against, the nature of their workpeople, were not eagerly welcomed by them as fitting their experience and as ultimately beneficial even to their pockets, but were, on the contrary, bitterly opposed by manufacturers as a whole, who were abetted in this by many of the economists, uttering the most dire prophecies of doom.

Because of the nature of eighteenth-century British society within which modern industrialism arose, because of the bitterly competitive nature of the market facing the typical manufacturer, because of the alienation from work involved in the change, and because, after all, they faced the employers as enemies within the distributive system of a capitalist economy, the modern industrial proletariat was introduced to its role not so much by attraction or monetary reward, but by compulsion, force and fear. It was not allowed to grow as in a sunny garden; it was forged, over a fire, by the powerful blows of a hammer. The marks of its origins largely determined the atmosphere within which the management of labour was attempted. There are few records of co-operation, and they almost appear eccentric. The typical framework is that of dominance and fear, fear of hunger, of eviction, of prison for those who disobey the new industrial rules. Hitherto, the experience of other countries at a similar stage of development has not, in essentials, been very different.

No social development ever proceeds entirely without doctrine, conscious or implicit. The unhappy nature of the acculturation of the first generation of factory workers is reflected in the uncertainties and contradiction of the doctrines with which it was attempted. On the one hand, the worker was treated as a piece of mechanism, who obeys the simplest behaviourist stimulus and response rules, and whose other mental capacities and interests could be ignored. On the other, a large-scale assault was made on his soul, occasionally by the employer directly, but more often by the religions of the day—a social role which did not in the long run benefit the religions, though it may have saved British society. The task was finally accomplished, though at a needlessly high cost, and a society of peasants, craftsmen and versatile labourers became a society of modern industrial workers: but it is doubtful whether, within the context of the present structure of society and industry, the dilemmas of its beginnings have been resolved even today.

6/ Accounting and Management

If the appointment and training of managerial staff was one of the two main responses of large firms to the problems of management in the industrial revolution, the development of accounting for industry was the other. In addition to being a potential aid to management, accounting represented for many entrepreneurs an element of certainty and assurance, a familiar landmark in an unfamiliar world, and an element of rationality in what must to many have appeared as a capricious environment, in which large fortunes could be made or lost by methods which previous generations had not even dreamt of.

Existing accounting methods available to the industrialist in the second half of the eighteenth century had developed along three main routes, each with its own objectives, its own logic and its own conventions, and to some extent he could pick from among them what best suited his needs, as indeed he had to pick his accountants and clerks from people trained in one or other of the older routines.[1] These three were the master and steward system, developed largely in the administration of large landed estates; the mercantile system, arising out of the practices of overseas merchants and bankers; and the accounting developed by manufacturers operating the putting-out system. None of these, however, fully met his problems, many of which were new or appeared on a new scale, and included the sheer volume of his operations, the quantity of fixed capital involved, and the inability of a single head to supervise, check and control a complex industrial enterprise.

This chapter will attempt to trace the development of these different strands of accounting procedure and techniques and their adaptation by the new industrialists. It will also discuss the extent to which they fulfilled their hopes for certainty, for powers of control, and for a basis for rational decision-making.

I

The master and steward system was based on the notion of stewardship of the servant towards the proprietor or, later, the firm. As it had developed in the Tudor period,[2] after which it did not change essentially until the end of the eighteenth century, it was based on double-entry book-keeping, but of a particular kind: on the debit side was the 'charge', or all the receipts of the agent on behalf of his master, at first both in money and in kind, but by the end of the period generally in money only; and on the credit side the 'discharge', or all the payments made, including the contributions towards the upkeep of the master's household and cash payments to him, leaving as balance usually cash still in the hands of the agent,[1] or, more rarely, the sum due to the agent from his master. A typical formula for this balance is the following, drawn from an ironworks in 1692: '. . . so that theire remaines due to your Worshipe from ye receiptes Before Mentioned ye sum of . . .'[2]

This form of account had become standard on British landed estates,[3] and had been routinized to the extent of being included in textbooks on land stewardship and, no doubt, taught in the appropriate schools.[4] When a system reaches this point it is difficult to develop it further, for what had been practical expedients become inviolable rules, and the comparability as between estates and the consequent mobility of trained stewards and accountants is a boon in its own right which it becomes imprudent to jettison. At the same time, methods become standardized to that extent only when they fulfil widespread or general needs.

The main and obvious achievement of this system was to provide a check against embezzlement by the staff. Where all items were entered in monetary form it could, in fact, be looked upon as an elaborate cash account, presented annually and running, on large estates, into tens of thousands of pounds. It also provided a general view of the estate, and since incomes, such as rents, sales of timber, etc., were usually grouped together in some commonsense way, e.g. by manors, unchanged over the years, it also provided a kind of check on the efficiency of the estate, as it was possible to compare from year to year the movement of rents between village and village, or the proportions of rents in arrears, or, on the expenditure side, the salaries or other expenses on the upkeep of the farms.

Further, in a very broad way, and on certain assumptions, the accounts in this form could also afford some view of the efficiency of the whole estate by comparing total incomes and outgoings year by year. Among the methods open to the landlord who might wish to maximize his surplus were collecting rents with a minimum of arrears, raising rents from a given acreage, keeping estate costs down, and preventing embezzlement: for the 'improving' landlord, efficient management might also mean raising output per acre on his home farm, or even on his tenants' farms. All these the accounts could be made to show. But, although with much additional work it was possible to go farther and test the profitability of certain enterprises within the estate, or even of certain experiments,[1] by and large the system was utterly unsuited to this and was, in fact, very rarely so used. Normally, the incomes and appropriate expenditures were not grouped together, or at all comparable, so that it was not possible to determine from the accounts which expenditure belonged to a certain wood or a certain farm. Capital expenditure had to be booked simply as that year's outlay, grossly and fatally distorting any possible conclusions as to efficiency or even profitability. Again, the return on investments could not be isolated and calculated, and there was no guidance on stocks, which might be run down or built up without showing in the accounts, yet greatly distorting the 'profitability' of the estate. The methods in use, even in the first half of the nineteenth century, 'were confusing the consumption of oats by race-horses with the payment of wages to coal-miners in a single tally, which effectively concealed his real financial status from the owner even if it served to square those of the steward'.[2]

The popularity of this system proves that it was well suited to the landed estate, though it could not have been much help to the improving landlord. Equally clearly, it was defective for the industrialist. Nevertheless, for historical reasons it was widely used in the industrial enterprises developed out of the estates themselves, such as coal-mines, iron- and copper-mines, and even ironworks, canals and tar distilleries, some of which grew to considerable size. Where these were directly managed for the estate-owner, as distinct from being let out to profit-making entrepreneurs paying a rent, the landlord's steward was usually the superior of the industrial manager, and because of this derivation the accounts were cast in the estate form. In turn, this influenced other enterprises; thus, typically, coal-mines tended to have no capital accounts,[3] entering any investment in the year's current outlay, and similar parallels could be found among a wide range of other enterprises with personal, organizational or historical links with the estate economy.[4]

While some of these enterprises might develop within this framework extremely sophisticated and well-designed accounts which showed the quality of output, e.g. the proportion of slack in the coal, or copper in the ore, and the skill with which they were being extracted, or could assist in storekeeping and stock holdings, they received no guidance from their accounting as to the benefits of innovation, nor as to the firm's position in the face of the innovations of others. Thus two of the central problems of the new industrialist, a check on his capital investments, and on technical and other innovation, were beyond the abilities of this system, and it was therefore felt increasingly to be unsatisfactory by the firms which were using it, and rejected by new firms searching for adequate accountancy methods.

The second root of accountancy practice, that arising from the counting houses of the merchants, was probably the oldest. In many ways it was also the most important, for not only had it developed double-entry book-keeping, the logical basis of all widely used systems, but it had also had to grapple at an early stage with the problems of large-scale enterprise, and the supervision of businesses at a distance; that is to say, it had to aid in the management of firms too complex to be directly controlled by a single head. It had therefore had to solve some of the problems that were to weigh most heavily on the entrepreneurs of the industrial revolution. Further, inasmuch as mercantile accounting was designed to eliminate errors, prevent embezzlement, and establish the value of a business for probate or similar purposes, it shared some objectives with the industrialist; whilst in controlling distant agents, merchants to some extent also used 'stewardship' accounting of the type favoured by the estates.[1] Finally, many, and perhaps most, of the accountants to be found in works offices, and much of the accountancy they learnt, had been derived from the merchants' counting houses.

Again, however, the problems of the merchants were basically different from those of the factory owners. The merchants and moneylenders of fourteenth-, fifteenth- and sixteenth-century Italy, among whom modern accounting practices first arose,[2] were indeed interested in profits and probably also in maximizing profits, but there was in their case no sense in which they could relate profits to any fixed investment or 'capital' of a firm as a whole: their calculations showed the costs and returns from individual journeys, or individual commodities, and were designed to allow an appropriate division of profits among the shifting groups of associates for each separate venture.[3] Even where fixed assets were used, such as houses or ships, they were not entered into the accounts, as they did not change hands during the transactions and no money value could be attached to them.

The benefits which the moneylenders expected from the accounting system were somewhat different. In their case they wanted records which might in case of need stand up in a court of law as to the amounts of the loans outstanding, their terms and repayments. These were essentially only memoranda, and did not require any analytical treatment unless combined with other commercial enterprise. All this remained true, in principle, until the beginning of the nineteenth century.[1]

Finally, at the height of the Renaissance, some of the leading merchants employing outworker producers, and some mints and similar enterprises, developed rudimentary cost accounts. In view of the small quantities of fixed capital involved, however, they tended to ignore the problems of overheads and thought in terms of direct cost largely. In any case, their achievements seem to have been lost, for very little in the way of industrial or production cost accounting was either taught or practised in the intervening centuries until well into the period of the British industrial revolution.

Among the wealth of accounting textbooks which came off the European presses between the sixteenth and the early nineteenth centuries nothing perhaps is more surprising than this absence of references to the needs of the industrialist and to the teaching of cost accounting. This gap has often been remarked on.[2] In Britain the only authors dealing with production costs at all, in however tenuous a form, were John Collier (1697), James Dodson (1750), Wardlaugh Thompson (1777), Robert Hamilton (1788) and F. W. Cronhelm (1818), but of these the first three dealt with producers external to the firm, i.e. domestic workers, and the fourth had only a minor reference to production which he dropped in the second edition. In 1796 Edward Farmer, an accountant, submitted an accounting textbook to Boulton & Watt, representing

> a set of books which I have just compleated, framed to answer the Mercht. or Manufr., with various ways to prove not only the correctness of it's debits and credits, but the real profit of the concern,[3]

but any hopes industrial accountants might have had of this work were unfulfilled. 'It is probable', commented one of the historians of Soho, 'that the methods were copied to a large extent from those of the bankers and merchants; in fact, just as more and more capital was diverted from commerce to industry, so the methods of commerce were applied to industry.'[4] Accountancy in Britain was dominated by the requirements of the merchant, all the formal training, all the prestige derived from him. The large, growing and respected body of professional accountants which had developed by then had not considered it worth while to adapt their system, complex and routinized as it had become, to the needs of industry, and the adventurous manufacturer who wished to use accounts as an aid to his management had to adapt them himself.

The third root of accounting practice existing in the later eighteenth century was that slowly evolved by the immediate predecessors of the factory-owners, the putting-out hosiers, clothiers, and others to be found over a wide range of industries. They came nearest to the problems of the large-scale industrialist, but they, too, could manage with a different and less ambitious approach. In practical terms, what they required was a check on the materials handed over to the outworkers, on the rent of their equipment (if any), and on the workmanship of the finished goods handed back. But at each stage the product was marketable, and its price therefore known, and in principle this was no different from the transactions of the merchant, with whom they also shared the need of establishing the profitability of various lines.[1] There was the further decisive difference between theirs and the factory-owner's problems that there was no fixed capital worth speaking of, that there was therefore also no problem of costs varying with output, and that there were no technical innovations of a major kind to be tested by their relative profitability. Further, the typical business was still small, and so was the range of the owner's activities, since the activities in the workers' households, and the subcontracting that might go on, were none of the putter-out's concern.

> Periodic calculations of a firm's profits and statements of the value of its assets are of little interest to the business man who is closely and continuously concerned with his own business operations,

as Professor Yamey has remarked in a different context. It is then not necessary to find the liquidity of a firm by calculation,

> and little thought would be given to the precise definition or careful and consistent measurement of periodic profit.[2]

Unlike the other two systems of accountancy, this one had not, by the end of the eighteenth century, developed into a body of doctrine, taught and transmitted by qualified practitioners, but had, on the contrary, evolved merely by the practical needs of the firms concerned, innovating as they went along, normally without knowledge of similar forward probings elsewhere. Mostly, there was in any case no qualified accountant, and the entrepreneur kept his own books, as the need arose. In all this there were strong similarities with the development of factory accountancy.

II

These, then, were the raw materials out of which the new industrialist had to build his own accounting system—three systems based on widely different needs, and on a different logic, and none of them dealing with some of his most pressing problems. The response of the industrialist to this challenge, or in other words, the development of accounting as a tool of industrial management in this period, was patchy and uneven. As in the field of management in its other aspects, there was no tradition, no body of doctrine, no literature worthy of the name developed to unify or even up the practices in different parts of the country or in different industries.[1] Each firm progressed at its own speed, neighbouring firms might be decades apart in their development, and generalization is, therefore, virtually impossible. Some lessons may, however, be learned from the comparative speeds with which different aspects and functions of accounting were evolved or became widespread.

Four main developments will be examined here. The first was the adoption of regular, periodic returns in place of the *ad hoc*, waste book or journal type of book-keeping, the forcing of the natural rhythm of work into a strait-jacket of comparable sections of time. Secondly, accounting had some severely practical tasks, such as the detection of error or fraud. Further, what was particularly significant in this period was the growing pressure for the use of accountancy in costing and in aiding management decisions, and here, thirdly, various approaches to 'partial' costing will be examined. Finally, we shall look at the determination of total costs and profits of a firm.

The regularity or periodicity of the accounts kept is the single feature which emerges most sharply from the evidence. This is to some extent inherent in any formal teaching of accounting, and entrepreneurs were increasingly being schooled in that way. But it should be remembered that the books of merchants and others, in earlier times, showed little of that neat division into equal periods, and many had no regular date for closing or comparison at all. Also, this regularity is unnatural to most economic activities, outside farming: cotton-spinning or mining, iron-smelting or the selling of manufactured goods does not proceed in regular weekly, monthly or yearly time spans, and to force them into this artificial paper mould requires some pressure and some initiative. Where did the pressure come from? The Sombart-Weber thesis of the capitalist as predominately a rational animal, seeking to reduce life to regular measurable patterns, no doubt played a part. More directly relevant was the fact that this was an age of uncertainty, of change more rapid than any previous age had known, and nowhere was this more true than in the industries chiefly considered here. In these conditions men looked for reassurance and regularity where they could impose it. Also, and related to this quest for certainty, there was the underlying sense of the inadequacy of existing powers of control over large works beyond the span of a single individual's command, which is but an aspect of the main theme of this book. Knowledge here could be power, and knowledge of the many facts thrown up by a large concern had to be systematized and regularized before it could be grasped by a single brain.[1]

It was, of course, true that agricultural estates, and accounts based on them, had one-year cycles, and joint-stock companies and similar institutions required the regular payment of dividends and therefore the regular closing of books. But the regularity noted here went much farther than this, and began to affect even sectors hitherto immune from it, such as the Cornwall or Derbyshire 'cost-book' systems of accounting, or the North Wales slate quarries.[2] Again and again, where long series of accounts survive, it will be seen that where they have not been regularly periodic before they become so at some time during the eighteenth century.

Most of all, however, it was practical needs which determined this regularity: that is to say, the book-keeping assumes the colouring of being partly a tool of management as well as a system of reckoning. We find it in many practical expedients, often of no great significance in themselves. Thus the Stanley (Copper) Co., controlled from Anglesey, returned fortnightly details of output, sales and salaries on regular printed forms; Coalbrookdale began regular four-weekly returns of production, consumption of raw materials, labour and wages from about 1718 onwards; by 1752 William Brown sent fortnightly returns of disbursements and quantities of coal led to the partners of his mines; the Shrewsbury workhouse steward was required to keep thirteen sets of books in the 1790s, beside journal and waste book; the Soho Foundry, in its heyday of early control, used twenty-two; while Ambrose Crowley, imposing his works order, a century before its time, on his unwieldy Tyneside enterprises, required no fewer than fifteen different sets of returns every week, and dispensed with the calendar altogether, dividing time into arbitrary ten-week periods, numbered from the founding date, and requiring different recurring tasks and returns on certain weeks of the ten-week cycle and a stock check every twenty weeks.[1] Every colliery, read a contemporary guide-book for managers, should have exact cost accounts, 'pay-by-pay, month-by-month, or yearly';[2] the exact period did not matter, since it had no relation to the cycle of production, as long as it was regular and reliable. Typically for another industry, George Smith, partner in James Massey & Son, Manchester cotton-spinners, stated that while they took stock once a year, he had a 'bird's-eye peep at the concern once a month'.[3]

In the absence of reliable managerial staff or settled routine, the owner-manager, away from the works to act as salesman or buyer, also required regular reports: Benjamin Gott had them weekly, and so had J. J. Guest and William Crawshay, permanently settled in London, but attempting to run Dowlais or Cyfarthfa at long distance. A similar problem of management from a distance arising out of the necessarily scattered units of the great ironworks combines, like those of the Foleys, or the South Yorkshire group, or the lead-mines and smeltworks of the Quaker Lead Co., led to standardized annual return forms for all major accounts to head office. Where stock holding was important, as on the banks or staithes of coal-mines, fortnightly or more frequent stock reports and accounts of inflows and outflows became the rule, and in turn led to other regular accounts, including those couched in monetary terms. In the large porter breweries the annual stocktaking was vital and correspondingly highly developed. Finally, where the payment of wages involved a large number of subsidiary calculations, such as deductions for 'subs', rents, truck-shop purchases, etc., it called for a more comprehensive regular periodic statement, including elaborate printed forms, every two, four, eight or twelve weeks, according to the traditional wage period.

The quest for order and regularity as one way of dealing with overwhelming detail and with numbers too large to be supervised directly, also led to other forms of book-keeping and accounting. Wedgwood, appointing a clerk of weights and measures in 1770, was sanguine that 'he will save me three times his wages in clay and ten times as much in credit'. The needs of a complex plant such as the Soho Foundry brought forth the most elaborately detailed and regularized system of costing and accounting of the age, so well described by Eric Roll. Others, with John Wilkinson, instituted checks and systems of account to watch their cash and the regularity of their clerks.[1] Watt's invention of the copying press, and its steady sales, are a further pointer to the demand for regularity and reliability in office work: 'Accurate machinery for industrial purposes was accompanied by a development of accurate machinery for office work. Bookkeeping became a science, and Watt's copying machine supplied a pre-existing want.'[2]

Among the second group of practical services required from book-keeping was the preservation of liquidity, to ensure that there were resources available to meet outstanding bills as they fell in; this was taken over as a well-developed practice from the merchants. It could be extended to include the need to ensure that a correct profit balance was established, so as not to pay out more in dividends than had been made in profits, but this raises some wider issues which are discussed below.[3]

Another was to prevent, or at least discover in due course, theft and embezzlement by the staff, again a problem well known to the merchants and the owners of large estates, though the large firms of the industrial revolution appear to have been more than usually prone to depredations from that quarter. At the same time, it was not always easy to distinguish between the errors of ill-trained managers and accountants and outright frauds; nor were employers always very particular to distinguish between them. Alexander Tarbuck, Sarah Clayton's colliery manager, was dismissed in 1772 for keeping books in an 'irregular manner', but two years later was prosecuted for fraud in buying timber for her; some inspectors of the worsted committees were reported to be 'dismissed quickly for neglect of duty, drunkenness, misbehaviour, screening offenders, mismanaging financial matters, and for being incapable of keeping proper accounts'; whereas Ambrose Crowley's plaint was: '. . . I have received great damages by reason of unskilful, negligent and corrupt surveyors. . . .' Fraud was accepted as a normal risk, and Matthew Boulton, proposing that his brass company should be subcontracted, and not run by a salaried manager, claimed the advantage that

> the Company will be placed on a certainty as regards expense, will have no clerks to pay, will be exempt from frauds, thieves and all other risks.[4]

No system of accounts can by itself prevent embezzlement, and although it was one of the most pressing problems in this period, it was only gradually solved in the course of the nineteenth century by giving clerks higher status and developing guarantee funds and insurances for them.

There were signs, also, that errors were slipping through remarkably often. Sombart had used the fact that errors were allowed to remain in the accounts, even where they should have been checked by the double-entry system, as a proof for his contention that early capitalism was not fully 'rational',[1] but, in fact, even in this period errors were common, though they were spotted more regularly: to some extent audit was instituted to show up errors rather than malpractice.[2] Even at Boulton & Watt's firm, where accounting, costing and office routine had been developed to a higher degree than elsewhere, it was found in 1802 that goods of £342 value had been 'omitted' from an inventory; that in 1828, when a clerk died, errors of a total of £91 were thought to have accumulated, though his brother put them nearer £35; and the cash book of 1820–5 contains this pleasantly human note:

> Sir, the books yet remain incomplete owing to the moneys yet to be entered. A balance has been made but owing to the largeness of the sum it is judged that an error must exist. Mr. Bennet's feelings are so excited that he finds himself incompetent to writing himself or examining the a/cs.[3]

III

All these and other similar practical objectives, however, were of minor importance compared with the major aims of accountancy as an aid to management. These included the estimates of costs and revenue, in order to establish which methods of production or which departments to adopt, enlarge, reduce or wind up. They would also include the calculation of total profits of the enterprise and its value, for the purposes of dividend distribution or for the valuation of partners' holdings,[4] for sale or probate.

We may usefully distinguish here between *ex ante* calculations, to estimate likely costs and returns in the future, and the *ex post* accounts of the actual figures of the past. It can be taken for granted that no new enterprise was started, or no major extension undertaken, without an estimate of expected costs and incomes. Many such estimates must have been made in a manner leaving no records, but innumerable such cost calculations have in fact survived.

It is of some interest that these cost estimates represented the highest forms of accounting of which records have survived. Many refinements were included which were never to be found in actual *ex post* accounts. In particular, not only did they take account of capital costs, both in the form of depreciation and a rate of interest, but in appropriate cases compound interest was also entered,[1] derived from the calculations well known among estate stewards as to the opportunity costs of growing timber and from the valuation of coal-mines and other extractive industries. Many examples have survived of detailed calculations of the probable comparative costs and revenues of different methods, different locations, or different alternative products of a given equipment, and calculations of this kind, brought down to costs per unit or per week, must have made the accountants familiar, if they were not familiar already, with the notion of variations of costs with size of output.[2] If one confined oneself to cost estimates, and ignored the actual *post-factum* accounts, much of the cost accounting of this period would appear extremely advanced.

Many of these estimates, of course, were only wild guesses, and this was particularly true of overhead costs, which usually appear only conventionally as a simple round sum per unit. Similarly, estimates of the size of the market, or of the extent of mineral reserves, appear wildly and childishly unrealistic. This is true not only of promotional literature, designed to attract subscriptions or other financial support, but also of calculations for internal consumption. While direct unit cost calculations often surprise the modern reader by their sophisticated accuracy, estimates of turnover, or of coal or mineral reserves assumed to be workable at constant unit costs over a vast range of output, or the quantity of output saleable at a given price, are equally unexpected in their crude *naïveté*. The same inability to see that a large sudden local demand for labour would in the circumstances, in rural areas at least, be likely to drive up wages, and *mutatis mutandis* in the case of land and materials, was to a large measure responsible for the ludicrous way in which the costs of the great civil engineering enterprises, the roads, canals, and railways, were underestimated by the engineers.

In these *ex ante* estimates, and even more so in the true *ex post* accounts, accountants and owner-managers were, in fact, quite capable of working out what might be called 'partial' cost analyses, such as, for example, detailed unit costs holding technique constant. Their great difficulty, and it was a difficulty they remained essentially unable to surmount, was the establishment of a reliable basis for total or overall calculations for the firm as a whole. This is perhaps the most significant distinction to emerge from the contemporary accounts: useful, and generally reliable 'partial' analyses, and primitive, potentially misleading general analyses. .

In the *post-factum* calculations the best results, perhaps, were achieved in the departmental allocation of costs. This had at least two sides: the attempt to take account of internal transfers of goods from one department to another, and the attempt to calculate which of the different departments or goods were, and which were not, producing their share of the profits.

The first seems to have existed from the beginning of firms large enough to have departments: it was derived from the putting-out system and from the better estate accounts, and was an obvious step whenever any accounts at all were contemplated.[1] Thus Coalbrookdale, from 1718 on, credited finished goods sales to the warehouses, and credited the 'Pigg Yard' both with sales of pigs outside and with transfer to the air furnaces for re-melting and casting. Boulton & Watt, representing an assembly industry, also adopted this method from the earliest days of the 'foundry', i.e. the full-scale engineering works, while in the years before its establishment the different partnerships of button and toymakers were debited with rents for their workshops at Soho. Similarly, the South Yorkshire ironworks partnerships credited and debited the individual units for pig iron or other materials transferred. The notebook relating to Earl Fitzwilliam's tar works records that the latter was to draw its supplies from the estate, but 'every article supplied by his Lordship must be valued and paid for, in account to him, the same as bought of any other person'.[2] In the same way, millowners would charge themselves the rent of their mill, even if they owned it, and mine-owners would calculate their royalties, though they might own the mineral. As Samuel Walker explained, '[we] charge ourselves with those royalties as being the general royalties of the country', though they belonged to the firm.[3]

The second, the determination of the profitability of different departments or commodities, was in principle based on the early merchant practices. As Wardlaugh Thompson, author of one of the most original accountancy textbooks, noted in 1777:

> Bookkeeping by Double Entry . . . is the art of keeping our accompts in such a manner, as will not only exhibit to us our net gain or loss upon the whole, but our particular gain or loss upon each article we deal in, by which we are instructed what branches to pursue, and which to decline; a piece of knowledge so very essential to every man in business, that without

it a person can only be said to deal at random, or at best can be called but guess'd-work.[1]

These merchant practices had been considerably refined well before the first large industrial works made their appearance, and the adoption of departmental accounts was thus not only fairly obvious from the industrialist's point of view, especially where his firm was in danger of making losses, as in the case of the Carron Company, but was also hallowed by accountancy tradition. Thus it was not only Babbage, turning over in his mind a degree of accounting control several generations ahead of his contemporaries, who emphasized that

> the evil of not assigning fairly to each tool, or each article produced, its *proportionate value* . . . is very considerable . . . It is of great importance to know the precise expense of every process, as well as the wear and tear of machinery which is due to it,[2]

but even relatively simple accounts would attempt to keep the returns of department separate, down to elaborate schemes of allocating overheads fairly and proportionately.[3]

In the most advanced works, departmental accounts were always separated and separately considered. In Soho, Boulton had from the beginning, in 1761, divided the annual rent between the manufactory and the house. Again, Marshall and Hives demanded accounts to show the input and output of each process, including hackling, spinning, weaving and bleaching, by quantity and value, then

> compiled a departmental abstract indicating average performance in physical and financial terms for both workers and machines, together with average factor prices. Simultaneously, John Marshall began a rudimentary profit and loss account, although to the end of its days, the firm's declared profit was calculated in customary merchant manner as the excess of assets over liabilities at the annual stock-take.[4]

Sometimes this was done at great inconvenience. Thus the Quaker Lead Company resolved in 1774

> that the Ore from the Company's Mines & from each Mine be kept in separate Bing steads at the several Mills; & also the Bought Ore likewise separate of them.[5]

It is clear that this trouble was taken because it was meant to lead to managerial decisions: which department to expand, which to reform and which to close down.

The breakdown of accounts by departments thus represents one of the most advanced accounting techniques then in use in industry. Even here much remained to be done. Overheads were still only guessed, and as far as the costing of joint products was concerned, not even the principles could be worked out.[1] But at least these accounts furnished a reasonably reliable guide to action.

In this they were typical of many other 'partial' comparisons and statements used in industrial accountancy. They all have two things, additionally, in common: they were based on some pre-existing mercantile practice, and they solved some immediate practical problem. It would not be out of place to reason that these are the main two causes for the early successful development of these techniques.

IV

By contrast, the problems of a satisfactory overall cost-and-revenue statement remained very far from a solution—if indeed, such solution has been found even today. This was not because of any lack of effort devoted to it. In many instances the tasks of the accounts were clearly thought out and defined and formed a connected and interlocking whole. The following four examples illustrate the way in which differing needs could determine the varying sets of books.

The Herculaneum Pottery, reorganized early in the nineteenth century, kept the following series:[2]

- (*a*) Share payments.
- (*b*) Cash accounts.
- (*c*) Building accounts (the cottages let to workmen were managed separately, and made their own profits).
- (*d*) Slag account.
- (*e*) Profit and Loss accounts, beside the usual ledgers, etc.

Written instructions to Mr. Foreman, the accountant of the productive side of the Soho Foundry, dated 5 November 1799, enumerated the following objectives of the accounting system there:[3]

- (*a*) Collective profit and loss account of the engine manufactory as a whole.
- (*b*) The same of the separate departments, smithing, fitting, brass, patternmaking, boilers and pneumatic.
- (*c*) Amount of materials used.
- (*d*) Amount of manufactured goods used.
- (*e*) Amount of labour used.

(*f*) Disbursements for machinery, including repairs, experiments, rent, overheads, salaries, etc.
(*g*) Sales.

The officers of the Aire and Calder Navigation[1] presented their new-style accounts in 1817,

> under such principal heads and abstracts as are produced and brought to a point from the nature of that system of Book-keeping which you (i.e. the shareholders) resolved should be pursued—a system the best adapted to prevent, as also to detect errors in accounts, and to exhibit the real state of your affairs, by showing:

(*a*) Net profit and loss, after deducting bad debts.
(*b*) Net revenue and expenditure.
(*c*) Cash balance account, showing where the funds are held.
(*d*) The so-called stock account, 'the increased or decreased value of your Property from year to year'.

The latter was also to 'prove' all the other accounts.

Finally, John Kitching, asked for his professional advice on the accounts which the Stockton and Darlington Railway Company should keep, in 1824, suggested the following:[2]

(*a*) Careful and detailed land registers.
(*b*) Treasurer's accounts, i.e. payments account, but of a kind which would not show the profitability of running, as capital and revenue accounts were all mixed up.
(*c*) Journals and ledgers.
(*d*) Monthly balances, to show up errors that might have crept into the other accounts.

Some brave attempts were also made to calculate total costs with accuracy, as distinct from workable guesses. The elaborate and intelligent calculations of the young James Watt and Matthew Robinson Boulton, to work out standard prices for engines and boilers of all sizes and types, '[proceeding] upon what appeared to be the real costs by Foreman's books', are well known as outstanding examples. Benjamin Gott's manager attempted a most ambitious calculation of costs in 1830, to give another example, and the large breweries and coal-mines also achieved considerable success.[3]

In most cases accuracy remained a pious hope, and those who were honest with themselves admitted that they could do little beyond guessing. Josiah Wedgwood had in 1776 been puzzling his brain all the last week to find out proper data and methods of calculating the expenses of manufacture, sale and loss, etc., to be laid upon each article of manufacture, but without success.

Pricing is difficult in the potteries even today,

and with the simple bookkeeping of the eighteenth century Wedgwood could do little more than guess at costs. Prices were, therefore, fixed arbitrarily and represented Wedgwood's judgment as to what the market would bear or what competitors were charging. Wedgwood even instructed Bentley 'in the future when any new articles come to you be so good to proportion the price yourself to the other things in the warehouse'![1]

Matthew Boulton's prices before the days of the steam-engine works were similarly fixed without any close relation to costs. Civil engineering and building contract prices were traditional, even for large programmes, and as late as 1840 one engineer could state that:

up to the present moment, few men, not even contractors, make out their estimates of expenditure and time upon any fixed principles—the accuracy of their estimates, in all cases, being dependent upon the conjectural instincts of the persons who may make them,

and, as a result, there arose

glaring discrepancies between the supposed and actual outlay required for their completion.

There were owners of large coal-mines who did not know the cost of bringing a ton of coal to market, admitting that 'it requires a great combination of calculations to answer that', and in copper-smelting Thomas Williams, the giant of the industry, stated (perhaps not quite truthfully) that he 'never calculates' the expenses of smelting copper ores, and this was confirmed in 1818 by Treweek, manager of the Mona Co.[2]

Perhaps most significant of all was the position in the cotton industry, which by the 1790s had become sufficiently large to have developed competitive market prices for the main ranges of quality and weight. Here most firms were no longer under any necessity of establishing their own prices, but merely accepted the market price and endeavoured to keep costs below them; but those which did calculate costs found them to differ widely from prices charged and, on certain reasonable assumptions, found all coarse yarns to be produced at a loss, while the profits per lb. rose steeply with the finer counts. It is fairly evident, however, that the normal mill calculations even of the larger firms were so crude and left out so many necessary factors as to have been misleading and therefore worthless.[1]

As the number of large industrial units and their problems multiplied in the second half of the eighteenth century, this absence of reliable cost (or profit or liquidity) accounts became increasingly evident and irritating to many of the most progressive entrepreneurs at different stages in the development of their firms. It is in this way that normally an atmosphere is created in which improvements are called forth and are adopted. We have also seen how widespread were the efforts to find technical solutions, and how advanced certain techniques in *ex ante* estimating and in partial costing had become. That improvements were nevertheless slow and minimal in overall management accounting in this period is perhaps due largely to three factors: the absence of accountancy tradition and knowledge within industry; the small number of accountants available; and the inability of industrial accountants to deal with the main new factor involved in cost calculations—the relatively large quantities of fixed capital.

With the exception of the firms which developed from merchants' houses, industrialists emerged from a world in which accounts had played little part. Charles Lloyd III, the ironmaster, found he was in debt in 1727, but it was only after 'much solicitation' that he 'discovered it to be to the extent of £16,000, or more by half than he was worth'. John Kelsall, his clerk, had at the time of his dismissal in 1719 not drawn up any accounts for two years, though there are more regular entries in the 1720s in his diary mentioning his book-keeping activities. Bersham was in difficulties in 1735, the cause being Hawkins 'failing to keep any clear or separate accounts in his own affairs'. Even among the much better organized South Yorkshire ironworks it was noted that 'a certain amount of indeterminacy seems to be revealed by some of the middle records, for two-fifths of the proceeds are charged to the account of "Queries, till settled" '.[2] These are all examples of successful, progressive firms.

In other industries the primitive practice of mixing private affairs with the company accounts survived well after the companies concerned had outgrown the size at which this was tolerable. Jedediah Strutt, who had struck only occasional balances for his large combine in the 1770s, took over virtually sole charge in 1781, and 'thenceforward the accounts became more complicated and mixed up, as if they were entirely his affair'. John Foster, attempting by 1828 to run a worsted putting-out business, a coal-mine and a shop, intermingled all three accounts with his private domestic housekeeping:

> Further, the nature of the accounts themselves, some kept on the double-entry principle, others in the form of a running balance, with some pages shared by several accounts kept on either plan, helps to make the muddle worse.[1]

Hague & Cook, another West Riding firm, also mixed their banking, farming, merchanting and manufacturing accounts in the period up to 1830. Again,

> few serge-makers kept any but the most piecemeal accounts. Even the Company of Weavers, Fullers and Shearmen had to be persuaded by Baring, after the middle of the eighteenth century, to adopt some system of accounting.[2]

In another industry, that of metal-smelting, John Read kept his ledger for 1760–78 in his own handwriting, but:

> Skey's tutorship had not taught him bookkeeping and he appears to have had little time to do more than record transactions. The accounts were seldom balanced, nor did he give consistent information.

Industrial concerns run as part of large estates might not be balanced at any regular period, while in questions of improving the home farm, 'the estate office staff itself was evidently not certain how much should be counted as spent'. Richard Trevithick, who with the death of his father became chief engineer of several large Cornish mines, and supreme technical adviser in the 'Western District' of Cornwall, never balanced his books beginning in 1797, though large sums for nineteen of the largest mines passed through his hands.[3]

It has been asserted that

> the frequency of early bank failures is partly to be explained by the scrappy, uncoordinated character of the bookkeeping. A general audit was so rare as to be almost unknown,

and the Great Eastern Railway Company, in 1839, could not untangle its accounts 'by the perplexity and confusion in which the accounts were left by the late secretary'. Even the cotton mills, which were perhaps among the leaders in introducing some kind of book-keeping, did not keep time-books of their workers' hours put in, though they were ordered to do so for children by Hobhouse's Act of 1831.[1]

This floundering in ignorance can be illustrated from various stages of development of the leading firms.

> How do you think, my dear Friend, [Wedgwood wrote to Bentley in perplexity in 1771], it happens that I am so very *poor*, or at least so very *needy* as I am at this present time, when it appears by the accounts that I clear money enough by my business to do anything with. The nett profits of last year appeared by the accts in which I cannot find any errors to be upwards of £4,000 in the Burslem Works only & yet I have not money to pay my debts & unless something extra can be done in collecting, must borrow money for the purpose![2]

In the following year, he confided,

> although I am very positive [that] what I have allowed for the expences of makeing and selling our goods is quite enough; yet it appears from comparing the expence of manufacture for a year, with the amo't of the goods made, to be little more than half the *real* expence attending the making and selling so many goods.

Further, the totals did not agree with the departmental summaries: 'we are now taking stock and shall then try another method'.[3]

Boulton & Fothergill, in Soho, struck a balance in 1765 and found £1,907 available for distribution:

> too much reliance must not, however, be placed upon the books and accounts of Boulton & Fothergill. In some years they were never closed. There was no provision for doubtful debts and it was subsequently found that colossal sums had been lost through bad debts.

In the years 1767–72, when large sums were lost from all sorts of causes, including the 'haphazard pricing' of goods, no accounts at all were presented to the partners; in 1780 Zachary Walker, the cashier, stated that in ten years there had been a loss of £11,000 out of a capital of £20,000; and even in the 1780s, despite James Watt's attempts to systematize the book-keeping at Soho, the firm did not know which departments were losing money.[4] The revolution in the management came only with the opening of the Soho

Foundry in 1796 by the younger generation of partners. Similarly, the Albion Mills suffered from bad accounting as much as from poor management: Mynd, sent from Soho, was 'seemingly the only person there with a bare knowledge of book-keeping', and he was kept busy elsewhere.[1]

The story of Carron is equally well known. Thus in 1767 Cadell estimated a possible profit of £10,500, when in fact a loss of £10,000 was made. No better results could be expected:

> the system had been haphazard, being at most a record of expenditure and income, with little attempt at coherent classification, and certainly with little indication of the current level of profits being earned either generally or departmentally. Budgeting . . . did take place, but no attempt was made, or has at least survived, to reconcile the estimates with the performance.

The first ten years, until Gascoigne's reforms of 1769, showed much 'financial carelessness if not irresponsibility'.[2]

At the Anglesey copper-mines, another power house of the industrial revolution, the early accounts were so badly kept as to be almost useless; but even in later years Pasco Grenfell and John Sanderson, Uxbridge's agent, complained of their inadequacy, and in the years following 1825 prolonged investigation failed to trace the apparent loss of copper from the Mona smeltworks. At Newton Chambers, Robert Scott, the moneyed partner, complained in 1820, with some justice, that the firm kept no regular accounts to show progress, and did not know how to take stock. The Gas Light & Coke Company in 1816 evolved a new method of accounts, employing a specialist accountant, and the resultant new figures so alarmed the company by their difference from the accepted ones that major measures were taken. As a final example, an entry in the books of the flourishing firm of the Walkers of Masbro' may be taken, dated 1 May 1776:

> In the beginning of Sepr. last, the book debts, estates, and the whole effects of the Company were look'd over and considered, and estimated at £82,189 (to our great surprise), in which we made a large allowance for loss in the wood trade, but now the loss seems as if it wd. be still more, and upon the whole we now suppose the effects of the Company to be £87,500.[3]

All these were leading, innovating firms, coping successfully with supreme challenges of technique and markets. The conservative heritage of other firms, including the absence of any tradition of accountancy or innovation there, must have been considerably more powerful still.

The second difficulty was the small number of clerical staff employed in the counting houses of even large firms. Many of these clerks were also occupied on so many other routine jobs, now performed by specialists, such as timekeeping, quality control, travelling, draughtsmanship, as well as copying out by hand duplicates of letters and preparing accounts in several fine copies, in multi-coloured copperplate hand, that the marvel is that they could perform their duties at all. Exceptional tasks are always likely to overburden an office working by routine, and calculating costs or taking stock correctly must have appeared as such.

Thus, at Soho, the elaborate and well-developed book-keeping was done by two book-keepers, one cashier and,

> a limited number of clerks. . . . The amount of work performed by this office staff [and also, of course, by the partners in the business] as it appears from the firm's records, is amazing when the absence of modern equipment and of labour-saving devices is borne in mind.

For years Watt made all his drawings himself, having no other draughtsman on the staff, while both the senior partners habitually wrote all their own letters.[1] Those who have investigated the industrial correspondence of that period will know that this was universal for firms of every size: all correspondence, no matter how voluminous, was conducted as a matter of course in the senior partners' own hand—except in cases like that of Josiah Wedgwood, in 1769, who suffered from a temporary eye disease, and who therefore had all his business letters written by his wife.[2] Nor was it likely that this practice should change, when James Watt discovered that

> Ld. D[artmouth] says the King writes a great deal & takes copys of all he writes with his own hand, so that he thinks it [i.e. the copying press invented by Watt] will be a very desirable thing to his Majesty.[3]

Employers, accountants and clerks performed prodigies of labour, at least of a routine nature. Large enterprises of international repute managed with a tiny handful of office and general staff. At Coalbrookdale a few clerks worked out the wages, based on different piece rates, for 2,000 workers in the 1830s, besides looking after all the other complex operations of an integrated firm. At the Clyde Ironworks in 1793, possessing two blast furnaces, David Mushet was left 'almost the sole occupant of the office'. The Arkwrights, in 1801–4, employed only three clerks to look after 1,063 workers, nearly all of whom, again, were paid by complicated piece rates, so that 'an immense amount of bookkeeping and calculation was involved'. At Gott's mill at Bean Ing, in 1813, three clerks looked after a staff of 744 workers plus an unknown number of outworkers.[1]

These clerks did more than book-keeping. At Whitbread's, a typical large porter brewery, there were two clerks, but they were mainly employed in 'collecting' the debts from the publicans whom the firm supplied direct, while the master looked after the accounts himself. Again, Fenton, Murray, the famous Leeds engineering firm spied on by James Watt, jun., in 1802, was reported by him to employ 160 men, with

> 4 bookkeepers or clerks. The cash keeper and his assistant, who I suppose keeps the waste book & journal, a clerk who overlooks both foundries in the capacity of A[braham] Storey, a time keeper who also assists in paying the men & regulates the police of the yard. Fenton is generally busied in the counting house and probably keeps the ledger & writes the letters. [The other two partners managed the production side.] The men are paid upon the Saturday about 11 o'clock by the clerks who go into each shop.[2]

Wage payments, in fact, were often less burdensome than might at first sight appear, since many firms and industries worked on an effective subcontract basis, and it was up to the subcontractor, butty, spinner, head melter, or similar under-manager to pay the men, women and children under him out of a lump-sum payment which often might be a simple piece rate or tonnage rate on work performed. Lady Charlotte Guest has left us an account of the opposition she met from her managers and clerks, and the large additional burdens she imposed on them, when she forced them in May 1853 to replace the current 'list' (group) payment by individual payments.[3]

On the other hand, even the group or subcontract payments were often based on detailed calculations of individual work, as in most of the textile mills, so that there was little real saving in the labour of clerks, while the system of deductions, advance payments, fines and truck imposed further burdens on the book-keeping staff which made wage payments almost as complex as those of modern firms plagued by bonuses, allowances, elaborate piece systems, income tax and national insurance deductions. Thus a typical fortnightly wage entry at the Mona Mine in 1825 had fourteen columns, of which eight represented amounts payable, at different contract and other rates, four represented deductions for cash and stores advanced, and two the totals, which might, at the end of each period, consist of either credit or debit items for each workman.[1] In cotton mills, also, entries for family earnings might run over a whole double page, when all the debits, purchases, rents, etc., were entered. In the more traditional mining areas, such as Cornwall and Derbyshire, it was the intricate share divisions of the proprietors which might represent a comparable amount of clerical work.

In these circumstances the technical facilities scarcely existed for thorough or sustained attempts to innovate more accurate methods of costing, forecasting or production control. There could have been little room to manoeuvre in this field when, as late as 1833, it was reported that at Messrs. Wilkins & Co., owning reputedly the largest factory in the West of England, the request for a list of employees occupied one clerk continuously for a fortnight—though many of these workers must have been outworkers.[2]

This comparative understaffing of the counting houses is not, of course, independent of the total problem of training and recruiting of clerical staff, which is treated elsewhere in this book. On the one hand, there existed, by modern standards, a grave shortage of qualified clerical workers or even of men sufficiently literate to be trained as such, and the needs of modern industry during the industrial revolution appear, on the evidence, to have outgrown the possible sources of supply, as was the case with many other vital skills.

Yet on the other hand this shortage of skilled staff, though frequently felt, was not felt as a major and oppressive bottleneck, not even to the extent of, say, the shortage of skilled engineers and metalworkers. In other words, employers were satisfied, by and large, with their quota of office staff, as long as wages and other outgoings were paid, books kept in order, and liquidity maintained to meet bills due. This in turn points to the fact that the notion of using accounts or other office work to ease the task of management was still foreign to the entrepreneurs of the day. Among the many innovations and schemes of rationalization of the age, the rationalization of management through accountancy and audit was stirring but faintly.

In part, this was an aspect of the general neglect of any systematic study of management as a science; in part it was also due to the unsuitability of the accounting practices inherited from merchants and estate stewards, while the special problems of industrialists largely remained unsolved in this period. Regarding this latter, one of the main problems has not been touched on yet: the inability to deal satisfactorily with large quantities of fixed capital.

V

Whatever the current notions of 'capital' may have been, industrial accountants seemed to be unable to integrate fixed capital into their scheme of things. Their practices were characterized by two main heresies: the treatment of capital as an auxiliary to entrepreneurship instead of the central motive force behind the firm and the confusion between capital and revenue.[1]

For purposes of exposition, it will be easiest to begin with the fact that the typical firm was a partnership. Joint-stock enterprises were rare, and often modelled on partnerships, while single proprietorships were perhaps rarer still among large firms. Normally a partnership would start with a round sum, divided in fixed proportions: in Cyfarthfa, for example. William Crawshay, sen., was to have had a capital of £100,000 and his partner Benjamin Hall £60,000. At the end of the year each partner was first credited with interest on his capital, and the net surplus then remaining was divided in a fixed proportion, in this case 5:3, and also credited to the partners' accounts. Since, however, dividends and interest were not paid out, but allowed to accumulate except for irregular withdrawals by partners to meet their living expenses, actual capital holdings very quickly diverged from their original round sums, both in absolute terms and in the proportions of the partners' holdings to each other. Further, all partners did not necessarily contribute the full amounts of their nominal share; this was especially so when they were admitted into an existing partnership as managerial experts or sons of partners. The withdrawal of a partner, by death for example, requiring the paying off of the share to the executors, might also greatly distort the actual shareholdings from the nominal for many years. Knight's Stourbridge partnerships, according to the surviving accounts of 1726–36, made up their nominal capital to round sums whenever a new works was added to the group, but normally actual holding tended to diverge increasingly from nominal capital, until partnership shares were adjusted at renewals and changes of the partnership. Throughout, however, partners continued to receive interest on the actual amounts held (an incentive to saving and the ploughing back of profits), while profits were shared out according to the original formula.

There was also a clear and parallel distinction between interest and profits in cost accounting. Interest was treated as a cost, universally in computing the advisability of planned ventures, but frequently also in accounts of the past. This was natural where capital was borrowed, or derived from an associated company, as in the case of the Soho Foundry, which drew its capital from Boulton & Watt, or where payment was in bills which had to be discounted. But it was widespread also in other cases, and there is much evidence to show that 'profits' in common parlance were often understood to be the surplus after interest was paid. Conversely, earnings less than the expected interest rate were termed 'losses'—an echo of the present practice relating to the nationalized industries.

Normally, this interest as a cost was computed, year after year, on the original investment, but occasionally it was based on current capital values: in the Mona Mine Co., for example,

> upon the Estimated Value of Stocks, Debts, buildings, stores and implements on 31st December, 1810.[1]

In the case of the Carron Co., indeed, it was charged in full as a cost against revenue even after it had become clear that much of the original capital, on which it had been computed, had been lost.

There are other clues to show the basic distinction made between interest and the remainder of the surplus. Thus Robert Owen, measuring his success at New Lanark, first allowed interest at 5 per cent and then included in the additional profit not only the increased capital value of the property but also the £7,000 paid out in wages relief during the cotton famine of 1806—a notion of profits which clearly embraced any disposable surplus, however spent. Again, John Curr, in presenting the Duke of Norfolk's coal accounts for 1781–90 in order to compare the returns of direct management with those of letting, called the surplus 'profits and interest', to show that interest had to be earned before a venture became profitable. Alexander Mason, the Scots projector, offered investors their interest even before payment of his managerial salary, while Samuel Walker believed that his returns as an ironmaster should provide separately for interest on capital, risk and management.

All these practices are linked by a common, though unspoken assumption: the assumption that profits are not directly related to the quantity of capital, and therefore are not payment for capital or created by capital. Capital is adequately rewarded by interest at the current rate, at which, incidentally, the supply is clearly assumed to be highly elastic and limited by personal and specific shortages rather than by price. Profits are distinct and are rewards of entrepreneurship *per se*, depending on skill, the concrete business situation or sheer luck, the entrepreneur using capital merely as a tool for which he pays the market rate. This contrasts directly with the classical economists' assumption that

> the sums received as 'wages' by particular undertakers seemed to depend on the quantity of capital at their disposal, and not upon the amount of labour they performed.

Further, the accountants' pattern of thought is not consistent with a market-ordained distribution of capital according to its marginal return, or any bidding for it based on promised earnings: the price offered is the same everywhere—though the risk might differ. Conversely, contemporaries did not attempt any calculations of the profit rate on capital in the modern sense, though, significantly, many such have been made on the basis of surviving records by modern authors. Yet the contemporary economists' view was that

> the rate of profit . . . is always reckoned or estimated by the proportion or ratio which it bears to the stock or capital from which it arises . . . The rate of profit was given by the ratio of the amount of profits obtained in a year to the amount of capital from which they were derived.[1]

Three causes of this, our first, heresy might be mentioned briefly. One was the method of partnership accounting mentioned above, which encouraged the distinction between interest on capital and profits of the partnership. The second was the legal limitation of interest. The third, *pace* the 'classical' doctrine, was the relatively small proportion of fixed capital (outside the public utilities) in relation to goods in process of production, stocks and debtors, and the fact that trade credits obtained by bills or by simple book entry formed a large share of the total capital of many firms.[2] In many cases the two items of creditors and debtors exceeded the partners' original capital several-fold, and since they tended to fluctuate wildly, they might leave the positive or negative residual of capital to be provided by the partners to fluctuate even more widely. Clearly, in these circumstances, it would be meaningless to speak in terms of 'capital employed', or of a rate of profit earned on it.

The second heresy was the confusion of capital and revenue. This

235

may be viewed in two ways, from the point of view of ownership, i.e. looking on capital as a balance-sheet liability, or from the point of view of actual equipment, i.e. looking upon it as a set of assets, though the two are connected. We shall take them in turn.

The partnership accounts as described above required the periodic determination of profits, to be credited to the partners in the firms' books, and this in turn required a valuation of the firm. Several methods were in use. The one found most commonly in the accounts examined consisted of valuing the whole firm *de novo* at the date of a striking the balance. From the total assets, including debtors, all liabilities except for the original partners' capital were deducted and the difference, if positive, was capital-cum-profits. This sum, compared with the sum similarly arrived at at the last balancing date, might show how far the concern had been profitable in the interim, provided no funds had been withdrawn by the partners, though few firms seem to have made the comparison. Among the larger firms using this method of valuation were Truman's brewery, John Marshall, the Carron Co., Broadbent & Lockwood, the Mona Mine Co. and (doubtfully) its associated Stanley and Ravenhead copperworks.

While this approach has a certain internal logic, it is very far removed from the modern concept of profit maximization as the driving force of capitalism: indeed, the notion of capital as a continuous, let alone autonomous, factor is virtually eliminated. Thus there might develop bewildering fluctuations of the 'capital' of a company from year to year, depending on trade, the valuation of assets, and the discount for bad debts. Kirkstall Forge, in a set of accounts for 1712–57, found its 'capital' fluctuating between £1,000 and £7,000. Again, some assets which could not easily be valued were left out of the calculation altogether: the Aire and Calder Navigation, valuing its 'clear and unencumbered surplus property' (a phrase much more realistic than 'capital') in 1817 at just under £30,000, including £20,000, in a round sum, for the sloops, yet excluded completely some real estate bringing in about £3,000 a year. The Parys Mine Co. computed the increase in its 'capital' between March 1816 and March 1824 simply by comparing the two stock valuations, wholly ignoring such items as debtors or the value of leases, perhaps for reasons noted in some accounts of the associated Mona Mine in 1782–9: 'What the Mine capital may be worth no idea can be found as no Balance appears to have been struck.'[1]

Nothing, perhaps, shows up the resulting confusion in the notion of capital better than the terminology used. The Herculaneum Pottery, having found a 'surplus of capital arising from profits, more than sufficient to meet the current exigences [*sic*] for the current year', turned it into a cash bonus, on top of the dividend. The Coalbrookdale Co. described as 'profits' (divisible by shares) the whole net surplus remaining after 'dividends' (also divisible by shares, but in round sums) had been paid out, while in the next century William Matthews, the ironmaster, considered 'the profits of the iron trade as part of the interest of capital'.[1] In the partnership later to become the Sheffield Smelting Co.,

> debts owing by Read and Lucas were deducted from the total value of stock plus the money owing to them. This was the gross profit. From it was deducted the capital of the partners. The difference was then divided in the agreed proportions and entered as the net profit.[2]

In other words, here capital becomes part of gross profit.

A second method was to value the firm's capital by its earning capacity. Sometimes this took the form of valuing the assets by conventional means and then adjusting values so arrived at; at other times the total valuation seems to have been built up on earning capacity alone. The Walkers of Masbro' entered a £14,000 increase in capital on 1 May 1778,

> as the works have answered very well this year (except the Fire Engine) it is hop'd it is not laid too high.

Two years later, the entry runs:

> I suppose [£120,000] is a moderate estimate. N.B. on the last acco'ts, settled May-Day 1780, turning out so well, think £2,000 should be added, then the Capital is £122,000.

By contrast, in 1816,

> in consequence of the general stagnation of trade, and the depreciation of every kind of property . . . this valuation may be considered as nominal rather than real.[3]

Similarly, Benjamin Gott wrote down the fixed capital of the Bean Ing mill from its long-standing book value of £26,500 to £10,000 in 1817 and £5,000 in 1818 because of bad trade conditions.[4]

When the Albion Mill was planned for London the 500 existing mills were 'valued at' £200 p.a. each, and the Albion Mill itself was 'valued' at £3,000 p.a., arrived at by calculating 5 per cent on a planned investment of £60,000. The former appears to be a valuation purely by earning capacity; it is difficult to assign a meaning to the 'valuation' of the latter. On a more sophisticated level, Thomas Fenwick, the famous northern coal-viewer, wrote in 1818:

> The mode of valuing coal in Northumberland is according to the system of valuing Annuities—the Duration of the Colliery being considered as the term of the Payment of the Annuity— the annual Rent of the Colliery is considered as the Annuity itself, and the p'centage is fixed according to the Hazard attending the coal property,

being 8 per cent normally, 10 per cent if risky. Sometimes several methods of valuation were used for the same asset.[1]

In considering capital in the sense of working assets most manufacturers of the industrial revolution were apt to confuse fixed investments and current expenditure as frequently as they confused capital and profits. Indeed, influenced by the historical fact that industrial accounting evolved from commercial accounting or, concretely, that the accountants in the works had been trained in, or with textbooks written for, merchants' counting houses, there was a common tendency to ignore the fixed equipment altogether, except for the annual interest in some firms, as noted above.

Whether or not interest charges on the initial capital were included, any additions and improvements to the capital equipment were normally entered in the current accounts. The identification of capital and current accounts was, perhaps, most complete in the Cornish 'cost-book' system, in which the adventurers contributed capital or drew dividends during the whole lifetime of the mine in proportion to their shareholding, according to the balance available, irrespective of whether the balances were due to capital or current items. Though the system was considered anachronistic at the time, it was in truth more so in the freedom of the Stannaries from the obstructions of contemporary law and lawyers than in its attitude to capital.

A high rate of profit and a relatively low ratio of fixed capital, as well as technical considerations, made it easy to enter capital additions in the revenue accounts. In mining, for example, where occasionally the cost of sinking a pit could be recovered in three months' working, the larger companies were constantly sinking new pits while working out the old ones. It then became normal practice to absorb capital costs in the current working of the whole enterprise: the Larwood colliery account for 1789, for example, included an expenditure of some £25 for sinking pits, £3 for boring to draw the water off the sinkings, and £6 for 11,000 pit bricks, with the note:

> N.B. These (3 items) are charg'd as the annual average expence, none of these expences having occurr'd in 1789.

As late as 1872, at the Dalcoath mine, employing 1,000 men, 'invested capital is only nominal, outlay for machinery being paid for as a working expense'. The occasional fluctuations in the apparent annual costs of the enterprise, owing to such discontinuous investment, then required explanation:

> The present Compt'g Ho., Carpt'rs Shop & Storehouse was built in this quarter and a considerable part of the cost included [in this quarter's current account].[1]

In the ironworks the fixed capital consisted largely of furnaces, bellows and hammers which required regular re-lining and repair and appeared as running costs even in the sophisticated accounts of the South Yorkshire ironmasters; even the cost of erecting a large cotton mill might appear largely as an item in the weekly wages bill, as at Mellor. It was for the same reason that the equipment of the Duke of Norfolk's collieries was valued according to the weight of iron and timber in the various engines and machines, showing the nature of the original outlay. Elsewhere, large profits were simply ploughed back in generous annual extensions of capital.

Even the public utilities, with their heavy fixed capital investment, found the distinction between it and the current costs difficult to maintain. The Stockton and Darlington Railway Co., conscious of a decade of this confusion, reported to the shareholders on 10 July 1830 that

> the statement presented of the Company's affairs is the result of constant care to keep the Accounts so as to distinguish between the current expenses of the concern, and the charges consequent upon the Works now in hand, and incompleted,

yet the following accounts were as confused as ever. Similarly the Aire and Calder Navigation went to great trouble to recast its accounts in 1817, in a form to show real income and expenditure, profit and loss, as well as 'the increased or decreased value of your Property from year to year', but by 1822 had still not succeeded in separating capital and revenue. Again, the Birmingham Canal Co. attempted a rigorous separation when it opened a new set of books in 1795, but in the half-year to March 1797 timber was still shown under new work, while in the next half-year it was entered under current expenditure.[1]

There were, indeed, examples of greater sophistication, to the extent not only of entering such capital costs as interest and depreciation, but collecting them in the central (as distinct from the branch) accounts with the other 'general' or overhead expenses, as in the varied enterprises of the Fitzwilliam estate near Sheffield or at the Cyfarthfa and Hirwain works. This method, however, invited the error of using the incomplete departmental accounts for comparative cost calculations and thus again failing to take capital costs into account.

Capital depreciation was by no means the rule even in the larger firms. Apart from the examples enumerated above, of firms entering maintenance costs of capital in revenue instead, and such well-known concerns as Crowleys' ironworks, there was, for example, the Imperial Continental Gas Association, established in 1824:

> In common with the generally accepted practice among the public utility companies operating in this country, the Association made no provision for depreciation in its accounts. Expenditure for renewals was charged against revenue as it was incurred and since substantial sums were involved when the periodic renewal of major items of gaswork equipment took place, there were quite serious fluctuations in profit for particular half-years and also . . . serious financial stringency was experienced at times because down to 1850 the association used to distribute in dividend almost all its profits and had no fund of retained profits with which to finance capital expenditure.[2]

The absence of reserve funds or depreciation charges was, in fact, typical of joint-stock firms at the end of the eighteenth century, a failing, it has been said, which meant that a 'complex business was not better than a blind man's buff'.[3] In 1793 the valuation of one of the largest and most advanced firms in Britain, the Ketley ironworks,

> was examined and subjected to the same objection as the Coalbrookdale one, that little or no allowance for depreciation of materials and tools had been made, so a revaluation was called for and lengthy rules for the valuation of different kinds of property were laid down.[4]

Pleasley Mills was running for six years before its buildings, and sixteen years before its machinery, began to be written off. The Stockton and Darlington Railway Co. in its early comparative cost calculations omitted to take into account any depreciation on locomotives, though by 1836 it had evolved a capital account in which engines and coaches were written off separately. The Midland Railway operated a depreciation fund for the permanent way between 1848 and 1857, in order to even out large changes in expenditure; but at other times it followed the general practice of simply charging capital repair and replacement costs to revenue: in the 'manias' any potential depreciation funds were raided for new building; in slumps they were raided for dividends. As late as 1884 a standard accounting textbook could state that

> . . . the capital accounts are not always deemed to be of such pressing importance; and variations in the value of plant, arising from the wear and tear and other causes, may be left unnoted.[1]

It will be evident that to some extent the errors in accounting cancelled out, a fact which allowed them to continue for so long without punishing the companies concerned by failure. What happened was that the absence of depreciation might, at a certain stage of growth, be neatly compensated by additions to capital not entered in the capital account, so that book values and real assets continued to correspond. Similarly, sharing out surpluses to the hilt would be neutralized by letting them accumulate, as book entries— until the revaluation of the next partnership change rectified the position. The example of the Gas Association above, however, shows that this fortunate complementarity did not always occur, and several companies had to take more drastic steps to protect their funds. Some of the large breweries, Benjamin Gott & Partners, and the Llangavelach copperworks divided partners' holdings into two parts, only one of which was withdrawable; the Carron partners agreed formally to re-invest all their surplus beyond the 5 per cent interest; and some joint-stock companies explicitly prohibited the payment of dividends out of capital. In well-run private partnerships balances were not necessarily struck, but drawings were made

> when the account would bear a certain amount of money being withdrawn from it.[2]

Even where the practice of depreciation had been introduced, it did not necessarily derive from a 'rational' view of capital. In some cases it was to get tax allowances:

> It is best to write off & not uphold all Accounts of the sort I
> point out [ordered William Crawshay in 1814], more par-
> ticularly while there is still property tax to pay,[1]

not before making certain, of course, of the real state of the property
before writing-off. In other cases depreciation had fraudulent
objectives: the machinations of the Stanton family with the Carron
Company have recently been described in some detail by Professor
R. H. Campbell.

Generally, however, the objects of depreciation ranged from the
wish for a true valuation to the more practical need to allow for
replacement, repair and maintenance without upsetting the balance
of any one accounting period or permitting an overdistribution of
dividends. An attempt at a true valuation, however, could be made
as easily by the mercantile practice of annual stock valuations as by
writing-off, which presupposes the more advanced notion of a continuous, fixed capital. Here, for example, are the fixed capital items
in the 'Stock Account' of the Mona Mine for 1829 and 1830 (shillings
and pence omitted):[2]

	1829	1830	Notes
Steam engine 'valued at'	£400	£350	
Whimseys & appurtenances	629	663	additional items
Schooner 'Hero', per valua-			in 1830
tion	£1,500	£1,500	
Furnaces	£1,600	£1,540	18 in 1829, 17 in
			1830

Despite first appearances, all items here are simple valuations,
extracted, in point of fact, from a long list in which they were
indiscriminately mixed with stores and stocks and from which the
notion of a permanent capital was clearly absent. Similar examples
may be found in larger porter breweries, at Crawshay's ironworks
and at the Herculaneum Pottery. Even where percentage depreciation had been introduced, it was often derived from merchant's
practice of reducing the book value of stocks in hand to allow for
discounts, obsolescence and lower manufacturing costs. 'True' percentage depreciation for the sake of valuation was rare; among the
best-known examples were Boulton & Fothergill, the Soho Foundry
and the Carron Co., after Gascoigne's reforms of 1769.

Depreciation to account for the practical needs of repair and
replacement was much more common. Inevitably, these two were
often confused, as were physical deterioration and technological

obsolescence. Joshua Milne, for example, the well-known Oldham cotton-spinner, justified his practice of depreciation by the need to provide for wear and tear, replacement, annual upkeep, the 'fall in value' and, in reply to a leading question, that without it he would soon have a 'fictitious capital', all at the same time. R. H. Greg, another cotton-spinner, more thoughtfully explained his depreciation on 'sunk' capital, i.e. 'the amount spent on buildings and machinery', as 'not only for actual wear and tear, but also for its deterioration arising out of new inventions'. The Albion Mill's boilers were depreciated for 'repair and fund for renewing'.[1]

With its rapid obsolescence (Heathcoat's patent bobbin net machine, reducing hand machines from £1,200 to £60 in value was often quoted), textile machinery was usually depreciated very rapidly. Elsewhere, 'wear and tear' tended to mean repair: this was true also of Wyatt and Paul, pioneers of industrial cost accounting as well as roller spinning.

Replacement came up against the problem of 'betterment', i.e. replacement by a superior piece of equipment of which the addition should be charged to capital. Where the additions were large in relation to the original capital, accountants found it hard to ignore the difference between capital and revenue, and the inability of the latter to provide for the former. The Birmingham Canal Company offers a useful illustration. In 1800 it opened a 'Sinking Fund', fed by irregular surpluses, for the repayment of borrowed funds. In 1820, the repayment completed, this was renamed a 'Surplus Fund', but its income virtually ceased. It was rescued in 1824, renamed 'Improvement Fund', given the income from thirteen shares held by the company itself and debited with expenditure on improvements, the whole being balanced independently and the balance being carried forward from period to period. Almost at once, however, in 1825 heavy expenditure on new vast capital projects completely swamped the original modest sums, yet the borrowings and expenditure were still being passed through this fund, though the interest alone, payable on the borrowings, quickly exceeded the total original outgoings on 'improvements'. It was at this stage that the company was slowly forced to consider a separate capital account.[2]

There were other examples of 'funds', established originally as security against losses or to even out cash flows, which drew the attention of their originators towards depreciation and separate capital accounts. In 1829, having just paid off a large liability arising out of some bad debts, Nevill & Co.

resolved that it will be expedient henceforward to divide a moiety only of the annual Profits, and to transfer the other moiety to the Sinking Fund accounts, till the same be sufficient to protect the concern against any loss which may occur upon any of the accounts in our ledgers.

The Gas Light & Coke Co., also, in 1821–9 made provision for a 'reserve fund' over and above 'wear and tear'.[1]

Finally, perhaps the differences in actual rates of depreciation may also be taken as an indication of the uncertain philosophy behind them:

Date	Firm or industry	Annual Rate of Depreciation on: Buildings %	Steam engines %	Machinery %
1769	Carron Ironworks	8	8	8
1780s	Soho	5(a)	—	—
1797–1800	Soho Foundry	5	8	—
1822–1831	Soho Foundry	10	15	—
1806	Copperworks	5	—	—
1814	Herculaneum Pottery	10	—	—
1825	Locomotives	—	15	—
1827	Marshall Flax Co.	—	—	$7\frac{1}{2}$
1831–1872	Tinplate works	5	—	—
1832	Greg Cotton Mill (b)	5	5	10
1832	Ashworth Cotton Mill	—	5(c)	5(c)
1833	Cotton industry	—	10	—
1833	Cotton mill	—	6	—
1833	Cotton mill	—	—	$10–33\frac{1}{3}$
1833	Ironworks	$2\frac{1}{2}$	—	—
1833	Ironworks	—	10(d)	—
1830–1880	Textile mills	$2\frac{1}{2}$	$2\frac{1}{2}$	$7\frac{1}{2}$

Notes:
(a) 'The same as the rate of interest.'
(b) not straight line, but on value remaining.
(c) expects to get: 5% interest
  5% depreciation
  15% clear profit.
(d) 15%, but that includes interest on capital.

Surviving accounts may not tell the whole story, but it seems unlikely that they were notably less advanced than those which have perished. Perhaps the outstanding fact to emerge from them is the enormous variety and ranges of practices in the counting houses in this period and the variety of assumptions on which they seem to have been based. The differences may be largely derived from the different practical demands which the accounts were designed to meet, but very few sets managed to deal adequately with the problems thrown up by fixed capital. It is not even possible to discern a clear movement in that direction. Yet as long as there was no purposeful capital accounting, there could be no rational use of accounts for managerial guidance.

VI

The evidence presented here appears to be largely negative. Accountancy in its wider sense was used only minimally to guide businessmen in their business decisions, and where it was so used the guidance was often unreliable. Before this verdict is accepted, however, with its corollary of a certain presumption of incompetence among business leaders, several major reservations must be made.

In the first place, it should be stressed that accuracy in accounting was less essential at a time when selling prices tended to be so far above total costs, no matter how calculated, that almost any pricing policy was bound to show a net surplus, at least among the leaders in their industries. Similarly, as far as dividend distribution was concerned, the typical partner would normally withdraw only a fraction of his nominal surplus, so that there was rarely any danger of illiquidity.

Total profits (and total rents, also) were very much higher in relation to total industrial incomes, i.e. in relation to wages, in the earlier stages of the industrial revolution, to about 1830, than they have become since,[1] particularly in the advanced, large firms, and this normally left a large margin for inefficient pricing and planning. In other words, the prize for the innovating entrepreneur was high, though his chance of failure was probably also much higher than it has become since. This was but an expression of the fact that possession both of capital and of entrepreneurship was still so scarce as to have evident monopolistic elements. Conversely, it was only precisely at the point at which serious competition set in, or at which profit margins for other reasons were depressed, as, for example, in a general industrial crisis, that firms began to calculate their costs more seriously and more exactly.[2]

These easy margins explain not only the cavalier attitude to exact costing and pricing, but also the rapid growth of firms out of ploughed-back capital: for it was precisely the high profits which allowed this rapid accumulation.[1] They also explain such phenomena as Robert Owen's success as a mill manager, in spite of his relatively generous treatment of his workers and their children. For the notion of his great ability as a businessman is a myth, as his later career surely adequately shows. What he possessed, apart from his humanity and an innate and almost uncanny insight into the psychological needs of the first generation of factory workers, was a monopolistic position at the fine end of the spinning industry, itself partly the result of his successful handling of labour, and there, as all the evidence shows, profit margins were so exceptionally high at the time that any policy would have produced large profits. As Mr. Frank Podmore showed long ago in a brilliant analysis ignored by almost all the later biographers, Owen not only did not know the exact cost of his innovations; he did not even trouble to find out. His abilities to get people to work willingly for him

> were no doubt sufficient, in an age when capital had an extra-ordinary monopoly value, and when enterprising manufacturers were making with ease 20 per cent and more on their capital, to explain his commercial success at New Lanark. In fact the margin of profit was so wide that we need scarcely look for any other explanation of Owen's success as a manufacturer.[2]

Not all advanced industrialists were in such an enviable quasi-monopoly position, but it is worth while recalling here how few were the exceptions. In coal-mining most of the large mines enjoyed local working monopolies, and the one area which did not, the North-East, had created an artificial one by its 'Vend'. Canals and early railways, and their builders, were almost secure as local monopolists; Wedgwood had succeeded in creating a monopoly by successful product differentiation,[3] while other business leaders, like Boulton or the Coalbrookdale works, had costs so much lower than their competitors at critical times, because of technical advantages, as to reap quasi-monopoly profits. In engineering, the silk, woollen and even the cotton industries, the leading firms enjoyed equal advantages, by technique or design, and in chemicals a monopolistic structure has been virtually permanent in Great Britain. There remains only the bulk of the cotton industry, and certain sections of the iron industry which were truly competitive, to the extent of driving prices down to somewhere near costs in most years of the trade cycle; and in these cases exact costing by individual firms was almost equally unnecessary, for the firms had to keep to market prices and merely tried to survive within them.

Secondly, as the result of the experience of this period, there were, towards its end, the first stirrings towards the use of accounts in aid of management decisions. Some of them, it is true, came from outside industry. Thus the journalist who visited a series of large London factories in 1843, mostly of the assembly type, realized that

> it must be obvious that where some hundreds of men are employed, some working by the day, and others by 'piece-work', and where scores of different materials are used, the commercial accounts of a factory must require extra care and a well-organised system, to prevent the most inextricable confusion . . . the manufacturer who makes an engine, consisting of many scores or even hundreds of parts, some of one metal and some of another, and made by men of whom some are paid by the day and others by the piece, has a task of no mean difficulty in estimating the cost of a machine.

Babbage, ten years earlier, had been well ahead of his time in suggesting not only detailed and accurate costs, particularly for new machinery, but also went a stage further in hoping that cost accounts would show at which stages of the process improvements should be attempted, as being those carrying the greatest present costs. Similarly, H. R. Hatfield was in advance of current practice when he wrote, in his *Historical Defence of Book-keeping*, that the functions of book-keeping were

> to locate responsibility, to prevent fraud, to guide industry, to determine equities, to solve the all essential conundrum of business: 'what are my profits?', to facilitate the government in its fiscal operations, to guide the business manager in the attempt to secure efficiency.[1]

Some traces of the same attitude could be found within industry also, particularly among the larger and more progressive firms. At Soho, the model firm in this respect, the costing figures were used not only to determine prices but also wages, and they became the starting-point for changes in the methods of work and of payments, and of technical changes. Wedgwood, by the end of the century, used his accounts to show which department was profitable and which was not, and, a most important matter in his type of industry, to help in the control of his stocks. John Marshall, the great flax spinner, developed his accounts from the traditional annual statement into close guides of real efficiency of machinery and labour in his works, as well as of the yield of the season's flax, for the purpose of determining the efficiency of new machines, and keeping laggard

247

labour up to the mark. Among the larger London breweries the hydrometer was used to calculate how far lowering of quality would save costs without reducing revenue correspondingly, and the actual quality produced was settled only after refined calculation.[1]

It would be misleading, however, to pretend that these were more than embryonic and hesitant attempts. The practice of using accounts as direct aids to management was not one of the achievements of the British industrial revolution; in a sense, it does not even belong to the later nineteenth century, but to the twentieth.

Thirdly, it has been shown that in 'partial' cost accounts and other statements, particularly those called forth by the concrete need of industry, quite advanced and fairly accurate techniques were developed and used. The problems that were solved included stock control and prevention of embezzlement, comparisons between departments or commodities produced. Accountancy, as in other ages, was responsive to the needs of its users, and it may therefore be legitimate to judge that if reliable overall cost accounts were not further developed the chances are that the need for them could not have been felt very strongly. The British experience would seem to bear out the general view that 'there is little to suggest that the course of accounting has been consciously influenced to any considerable extent by economic thought. The fact is, rather . . . that accounting is a tool of business, and that the development of accounting . . . has been determined by the practices of businessmen.'[2]

With these qualifications in mind, we must conclude that entrepreneurship in the industrial revolution did not develop to any significant extent the use of accounts in guiding management decisions. At the end of the period various methods had been tried out and in several cases practised for lengthy spells, but no acceptable improved system had emerged, and there was no new systematized technique developed in parallel with new techniques in the production field.

Among the causes for this, apart from the technical difficulties and the absence of a tradition, was the fact that the problem calling for a solution was not widely or continuously felt. In the early years of the industrial revolution those using the new techniques and new capital equipment enjoyed a monopolistic position not only in this country but throughout the world. Apart from certain crisis years, anyone with a better technique had no problem in selling, and new techniques were so obviously 'better' that it did not need elaborate accounts to prove this before the innovations were adopted. There are indications that it was precisely at the time when firms departed from routine and innovated that accounting was neglected, until a new routine had been established.[1] It is, of course, of the very nature of Schumpeterian entrepreneurship that there are no precedents to go on, no easy comparisons to be made, and no means of bringing the future into the framework of existing accounts, and in this period an unusually high proportion of the large firms discussed here were entrepreneurs in the Schumpeterian sense.

At the same time, however, the conclusion is difficult to resist that here was but another aspect of the absence of any management science or even a widespread feeling of need for one which has been stressed elsewhere in this book. The success of a concern, it was firmly believed, would stand or fall with the 'quality' of its partners, and there was little that any organized science or even art, like accountancy, could do to help them beyond the industrial technology itself.

7/ Conclusion: Management in Theory and Practice

We have had occasion, in the course of this survey, to refer several times to the absence of any attempt to generalize or rationalize the experiences of industrial management into a management science or at least a management technology in the period of the industrial revolution. We have also noted that a managerial class as such was slow to develop and even by 1830 could hardly be said to be in existence, though well-defined classes of managers had emerged in various specific industries. Could we go on from there to question the whole concept of industrial management in that period as a logically connected set of problems? Have we been chasing a mirage?

Perhaps it is no accident that most of the literature about the industrial revolution tells us so little about the progress of management, and 'still less about the attitudes of the early industrialists themselves, about their problems of control'. The literature of the seventeenth and eighteenth centuries contains many indications of an awareness among the mercantile community 'of the significance of methodical accounting and of the need of at least some specific training for the discharge of executive responsibilities', but among the manufacturers of the industrial revolution it seems as though the interest has vanished.[1] Was no one aware of the emergence of new social and industrial relations and new methods of handling them? Did others share the contempt for management which William Crawshay, sen., exhibited when he wrote, about proposals to save on managerial salaries:

> John Homfray may surely aid in services beyond mere Farm and horses which are more for direction than actual doing; mere superintendence?[2]

Alternatively, are we to agree with those students of the history of entrepreneurship who draw the dividing line between the entrepreneur and the manager not, as we have already done,[3] along the differences between strategic and tactical decisions, but by equating

250

entrepreneurship with innovations, and management with routine?
Thus John H. Dales stresses that management,

> the maintenance of a going concern in a healthy stable condi-
> tion, is an important business function clearly distinct from
> innovating change,

while Karl W. Deutsch distinguished the 'manager-entrepreneur'
precisely by his many routine decisions of management and the
'sheer momentum' of going concerns:

> with the growing proportion of capital invested in relatively
> immobile equipment,the aim above all is continuity of operation.
> Management's aim is first to survive, and second to strengthen
> its trade position.[1]

If the manager, or the entrepreneur in his managerial capacity, was
indeed the one member of society whose energies were directed
towards preserving continuity and who personified routine during
the industrial revolution, then there is truly little of value to be said
about him in this context.

Before pursuing the degree of innovation in management practice, however, it would be best to deal with the strange absence of
management theory. Why was there no consciousness of its need, or
of its possible utility?

I

Let us begin with the few isolated examples of conscious thought on
management and the attempts to systematize it. The best-docu-
mented case, without a doubt, is that of the Boulton & Watt partnership, described with such insight by Lord, Roll and others. It was in
the 1770s, when the two partners were regularly away from Soho,
supervising the erection of engines, that the need arose to organize
the works so as to continue running smoothly even in their absence.
By grappling with the resulting periodic emergencies, the partners
learnt to introduce regularity, delegation and division of functions.
In the measure that their own enterprise began to be managed
efficiently, they became increasingly critical of the mismanagement
of other concerns, like the Albion steam mill and the copper-mines
in Cornwall and smelting plants in South Wales with which they
were associated.[2] The most significant innovations, however, were
introduced in 1795–1800, when the Soho Foundry, i.e. the engine

works, was set up, largely by the sons of the senior partners. This was a manufacturing plant in which accurate workmanship, stock control, assembly methods and detailed costing were necessary for profitable survival. The solutions to these problems, consciously adopted, have rightly been compared with the best practices of the twentieth century.

A second example is Robert Owen, as a manager of cotton mills, firstly in Manchester and then in New Lanark. By contrast with Boulton & Watt, his work is virtually not documented at all. Nevertheless, it seems clear, from various hints in Owen's own autobiography and in the description of visitors to New Lanark, that his competitive advantage could not have come either from a harsh bargaining ability or from particularly effective marketing arrangements, but arose out of his ability to win the co-operation of his workers while paying them no more than competitive wages, as well as out of the 'orderly arrangement' of the works, an alert policy of technical up-to-dateness and a careful selection and training of under-managers.

> It is probable . . . that his success was owing in great measure to his capacity to handle the administrative techniques of the factory system, techniques which were, at the time, completely outside the experiences of the men who were pioneering in this new form of social organisation. . . .
> When Owen left Drinkwater to enter into the management of the New Lanark Mills, he . . . was . . . equipped with an understanding of the administrative processes of factory management which must have been very largely unique at the time.

These allowed him to produce the finest counts of yarn on which the large profits were earned which formed the basis of his philanthropic schemes.[1]

Surviving manuscript notebooks also show that some consideration of management problems went on at Benjamin Gott's leading woollen mill in Leeds. The most interesting insight into current thinking about them, however, comes from the notebooks of William Brown, a Dundee flax-spinner, whose small 'East Mill', managed jointly with his brother, later became a centre of management consultancy in his own industry. In a series of manuscript essays, written between 1818 and 1823, Brown discussed with a remarkable degree of maturity and depth a wide range of management problems of the type considered in this book.

The manuscripts

> illustrate Brown's essentially scientific attitude to technical and managerial problems.[1]

At the start, Brown promised himself that

> These Essays . . . will embrace everything of importance relating to the management of the East Mill . . . respecting machinery, hands, operations or flax,

and while he included much systematized knowledge regarding the technical processes, he went beyond the practice of most of his contemporaries by taking this list seriously and dealing with organization, supervision and labour problems also. Systematic himself, he believed that

> surely all managers of extensive well-conducted works must write much, otherwise they could never establish order and discipline among their Hands, nor improvement and regularity in the construction and arrangement of their machinery.

For his part, he wrote out, for example, the duties of his under-manager in a document eighteen pages long, in January 1818, with precise details of daily routines and of the duties of other employees.

For his own purposes, he began with an admirably clear summary of the aim of the enterprise:

> The first and great object to be aimed at by the Manager of East Mill is PROFIT.

To achieve this aim the mill was subdivided into eleven departments, each of which was examined in rotation at set intervals. The clerk was ordered to keep five sets of books, and the managers and supervisors were also given instructions for regular checking over work performed, material used, quality, etc. Brown was aware of the need for co-ordination between the departments, particularly sales and production, and in describing the qualifications of a good manager, he implicitly stresses not only his personal qualities and technical and business knowledge, but also his administrative ability and his social skills. Much attention, indeed, is devoted to methods of keeping discipline without undue friction or severity. Perhaps the most unusual feature was the 'Improvement or Alteration Department', one of the eleven, created for the purpose of keeping abreast of the improvements of others and developing the firm's own.

It may be significant that Brown's observations were not published at the time, though later some of his technical essays were. Further, it seems unlikely that the selectivity of survival should have worked exclusively against firms which attempted a deliberate systematization of managerial experience within industry, so that while there may have been another half a dozen or so unknown cases, they were exceptional, and unpublished. As far as we know, the management pioneers were isolated and their ideas without great influence.[1]

Towards the end of the period, studies covering all the important innovating large-scale industries began to be published. In cotton we have the works of Ure and Montgomery; in coal-mining, Benjamin Thompson; in ironmaking, Gibbons, and in engineering, Oliver Evans among others. On the early railways, the Stockton and Darlington Company were given detailed advice in 1830 by an expert in colliery management, how to find a manager with 'complete *scientific* and mechanical abilities', who could also *manage*, organize and develop least-cost methods, in contrast with the existing haphazard and unsatisfactory organization of the line, while in 1825 a transport contractor had written in to the company, offering to 'methodize' their concern. All of these were mainly concerned with technical knowledge and codification of manufacturing practices; but all equally codified some managerial experiences also.[2] Moreover, there were the encyclopaedias, and above all there was Babbage's pioneer study,[3] generations ahead of its time in some respects certainly, yet, running into four editions in as many years and based on at least some practical observations and discussions with active industrialists.

All this, however important in itself, does not add up to a technology, still less to a science which could be taught or even summarized in textbooks. Why, then, did the age fail to produce a tangible awareness of this set of problems? The answer appears to be that there was no single cause, but several interrelated causal factors, powerful enough to keep the subject out of public discussion, not only until 1830, but in effect until the beginning of the twentieth century.

First, in an age of basic structural changes of technology, it was difficult to isolate the 'managerial' function from that of technical supervision or commercial control, which were often more critical. The 'distinctive characteristics' of entrepreneurs at that time 'was that they fulfilled in one person, the functions of capitalist, financier, works manager, merchant and salesman'.[4] Moreover, as we have shown in chapter 5 above, even among the problems that could

254

broadly be called managerial, the most pressing ones were not always the 'internal' ones, corresponding to the tasks of present-day managers, but such as would nowadays be left to public authorities or specialist firms, like the building of roads, canals, docks and whole villages, the provision of churches and of schools, banking and shopkeeping and the like. A textbook on management, had it been written, would have quite properly paid more attention to those 'external' problems, which took up so much more of the resources, time and energies of managing entrepreneurs, than to the kind of problems discussed by modern writers on the subject. In fact, those external tasks were quite widely discussed, though in the nature of the case no systematized science emerged, or could emerge.

Secondly, in a period dominated largely by pioneers and founder-managers apt to stress the differences in individual 'character', rather than the similarities generalized in a science of psychology, such questions as the structuring and management of firms must have seemed too individual, too unclassifiable, to repay further generalized study. As has been said about Egypt today, in any industrializing society

> the manager is a dominant individual who extends his personal control over all phases of the business. There is no chartered plan of organization, no formalized procedures for selection and development of managerial personnel, no publicized system of wage and salary classifications. The status of individuals in the managerial hierarchy is based not so much upon function as upon the nature of their relations with the owner-manager.[1]

With certain obvious exceptions, this was true of the British industrial revolution period also: each firm (much more so than today) was a law unto itself.

Thirdly, on one of the fundamental issues, the treatment of labour, not only had there been no general attitude crystallized out, but there were two distinct poles of schools of thought, towards which current practice was tending to move. On the one hand, the views of the majority were bounded by the realization that they were dealing with a recalcitrant, hostile working force whose morale, whose habits of work and whose culture had to be broken in order to fit them for a form of employment in which they had to become obedient servants of the machine, of its owners and of crude monetary incentives. What was necessary, according to this view, was a reform of 'character' on the part of every single workman, since their

255

previous character did not fit the new industrial system. In the words of one of the more thoughtful and humane of factory owners,

> It is a mistaken humanity to indulge [the hands] in ease, idleness or play. When in fault they should be reprimanded, first calmly, then seriously, then sharply—great care should be taken to point out faults—explain duties—to young ones or beginners especially. There is scarcely anyone so backward or corrupt that may not be improved by unremitting attention.[1]

Whether by kindness, as in this case, or by harsh punishment, as in others, the vision was that of a whole class, endowed by nature with a deficient character, which had to be reformed, individual by individual, into the ideal hard-working, regular and undemanding labour force of large-scale industry.

One way of looking at this would be to say that the new large-scale organizational structure was still so uncertain and untried that no allowance could be made within it for human labour for fear of breaking the still fragile framework altogether. Labour just had to be made to fit the Procrustean bed assigned to it. Alternatively, and perhaps more accurately, it could have been that the successes of mechanical invention in industry encouraged a mechanistic view of psychology, which was untempered by any excess of humanity felt by a newly arrived entrepreneur class for its least predictable factor of production, its labour.

Be that as it may, it was this view of the primacy of the factory and the machine, that would force human character into the mechanical mould, rather than build the factory round a study of the human character, which was observed so acutely by Carlyle and called forth his splendid wrath:

> Not the external and physical alone is now managed by machinery, but the internal and spiritual also . . . The same habit regulates not our modes of action alone, but our modes of thought and feeling. Men are grown mechanical in head and heart, as well as in hand. They have lost faith in individual endeavours, and in natural force, of any kind. Not for internal perfection, but for external combinations and arrangements, for institutions, constitutions, for Mechanism of one sort or other, do they hope and struggle.

And he goes on to deplore the

> inward persuasion . . . that, except the external, there are no true sciences; that to the inward world (if there be any) our

only conceivable road is through the outward; that, in short, what cannot be investigated and understood mechanically, cannot be investigated and understood at all.[1]

Carlyle, searching in vain for his hero within the framework of modern industrialism, greatly exaggerates or anticipates the decline in the belief in character, as against the efficacy of organization, which he noticed with reference to industrial leadership; but he is correct if his appraisal is intended to refer to the typical current views on labour psychology.

In contrast with this we have the other pole, represented by Robert Owen and his well-known plea to his fellow industrialists to treat their labour no worse than their machinery. In our period, as our survey has shown, this view represented a tiny minority only. It was only in the last quarter of the nineteenth century, or perhaps even later,

as the productivity of workers becomes as important as the productivity of the machines, [that] there is widespread recognition of the value of conscious investment in the development of enterprise, managers and workers.[2]

Perhaps we have indeed hitherto overstressed

the entrepreneur as a bold, rugged and ruthless individual,

and have neglected his

ability to engineer agreement among all interested parties, such as the inventor of the process, the partners, the capitalists, the suppliers of parts and services, the distributors etc.; . . . the ability to hold together an able staff, to delegate authority, to inspire loyalty, to handle successfully relations with labour and the public and a host of other managerial talents.[3]

Yet such evidence as does survive suggests the typical entrepreneur to have been ruthless, if not necessarily 'bold' or 'rugged'. The necessary embattled posture against his own labour seemed to have determined his attitude towards his fellow industrialists, partners and even members of his own family, overriding any mollifying influence in the reverse direction.

In the main growth industries entrepreneurs were acutely conscious of the dangerous competitive environment within which they operated. Matthew Boulton, in 1768, was certain that to succeed in his type of business a man had either to be a practical man or to possess a fortune—and he himself, though he had both, came very near to ruin. Gaskell similarly explained that in cotton-spinning,

> few of the men who entered the trade rich were successful. They trusted too much to others—too little to themselves: whilst on the contrary, the men who did establish themselves were raised by their own efforts—commencing in a very humble way and pushing their advance by a series of unceasing exertions. . . . The celerity with which some of these individuals accumulated wealth in the early times of steam spinning and weaving are proofs—if any such are wanting—that they were men of quick views, great energy of character, and possessing no small share of sagacity. . . . Very few who brought large capital into the trade were fortunate—or even made satisfactory progress. Neither will this fact be considered singular, when it is remembered with whom the battle had to be fought.

Similarly, it was asserted, Wyatt had failed because

> he was of a gentle and passive spirit, little qualified to cope with the hardships of a new manufacturing enterprise. It required, in fact, a man of a Napoleon nerve and ambition . . .[1]

Many of the more successful pioneers succeeded in creating for themselves a quasi-monopoly position in which the immediate pressure was less,[2] and it was usually among them that a more human, and humane, attitude to business and to labour was to be found, if it was found at all; but by the time they had reached this position, they had mostly become settled in their habits. The stock figure of literature, the hard-bitten owner of dark, satanic mills, while not universally true, was common enough to be representative.

The dialectical struggle sometimes within the same firm, perhaps even in the mind of the same man, between these two poles of approach towards labour management reflects a struggle between real issues. On the one hand, the necessary mechanism of industrial change had imposed a major social revolution on the working population of Great Britain, accompanied by the partial expropriation, the degradation (at least in their own eyes) and the forced transformation of the many groups which were to coalesce into the industrial proletariat of the large factories and mines. This was a real class battle, in which there were victors and vanquished, and in which the victor imposed his own terms, and safeguarded them by breaking the social bonds which had held the peasants, the craftsmen and the town poor of the eighteenth century together in opposition to the new order. But, on the other hand, we have the dawning realization that such a victory could not be static or permanent, that it raised new problems even before it could be consolidated, and that on this new plane it might pay to work *with* the social ambitions of the workforce, rather than against it: the slow discovery of the reality of the economy of high wages, in the wider sense, on which much of recent scientific management has been based.

In the early heroic years up to 1830 the second attitude had very little influence, but it was known and it made its uneasy presence felt among the manufacturers as well as among their outside critics. At the same time, the very existence of the conflict made it even more difficult than it would have been otherwise to develop a managerial theory which would represent generalized practice or a consensus of opinion about it.

II

If there was no theory to help, how systematic and how self-conscious was 'management' practice in the industrial revolution? Further, how much of it was novel, and therefore likely to impose additional strains on busy innovators?

Some aspects of internal management could be continued more or less unchanged from earlier ages. Thus the logic of accountancy and even some of its detailed methods were taken over from the merchants, who also supplied much of the technique for stock keeping and control, developed over the previous century or so of mercantile expansion. Indeed, it could be held that mercantile accounting techniques were too slavishly followed and too imperfectly adapted and that the early factory-owner continued to use practices which might perhaps have offered adequate checks on the activities of merchanting, but were plainly inadequate as tools of management for businesses owning much fixed capital.

Again, many ideas on discipline were taken over from older organizations with comparable problems. Thus, there is the widespread realization that a manager must be given firm authority, and must not be overruled by his superiors:

> I have always considered that, for the maintenance of a proper authority in agents upon the spot, all business of an ordinary nature sh'd be left to their adjustment,

Sanderson, Lord Uxbridge's agent, wrote to Treweek, manager of the Mona Mine Co. Like views were expressed by William Brown

259

in regard to textile mills, by Gibbons in his discussion of management in ironworks, and by Hall in his advice to railway proprietors.[1] Similarly, it was realized, in the Cornish mines, for example, that a newly appointed 'captain' would have some initial difficulty in establishing his authority with his former workmates.[2]

But none of these problems was in any way limited to the new industrial enterprises. We have attempted to concentrate on those which were, and among them perhaps the outstanding first need was the achievement of some order, so that control could become rational and purposeful. Without it, the management could not even begin to handle the new large industrial complexes.

> The essence of technology lay in precise and orderly manipulation of the factors of production. Industrial leaders tried to control an ever larger number of elements bearing on the business undertaking—prices, markets, sources of raw materials, labour's willingness to work, legal conditions and public opinion.[3]

As these exceeded the span of control of a single individual, and as the needs of business created new structures of their own, a new order in business became both a symbol of rational capitalism and a necessity imposed by technological considerations.

We have noted above the widespread consensus of opinion that Owen's success as a manufacturer was largely due to the orderliness of his factory. Richard Arkwright before him equally impressed his visitors by the ingenuity of the layout and the order and regularity of the mills. His own pattern of factory design and disposition became the model of a whole industry for two generations to follow.

> He was introducing into every department of the manufacture, a system of industry, economy, order and cleanliness till then unknown in any great establishment where many people were employed together; but which he so effectively accomplished, that his example may be regarded as the pattern of almost all subsequent improvement.[4]

Many observers ranked this among the highest of Arkwright's achievements. When the water frame was being superseded by the mule in the mills,

> order, system and cleanliness in their arrangement became more necessary and more generally cultivated. This has been attended with good effects on the habits of the people. Being obliged to be more regular in their attendance on their work, they became more orderly in their conduct.[5]

Similarly, in the linen industry, John Marshall, as soon as he found his mills too large to be managed directly, 'relied instead on an elaborate system of rules and accounting'.[1]

In engineering, the Soho plant was the pioneer in 'establishing regulations . . . and bringing them to perfection'.[2] but it was not the only one. James Nasmyth, entering Maudslay's, another innovating enterprise, in 1828, was particularly impressed by

> the admirable order in the management that pervaded the whole establishment.[3]

In turn,

> Boulton explained to Wedgwood his book-keeping, his method of finance, his agencies, his system of accounts, and all the other points of business organization that were developing his rapidly expanding business.

As a result, inside Etruria, 'a minute division of labour and the development of factory discipline and control', showed that the lessons had been learned.[4] The potteries as a whole saw in this period

> a greater division of labour, a growth of the factory and the development of methods of control, i.e. the beginnings of scientific management and cost accounting.
>
> The records of that time also show a decided advance in the direction of works organisation and control.

G. Forrester's pottery was

> the first in which a regular plan for the arrangement of the separate places for the distinct processes was adopted,

and at Minton's, in 1829, there was

> a regular plan for usefulness, and reduction of labour.[5]

In ironmaking, Coalbrookdale had by 1800 developed regular cycles of furnace charging, and by about 1830 had developed norms of work and a rational management structure, including exact details of the position and duties of foremen. At the Carron ironworks, an exact routine was established early: the baskets with the charges were carefully measured and counted and a clock struck to determine the moment of charge and the time of tapping. Regular meetings and regular accounts were established in the 1760s and a

carefully-thought-out stock policy ensured that the stock assort-
ments were always balanced. At William Foster's ironworks, one of
the largest in the country in 1821, it was reported that 'an order and
regularity prevails throughout we have not seen in any other'. Other
works, like Dowlais, attempted to improve their performance by the
careful timekeeping of men and more careful stock-keeping.[1]

Similar advances in regularity, orderliness and consequent
potential powers of control could be quoted from coal-mining,
slate-quarrying, glassmaking and even canal-building. Elsewhere,
we have the first examples of printed forms for branch returns,
engine performances, instructions and contracts.[2] In some respects,
orderliness and regularity in one firm or industry depended on
similar order in parallel or supplying industries, and there is here
one of the key mechanisms for the development 'blocks' of industries
in industrializing economies. Thus, in naval block-making, perhaps
the first real mass-production industry outside textile spinning, the
benefits of the technical improvements were lost because of the
inability of the dockyard to organize the required regular supplies
of timber and other raw materials.

Perhaps even more significant than the orderly layout and
management of the plants was the fact that, in order to be worked
effectively and economically, some of the most important and
complex of them had to be pre-planned, in their entirety, as working
units before they were actually laid down. Such planning presup-
posed a modicum of conscious thought about the organization and
purpose of an industrial unit. The Soho Foundry is again the
classical example. As early as 1794 Boulton had written,

> to a person totally unacquainted with the Nature of a Manu-
> factory, it is not easily comprehensible what the requirements
> are of erecting and fully establishing a new Branch of Manu-
> facture; even to a Manufacturer himself it is not an easy task
> to form a direct and accurate judgment of the Buildings and
> Machinery that may be necessary for this purpose.

His own metalware manufactory was, in fact, anything but efficiently laid out. The Foundry, on the other hand, was the

> result of a definite systematic and preconceived plan of what the
> Soho Engine Manufactory should be.[3]

Other famous works planned beforehand were Etruria, built round
a number of courts, along a canal basin, with each workroom carefully sited as to light and the flow of the material, and Carron, for

which even ore assays were undertaken in Birmingham before the site was finally chosen.

In mining, the nature of the industry, as well as the cost of internal transport, made it necessary to develop a policy of looking years ahead in the sinking of new pits and the tapping of new strata. In Anglesey, for example, some miners were constantly preparing new workings well ahead of the completion of old ones, and at Wanlockhead 'some spare pickmen are always at work for making new discoveries of lead'. It was, however, in the large coal-mines that the viewers had to think farthest ahead.[1] In the iron industry technical need might require pre-planning of the flow of work, if not of the layout of the plant.[2] Brewing was another industry in which technical considerations, notably the early use of the steam engine, made complete pre-planning necessary. As early as 1742 a book of instructions noted:

> In erecting a large works of this kind, everything is to be considered that can save the labour of the people employed, for as everything is done in quantities, the difficulty of removing the ingredients from place to place would be very great, but for the help of such early care.[3]

Multi-storied cotton mills, like breweries, had to be designed to full size from the start. The standard layout, developed since Arkwright's day, did, however, require little more than a rectangular block with large rooms on each floor and easy communications between the floors. Such mills could be easily adapted to other uses or shared out between smaller firms hiring space and power. Nevertheless, rational planning was still essential for the siting:

> The site of the factory ought to be carefully selected in reference to the health of the operatives[!], the cheapness of provisions, the facilities of transport for the raw materials, and the convenience of the market for the manufactured articles,

and the supply of clean water and of fuel and water power ought to be 'primary considerations', wrote Ure. By the 1820s, in fact, not merely the siting, but also the general design of large cotton mills had ceased to be 'natural', and had become planned. A textbook on cotton mills of 1833 stressed the layout as important for the speed of work.

> It will be necessary that the various departments be so situated, as to prevent all unnecessary going to and from any apartments of the work by the workers employed about the establishment,

and, adding a touch of ergonomics over a century ahead of its time,

> whatever gives freedom to a workman in the performance of
> any piece of labour or removes incumbrances out of his way,
> will enable him to perform a greater quantity of labour at the
> same time.[1]

This was theoretical advice rather than actual practice; but of
Marshall's famous flax mill it was said in 1821,

> every man chases his business—in the others every man's
> business chases him. . . . The hands had very particular printed
> instructions set before them which are . . . particularly
> attended to.

When a machine shop was added in 1825 the large number of boys

> had their work regularly laid out and planned . . . so that they
> may go straight forward with it.[2]

A few years later the visitor to the various large London assembly
industry factories was struck particularly by the planned order of the
store-rooms. Thus at Broadwood's piano factory there was timber
enough for two years' output, or 5,000 pianos.

> Near the principal entrance to the premises . . . is the store-
> room of the principal foreman, in which all the smaller articles
> required in the manufacture are kept. This room, and the
> whole arrangements connected with it, are conducted on the
> most scrupulous system, an indispensable requisite where
> several hundred workmen are to be supplied with working
> materials.

Even in the relatively simple cotton industry

> There are generally various qualities of goods manufactured at
> the same time; so that the waste made from the finer, may be
> used up in the coarser; and the warp and weft are always made
> from different qualities of cotton.[3]

It will be clear how closely any pre-planning or orderly layout
in almost every single example given here is dependent on the
technical needs of the firm concerned. This close interdependence
between organizational planning and technology is even more
clearly illustrated in the highest form of organization and pre-

planning achieved at the time, the development of true industrial mass production. Among the forerunners was John Taylor, the Birmingham button-maker who divided his work into seventy different operations, in 1755, performed by seventy people. Matthew Boulton, his great rival, did not quite achieve such division of labour at the time, but had plans to mass-produce parts of clocks in the 1760s. Similar ideas were discussed between Boulton and Watt in the early days of the engine partnership, and it was the upsurge of demand for the rotative engines in 1782–6 which finally persuaded the partners to begin the standardization of the sizes of engines and components of engine parts: in 1786 James Watt proposed to his partner to 'methodize the rotative engines so as to get on with them at greater pace. Indeed that is already in some degree the case'.[1] The standardization of engines, the production of small engines for stock and the increasing exactitude of finish to allow interchangeability which were achieved in the Soho Foundry from about 1800 onwards had their origins in the firm's experience of a (relative) mass demand then. Brunel's and Maudslay's method of mass-producing naval blocks, developed just after the turn of the century, formed an early example of the woodworking industry, and large ironworks, like Carron, could combine the techniques of the foundry with the market needs of several types of cast products to go in for mass production even earlier. But it was engineering in which progress was most spectacular and most necessary. By the mid-thirties, Nasmyth's Manchester foundry had developed an assembly line for mass-producing pumps, lathes and other big items ahead of orders, while Vignoles, one of the great railway builders of the age, consulting a railway engineer over engines for the Dublin and Kingstown Railway, found that

> Mr. Dodds made a sketch for him, so that each locomotive should be a perfect duplication of the other, and that each detailed part of an engine should also be the duplicate of any other engine, so that the whole family should be exactly the same size, weight and kind, and thus a very small stock of detached parts need be kept in the stores.[2]

Mass production and the division of labour in greater or lesser degree of perfection did, of course, together with the new mechanical and chemical techniques, lie near the centre of the industrial revolution: Wedgwood, for example, who was helped by no startling mechanical invention, imposed a system of 'specialization and hitherto unheard-of division of labour',[3] and the same was even true of industries which did benefit from new capital equipment and new processes. It was these developments, occurring against a highly elastic and buoyant market, which caused the aggrandizement of some firms, and it was, in turn, this process of accretion and growth which had called forth the problems of management in the first place, together with the problems of differentiation of skill, both among workers and among managers. It implied that growth was no mere addition of like units, but a structuring as well. Whilst an older firm could be treated as consisting of separate units, as, for example, an ironworks strung out along a river for power, new methods, new steam power and the vastly greater scale of operations required their reconstruction as an organic whole, an 'organization'.[1] Again, whereas in the mid-eighteenth century industrialists were still usually in personal contact with their men, the growing

> number of different processes carried on by one employer, and the increase in the ground to be covered in supervision, made the introduction of wage-earning foremen and managers essential.[2]

As a result, there occurred simultaneously the creation of a managerial class[3] and departmentalization and experiments with management structure.

Departmentalized structure in this period developed in two main forms. One was a division of functions among partners and the members of their families, so that each became in effect a departmental head, with one or two paid managers under him. The other, in its ideal type form, centred on a single managing director, partnered by essentially inactive directors, and a group of fairly evenly matched managers branching out below him.

Typical examples of the former included the Walkers of Masbro', among whom a formidable list of family members' divided among themselves a large number of departments, Newton-Chambers after the reconstruction in 1831, and the Carron Company as a result of Gascoigne's reform of its management in 1769, all in the iron industry. In textiles the better-known examples included the Horrocks brothers, administering between them ten different mills by 1810, the Strutts, who shared the management of their five mills among the three brothers on the death of Jedediah in 1797, the large Scottish water-spinning combines, and the Marshalls of Leeds, dividing up control of their father's heritage in the 1830s. At Coalbrookdale the pendulum swung between the two methods. Prior to 1789 everything had been the direct responsibility of the manager, with no one in the position of head of department, to whom he could delegate oversight and decisions on running policy.

In that year, the firm became departmentalized, with

foremen and managers over several parts, and the general manager reported regularly to the meetings of the Darby owners.

From 1803 onwards, however, several more members of the family took up active management posts,

but maintained and extended the departmental divisions with the delegation of some parts of the works to under managers.

About 1830 central control appears to have been shared again by several partners dividing their functions.[1] At Dowlais the movement was clearly all one way. There was much confusion, and many tensions arose in the early years, 1760–4, when the several partners each took on some duties of management; they then transferred them to a single manager, continuing the obligation of buying their share of the output at a fixed price, and in 1767 the management was transferred to John Guest as manager-contractor, from which position he gradually proceeded to buy out the other partners.[2]

The other method, of a single managing partner controlling lower echelons of managers, ultimately proved to be more flexible in practice and therefore more favoured by go-ahead firms. Thus Gott considered himself to have merely provided the capital and kept ultimate control, and to have 'paid for the talents of others in the different branches of manufacture'. Robert Owen trained up four under-managers, one for each department, whom he could leave detailed instructions for the duration of his absences, and a similar development took place in the Boulton & Watt firm. In the large porter breweries more 'articulate' management allowed specialization of functions between the very different jobs of brewing, buying and accounting. At Dowlais the flexibility of the system was shown by the fact that the 'foundry' manager was given only very limited duties in 1784,

to manage the workmen, take orders, and see them Properly Executed and to keep the Books,

whilst, by contrast, in 1803 it was decided that whoever was to manage the subsidiary collieries must have as one of his qualifications, sufficient knowledge of men so as to be able to procure some when wanting.

A note of higher sophistication was struck at Nasmyth's foundry in 1839:

> the whole establishment is divided into departments, over each of which a foreman, or responsible person, is placed, whose duty is not only to see that the men under his superintendence produce good work, but also to endeavour to keep pace with the productive powers of all the other departments.[1]

Other pioneers of division and departmentalization include the Wedgwood works, the Bridgewater enterprises, and the Herculaneum Pottery.

Joint-stock companies and others with a multiple ownership tended to adopt a similar structure. Thus the Quaker Lead Co. appointed a 'general agent' for the North, i.e. the productive area, with 'overmen' (foremen) appointed from the more experienced miners and other workers, and between them another layer of 'mill agents', 'washing agents' and 'underground agents', respectively. Coalbrookdale, in the early nineteenth century, also began to take on the appearance of an impersonal firm, managed by a self-contained managerial hierarchy with well-defined duties. The Gas Light and Coke Co. quickly developed a similar structure, aided by subcommittees of directors.

Mining, in which most of the work was done out of sight, and in which a high degree of technical competence was essential, both for economical working and for safety, was among the earliest to develop a clearly defined management structure. This was true even of the earlier types of organizations owned by 'adventurer'-shareholders in the tin- and copper-mines of Cornwall, and in the lead-mines of Derbyshire and Scotland, as well as in the large Anglesey mining companies. It was even more true of coal, where large-scale organization under unified ownership made an early appearance and where safety was particularly important.

> [I] has one [overman] in each pit [William Brown wrote to Carlisle Spedding in 1754, in his rambling ungrammatical fashion], whose office is to keep the ways in proper order see the air courses and stoppings is right see the men works the coal to the most advantage place the work among the men so that one may not worry another in short has the whole and Sole Direction and charge under the Principal Viewer. Sometimes we are forced to sett an Assistant or two to a pit to help the overman and these we call Deputies or underovermen.

Ten years later he reported to Spedding's son that all the overmen and deputies went into Walker pit after an explosion and were killed by a second explosion, so that the work would have come to a halt unless Spedding could lend two or three experienced men for a short period.[1]

It was not only in the North-East that deeper mining meant the creation of a 'hierarchy of officials and workers'.[2] On the Fitzwilliam estates near Sheffield, for example, the 'overseer' put in charge of opening the Elsecar colliery in 1752 was paid an ordinary workman's wage plus £20 a year; but by 1797 the estate employed not only a 'General Inspector of all the collieries', 'whose business it must be to take the Accounts from the different Banksmen, make contracts, pay all wages and regulate the same from time to time with the workmen', but also an 'underground superintendent', and banksmen at all the pits. The Staff Instruction Book of the 1840s lists further posts, still within the estate.[3]

Thus the need for delegation of managerial power brought new skills and new forms of organization into existence. In the nascent civil engineering industry Telford's formidable list of duties as 'general Agent' for the Ellesmere canal in 1793 laid it down that he was to be

> General Agent, Surveyor, Engineer, Architect & Overlooker of the Canal and Clerk to this Committee and the Sub-Committee when appointed. To attend meetings, make reports, to superintend the cutting forming and making of the Canal and taking up and seeing to the due observance of the levels thereof, to make the Drawings and to submit such drawings to the consideration and correction of Mr. Wm. Jessop or the person employed by the said Company for the time being as their Principal Engineer.[4] To give instructions for contracts to attend himself (or some confidential person by him employed) to the execution of all the Contracts relative to the making and completing the said Canal. To pay Contractors and workmen and to keep accounts, His engagement to extend to all Architectural and Engineering business, reservoirs, wharfs and other works.

Yet within a short time he had not only subdelegated many of his duties but had in the process created the ranks of local engineers and specialist contracting firms with more or less permanent staffs and connections with engineers.[5] Large-scale building also depended on a hierarchy of reliable foremen and subcontractors.

In the cotton industry a class of mill (or works) managers was created which was said to 'form the soul of our factory system'.

Below them were the 'overseers', in charge of particular rooms or classes or workers, who were the men directly in contact with the women and children of the mills and gave the early cotton industry much of its ill repute. Even one of the most powerful masters, Sir Robert Peel the elder, complained that

> in my concerns, I have no opportunity of managing [the children] but through the medium of overseers; and I believe every other man must, in that situation, adopt that practice,

and suffer the overseers to overwork the children against the orders of the proprietors.[1]

The time taken to fashion out of the needs of the industry and the managerial personnel available an instrument of production which was organized rationally to carry out the intentions of its owners and managers might vary enormously, but might be as much as twenty to thirty years. After such a period, the more successful industrialists felt, with Marshall, that

> a concern directed, in the general plan of conducting it, by a good judgment, may be well and profitably managed in the detail by servants.[2]

The wheel had turned full circle since the days when it was held to be axiomatic that control by salaried managers was the quickest way to ruin. The more advanced industries, and the larger firms, had learnt to detach the function of management from the person of the proprietor and to see it as a separate set of activity, sensibly and rationally performed, if necessary, by a separate set of individuals.

III

We began by stressing the limited nature of this study and the narrow definitions of 'management' to which it was confined. Large areas of managerial responsibility, including sales, purchases, the provision of finance and technical innovation, have been left out. The remaining managerial functions discussed here, while they might appear to be a mixed bag, have at least two qualities in common. They have all been neglected both by historians and by nearly all articulate contemporaries, and they were essentially new during the industrial revolution, their novelty deriving directly from the novelty of large-scale centrally controlled industry itself.

The evidence assembled here shows that these problems of management, though widely ignored, were not negligible. They occupied much of the energy of the first generations of industrial entrepreneurs and managers at a time when they were already fully stretched by complex technological innovations and by social change. Some of the important features of the age, which may perhaps have appeared puzzling or inadequately accounted for in the past, can be explained by precisely this overloading of the managerial capacity. At the same time some important and lasting aspects of British industrial management, current until the present day, can be shown to derive directly from the conditions under which its genesis took place.

British society at the time of the industrial revolution was vigorous, mobile and inventive. The responses to the managerial challenges discussed here were immensely varied. Not all were equally successful and some were undoubtedly responsible for the failures of that period as well as for its achievements. While many of the practices have survived, more or less unchanged, to form the basis of managerial practices of the present day, others have been altered, though perhaps not improved, since.

Perhaps the most important conclusion to emerge is that 'management', in our sense, though not a barrier to progress, yet could not be shown to have been an initiator of change either. The pragmatic discovery of new methods was no doubt adequate, but management appears everywhere to have adapted itself merely to the needs of technology, discipline or financial control. Among the many competing explanations there can surely nowhere be a managerial theory of industrial revolutions.

This has further implications. The managerial methods adopted were sufficient for the needs of the day, for after all the industrialization of Great Britain did take place; but they were rarely very brilliant or very central. This may be another way of saying that they were nowhere very important. Needs which arose were adequately met, but it was other factors, such as technical invention, social tension, or the opening up of new markets which determined the need. It may be some such unspoken reasoning as this which may have been responsible for the neglect of the subject in the past.

This would be an underestimate of the role of management in the British industrializing economy. It is true that 'management' cannot explain industrial progress, still less the industrial revolution or the unique nature of the 'take-off'. It is not the mainspring to the mechanism so diligently looked for in so many quarters in recent years. But its influence on the texture of the new industrialism, on the new society created by it, was enormous. As far as our evidence goes, it seems to show that 'management' was the instrument, if not the originator, of many of the forces which shaped the peculiar forms of rational self-interest, the ambiguities of ownership and control of firms, and above all the class relations within industry, which became peculiar to Western industrial capitalism. There may be little autonomous causation in the field of 'management', but it is still worthy of study as a vital instrument through which social forces expressed themselves. With different management practices, things might have fallen out otherwise.

Unfortunately, our evidence does not go very far. The firms covered and the evidence surviving are highly selective, and not all the evidence which is available could be sifted: it is, perhaps, beyond the powers of a single pair of eyes. It may be, however, that this study has drawn attention to areas of research which might prove fruitful if tilled by other hands—even if some of the new evidence does require a revision of our own first tentative conclusions.

Notes

1   1 Reinhard Bendix, *Work and Authority in Industry. Ideologies of Management in the Course of Industrialization* (New York and London, 1956); L. Urwick and E. F. L. Brech, *The Making of Scientific Management* (1959 ed.), vol. 2, chapter 1; N. J. Smelser, *Social Change in the Industrial Revolution, an Application of Theory to the Lancashire Cotton Industry 1770–1840* (1959).

1   2 L. Urwick and E. F. L. Brech, *The Human Factor in Management, 1795–1943* (1944), p. 5; cf. also N. S. B. Gras, *Business and Capitalism, an Introduction to Business History* (New York, 1939), p. 189.

2   1 Bendix, pp. xvii–xviii, and Werner Sombart *Das Wirtschaftsleben im Zeitalter des Hochkapitalismus* (Munich and Leipzig, 1927), chapter 52.

2   2 F. Harbison and C. A. Myers, *Management in the Industrial World: An International Analysis* (New York, Toronto, London, 1959), p. 15, and the excellent summary of past and present views, pp. 8–15.

3   1 W. T. Easterbrook, 'The Entrepreneurial Function in Relation to Technological and Economic Change', in B. F. Hoselitz and W. E. Moore (ed.), *Industrialization and Society* (Unesco-Mouton, 1963), p. 62.

3   2 Arthur H. Cole, 'An Approach to the Study of Entrepreneurship', *J.Ec.H.* VI (Supplement, 1946), reprinted in F. C. Lane and J. C. Riemersma (ed.), *Enterprise and Secular Change* (1953), pp. 186, 193.

3   3 *The Entrepreneur* (Harvard University, Cambridge, Mass. 1957), pp. 50–51; Fritz Redlich, *Der Unternehmer* (Göttingen, 1964), pp. 97, 99, repr. from *American Journal of Economics and Sociology*, VIII (April, 1949).

4   1 Gras, pp. 193–4.

5   1 Bert F. Hoselitz, 'Main Concepts in the Analysis of the Social Implications of Technical Change', in *Industrialization and Society*, p. 23.

5   2 Harbison and Myers, p. 22. Italics in original.

7   1 J. U. Nef, 'The Progress of Technology and the Growth of Large-scale Industry in Great Britain, 1540–1640', *Ec.H.R.* VI (1934), p. 3. This is not the place to discuss the many doubtful methods by which Nef succeeds in enlarging the scale of early industrial enterprises.

7   2 Max Weber, *General Economic History* (1928), p. 334. Cf. his criticism of Sombart on those grounds, p. 309.

7   3 Ibid., p. 302.

8   1 W. B. Crump (ed.), *The Leeds Woollen Industry, 1780–1820* (Leeds, 1931), pp. vii, 26.

8   2 W. H. B. Court, 'Industrial Organization and Economic Progress in the Eighteenth-Century Midlands', *Trans.R.H.S.* 4th ser. XXVIII (1946), esp. p. 94.

8   3 Urwick and Brech, *The Making of Scientific Management*, vol. 2, pp. 8–12, 15.

9 1 Gras, pp. 190–1; T. S. Ashton, *An Economic History of England: The 18th Century* (1955), p. 122.

10 1 J. R. Immer, *The Development of Production Methods in Birmingham 1760–1851* (D.Phil. Thesis, Oxford, 1954), p. 294.

10 2 G. C. Allen, *The Industrial Development of Birmingham and the Black Country, 1860–1927* (1929), p. 114.

11 1 *Committee on the Woollen Manufacture of England*, B.P.P. (1806), III, p. 10; Herbert Heaton, 'Benjamin Gott and the Industrial Revolution in Yorkshire', *Ec.H.R.* III (January 1931), p. 51; *idem. The Yorkshire Woollen and Worsted Industries* (Oxford, 1920), p. 352; D. C. Coleman, 'Technology and Economic History', *Ec.H.R.*, 2nd ser. XI (April, 1959), 509.

11 2 W. J. Ashley, *The Economic Organisation of England* (1914), pp. 149–53; Henry Smith, *Retail Distribution, a Critical Analysis* (1948 ed.), p. 121.

12 1 N. S. B. Gras, *Industrial Evolution* (1930), p. 77.

12 2 H. D. Fong, *Triumph of the Factory System in England* (Tientsin, 1930), p. 16.

12 3 Sombart, *Hochkapitalismus*, pp. 38–41.

12 4 See the brilliant analysis in Josef Kulischer, *Allgemeine Wirtschaftsgeschichte des Mittelalters and der Neuzeit* (Munich 1928, repr. 1958), vol. 2, p. 156.

13 1 Adam Smith, *Wealth of Nations* (Cannan ed. 1904), vol. 2, pp. 233, 246, 248, cf. also A. B. Dubois, *The English Business Company after the Bubble Act, 1720–1800* (New York, 1938), p. 91.

13 2 Josiah Tucker, *A Brief Essay on Trade* (3rd ed. 1753), pp. 70–71.

13 3 Cf. George Unwin, *Studies in Economic History* (1927), Part II, chapter V (iv).

13 4 *Wealth of Nations*, vol. 2, p. 246. Adam Smith did not think the Abbé's list quite accurate.

15 1 M. B. Donald, *Elizabethan Monopolies. The History of the Company of the Mineral and Battery Works from 1565 to 1604* (Edinburgh and London, 1961), p. 93.

15 2 Or to learn them: 'The Elizabethan statesmen imported technicians to develop not only copper smelting but a number of other industries. To safeguard their interests, so they thought, they put Englishmen on the board of directors to observe what was being done. Their mistake was that no amount of observation by a non-technically trained person will make him adequate to take over and develop new ideas. When the Germans died their skill died with them.' M. B. Donald, *Elizabethan Copper, the History of the Company of Mines Royal, 1568–1605* (1955), p. 3, also p. 368.

15 3 Quoted in D. Glyn John, *Contributions to the Economic History of South Wales* (D.Sc. Thesis, Wales, 1930), vol. 1, Part I, pp. 20–21.

15 4 H. Hamilton, *The English Brass and Copper Industries to 1800* (1926), esp. pp. 12–13, 37, 44–48, 82–85; Donald, *Elizabethan Copper*, esp. pp. 23, 252; *Elizabethan Monopolies*, pp. 93, 117; S. R. Meyrick, *The History and Antiquities of the County of Cardigan* (1810), pp. ccxviii ff; W. G. Collingwood, *Elizabethan Keswick* (Kendal, 1912) esp. pp. 190–1; D. G. John, vol. 1, esp. Parts 2, 5; Rhys Jenkins, 'The Society for the Mines Royal and the German Colony in the Lake District', *Trans.N.S.* XVIII (1937–8), 225–

15   4 234; Lionel Williams, 'The Exploitation of Cornish Copper and Lead Ores and Copper Smelting at Neath, 1583–1587', *Trans. Glamorgan Local History Society*, III (1959); W. R. Scott, *The Constitution and Finance of English, Scottish and Irish Joint-stock Companies to 1720* (vol. 2, Cambridge, 1910), pp. 383 ff., 413 ff.

15   5 D. S. Davis, 'The Records of the Mines Royal and the Mineral and Battery Works', *Ec.H.R.* VI (April, 1936), p. 211.

15   6 Samuel Smiles, *Lives of the Engineers* (1904 ed.) I, 111–12; D. J. Davies, *The Economic History of South Wales Prior to 1800* (Cardiff, 1933), pp. 72 ff.

15   7 Edward Hughes, 'The Monopoly of Salt in the Years 1563–71' *English Historical Review* XL (June 1925).

15   8 Maud Sellers, 'Industries', in *V.C.H. Durham* (1907), II, 297; W. R. Scott, vol. 1, p. 210, vol. 2, pp. 469–70.

16   1 George Unwin, *Industrial Organisation in the Sixteenth and Seventeenth Centuries* (Oxford, 1904), pp. 155 *passim*.

16   2 G. N. Clark, 'Early Capitalism and Invention', *Ec.H.R.* VI (1936), 151. Some eighteenth-century schemes fared a little better, e.g. that of the Framework Knitters' Company in 1720–30, but this affected only trade and not production, F. A. Wells, *The British Hosiery Trade* (1935), pp. 45–47.

16   3 John Lord, *Capital and Steam-Power* (1923), p. 70, note 1.

17   1 W. R. Scott, vol. 3, pp. 418–434; David Murray, *The York Buildings Company, A Chapter in Scotch History* (Glasgow, 1883).

17   2 K. G. Davies, 'Joint-Stock Investment in the later Seventeenth Century', *Ec.H.R.* 2nd ser., IV (1952); W. R. Scott, vol. 1, chapter 17, vol. 2, Division IV, sections 5, 6, 8–12, vol. 3, Div. VIII, secs. 3–9, Div. IX, secs. 3, 4B, 7.

17   3 *Report of the Committee appointed to enquire into the State of the Copper Mines and Copper Trade of this Kingdom*, B.P.P. 7th May 1799, Ev. Thos. Williams, p. 47; R. A. Mott, 'Abraham Darby (I and II) and the Coal-Iron Industry', *Trans. N.S.* XXXI (1957–9), p. 59; Rhys Jenkins, 'The Copper Works at Redbrook and at Bristol', *Trans. Bristol and Glos. Arch. Soc.* LXIII (1942), p. 158; W. R. Scott, II, 430 ff.

18   1 Arthur Raistrick, *Quakers in Science and Industry* (1950), p. 166; *Two Centuries of Industrial Welfare, The London (Quaker) Lead Company, 1692–1905* (1938), p. 117 and his 'The London Lead Company, 1692–1905', *Trans.N.S.* XIV (1933–4), 125.

18   2 'London Lead Company', p. 140. Yet close inspection continued, cf. the visit of two Directors to the North, with power to 'place, displace, suspend or discharge such of the Company's Agents, Accountants and Servants, as they shall find occasion to do', Quaker Lead Company, *Court of Assistants' Minute Books* (MS), 6/8/1778. Also, e.g. inspection of Derbyshire, ibid. 5/8, 2/9, 15/11/ 1773, 21/3, 5/5, 9/5, 12/5, 16/5, 19/5/1774, 31/1/1775.

18   3 'London Lead Company', p. 147.

19   1 e.g. William Shiers, *A Familiar Discourse or Dialogue concerning the Mine Adventure* (1709), esp. pp. 18–19, 37; and the reply by William Waller, *The Mine Adventure Laid Open* (1710); Sir Humphrey Mackworth, *A Short State of the Case and Proceedings of the Company of Mine Adventurers* (1710), pp. 10, 20.

Notes

19 2 Shiers, op cit., p. 37, also pp. 54–5 below.
19 3 All based on William Waller, *An Essay on the Value of the Mines, late of Sir Carbery Price* (1698), pp. 8–9, 26–27.
19 4 *Report of the Committee of the House of Commons, re the Petitions of Several Creditors and Proprietors of the Mine-Adventurers of England* (Feb. 1709/10).
19 5 D. J. Davies, p. 132.
20 1 J. M. Norris, 'The Struggle for Carron, Samuel Garbett and Charles Gascoigne', *Scottish Hist. Review*, XXXVII (1958), 136.
20 2 R. H. Campbell, *Carron Company* (Edinburgh and London, 1961).
20 3 H. W. Dickinson, *James Watt, Craftsman and Engineer* (Cambridge 1935), p. 149; A. D. Insull, *The Albion Mill Story* (B. A. Dissertation, Nottingham, 1955).
20 4 Hamilton, esp. pp. 169–201; S. Timmins (ed.), *Birmingham and the Midland Hardware District* (1866), p. 252; T. C. Barker and J. R. Harris, *A Merseyside Town in the Industrial Revolution: St. Helens, 1750–1900* (Liverpool, 1954), pp. 144–6.
20 5 Charles Hadfield, *British Canals, an Illustrated History* (1950), p. 65.
21 1 e.g. A. H. Dodd, *The Industrial Revolution in North Wales* (Cardiff, 1933), p. 216.
21 2 Henry English, *A Compendium . . . Relating to the Companies Formed for Working British Mines* (1826), pp. 1–3, 84.
21 3 e.g. N. McKendrick, 'Josiah Wedgwood and Factory Discipline', *Historical Journal*, IV (1961), 39; A. E. Musson and Eric Robinson, 'The Early Growth of Steam Power', *Ec.H.R.*, 2nd Ser. XI (1959), 434; Campbell, *Carron Company*, pp. 110–111; Stirling Everard, *The History of the Gas, Light and Coke Company, 1812–1949* (1949), p. 157. See also pp. 218–9 below.
21 4 E. Baines, jun., *History of the Cotton Manufacture in Great Britain* (1835), p. 126; John Kennedy, *Miscellaneous Papers* (Manchester, 1849), p. 24.
21 5 *Co-operative Magazine*, March 1826, p. 91.
21 6 *S.C. on the Children Employed in the Manufactories of the United Kingdom*, B.P.P. (1816) 111, Ev. Sir Robert Peel, p. 136.
21 7 *S.C. on the Silk Trade*, B.P.P. (1831–2) XIX, QQ. 2393–4.
22 1 J.C., *The Compleat Collier* (1708, Ed. 1845) pp. 9–10; *Tyne Mercury*, 22nd September, 1829. Letter by John Bedlington.
22 2 D. C. Coleman, *The British Paper Industry 1495–1860* (1958), p. 234.
22 3 M. W. Flinn, *Men of Iron, the Crowleys in the Early Iron Industry* (Edinburgh, 1962), pp. 100, 194.
22 4 Alan Birch, 'The Haigh Iron Works, 1789–1856; A Nobleman's Enterprise During the Industrial Revolution', *Bull. John Ryland's Library*, XXXV (March 1953), pp. 323, 330.
22 5 *Wentworth-Woodhouse Muniments* (MS) F. 107c, William Newman to Earl Fitzwilliam, 9th June, 1819; John P. Addis, *The Crawshay Dynasty. A Study in Industrial Organisation and Development, 1765–1867* (Cardiff, 1957), p. 134.
23 1 *British Transport Commission Archives* (York)(MS) SAD/1/28, Letter 28th July, 1821.
23 2 Clark, 'Early Capitalism', p. 153.
23 3 George Unwin, *Studies in Economic History*, p. 324.

276

CHAPTER 2

26 1 G. E. Fussell (ed.) *Robert Loder's Farm Accounts, 1610–1620* (Camden Society, Third Series, vol. 53, 1936) pp. xxiii, xxx; Conyers Read 'Lord Burleigh's Household Accounts', *Ec.H.R.* (December, 1956); A. C. Littleton, *Essays in Accountancy*, (Urbana, Illinois, 1961), pp. 40 ff.

26 2 G. E. Mingay, *English Landed Society in the Eighteenth Century* (1963), p. 174.

26 3 W. H. B. Court, *The Rise of the Midland Industries, 1600–1838* (1938), p. 153; *Arundel Castle Muniments* (MS. Sheffield City Library) S. 185; R. A. C. Parker 'Coke of Norfolk and the Agrarian Revolution', *Ec.H.R.*, Second Series, VIII (December, 1955), pp. 160–3; also his *Financial and Economic Affairs of the Cokes of Holkham, Norfolk, 1707–1842* (D.Phil. Thesis, Oxford, 1956), pp. 7 ff., 186 ff.; F. J. Monkhouse, 'An Eighteenth Century Company Promoter', *Transactions of the Cumberland and Westmorland Antiquarian and Archaeological Society*, NS, vol. 40 (1940), p. 142.

27 1 Edward Laurence, *The Duty of a Steward to His Lord* (1727), originally written for the several Stewards of the Duke of Buckingham; also cf. R. S. Edwards, 'Some notes on the early literature and development of Cost Accounting in Great Britain', *The Accountant*, vol. 97, N.S. (1937), p. 226; G. E. Mingay, 'Estate Management in Eighteenth-Century Kent', *Agricultural History Review*, 4 (1956); 'The Surveyor', *Ec.H.R.*, XVII (1947), 121; George Clarke, *The Landed-Man's Assistant, or, The Steward's Vade Mecum* (1715); J. Richards, *The Gentleman's Steward and Tenants of Manors Instructed* (1730).

27 2 Many Estate Offices possess long runs of Accounts, kept in identical form for very long periods. As a good example, cf. *Middleton of Woollaton Muniments*, (Nottingham University) MiA 220–57, Middleton Estate 1678/9 to 1716.

27 3 *Wentworth-Woodhouse Muniments A.* 1389. Also, *Tehidy Estate MSS.* (Camborne) Memorandum Book, 1756; Edward Hughes, *North Country Life in the Eighteenth Century* (1952), p. 74; idem 'The Eighteenth-Century Estate Agent' in *Essays in British and Irish History* ed. Cronne, Moody and Quinn, pp. 195–6; E. M. Jancey, 'An Eighteenth-Century Steward and his Work', *Transactions of the Shropshire Archaeological Society* 56/Part I (1957–8), pp. 36 ff..

28 1 J. D. Bailey, 'Australian Borrowing in Scotland in the Nineteenth Century', *Ec.H.R.*, Second Series, XII (December, 1959), p. 268. Also, Robert Robson, *The Attorney in Eighteenth Century England* (Cambridge 1959), pp. 68 ff., 85 ff.

28 2 Hughes, 'Estate Agent', pp. 189–92; Parker, *Cokes of Holkham*, pp. 213 ff.; Sydney B. Donkin, 'Bryan Donkin, F.R.S., M.I.C.E., 1768–1855', *Trans.N.S.*, XXVII (1949–59), p. 85; David Solomon, 'The Historical Development of Costing', in David Solomon (ed.) *Studies in Costing* (1952), p. 5. For a similar eminence in Plantation Economy and a veritable 'school of Plantership in the West Indies' cf. R. B. Sheridan, 'The Rise of a Colonial Gentry;

Notes

28 2 A case study of Antigua, 1730–1775', *Ec.H.R.*, Second Series, XIII (April, 1961), p. 353.
28 3 Peter Mathias, *The Brewing Industry in England, 1700–1830* (Cambridge, 1959), p. 156, n. 1.
28 4 Mingay, op. cit., p. 59.
28 5 F. M. L. Thompson, *English Landed Society in the Nineteenth Century* (1963), p. 166.
29 1 Crump, *Leeds Woollen Industry*, pp. 268–70; C. F. Dendy Marshall, 'The Liverpool and Manchester Railway', *Trans.N.S.*, II (1921–2), p. 12; *Trans.N.S.*, XI (1930–1), p. 165; Hugh Malet, *The Canal Duke. A Biography of Francis, Third Duke of Bridgwater* (Dawlish, London, 1961), pp. 100–1; G. G. Hopkinson, 'Lead Mining in Eighteenth-Century Ashover', *Journal of the Derbyshire Archaeological and Natural History Society*, LXII (1952), p. 2; *idem* 'Five Generations of Derbyshire Lead Mining and Smelting, 1739–1858', ibid. LXXVII (1960), p. 9–11; A. G. Davis, 'William Smith, Civil Engineer, Geologist (1769–1839)' *Trans.N.S.*, XXIII (1942–3).
29 2 A. H. John, *The Industrial Development of South Wales, 1750–1850* (Cardiff, 1950), p. 7; Hughes, 'Estate Agent', p. 197; *Middleton of Woollaton Muniments*, Mi Ac 135; G. G. Hopkinson, *The Development of Lead Mining and the Coal and Iron Industries of North Derbyshire and South Yorkshire, 1700–1850* (Ph.D. Thesis, Sheffield, 1958), pp. 233, 333.
29 3 Parker, *Cokes of Holkham*, pp. 68–69; *Tehidy Estates MSS.* Proposals and Answers, 1756–1790, 18th June, 1762.
30 1 *Wentworth-Woodhouse Muniments*, F70e, 70i, 98, 99a, 105; John Rowlands, *Study of some of the Social and Economic Changes in the Town and Parish of Amlwch, 1750–1850* (M.A. Thesis, Wales, 1960), pp. 89–91, 140–1; *Mona Mine MSS.* (University College of North Wales, Bangor), nos. 1271, 1279, 2244–51, 3755; Malet, op cit., pp. 91, 102, 129–30.
30 2 W. E. Minchinton, 'The Merchant in England in the Eighteenth Century', in *The Entrepreneur*, p. 22; R. Campbell, *The London Tradesman* (1747), pp. 82–83; Malachi Postlethwayt, *The Merchant's Public Counting-House* (1750); J. Aikin, *A Description of the country from 30–40 Miles Round Manchester* (2 vols., 1795), p. 184; R. B. Westerfield, *Middleman in English Business, 1660–1760* (New Haven, 1915), p. 395; R. M. Hartwell, *The Yorkshire Woollen and Worsted Industry, 1800–1850* (D.Phil. Thesis, Oxford, 1955), p. 300; Hughes *North Country Life*, pp. 104–5.
30 3 S.C., *House of Lords, on The State of the Wool Trade* (B.P.P., 1828, 515), p. 289; cf. also Heaton, 'Benjamin Gott', pp. 47–48; Paul Mantoux, *The Industrial Revolution in the Eighteenth Century* (1961 ed.), pp. 265–6.
31 1 L. B. Namier, 'Anthony Bacon, M.P., an Eighteenth Century Merchant', *Journal of Economic and Business History*, II (November, 1929).
31 2 Lord, *Capital and Steam-Power*, p. 132; Jacob Strieder, 'Origin and Evolution of Early European Capitalism', *Journal of Economic and Business History*, II (November, 1929), p. 18; S. M. Ames, 'A Typical Businessman of the Revolutionary Era: Nathaniel

31 2 Littleton Savage and His Account Book', ibid, III (May 1931), pp. 410–11; J. H. Soltow, 'Scottish Traders in Virginia, 1750–1775', *Ec.H.R.*, Second Series, XII (August, 1959); Gras, op. cit., pp. 132–3.

31 3 e.g. G. W. Daniels, *The Early English Cotton Industry* (Manchester, 1920), pp. 36, 143; Mantoux, op. cit., pp. 57–62; G. H. Tupling, *The Economic History of Rossendale* (Manchester, 1927), p. 188; Wells, *British Hosiery Trade*, pp. 77 ff.; G. I. H. Lloyd, *The Cutlery Trades* (1913), pp. 14 ff.; Carl Bücher, *Industrial Evolution* (1901), pp. 171 ff., 198 ff.; Coleman, 'Technology', p. 509.

31 4 Ashley, *Economic Organisation of England*, p. 145.

32 1 A. P. Wadsworth and J. De L. Mann, *The Cotton Trade and Industrial Lancashire: 1600–1780* (Manchester, 1931), p. 211. Also, Daniel Defoe, *A Plan of the English Commerce* (Oxford, 1928 reprint), p. 63; and p. 96 below.

32 2 William Radcliffe, *Origins of the New Systems of Manufacture Commonly Called Powerloom Weaving*, (Stockport, 1828), p. 231; Wadsworth & Mann, op. cit., pp. 282, 302; Frank Atkinson (ed.), *Some Aspects of the Eighteenth Century Woollen and Worsted Trade in Halifax* (Halifax, 1956), p. VIII; *S.C. on the Wool Trade* (1828), p. 146; *S.C. on Manufactures, Commerce and Shipping* (B.P.P. 1833, p. 690), evid. Henry Hughes, Q. 1, 320; *Committee on Orders in Council* (B.P.P. 1812, III. 210), evid. James Kay, p. 217, Thomas Cardwell, p. 282; *S.C. on the Silk Trade* (1831–2) evid. R. S. Cox, Q. 2,055, J. S. Ward, *passim*, Joseph Grout, 10,285; *J.H.C.*, 1765, pp. 212–19; *Committee on Cotton Weavers' Petition* (B.P.P., 1802–3, VIII) evid. Patrick Murran, p. 112; K. H. Burley, 'Some Accounting Records of an Eighteenth Century Clothier', *Accounting Research*, IX (1958), pp. 50–51; P. Russell (ed.), *England Displayed* (1769), p. 90; N. L. and Archibald Clow, 'George Mackintosh (1737–1807) and Charles Mackintosh (1766–1842)', *Chemistry and Industry*, 62 (1943), p. 104; Wells, op. cit., p. 83; D. F. McDonald, *Scotland's Shifting Population, 1770–1850* (Glasgow, 1937), p. 80; E. M. Sigsworth, *Black Dyke Mills* (Liverpool, 1958), p. 141.

32 3 Court, op. cit., p. 202; R. S. Fitton and A. P. Wadsworth, *The Strutts and the Arkwrights, 1758–30. A Study of the Early Factory System* (Manchester, 1958) pp. 56–57; George Unwin, 'The Transition to the Factory System', *English Historical Review*, XXVII (1922), p. 384; Louis W. Moffit, *England on the Eve of the Industrial Revolution* (1925), p. 198; Daniels, op. cit., pp. 39, 143.

32 4 Evelyn Gibson Nelson, 'The Putting-Out System in the English Framework-Knitting Industry', *Journal of Economic and Business History*, II (1930), p. 485; Wadsworth and Mann, pp. 274–6, 284; J. D. Chambers, *Nottinghamshire in the Eighteenth Century* (1932), pp. 127–33; *S.C. on Manufactures* (1833) evid. George Smith, QQ. 9033, 9270, 9344–5, 9365; Pinchbeck, op. cit., p. 137; Tupling, op. cit., p. 200; Wells, op. cit., p. 72. In the Northern coalfield, however, the 'undertaker' was an independent firm leasing a complete pit from the landowner.

32 5 K. H. Burley, 'An Essex Clothier of the Eighteenth Century', *Ec.H.R.*, Second Series, XI (December, 1958), p. 292; *idem*,

32 5 'Some Accounting Records of an Eighteenth Century Clothier', *Accounting Research* IX (1958), pp. 55–56; George Unwin *et al*, *Samuel Oldknow and the Arkwrights* (Manchester, 1924), p. 49.

32 6 T. S. Ashton, *An Eighteenth Century Industrialist, Peter Stubs of Warrington, 1756–1806* (Manchester, 1939), pp. 9, 21, 34–36, 71; *idem*, 'The Domestic System in the Early Lancashire Wool Trade' *Economy History*, I (January, 1926), p. 137, n. 1; and 'The Records of a Pin Manufactory, 1814–21', *Economica* V (1925), p. 281–3, 288; Fitton and Wadsworth, op. cit., pp. 47–49.

33 1 J. De L. Mann, 'Textile Industries since 1550' in *V.C.H. Wiltshire*, IV (1959), p. 162.

33 2 Joseph Koulischer, 'La Grande Industrie aux XVIIe et XVIIIe Siècles: France, Allemagne, Russie', *Annales d'Histoire Economique et Sociale*, III (January, 1931), p. 29; *Committee on Woollen Manufacturers* (1806), evid. Law Atkinson, p. 220; W. B. Crump and Gertrude Ghorbal, *History of the Huddersfield Woollen Industry* (Huddersfield, 1935), p. 92.

33 3 *Committee on Woollen Clothers' Petition* (B.P.P., 1802–3 V.) evid. Edward Shephard, p. 15.

33 4 Hopkinson, *The Development*, p. 230; Ashton, *Peter Stubs*, pp. 26–27; *idem*. 'Domestic System', p. 139.

34 1 Smelser, op. cit., p. 142.

34 2 A. B. Levy, *Private Corporations and their Control* (1950, 2 vols.), p. 339; P. Mantoux, op. cit., p. 63; Julia De L. Mann (ed.), *Documents Illustrating the Wiltshire Textile Trades in the Eighteenth Century* (Devizes, 1964), p. xxiv.

34 3 *S.C. on Artizans and Machinery* (B.P.P. 1824, V., 51), evid. Obediah Williams, pp. 283–4; *Committee on Woollen Clothiers* (1802–3), evid. A. L. Edridge, pp. 7–8; *Minutes of Committee on Cotton Weavers' Petition* (B.P.P., 1802–3, VIII).

34 4 W. Sombart, *Der Moderne Kapitalismus* (Munich and Leipzig, third ed., 1919) II, 2, 727; Maurice Dobb, *Studies in the Development of Capitalism* (1946), pp. 143–5; W. G. Hoskins, *Industry, Trade and People in Exeter, 1688–1800* (Manchester, 1935), pp. 14–16.

34 5 Charles Wilson 'The Entrepreneur in the Industrial Revolution', *History*, XLII (1957), p. 105; Fong, op. cit., p. 71; Charles Babbage, *On the Economy of Machinery and Manufacturers* (1833, third ed.), p. 223; H. Sée, *Les origines du capitalisme moderne* (Paris, 1926), p. 139.

35 1 H. Hamilton, *The Industrial Revolution in Scotland* (Oxford, 1932), pp. 125, 137–8; and *Economic History of Scotland in the Eighteenth Century* (1963), pp. 171–8; Alexander Cullen, *Adventures in Socialism* (Glasgow, 1910), pp. 3–4; G. M. Mitchell, 'The English and Scottish Cotton Industries: A Study in Interrelations', *Scottish Historical Review*, XXII (January, 1925), pp. 102–3; J. H. Clapham, 'Some Factory Statistics of 1815–16' *Economic Journal*, XXV (September, 1915), p. 476; D. F. McDonald, op. cit., pp. 53, 59; *Factories Inquiry Commission*, I, A2, p. 37, Alexander Cooper; Wadsworth and Mann, p. 171; *S.C. on Manufactures* (1833) evid. Kirkman Finlay, Q. 1204; Sir John Sinclair, *(Old) Statistical Accounts of Scotland* (Edinburgh, 1795) XV, 37.

35 2 Tupling, op. cit., p. 210.

35 3 Unwin, 'Transition', pp. 215, 384, 387; Pinchbeck, op. cit., p. 152; *Lords' Committee on the Factories Bill* (B.P.P. 1818, XCVI), p. 23; Wadsworth and Mann, pp. 284–307; *Lords' Committee on Apprentices* (1818–19), p. 23; *S.C. on Manufactures* (1833), evid. George Smith, Q. 9032–5, 9270, James Grimshaw, Q. 10050; Unwin, *Oldknow*, esp. p. 45; M. H. Mackenzie 'The Bakewell Mill and the Arkwrights', *Journal Derbyshire Archaeological and Natural History Society*, 79 (1959), pp. 77–78; *Factories Inquiry Commission*, I, A1, p. 69.

36 1 *Factories Inquiry Commission*, I, B1, p. 105; John Horner, *The Linen Trade of Europe during the Spinning-Wheel Period* (Belfast, 1920), p. 95; N. K. A. Rothstein, *The Silk Industry in London, 1702–1766* (M.A. Thesis, London, 1961), pp. 136–9, 170–1; *Committee on Petition of (Silk) Ribbon Weavers* (B.P.P. 1818, 134, IX), evid. Henry Critchley, p. 76.

36 2 Fitton and Wadsworth, pp. 55–56, 198; *Factories Inquiry Commission*, I, B1, pp. 69, 80, 83, 84; Chambers, *Nottinghamshire*, p. 133.

36 3 *Committee on Woollen Manufactures* (1806), Report, pp. 4–5; Wadsworth and Mann, pp. 384–5.

36 4 John Prest, *The Industrial Revolution in Coventry* (1960), ch. 6; Thomas Kelly, *George Birkbeck, Pioneer of Adult Education* (Liverpool, 1957), pp. 2–3; David Loch, *Essay on the Trade, Commerce and Manufacturers of Scotland* (Edinburgh, 1775), pp. 46–47; A. P. Usher, *An Introduction to the Industrial History of England* (1921), p. 348.

36 5 Crump, *Leeds Woollen Industry*, p. 23; H. Heaton, 'Benjamin Gott and the Anglo-American Cloth Trade', *Journal of Economic and Business History*, II (November 29), p. 149; Crump and Ghorbal, p. 93; J. Morris, *The West of England Woollen Industry* (M.Sc. Econ. Thesis) reported in *Bulletin of the Institute of Historical Research*, XIII (1935–6), p. 108; Tupling, op. cit., pp. 196–9.

37 1 William Turner, *The Warrington Academy, 1757–1786* (Warrington, 1957), pp. 47–49; J. L. and B. Hammond, *The Skilled Labourer, 1760–1832* (2nd ed. 1920), p. 198; Clapham 'Factory Statistics', p. 477; *Factories Inquiry Commission*, I, B1, pp. 59, 62, 89–99; R. M. Hartwell, op. cit., pp. 623, 630–2; *S.C. on Manufactures* (1833) evid. John Brooke QQ. 1919–23; *Committee on Woollen Manufactures* (1806) evid. Law Atkinson, p. 220, James Walker; Mann, 'Textile Industries', p. 172; R. P. Beckinsale (ed.) *The Trowbridge Woollen Industry as Illustrated by the Stock Books of John and Thomas Clark 1804–1824* (Devizes, 1951), p. xxxii.

37 2 Crump and Ghorbal, pp. 116–19; Sir Richard Phillips, *A Personal Tour Through the United Kingdom* (1828), p. 50; *Factories Inquiry Commission*, I, B1, Details of Messrs. George Hooman, Donald MacLean, Thomas Jones, D. P. Watkins and Edward Bernard, all Kidderminster Carpet Weavers, pp. 14, 35, 36, 38, 40; A. P. Usher, op. cit., p. 351; Maud Sellers, in *V.C.H. Durham*, II, 318.

37 3 Warmley Co. Petition ((M.S. 1769, B.M. Add MSS. 36221).

38 1 A. J. Taylor, 'The Sub-Contract System in the British Coal Industry' in L. S. Pressnell (ed.) *Studies in the Industrial Revolution. Essays presented to T. S. Ashton* (1960), p. 216, quoting esp. D. F. Schloss, G. C. Allen, and A. H. John, also cf. pp. 229—30;

38   1 Wilhem Abel, 'Die Landwirtschaftlichen Grossbetriebe Deutschlands' in *Contributions to First Conference of Economic Historians, Stockholm 1960* (Paris, 1960), p. 317.

39   1 Taylor, loc. cit, p. 233; W. E. Minchington, *The British Tinplate Industry, A History* (Oxford, 1957), p. 20; Bendix, op. cit, p. 53 and fn. 81 for examples.

39   2 Dobb, op. cit., pp. 242–9.

40   1 Hopkinson, *Developments*, p. 199; *Spencer-Stanhope Muniments* (MSS., Sheffield City Library); Rhys Jenkins, 'Iron Making in the Forest of Dean', *Trans.N.S.*, VI (1925–6), pp. 57–58; A. H. John (ed.), *The Walker Family, Ironfounders and Lead Manufacturers 1741–1893* (1951), Introduction; R. L. Downes, 'The Stour Partnership, 1726–36, a note on landed capital in the iron industry', *Ec.H.R.*, second series, III (1950), pp. 90–96; R. A. Mott, 'The Coalbrookdale Group Horsehay Works', *Trans.N.S.*, 31 (1957–9), p. 273; R. G. Awty, 'Charcoal Iron Masters of Cheshire and Lancashire, 1800–1785', *Trans. of Historical Society of Lancashire and Cheshire*, 109 (1957), pp. 71–124; B. L. C. Johnson, *The Charcoal Iron Trade in the Midlands: 1690–1720* (M.A. Thesis, Birmingham, 1950), pp. 4 ff., 167–8; 'Foley Partnerships, The Iron Industry at the end of the Charcoal Era', *Ec.H.R.*, 2nd series, IV (1952); A. Raistrick, 'South Yorkshire Iron Industry', *Trans. N.S.* 19, (1938–9); Court, *Midlands Industries*, p. 105; A. Raistrick and E. Allen, 'The South Yorkshire Iron Masters (1690–1750)', *Ec.H.R.* IX (May, 1939).

40   2 G. Jars, *Voyages Métallurgiques* (Lyons, 1774), p. 277; Raistrick, *Quakers in Science and Industry*, p. 120; idem., *Dynasty of Ironfounders, The Darbys and Coalbrookdale* (1953), pp. 42–44, 87–88; P. S. Bebbington, *Samuel Garbett, 1717–1803, A Birmingham Pioneer* (M.Com. Thesis, Birmingham, 1938), p. 13; T. Rees, *A. Topographical and Historical Description of South Wales* (1815), p. 607; M. W. Flinn, *Men of Iron*, pp. 7–8, 30; W. H. Chaloner, 'Isaac Wilkinson, Pot Founder' in *Studies in the Industrial Revolution*, p. 41; M. W. Flinn, 'The Lloyds in the Early English Iron Industry', *Business History*, II (December, 1959), p. 31; Samuel Lloyd, *The Lloyds of Birmingham* (Birmingham, 1907); A. S. Davies, 'The Early English Iron Industry in North Wales', *Trans.N.S.* 25 (1945–7).

41   1 Court, *Rise of Midlands Industries*, p. 124; Rhys Jenkins, 'Early Engineering and Ironfounding in Cornwall', *Trans.N.S.*, XXIII (1942–3), p. 28; Robert Owen, *Life of Owen, by Himself* (1920 ed.), pp. 81, 101; Erich Roll, *An Early Experiment in Industrial Organisation, being a History of the firm of Boulton & Watt, 1775–1805* (1930), p. 90.

41   2 John Rowe, *Cornwall in the Age of the Industrial Revolution* (Liverpool, 1953), p. 65.

41   3 Ibid., pp. 17, 22–23; J. R. Harris, *The Copper Industry in Lancashire and North Wales, 1760–1815* (Ph.D. Thesis, Manchester, n.d.), p. 185; H. W. Dickinson and Arthur Titley, *Richard Trevithick* (Cambridge, 1934), p. 8; George R. Lewis, 'Tin Mining' in *V. C. H. Cornwall* I (1906), pp. 554–5; idem, *The Stannaries, A Study of the English Tin Miner* (1907), pp. 205–7; John Postlethwaite, *Mines and Mining in the (English) Lake District* (Whitehaven,

41 3 third ed. 1913), pp. 80–81; Robert Hunt, *British Mining* (1884), pp. 109–11; *V. C. H. Derbyshire* (1907), 'Industries'; W. H. G. Armytage, *The Social History of Engineering* (1961); *Bagshaw Collection* (MSS, Sheffield City Library), esp. No. 392, beginning for 1772; Hopkinson, 'Leadmining', pp. 4, 8–11.

41 4 T. S. Ashton and Joseph Sykes, *The Coal Industry in the Eighteenth Century* (Manchester, 1929), p. 111; John Holland, *The History and Description of Fossil Fuel, The Collieries, and Coal Trade of Great Britain* (1835), p. 295.

42 1 Dodd, *Industrial Revolution*, p. 365; John, *Industrial Development*, pp. 18, 76–78, 80, 142, 147; Mathias Dunn, *View of the Coal Trade of the North of England* (Newcastle, 1844), p. 144; W. H. B. Court, 'A Warwickshire Colliery in the Eighteenth Century', *Ec.H.R.* VII (May, 1937), p. 227; A. H. John, 'Iron and Coal on a Glamorgan Estate, 1700–1740', ibid., XIII (1943), 100; Edith Malley, *The Financial Administration of the Bridgwater Estate 1780–1850* (M.A. Thesis, Manchester, 1929), p. 98; T. S. Ashton 'The Coal Miners of the Eighteenth Century', *Economic History*, I (January, 1928), 311–13; *Factories Inquiry Commission* I, B2, p. 81, Foster Jones and Company; Davies, *Economic History of South Wales*, pp. 80–81.

42 2 Jars, op. cit., p. 267; Hardy, 'Derbyshire Colliery', *University of Birmingham Historical Journal* (1957), pp. 151–4; Hammond, *Skilled Labourer*, p. 12; *William Brown's Letterbook* (MS., North of England Inst. of Mining and Mech. Engineers, Newcastle) from Leonard Hartley, 14th July 1753.

42 3 e.g. *Lambton Colliery Accounts* (ibid., MS.), No. 17; Crawcrook Colliery, Accounts 1821–5 (MS., ibid.); A. J. Taylor, op. cit.,; Oliver Wood, *The Development of the Coal, Iron and Shipbuilding Industries of West Cumberland, 1750–1914* (Ph.D. Thesis, London, 1952), p. 133.

42 4 Rowe, *Cornwall*, pp. 25–28; Lewis, *Stannaries*, pp. 185–6, 200–4; Clapham, *Economic History*, p. 187; Lewis, 'Tin Mining', pp. 555–6; Babbage, op. cit., p. 252; *Boulton and Watt Correspondence* (Birmingham Assay Office, MSS.), Boulton to Dr. William Withering, 5th July, 1784.

42 5 *Mona Mine MSS.* Nos. 1 ff., 186, 1027, 1274, 1599, 1472 ff., 2254–65, 2633; Archibald and L. Clow, *The Chemical Revolution, A Contribution to Social Technology* (1952), pp. 366, 369; Robert Clutterbuck, *Journal of Four Tours, Chiefly in Wales and the West of England* (MS. 1794–9, Cardiff Public Library) p. 48; Rowlands, op. cit., pp. 228–9; J. R. Harris, op. cit., p. 234; English, *British Mines*, pp. 35, 84, 101, 105; Dodd, *Industrial Revolution*, p. 365.

43 1 Hopkinson, *Development*, pp. 169–70; Hamilton, *English Brass and Copper Industries*, p. 309; Postlethwaite, *Mines in the Lake District*, p. 89; Rhys Jenkins, 'Francis Thompson's Visit to the Cardiganshire Mines in 1788', *Trans.N.S.*, XI (1930–1), p. 159; Dodd, *Industrial Revolution*, pp. 205, 214; Evan J. Jones, *Some Contributions to the Economic History of Wales* (1928), p. 88; Dylan Pritchard, *The Slate Industry of North Wales, A Study of the Changes in Economic Organisation from 1780 to the Present Day* (M.A., Wales, 1935), p. 61.

43 2 Frances Collier, 'Workers in a Lancashire Factory at the beginning of the Nineteenth Century', *Manchester School*, VII (1936),

43   2 p. 51; *idem, The Family Economy of the Workers in the Cotton Industry During the Period of the Industrial Revolution, 1784–1833* (M.A. Thesis, Manchester, 1921). p. 40; Pinchbeck, op. cit., p. 122.

43   3 John W. McConnell, *A Century of Fine Cotton Spinning* (Manchester, 1906), p. 53; *Lords' Committee on Factory Bill* (1818), evid. John Stuart, p. 181.

43   4 For some details of this system, cf. Andrew Ure, *The Philosophy of Manufactures* (2nd ed., 1835), pp. 289–90, 317, 423; *Factories Inquiry Commission*, I, A2, Alexander Cooper, p. 37, C2, p. 3, D1, John Redman, p. 41, D2, pp. 2, 22, T. W. Hodgson, p. 47; Thomas Marsland & Son, p. 49, Joseph Shepley, p. 53, James Bray, p. 63, Harrison's Mill, p. 74, Thomas Ashton, p. 84, E. Henry M'Connell, p. 7, Rowland Detroisier, p. 13; II, Medical Reports, p. 40; John J. Monaghan, 'The Rise and Fall of the Belfast Cotton Industry', *Irish Historical Studies*, III (1942–3), 11–12; *Committee on the Labour of Children in the Mills and Factories of the United Kingdom* (B.P.P., 1831–2, XV, 706), evid. G. S. Bull, Q. 10, 286; *House of Lords Committee on Apprentices* (1818–19), evid. Archibald Buchanan, p. 86, Thomas Scott, p. 167, John Stewart, p. 186; *S.C. on Manufactures* (1833) evid. James Thomson, Q. 3807, William Graham, Q. 5406, George Smith, Q. 9419, *Wages Lists* on page 319; *Lords, Committee on Factory Bill* (1818), evid. Edward Hume, pp. 16–17.

43   5 E. Baines, *Cotton Manufacture*, pp. 369–75; J. L. and B. Hammond, *The Town Labourer, 1760–1832* (1919), pp. 33–34; A. Ure, *The Cotton Manufacture of Great Britain* (1861 ed.), 2 vols, p. 398; *Factories Inquiry Commission*, IV, D1, p. 221 evid. Henry Houldsworth; Smelser, op. cit., p. 200; *S.C. on Children in Manufactories* (1816) evid. William Taylor, p. 261.

43   6 Crump, *Leeds Woollen Industry*, pp. 34, 38, 58, 185, 286.

44   1 *Factories Inquiry Commission*, I. B1, James Morton, p. 13, T. S. Lea, p. 18, Joel Viney, p. 23.

44   2 William Felkin, *A History of the Machine Wrought Hosiery and Lace Manufactures* (1867), p. 245.

44   3 John, *Industrial Development of South Wales*, pp. 75–76. Also, *Rhymney Ironworks MSS.* (Cardiff Public Library), Payment Book 1801.

45   1 J. J. Ferber, *Beschreibungen . . . einer Reise . . . in England und Schottland* (Halberstadt, 1793), p. 124; *Boulton and Watt Correspondence* (Assay Office), James Watt to Boulton, 24th March 1781; M. W. Flinn, *The Law Book of the Crowley Ironworks* (Surtees Society Publications, vol. 167, Durham and London, 1957), p. XXV; John England 'The Dowlais Ironworks, 1759–93', *Trans. Glamorgan Local History Society*, III (1959), 46–52.

45   2 V. W. Bladen 'The Potteries in the Industrial Revolution', *Economic History*, I (January, 1926), p. 129; Unwin, *Samuel Oldknow*, p. 163; *Factories Inquiry Commission*, I, B2, evid. R. Stevenson, p. 50; John Thomas, *The Economic Development of the Staffordshire Potteries since 1730, with special reference to the Industrial Revolution* (Ph.D. Thesis, London, 1934), pp. 204, 213, 553; George Dodd, *Days at the Factories* (1843), *passim.*

45   3 *Galway of Serlby Muniments* (MSS., Nottingham University Library), No. 12,863.

45 4 Stirling, Everard, *History of the Gas, Light and Coke Company* (1949), p. 69; *British Transport Commission Archives* (MSS., London), KAC/23/32, cost of building the Kennet and Avon Canal in 1806.

46 1 *British Transport Commission Archives* (MSS., York), SAD/3/22, 3/9, 3/14, 3/16–18, 3/6; Robert Young, 'Timothy Hackworth and the Locomotive', *Trans. N.S.*, II (1921–2), 76.

46 2 Thomas Brassey, *Lectures on the Labour Question* (1878), pp. 137, 140; Arthur Helps, *Life and Labours of Mr. Brassey, 1805–1870* (1872), pp. 40–51.

46 3 W. R. Scott (ed.) *The Records of a Scottish Cloth Manufactory at New Mills, Haddingtonshire, 1681–1703* (Edinburgh, 1905), p. 35; Oliver Wood, op. cit., p. 149; Gordon Rimmer, 'Middleton Colliery, Near Leeds (1770–1830)', *Yorkshire Bulletin of Econ. & Social Research*, VII (March, 1955), 45; Hughes, *North Country Life*, pp. 254–5.

47 1 Raistrick, *Dynasty of Ironfounders*, p. 231; Fong, op. cit., p. 237, fn; John, *Industrial Development*, p. 19; Charles Wilkins, *South Wales Coal Trade* (Cardiff, 1888), p. 67; E. F. Söderlund 'The Impact of the British Industrial Revolution on the Swedish Iron Industry', in *Studies in the Industrial Revolution*, p. 55; J. D. Marshall, *Furness and the Industrial Revolution* (Barrow-in-Furness, 1958), p. 39; *Wharncliffe Muniments* (MSS., Sheffield City Library), No. 56, Cockshutt Lease of 1793.

47 2 D. Pritchard, op. cit., p. 42; William Bray, *Sketch of a Tour into Derbyshire and Yorkshire* (2nd ed. 1783), p. 147; *Mona Mine MSS.*, No. 1275; Rowlands, op. cit., pp. 197–8.

47 3 J. A. G. Harvey, 'Samuel Whitbread's First Enterprise. A Survey of the Organization and Methods of an Eighteenth-Century London Brewery, 1742–50', *Guildhall Miscellany*, IX (July, 1958), 22–23; E. W. Swann, 'A Durham Colliery Stocktaking of 1783–4', *Trans. N.S.* XXIV (1943–5), p. 111.

49 1 Henri Sée, 'Hat Manufacturing at Rennes, 1776–1789', *Journal of Economic and Business History*, I (February, 1929).

49 2 Weber, op. cit., p. 171; Kulischer 'Grande Industrie', pp. 11–20; Louis Mosnier *Origines et Developpements de la Grande Industrie en France* (Paris, 1898), pp. 41 ff. 140–50; Sombart, op. cit., II, 773 ff, 786, 795; J. U. Nef, 'Industrial Europe at the time of the Reformation' Part 2, *Journal of Political Economy*, 49 (1941), p. 219; Kulischer, *Wirtschaftsgeschichte*, II, ch. 10, pp. 400–6; W. C. Scoville, *Capitalism and French Glass Making, 1640–1789* (Berkeley and Los Angeles (1950), esp. pp. 72 ff., 143 ff.

49 3 B. Foujas de Saint-Fond, *Travels in England, Scotland and the Hebrides* (1799), p. 136 cf. also, Mantoux, op. cit., pp. 30–32.

50 1 Even these figures are suspect. cf. F. Nicolai, *Beschreibung einer Reise durch Deutschland . . . im Jahre 1781* (12 vols., Berlin and Stettin, 1783–96), II, pp. 511—18.

50 2 W. C. Scoville, *The Persecution of the Huguenots and French Economic Development, 1680–1720* (Berkeley and Los Angeles, 1960), pp. 227–37; Germain Martin, *La grande industrie en France, sous le règne de Louis XV* (Paris, 1900), pp. 120–1, 203–4.

50 3 W. O. Henderson, *The State and the Industrial Revolution in Prussia* (Liverpool, 1958), esp. ch. 1, 4.

50 4 L. T. C. Rolt, *Thomas Telford* (1958), p. 98. But see the account of Russian experience in A. Kahan, 'Entrepreneurship in the Early Development of Iron Manufacturing in Russia', *Economic Development and Cultural Change*, X (1962) esp. pp. 414–15.

51 1 Scoville, *Capitalism and French Glass Making*; Paul W. Bamford, 'Entrepreneurship in Seventeenth and Eighteenth Century France', *Explorations in Entrepreneurial History*, IX (1957), 208–9. Cf. also, Nef, 'Industrial Europe', p. 218; N. J. G. Pounds and W. M. Parker, *Coal and Steel in Western Europe* (1957), pp. 92–93; Rudolf Forberger, *Die Manufaktur in Sachsen vom Ende des 16. bis Zum Anfang des 19. Jahrhunderts* (Berlin, 1958), Appendix.

51 2 The following account is based on Scott, *Cloth Manufactory*, quoted above. Cf. also, *idem.*, *Joint Stock Companies*, III, 138–58.

53 1 The best summary account is in Davies, *Economic History of South Wales*, pp. 80 ff., 125 ff. Cf. also, George Grant Francis, *The Smelting of Copper in the Swansea District* (2nd ed. 1881), pp. 82 ff.; T. S. Willan, *River Navigation in England, 1600–1750* (1936), p. 94; Sir Humphrey Mackworth, Tracts in the British Museum, esp. *Affidavits, Certificates and Presentments Proving the Facts mentioned in the Case of Sir Humphrey Mackworth and the Mine Adventurers* (1705) and Sir Humphrey Mackworth, *A Short State of the Case and Proceedings of the Company of the Mine Adventurers* (1710), pp. 26–27; *D.N.B.*, Sir Humphrey Mackworth; D. Trevor Williams, *The Economic Development of Swansea and the Swansea District to 1921* (Cardiff, 1940), pp. 27–29; Waller, *Value of the Mines*, 'Epistle Dedicatory'; Mary Ransome, 'The Parliamentary Career of Sir Humphrey Mackworth, 1701–1713', *University of Birmingham Historical Journal*, I (1948).

54 1 Cf. p. 19 above.

55 1 Cf. esp. John, *Economic History of South Wales*, pp. 8–9, 15–28.

55 2 *Crowley Ironworks, Law Book* (MS. British Museum, Add. MSS. 34,555), printed almost completely in M. W. Flinn (ed.), *Crowley Law Book*. Cf. also, Flinn, *Men of Iron*; Robert Surtees, *The History and Antiquities of the County Palatine of Durham* (1820, vol. 2), pp. 246, 272–3; W. P. Kingsford, 'Sir Ambrose Crowley: Pioneer of Modern Management', *The Manager* (July, 1954), 435–41; W. A. Young, 'Works Organisation in the Seventeenth Century. Some Account of Ambrose and John Crowley', *Trans.N.S.*, IV (1923–4).

55 3 Russell, *England Displayed*, p. 187; M. W. Flinn, 'Industry and Technology in the Derwent Valley of Durham and Northumberland in the Eighteenth Century', *Trans.N.S.*, XXIX (1953–5).

56 1 M. W. Flinn, *Crowley Law Book*, p. xxvi.

59 1 Ambrose Crowley, *Printed Matter Collection* (Newcastle on Tyne Public Library), pp. 148–9; Ambrose Crowley, *Minutes of Council of Arbitration, 1806–1843* (MS., Newcastle on Tyne Public Library); *V. C. H. Durham*, II, pp. 281–7.

60 1 Nef, 'Industrial Europe', p. 218.

CHAPTER 3

61 1 Nef, 'Technology', pp. 10–11; and 'Dominance of the Trader in the English Coal Industry in the Seventeenth Century', *Journal of Economic and Business History*, I (1929).

62 1 Hughes, *North Country Life*, pp. 167 ff.; Paul M. Sweezy, *Monopoly and Competition in the English Coal Trade, 1550–1850* (Cambridge, Mass., 1938); G. R. Porter, *The Progress of the Nation* (1912 ed.), pp. 218–19.

62 2 Asta Moller, 'Coal Mining in the Seventeenth Century', *Trans. R.H.S.*, Fourth Ser. 8 (1925) p. 81–85; *Trans.N.S.*, XXXI (1957–9) discussion, pp. 88–89.

62 3 R. L. Galloway, *A History of Coal Mining in Great Britain* (1882), p. 56; J. B. Simpson, *Capital and Labour in Coal Mining* (Newcastle, 1900), pp. 14–15; R. V. Simpson, 'Old Mining Records and Plans', *Trans. Institute of Mining Engineers*, LXXXI (?1931), p. 76; *V. C. H. Durham*, II, Maud Sellers, 'Industries'. But see Hughes, *North Country Life*, pp. 195–6.

62 4 J. C., *Compleat Collier*, p. 29. cf. also Hughes, op. cit., p. 156.

62 5 A. Raistrick, 'The Steam Engines on Tyneside 1715–1778', *Trans.N.S.*, XVII (1936 and 7); Dunn, *View of the Coal Trade*, pp. 24, 41; R. L. Galloway, *Annals of Coal Mining and the Coal Trade* (1898), p. 262; M. Dunn, *History of the Viewers* (MS. North of England Institute of Mining and Mechanical Engineers, Newcastle) f. 8. The first engine to draw coal was built by Smeaton in 1777, and the first mechanical ventilation was probably that at Walker in 1769. John Fairey, *A Treatise on the Steam Engine* (1827), p. 297; Galloway, *History*, p. 107.

62 6 Russell, *England Displayed*, p. 180; Jean Chevalier, 'Le Mission de Gabriel Jars dans les mines et les Usines Britanniques en 1764', *Trans.N.S.*, XXVI (1947–9), p. 59; A. P. M. Fleming and H. J. Brocklehurst, *A History of Engineering*, (1925), p. 119.

62 7 Dunn, *History of the Viewers*, f. 12. William Brown reported a sinking of 83 fathoms in 1750 as a curiosity, and Spedding sunk a pit to 123½ fathoms in 1752. *William Brown's Letter Book* (MS.), 30th October 1750, 17th March 1752.

63 1 J. Holland, *Coal Trade*, pp. 187–9; Rev. Richard Warner, *A Tour Through the Northern Counties of England and the Borders of Scotland* (2 vols., 1802), I, p. 312.

63 2 *William Brown's Letter Book*, Brown to Spedding, 10th April 1755; R. Dodd, *A Treatise on Newcastle Coal Pits* (Newcastle, 1757), pp. 11–12; Gabriel Jars, *Voyages Métallurgiques* (Lyons, 1774), esp. pp. 187, 207; Saint-Fond, *Travels in England*, I, p. 139.

63 3 T. H. Hair, *Views of the Collieries in the Counties of Northumberland and Durham* (1844); C. F. Dendy Marshall, *Two Essays in Locomotive History* (1928), p. 42; *idem.*, *A History of British Railways down to the year 1830* (1938), p. 7.

64 1 O. Wood, *Coal, Iron and Shipbuilding Industries of West Cumberland*, p. 2; J. E. Williams, 'Whitehaven in the Eighteenth Century', *Ec.H.R.*, 2nd Ser. VIII (1956), pp. 394, 400.

64 2 *Historical MS. Commission* 13th Report, Lonsdale MSS. Appendix, part VII (1893), p. 96; Moller, op. cit., pp. 87–88; Galloway, *Annals*, p. 218.

64 3 Ferber, *Reise*, pp. 98–99; *William Brown's Letter Book*, Spedding to Brown, 5th April 1753, 30th July 1754; Joshua Dickson, *The Literary Life of William Brownrigg, M.D., F.R.S.*, to which are added *An Account of the Coal Mines Near Whitehaven* (London, Dublin,

64 3 Edinburgh and Whitehaven, 1801), pp. 95 ff.; *V. C. H. Cumberland*, II, 359–62; *Annual Register*, No. 36 (1794), 326–33; Richard Ayton, *A Voyage Round Great Britain, undertaken in the Summer of the Year 1813* (2 vols., 1814–15), p. 149–59.

65 1 G. G. Hopkinson, *Development*, pp. 233 ff., 329 ff.; Edwin Sorby, 'Coal Mining Near Sheffield from 1773 to 1820', *Trans. Institute of Mining Engineers*, 65 (1923); William Philip Jeffcock, *Family Recollections* (1941); *Arundel Castle Muniments*, S. 214, 185, 235, 205, S. D. 13.

65 2 J. T. Ward, 'The Earls Fitzwilliam and the Wentworth Woodhouse Estate in the Nineteenth Century', *Yorkshire Bulletin*, 12 (1960) 21; *Wentworth Woodhouse Muniments*, ST. 13a, F.106d; Mingay, p. 195.

65 3 Frank Machin, *The Yorkshire Miners, A History* (Vol. 1, Barnsley, 1958).

66 1 Rimmer, 'Middleton Colliery'.

66 2 James Hogg (Ed.), *Fortunes Made in Business. First Series* (2nd ed., 1885?), p. 106; Philip Robinson, *The Smiths of Chesterfield. A History of the Griffin Foundry, Brampton, 1775–1833* (Chesterfield, 1957), p. 25.

66 3 Herbert Green, 'The Nottinghamshire and Derbyshire Coal Fields before 1850', *Journal of the Derbyshire Archaeological and Natural History Society*, LVI (1936); G. W. Daniels and T. S. Ashton, 'The Records of a Derbyshire Colliery, 1763–1779', *Ec.H.R.* II (1929–30); Hardy, 'Derbyshire Colliery'.

66 4 John, *Industrial Development*, p. 28; Davies, *Economic History of South Wales*, p. 141; Daniel Carless Webb, *Four Excursions made to Various Parts of Great Britain in the years 1810 and 1811* (1812), pp. 343–5, 358.

66 5 Elizabeth Phillips, *A History of the Pioneers of the Welsh Coalfield* (Cardiff, 1925), pp. 16–17; Hon. John Bing, *The Torrington Diaries, containing the Tours through England and Wales*, (4 vols. 1934) I, pp. 298–9; *Committee on the Petition of the Owners of Collieries in South Wales* (B.P.P. 1810; 344. IV), evid. Henry Smith, pp. 2–3.

66 6 *Committee on South Wales Colleries*, evid. R. Beavan, p. 20, Edward Jones, pp. 50–51, John Barnaby, p. 53.

66 7 H. English, *British Mines*, pp. 75, 119–20; R. R. Rawson, 'The Coal-Mining Industry of the Hawarden District on the Eve of the Industrial Revolution', *Archaeologia Cambrensis*, XCVI (1941); Dodd, *Industrial Revolution in North Wales*, p. 365; A. S. Davies, 'The First Steam Engine in Wales, 1714 and its Staffordshire Owner', *Trans.N.S.*, XVIII (1937–8), p. 67.

67 1 Peter L. Payne, 'The Govan Colleries, 1804–1805', *Business History* III (1961).

67 2 Henry M. Cadell, *The Rocks of West Lothian* (Edinburgh, 1925), pp. 328–37; Jars, p. 290; Campbell, *Carron Company*, pp. 228–9.

67 3 Robert Bald, *A General View of the Coal Trade of Scotland* (Edinburgh, 1812), pp. 91–94 *et. passim*; Lord, *Capital and Steam-Power*, p. 191; Farey, op. cit., pp. 228–30.

67 4 Jars, p. 253; Samuel Smiles, *Lives of the Engineers*, I, 272–3; Edith Malley, op. cit., pp. 88 ff.; *Factories Inquiry Commission* (1833–4) I, D2, p. 79; John Campbell, *A Political Survey of Britain* (2 vols., 1774), II, p. 269.

67 5 A. J. Taylor, loc. cit., pp. 216–17; Court, 'Warwickshire Colliery'; *idem., Rise of Midlands Industries*, pp. 73, 94–97, 160–2; Farey, op. cit., p. 297.

68 1 Dunn, *View of the Coal Trade*, p. 154; (British Museum) *Tracts on Trade*, 816. m. 12/94; English, *British Mines*, pp. 81–84; George O'Brien, *The Economic History of Ireland from the Union to the Famine* (1921), pp. 403–6.

69 1 Dunn, *View of the Coal Trade*, pp. 144 ff.

69 2 A. E. Dobbs, *Education and Social Movements, 1700–1850* (1919), p. 46; Ashton, 'Coal Miners', pp. 309–10; Hylton Scott 'The Miners' Bond in Northumberland and Durham', *Proc. of the Society of Antiquaries of Newcastle upon Tyne* (4th Ser.), XI (1947).

69 3 J. Campbell, op. cit., II, p. 31.

69 4 Rowe, *Cornwall in the Age of the Industrial Revolution*, p. 11.

69 5 See pp. 42 above.

70 1 *V. C. H. Cornwall*, I, G. R. Lewis, 'Tin Mining' and 'Copper Mining'; *Boulton and Watt Correspondence* (Birmingham Assay Office), James Watt to Boulton, 26th June, 1778, 6th September 1778, 18th May, 1783; F. Trevithick *Life of Richard Trevithick, with an Account of his Inventions* (1872), p. 4; *Copper Committee* (1799), evid. John Vivian, p. 13, M. Boulton, p. 35.

70 2 Arthur Titley, 'Cornish Mining: Notes from the Account Books of Richard Trevithick Senior', *Trans.N.S.* XI (1930–1), p. 31; John Grisco, *A Year in Europe* (2 vols.), New York, 1823), I, p. 186 f.; English, *British Mines, passim; Boulton and Watt Correspondence*, Watt to Boulton, 16th September, 1778; Robert Clutterbuck *Journal of Four Tours*: III, *Journal of a Tour Through the Western Counties of England*, 1796, ff. 294–5.

70 3 Joseph Carne, 'Statistics of the Tin-Mines in Cornwall, and of the Consumption of Tin in Great Britain', *Journ. Royal Statistical Society*, II (1839) and Sir Charles Lemon, 'The Statistics of the Copper Mines of Cornwall', in ibid. I (1838).

71 1 Rowe, op. cit., pp. 88–89; *Boulton and Watt Correspondence* (Assay Office), Boulton to M. Dupont, 21st July 1792; *Copper Committee* (1799), Appendix, pp. 102–5; J. E. Cule, *The Financial History of Matthew Boulton, 1759–1800* (M.Com. Thesis, Birmingham, 1935), pp. 250–1.

71 2 Lemon, loc. cit., pp. 78–79.

71 3 G. C. Allen, 'An Eighteenth Century Combination in the Copper-Mining Industry', *Economic Journal*, XXXIII (1923).

71 4 'We are here completely shut up in a corner and no one leaves home for any time to see or to make any enquiry of the improvements of the day', Treweek to Sanderson, 14th May, 1833, *Mona Mine MSS.*, No. 2690.

72 1 E.g. Richard Ayton, *A Voyage Round Great Britain* (2 vols., 1814–15), II, pp. 11 ff.; Thomas Pennant, *Tours in Wales* (3 vols., Caernarvon, 1883), III, pp. 56 ff., 395 ff.; R. E. Yates, *An Account of a Tour of Parts of Wales, England and Ireland, 1805* (MS., National Library of Wales, No. 687), ff. 42 passim; Clutterbuck, op. cit., 43 ff.; *Mona Mine MSS.*, esp. Nos. 1282, 3039, 3544.

72 2 Nellie Kirkham, 'Ecton Mines', *J. Derbyshire Archaeological Natural History Society*, LXVII (1947); *Torrington Diaries*, II, p. 58;

Notes

72　2 Hunt, *British Mining*, pp. 118–19; W. Bray, *Tour of Derbyshire*, pp. 147–8.
72　3 C. M. C. Bouch and G. P. Jones, *A Short Economic and Social History of the Lake Counties, 1500–1830* (Manchester, 1961), pp. 68, 72; *William Brown's Letter Book*, from Hartley, 4th March 1753, 28th May, 1753, 14th July, 1753; H. G. Jones, 'The Llandudno Copper Mines in the Eighteenth Century', *Bulletin of the Board of Celtic Studies*, X (1939).
72　4 pp. 17–19 above.
73　1 *Bagshaw Collection* (Sheffield City Library), esp. Nos. 377–9, 392–3, 427–8, 579–82; F. M. Fisher, 'Sir Cornelius Vermuyden and the Dove Gang Lead Mine', *J. Derbyshire Archaeological and Natural History Society*, LXII (1952); Nellie Kirkham, 'The Tumultuous Course of Dove Gang', ibid, LXIII (1953); G. G. Hopkinson, *Development*, pp. 140 ff.; 'Five Generations of Lead Mining'; idem. 'Lead Mining in Ashover'; *V. C. H. Derbyshire*, II, p. 331 ff.; Frank Nixon, 'The Early Steam-Engines in Derbyshire', *Trans.N.S.*, XXXI (1957–9); *V. C. H. Durham*, II, 'Mining', by Henry Louis, p. 352.
73　2 David Murray, *The York Building Company*, pp. 67–70; A. & N. Clow, *Chemical Revolution*, pp. 364 ff.; *Boulton and Watt Correspondence*, Watt to Boulton, 28th March, 1788; Ferber, op. cit,. pp. 159–66; T. Garnett, *Observations on a Tour Through the Highlands and part of the Western Isles of Scotland* (2 vols., 1811), pp. 238–9.
74　1 Davies, *Economic History of South Wales*, p. 133; Dodd, *Industrial Revolution in North Wales*, p. 175; Rhys Jenkins, 'Francis Thompsons' Visit to the Cardiganshire Mines in 1788', *Trans.N.S.* XI (1930–1), p. 159; F. J. Monkhouse, 'Eighteenth Century Company Promoter'; William Waller, *Value of the Mines* (1698), pp. 15–20.
74　2 E. J. Jones, *Economic History of Wales*, pp. 88–91; Lewis, *Topographical Dictionary, s.v.* 'Festiniog'; D. Pritchard, *Slate Industry of North Wales*; Dodd, op. cit., pp. 205–19; English, *British Mines*, pp. 76–77, 122; W. Morgan Richards, 'Some Aspects of the Industrial Revolution in South-East Caernarvonshire', *Trans. Caernarvonshire Historical Society*, 4 (1942–3) and 5 (1944); J. D. Marshall, *Furness and the Industrial Revolution*, p. 43.
74　3 Ferber, p. 100; Hughes, *North Country Life*, pp. 67–68; *William Brown's Letter Book*, John Burrel, 26th April 1755; J. Aikin, *A Description of the Country from Thirty to Forty Miles Round Manchester*, pp. 428–31; W. H. Chaloner, 'William Furnival, H. E. Falk and the Salt Chamber of Commerce, 1815–1889', *Trans. Historical Society Lancashire and Cheshire*, 112 (1960), p. 128.
75　1 R. A. Mott, 'Abraham Darby, I and II'; Henry Scrivenor, *A Comprehensive History of the Iron Trade* (1841 ed.), pp. 57, 86–87, 95–97, 134–5; E. W. Hulme, 'Statistical History of the Iron Trade of England and Wales, 1717–1750', *Trans.N.S.*, IX (1928–9).
75　2 cf. pp. 39–40 above.
75　3 Raistrick and Allen, 'South Yorkshire Ironmasters', p. 178; R. L. Downes, 'Stour Partnership, 1726–36'; B. L. C. Johnson, 'The Charcoal Iron Industry in the Early Eighteenth Century',

290

75   3 *Geographical Journal*, 117 (1951); *idem.*, 'Foley Partnerships'; A. Fell, *The Early Iron Industry of Furness and District* (Ulverston, 1908).

76   1 Raistrick, *Dynasty*, pp. 15, 87, 214–15, 226, 266; Court, *Rise of Midlands Industries*, p. 177; M. W. Flinn and Alan Birch, 'The English Steel Industry before 1856', *Yorkshire Bulletin*, VI (1954), p. 176; *S.C. on Artisans and Machinery* (1824), evid. Samuel Walker and William Yates, pp. 116–18; *S.C. on Manufactures* (1833), evid. Samuel Walker, QQ. 9511, 9525–6, 9575; A. H. John, *Walker Family*.

76   2 Jars, pp. 272 ff.; James Mackinnon, *The Social and Industrial History of Scotland from the Union to the Present Time* (1921), p. 19; Scrivenor, *History*, pp. 82–83; H. M. Cadell, *Rocks of West Lothian*, pp. 3–8 ff.; *idem.*, *The Story of the Forth* (Glasgow, 1913); James Cleland, *Rise and Progress of the City of Glasgow* (Glasgow, 1840), pp. 27–28; Saint-Fond, *Travels*, I, pp. 181 ff.; Henry Hamilton, 'The Founding of Carron Ironworks', *Scottish Historical Review*, XXV (1928); Bebbington, *Samuel Garbett*; Morris, 'Struggle for Carron'; Campbell, *Carron Company; idem.*, 'The Financing of Carron Company', *Business History*, I (1958); Clutterbuck, I. f. 203–5.

76   3 Court, *Rise of Midlands Industries*, p. 177.

77   1 Robinson, *Smiths of Chesterfield*; A. E. Musson and E. Robinson, 'The Origins of Engineering in Lancashire', *J.Ec.H.*, XX (1960), p. 226; D. C. Webb, *Four Excursions*, pp. 186–90; Sir R. Phillips, *Personal Tour*, p. 213–14; Jack Simmons, *Parish and Empire* (1952), p. 149; John W. Hall, 'Diary of a Tour by Joshua Field in the Midlands, 1821', *Trans.N.S.*, VI (1925–6), p. 28; *S.C. on Manufactures* (1833), Anthony Hill, evid. QQ. 10,238–40, William Hanberry Sparrow, QQ. 10, 728–35.

77   2 H. W. Dickinson, *John Wilkinson, Ironmaster* (Ulverston, 1914); A. N. Palmer, 'John Wilkinson and the Old Bersham Ironworks', reprinted from *Trans. of the Hon. Society of Cymmodorion* (1899); John Randall, *The Wilkinsons* (Madeley, 1876); W. H. Chaloner, 'Isaac Wilkinson, Potfounder', pp. 37 ff. in L. S. Pressnell, *Studies in the Industrial Revolution; * E. J. Jones, *Economic History of Wales*, p. 75; *Boulton and Watt Manuscripts* (Birmingham Reference Library), James Watt Junior to Watt Senior, 24th September, 1795.

77   3 Charles Wilkins, *The History of Merthyr Tydfil* (Merthyr Tydfil, 1908), pp. 227 ff.; *idem.*, *The History of the Iron, Steel, Tinplate and Other Trades of Wales* (Merthyr Tydfil, 1903), pp. 47 ff.; Namier, 'Anthony Bacon'.

77   4 Edgar L. Chappell, *Historic Melingriffith* (Cardiff, 1940); F. W. Gibbs, 'The Rise of the Tinplate Industry, IV, An Eighteenth-Century Tinplate Mill', *Annals of Science*, VII (1951); L. J. Williams, 'The Welsh Tinplate Trade in the Mid-Eighteenth Century', *Ec.H.R.*, 2nd Ser. XIII (1961).

78   1 Porter, *Progress*, p. 238.

78   2 Scrivenor, *Iron Trade*, pp. 123, 131; D. G. John, *Economic History of South Wales*, I (7); Lewis, *Topographical Dictionary*, *s.v.* 'Merthyr Tydfil', 'Neath'; *S.C. on Manufactures* (1833) evid. Anthony Hill, QQ. 10,210—22; Davies, *Economic History of South Wales; * John

78 2 Lloyd, *The Early History of the Old South Wales Iron Works (1760–1840)* (1906), p. 94; T. Rees, *Topographical Description of South Wales*; *Mechanics Magazine*, 25th June 1831; Addis, *Crawshay Dynasty*; Madeleine Elsas (ed.), *Iron in the Making: Dowlais Iron Company Letters, 1782–1860* (Cardiff), 1960.

78 3 A. Wolf, *A History of Science, Technology and Philosophy in the Eighteenth Century* (1938), pp. 612–16.

79 1 E. Roll, *An Early Experiment in Industrial Organisation, Being a History of the Firm of Boulton & Watt, 1775–1805* (1930).

79 2 Raistrick, *Dynasty*, pp. 156–69; Musson and Robinson, 'Growth of Steam Power', and 'Engineering in Lancashire'.

79 3 *Boulton and Watt Correspondence* (Birmingham Assay Office), James Watt to Boulton, 10th September 1777, 2nd May 1780, 12th September 1780, 24th March 1781.

79 4 T. H. Marshall, *James Watt (1736–1819)*, (n.d.); J. P. Muirhead, *The Life of James Watt* (1859), p. 250; H. W. Dickinson, *Matthew Boulton* (Cambridge, 1937); *Boulton and Watt Correspondence* (Assay Office), Boulton to J. Edwards, 14th September 1795.

79 5 *Boulton and Watt Accounts* (MS., Birmingham Reference Library); *Correspondence* (Birmingham Reference Library), James Watt Junior to James Watt, 3rd May 1795, reply 10th May; John W. Hall, *Diary*, p. 12; J. R. Immer, op. cit., pp. 57, 184.

79 6 Wolf, op. cit., p. 565, cf. also N. J. Smelser, *Social Change*, p. 117; *S.C. on Artisans and Machinery* (1824), evid. Peter Ewart and John Kennedy.

80 1 For this episode, see Webb, *Four Excursions*, pp. 222–3; Richard Beamish, *Memoir of the Life of Sir Marc Isambard Brunel* (1862), pp. 46 ff.; J. W. Hall, loc. cit., pp. 1–2; E. M. Forward, 'Simon Goodrich and his work as an Engineer', *Trans.N.S.*, III (1922–3) p. 8; H. W. Dickinson, 'Joliffe & Banks, Contractors', *Trans.N.S.*, XII (1931–2), and *idem*, 'The Taylors of Southampton', ibid., XXIX (1953–5); J. T. M. Pannell, 'The Taylors of Southampton', *Proc. Institute of Mechanical Engineers*, 169 (1955).

80 2 W. H. Chaloner, 'John Galloway, (1804–1894) Engineer of Manchester and His "Reminiscences",' *Trans. Lancashire and Cheshire Antiquarian Society*, LXIV (1954), p. 103; *S.C. on Artisans and Machinery* (1824), evid. Alexander Galloway, p. 26; Committee of the House of Commons on the Liverpool and Manchester Railroad Bill (1825), evid. J. U. Rastrick, p. 148; Charles Wilson and William Reader, *Men and Machines, A History of D. Napier & Son, Engineers, Limited* (1958), p. 27; S. M. Tomkin, 'Trevithick, Rastrick and the Hazeldine Foundry', *Trans.N.S.*, XXVI (1947–9).

80 3 W. G. Rimmer, *Marshalls of Leeds, Flax Spinners 1788–1886* (Cambridge, 1960), p. 49; E. Kilburn Scott, *Matthew Murray, Pioneer Engineer, Record for 1765–1826* (Leeds, 1928), p. 40; A. E. Musson, 'An Early Engineering Firm: Peel, Williams & Co., of Manchester', *Business History*, III (1960), 12–14; Musson and Robinson, 'Engineering in Lancashire', p. 223; *S.C. on Artisans and Machinery* (1824), evid. T. C. Herves, p. 16, Henry Houldsworth, pp. 378–9.

80 4 Elijah Galloway, *History and Progress of the Steam Engine* (1833), p. 628; Alfred E. Pease (ed.), *The Diaries of Edward Pease* (1907),

80   4 pp. 87, 94–95; J. G. H. Warren, *A Century of Locomotive Building,*
      by Robert Stephenson & Co. Limited, 1823–1923 (Newcastle, 1923),
      p. 71; C. F. D. Marshall, *Locomotive History*, p. 6; L. T. C. Rolt,
      George and Robert Stephenson; the Railway Revolution (1960), p. 146.
80   5 E.g. Stebbin Shaw, *History and Antiquities of Staffordshire* (2 vols,
      1798, 1801), II, p. 117; Ferber, op. cit., p. 123; Clutterbuck, op.
      cit, p. 120; *Torrington Diaries*, I, p. 149; R. Warner, *Tour,* II,
      p. 215.
81   1 W. H. B. Court, 'Industrial Organisation and Economic Progress
      in Eighteenth Century Midlands', *Trans.R.H.S.*, Fourth Series,
      XXVIII (1946), p. 89.
82   1 Rowe, *Boulton and Watt*, pp. 5–6. Also, cf. *Boulton & Watt Accounts*
      (MS., Birmingham Assay Office), 'M. Boulton, Inventory,
      22nd June 1782'; *Boulton & Watt Accounts* (Birmingham Reference
      Library) Inventory of Goods Belonging to Boulton & Watt,
      Soho'; *Boulton & Watt Correspondence* (Assay Office), Boulton and
      J. Adam, 1st October 1770, to J. H. Ebbinghaus, 26th June 1766,
      2nd March 1768, to Thomas Loggan, 14th December 1794;
      Eric Robinson, 'Matthew Boulton, Patron of the Arts', *Annals of*
      Science, IX (1953), and 'Boulton & Fothergill, 1762 to 1782',
      University of Birmingham Historical Journal, VII (1959); *Copper*
      Committee (1799) evid. Matthew Boulton, pp. 24, 36–37.
82   2 Court, *Rise of Midlands Industries*, p. 263; Lord Fitzmaurice, *Life*
      of William, Earl of Shelburne (2 vols., 1912 ed.), I, 276–8; William
      Hutton, *The History of Birmingham* (6th ed., Birmingham, 1835),
      p. 170; *Committee on Orders in Council* (1812), evid. Thomas
      Messenger, p. 63.
82   3 L. Simiand, *Journal of a Tour and Residence in Great Britain* (2 vols.,
      New York, 1815), II, p. 92; Immer., op. cit., chapter 9; *Factories*
      Inquiry Commission (1833–4), I, B1, pp. 2–6.
82   4 *Committee on Orders in Council* (1812), evid. William Whitehouse,
      p. 19, George Naylor, p. 145; MacKinnon, *Social and Industrial*
      History of Scotland, p. 19; Ashton, *Peter Stubbs*; Hamilton, *English*
      Brass and Copper Industry, p. 313; Russell, *England Displayed*, II, p. 90.
84   1 E.g. *Mona Mine MSS.*, No. 3041–2.
84   2 There is a large literature on the development of this industry in
      this period. See, among others, the works listed in footnotes 38–46
      above, also, Dubois, *English Business Corporation*, pp. 232–4;
      Raistrick, *Quakers in Science and Industry*, pp. 193 ff.; Barker and
      Harris, *St. Helens*, pp. 75 ff.; G. G. Francis, *The Smelting of Copper*;
      Robert Plant, *History of Cheadle in Staffordshire* (Leek and London,
      1881); Ferber, op. cit., pp. 106, 139–40; *Mona Mine MSS.*, esp.
      Nos. 564–71, 840, 1319, 1552, 3028, 3048–56, 3544, 3762–5;
      Boulton and Watt Correspondence (Birmingham Assay Office) from
      John Hurd to Boulton, 22nd October 1785, from Rupert Leigh,
      5th November 1785; Rhys Jenkins, 'Copper Works at Redbrook';
      Nevill MSS. (National Library of Wales); (Thomas Martyn?),
      A Tour to South Wales, 1801 (MS. National Library of Wales,
      No. 1,340), p. 85; Rhys Jenkins, 'The Zinc Industry in England:
      The Early Years up to about 1850', *Trans.N.S.*, XXV (1945–7);
      idem. 'Copper Smelting in England: Revival at the end of the
      17th Century', ibid., XXIV (1943–5); T. R. Harris, 'John

84 3 Edwards' (1731–1807), Cornish Industrialist', ibid., XXIII
(1942–3); De Soyres, 'History and Particulars of the Brass Battery
Process', ibid., XXVIII (1951–3); A. H. John 'War and the
English Economy, 1700–1763', *Ec.H.R.* 2nd Series, VII (1955),
330–1; *Torrington Diaries*, I, 298, III, 122; *Copper Committee* (1799),
evid. Thomas Williams; W. H. Chaloner, 'Charles Roe of
Macclesfield (1715–81); An Eighteenth-Century Industrialist',
Trans. Lancashire and Cheshire Antiquarian Society, LXII–III (1950–
3); L. St. L. Pendred, 'The Order Book of the New Wire Com-
pany, Cheadle, 1788–1831', *Trans.N.S.*, XV (1934–5); G. H.
Tupling, 'The Early Metal Trades and the Beginning of Engineering in Lancashire', *Trans. Lancashire and Cheshire Antiquarian
Society*, 61 (1949); D. G. John, *Economic History*, I (4).

84 3 D. C. Coleman, 'Naval Dockyards under the Later Stuarts',
Ec.H.R., 2nd Series, VI (1953); A. H. John. 'War and the
English Economy', p. 333; *P.R.O.* Adm. 42.

85 1 Henry Green and Robert Wigram, *Chronicles of Blackwall Yard*,
Part 1 (1881); Dodd, *Days at the Factories*, pp. 389 ff., 432 ff., 463;
Clapham, *Economic History*, I, p. 185, 191.

85 2 H. M. Colvin, *A Biographical Dictionary of English Architects, 1660–
1840* (1954), p. 5 cf. also Mingay, op. cit., p. 209; *Manvers of
Thoresby MSS.* (Nottingham University) MA. 2X (2), Ma.4,
420–1; *Wharncliffe Muniments*, Nos. 142–4; Barrington Kaye, *The
Development of the Architectural Profession in Britain: A Sociological
Study* (1960), pp. 44 ff.

85 3 E. W. Cooney, 'The Origins of the Victorian Master Builders',
Ec.H.R. 2nd Series, VIII (1955), p. 170.

85 4 Ibid., p. 172.

86 1 *S.C. on Manufactures* (1833), evid. Thomas Burton, Q. 1664; H. W.
Dickinson, 'Joliffe and Banks', pp. 3–5; John Summerson,
Georgian London (1944), pp. 56 ff., 152–6, 174–9.

86 2 *S.C. on Manufactures* (1833), evid. John Stewart, QQ. 4,834,
4,853, 4,887.

86 3 Roy Devereux, *John London McAdam* (1936), p. 68.

86 4 H. C. Darby, *The Draining of the Fens* (Cambridge, 1940), p. 44.

86 5 *British Transport Commission MSS.* (York), ACN/4/100 and 101.
Also ACN/3/13 (9th May 1699) ACN/1/3 (21st September 1715,
27th October 1716, 16th November 1743), ACN/1/32, Report
1822, CHN (Calder and Hebble)/4/1.

87 1 M. Richards, 'Industrial Revolution in Caernarvonshire'; A. W.
Skempton, 'The Engineers of the English River Navigation,
1620–1760', *Trans.N.S.*, XXIX (1953–5); L. T. C. Rolt, *Isam-
bard Kingdom Brunel, A Biography* (1957), pp. 20 ff.; R. A. H. Page,
The Dock Companies in London, 1796–1864 (M.A. Thesis, Sheffield,
1959), pp. 91–94, 110–14, 123; *Federation of Civil Engineering
Contractors, British Civil Engineering Contracting Industry. Illustrated
History* (1956), pp. 21–22, 30.

87 2 T. C. Barker, The Beginnings of the Canal Age in the British
Isles', in L. S. Pressnell, *Industrial Revolution*; Aikin, *Manchester*,
pp. 317 ff.

87 3 Sir Alexander Gibb, *The Story of Telford: The Rise of Civil Engineering* (1935), p. 186; cf. also Rolt, *Thomas Telford*, pp. XV, 158.

87   4 Hans Straub, *A History of Civil Engineering* (1852 ed.), pp. 136–7.
87   5 Gibb, op. cit., pp. 186–7.
88   1 Dickinson, *James Watt*, p. 72, also Marshall, *James Watt*, p. 96 and Muirhead, *James Watt*, p. 236.
88   2 Smiles, *Lives*, I, p. 252.
88   3 Raistrick, *Dynasty*, p. 189.
88   4 Eliza Meteyard, *The Life of Josiah Wedgwood* (2 vols., 1865–6), I, p. 449; Josiah C. Wedgwood, *Staffordshire Pottery and its History* (1913), p. 97.
88   5 Hadfield, *British Canals*, pp. 39–40, 126 ff.; *idem.*, *The Canals of Southern England* (1955), p. 186. E. C. Smith (ed.), 'Joshua Field's Diary of a Tour in 1821 Through the Provinces', *Trans.N.S.*, XIII (1932–3), p. 43; Edith Malley, *Bridgwater Estate*, p. 22; British Transport Commission MSS. (London) BCN/4/121 (Birmingham Canal 1768), GJC/23/10 (Grand Junction Canal 1810–11) KAC/23/32 (Kennet and Avon Canal, 1806), GBC/3/1 (Gloucester and Berkely Canal, 1794); *B.T.C. MSS.* (York) ACN/1/32 (Ayre and Calder Navigation 1822).
88   6 John Phillips, *A Treatise on Inland Navigation* (1785), p. 37; Russell, *England Displayed*, II, p. 98; Simeon Shaw, *History of Staffordshire Potteries* (1900 ed.), pp. 23–24; Hugh Malet, *The Canal Duke*, pp. 86, 104, 215. Canals themselves might develop into substantial enterprises, but do not fall strictly within the limits of this book, Edith Malley, op. cit., pp. 78–83; Warner, *Tour Through the Northern Counties*, II, p. 158; *B.T.C. MSS.* (London) CVC/4/1 and 6.
88   7 Sir Frederick Morton Eden, *The State of the Poor, A History of the Labouring Classes in England, with Parochial Reports* (2 vols., 1797), II, 565; Arthur Redford, *Labour Migration in England, 1800–50* (Manchester, 1926), p. 130.
88   8 Chevalier, 'Gabriel Jars', p. 60; Charles E. Lee, 'Tynside Tramroads of Northumberland', *Trans.N.S.*, XXVI (1947–9); Rolt, *George and Robert Stephenson*, p. 5.
89   1 Charles Landale, *Letter to the Committee of the Dundee and Newtyle Railway Company* (Dundee, 1829), p. 6; E. Chadwick, *The Demoralisation and Injuries Occasioned by the Construction and Working of Railways* (Manchester); Henry Booth, *An Account of the Liverpool and Manchester Railway* (Liverpool, 2nd ed., 1831), pp. 37, 44; *B.T.C. MSS.* (York) SPC/1/11 (Leeds and Selby 1830), SAD/3/9 and 14 (Stockton and Darlington 1822 and 1824), SAD/1/6 (25th May 1821); Pease, *Diary*, Appendix IX pp. 371–81; Rolt, *Stephenson*, pp. 67 ff., 227–8; Harold Pollins, 'Railway Contractors and the Finance of Railway Development in Britain', *Journal of Transport History*, III (1857–8).
89   2 Frederick McDermot, *The Life and Work of Joseph Fairbank, Railway Contractor* (1887); Arthur Helps, *Life and Labour of Mr. Brassey, 1805–1870* (1872); *B.T.C.* (York) SAD/8/86, Thomas Storey to Company, 29th March, 1824, 6th April 1824, LIB(Y)/15/26 p. 7; Brassey, *Labour Questions*, p. 137; Eleanor Eden, *The Autobiography of a Working Man* (1862), pp. 70–73.
89   3 Rolt, *Stephenson*, p. 186.
89   4 Ernest F. Carter, *An Historical Geography of the Railways of the British Isles* (1959), p. 211.

89   5 Fleming & Brocklehurst, op. cit., pp. 211–13; Dodd, *Days at the Factories*, chapter XVIII; Thomas Peckston, *A Practical Treatise on Gas-Lighting* (1841), pp. 91–93; Everard, *Gas, Light and Coke Company*; Thomas B. Mackenzie, *Life of James Beaumont Neilson, F.R.S.* (1928), p. 7; Clow, *Chemical Revolution* pp. 435–6.

90   1 Lord, *Capital and Steam-Power*, p. 186; Peter Gorb, 'Robert Owen as a Businessman', *Bulletin of the Business Historical Society*, XXV (1951) p. 129.

90   2 John Hodgson, *Textile Manufacture and other Industries in Keighley* (Keighley, 1879), pp. 212 ff.; Parakunnel J. Thomas, 'The Beginnings of Calico Printing in England', *English Historical Review*, XXXIX (1924); Lewis, *Topographical Dictionary of Wales*, *s.v.* 'Flint'.

91   1 P. Gaskell, *The Manufacturing Population of England* (1833), pp. 45, 53–54. Also, e.g. G. D. H. Cole, *Robert Owen* (1925), p. 57; Owen, *Life of Owen*, pp. 57–58.

91   2 (P. Colquhoun), *Considerations Relative to a Plan of Relief for the Cotton Manufactory* (1788), p. 44; Richard Guest, *Compendious History of the Cotton Manufactore* (Manchester, 1823), p. 31; J. D. Marshall, 'The Cotton Mills of the Upper Lean', *Trans. Thoroton Society*, LX (1956).

91   3 Frank Podmore, *Robert Owen, A Biography* (1923 ed.), p. 81; Henry Grey MacNab, *The New Views of Mr. Owen of Lanark Impartially Examined* (1819), pp. 61–66; Sir John Sinclair, *Old Statistical Account of Scotland*, XV, p. 36; W. H. Marwick, 'The Cotton Industry and the Industrial Revolution in Scotland', *Scottish Historical Review*, XXI (1924); Mitchell, 'Cotton Industry', ibid. (1925); Garnett, *Tour Through the Highlands*, II, pp. 169 ff.; *S.C. on Manufactures* (1833) evid. Kirkman Finlay, Henry Houldsworth; *Committee on Orders in Council* (1812), evid. Kirkman Finlay; *Inspectors of Factories, Reports* (1834), p. 11; Frances Collier, 'An Early Factory Community', *Economic History*, II (1930), pp. 117 ff.; J. Montgomery, *The Theory & Practice of Cotton Spinning; Or the Carding and Spinning Master's Assistant* (Glasgow, 1833), pp. 276–7;

91   4 Unwin, 'Transition to the Factory System'; Unwin, *Samuel Oldknow*; Collier, 'Workers in a Lancashire Factory', p. 50; *Calico Printers' Committee*, (B.P.P.), 1806–7 (129), II, p. 3; W. A. Hunter, 'James Hargreaves and the Invention of the Spinning Jenny', *Trans.N.S.*, XXVIII (1951–3), 143–4, 150; Sir Lawrence Peel, *A Sketch of the Life and Character of Sir Robert Peel* (1860), pp. 16 ff.

92   1 Warner, *Tour Through the Northern Counties*, II, p. 145; W. H. Chaloner, 'Robert Owen, Peter Drinkwater and the Early Factory System in Manchester', *Bull. John Rylands Library*, 37 (1954–5), p. 80; *Boulton and Watt Correspondence* (Assay Office), Boulton to John Porter, 16th November 1805; Fitton & Wadsworth, op. cit., p. 2820.

92   2 Guest, op. cit., p. 46; Radcliffe, *Origins of the New System of Manufacture*, p. 20; James Butterworth, *The Antiquities of the Town and a Complete History of the Trade of Manchester* (Manchester, 1822), 135.

92   3 *House of Lords Committee on Apprentices* (1818–19); *S.C. on Children in*

92   3 *Manufactories* (1816); *Lords' Committee on Factory Bill* (1818); Clapham, *Economic History of Modern Britain*, I, pp. 184—5; *idem.*, 'Some
Factory Statistics of 1815–16.'

92   4 *S.C. on Manufactures* (1833); Jean Lindsay, 'An Early Industrial
Community. The Evans' Cotton Mill at Darley Abbey, Derbyshire, 1783–1810', *Business History Review*, XXXIV (1960).

92   5 *Factories Inquiry Commission* (1833–4); *S.C. on Manufactures* (1833).

93   1 Clapham, *Economic History*, I, p. 184; Ure, *Cotton Manufacture*, I,
pp. 390–7.

93   2 *Factories Inquiry Commission*, I, D2, evid. R. H. Greg, p. 30.

93   3 *S.C. on Manufactures* (1833), evid. William Graham, Q.5408.

93   4 *Factories Inquiry Commission*, I, D2, evid. R. H. Greg; M. Blaug,
'The Productivity of Capital in the Lancashire Cotton Industry
During the Nineteenth Century', *Ec.H.R.*, 2nd Series, XIII (1961),
p. 359; E. Baines jun., *Cotton Manufacture*, p. 184; Roland Smith,
'Manchester as the Centre for the Manufacture and Merchanting
of Cotton Goods, 1820–30', *Univ. of Birmingham Historical Journal*,
IV (1953–4), p. 52.

94   1 Hammond, *Skilled Labourer*, pp. 140–54; Heaton, *Yorkshire
Woollen and Worsted Industry*, p. 283; Crump, *Leeds Woollen In-
dustry*; Crump and Ghorbal, *Huddersfield Woollen Industry*; Sigs-
worth, op. cit., pp. 3–4; Edward Collinson, *History of the Worsted
Trade* (Bradford, 1851), pp. 69–70; Hartwell, *Yorkshire Woollen and
Worsted Industry*; John James, *History of the Worsted Manufacture in
England* (1857); J. T. Ward, *The Factory Movement 1830–1855*
(1952), pp. 8–12; Mantoux. op. cit., pp. 264 ff.

94   2 Heaton, 'Benjamin Gott'; *Gott Papers* (MSS., Brotherton Library,
University of Leeds).

95   1 Fong, op. cit., pp. 62, 85; *Factories Inquiry Commission, passim.*; Sir
Richard Phillips, *Personal Tour*, pp. 52; *V. C. H. Durham*, II, p.
316; *Commission on Children in Factories* (1832), evid. John Hall;
V. C. H. Wiltshire, IV, 'Textile Industry'; *Committee on Woollen
Clothiers*, (1802–3), evid. Edward Sheppard, p. 3; *S.C. on Manu-
factures* (1833), evid. John Brooke, Q. 1859; *Committee on Orders in
Council* (1812) evid. John Parker, p. 192, William Midgely, p. 196,
William Walker, p. 202, William Hastings, p. 205, John Grundy,
jun., p. 213, William Thompson, p. 229, David Sheard, p. 260.

95   2 Rimmer, *Marshalls; idem.*, 'Castle Forgate Flax Mill, Shrewsbury
(1797–1886)', *Trans. Shropshire Archaeological Society*, LVI/I (1957–
8); Alexander J. Warden, *The Linen Trade, Ancient and Modern*
(1864), p. 694; *Boulton and Watt Correspondence* (Assay Office),
from John Kendrew & Company, 24th January 1794; *Marshall
Papers* (MSS., Brotherton Library, University of Leeds); Ure,
Philosophy of Manufacturers, p. 442; G. R. Porter, *The Progress of
the Nation* (1828), p. 269; *S.C. on Manufactures* (1833), evid. John
Marshall, Q. 2,367.

95   3 Ada K. Longfield, 'History of the Irish Linen and Cotton Printing
Industry in the 18th Century', *Journal of the Royal Society of
Antiquaries in Ireland*, Ser. 7, Vol. 7, 67/1 (1937).

95   4 Clapham, 'Factory Statistics', p. 477; *S.C. on Children in Manufactories* (1816), pp. 240–3; Ure, *Philosophy of Manufacturers*, p. 467.

96   1 Wadsworth & Mann, op. cit., p. 304; Gerald B. Hertz, 'The

96   1 English Silk Industry in the 18th Century', *English Historical Review*, XXIV (1909); Llewellyn Jewitt (ed.) *The Life of William Hutton* (1872), p. 105; Bray, *Tour of Derbyshire*, p. 107; Russell, *England Displayed*, II, pp. 104–12.

96   2 *Commons' Journal*, 1773, p. 240, 1765, XXX, 216–19; N. K. A. Rothstein, *Silk Industry in London*, pp. 136–7; Fong, op. cit., pp. 98–100; Horner, *Tour Through the Northern Counties*, I, p. 113; *Committee on Children in Factories* (1832), evid. James Turner, Q. 7,292; *Wentworth Woodhouse Muniments*, R. 174–2, July 19th, 1764; Eden, *State of the Poor*, II, p. 129; Clutterbuck, *Journal*, II, pp. 128–30; Chaloner, 'Charles Roe', I, p. 139; *S.C. on Manufactures* (1833), evid. William Haynes; *S.C. on Children in Factories* (1816), evid. James Pattison; Unwin, 'Transition to the Factory System', p. 213.

96   3 Charlotte Erickson, *British Industrialists—Steel and Hosiery, 1850–1950* (Cambridge, 1959), p. 87; Wells, *British Hosiery Trade*, p. 83.

97   1 Bebbington, *Samuel Garbett*; Cadell, *Story of the Forth*, p. 145; Saint-Fond, *Travels in England*, I, p. 77; Court, *Rise of the Midland Industries*, p. 228; H. W. Dickinson, 'The History of Vitriol Making in England', *Trans.N.S.*, XVIII (1937–8), 48–50; L. F. Haber, *The Chemical Industry During the 19th Century* (Oxford, 1958), p. 4; Clow, *Chemical Revolution*.

97   2 E. W. D. Tennant, 'The Early History of the St. Rollox Chemical Works', *Chemistry and Industry*, 1st November 1947; George Macintosh, *Biographical Memoir of the Late Charles Macintosh, F.R.S.* (Glasgow, 1847); Devereux, *J. L. MacAdam*, pp. 42–43; MacKinnon, op. cit., p. 119; Hamilton, *Industrial Revolution in Scotland*, p. 145; Clow, 'George Macintosh'; *idem.*, 'Lord Dundonald', *Ec.H.R.*, XII (1942); *V. C. H. Durham*, II, p. 276.

97   3 R. Campbell, *London Tradesman* (1747), pp. 264, 331 ff.; Also. Lord, op. cit., p. 188.

98   1 Peter Mathias, *Brewing Industry*; *idem.*, 'The Entrepreneur in Brewing', pp. 35–36; Saint-Fond, op. cit., I, pp. 101 ff.

98   2 Clow, *Chemical Revolution*, pp. 564–8; Dodd, *Days at the Factories*, II, III, V, VI.

98   3 A. D. Insull, *The Albion Mill Story*; A. O. Westworth, 'The Albion Steam Flour Mill', *Economic History*, II (1932); Farey, op. cit., p. 514; *Annual Register*, Vol. 3, for 3rd March 1791.

98   4 John Thomas, 'The Pottery Industry and the Industrial Revolution', *Economic History*, III (1937).

99   1 Meteyard, *Life of Wedgwood*; Neil McKendrick, 'Josiah Wedgwood, An Eighteenth-Century Entrepreneur in Salesmanship and Marketing Techniques', *Ec.H.R.*, 2nd Ser. XII (1960) and 'Josiah Wedgwood and Factory Discipline', *Historical Journal*, IV (1961); Ralph M. Hower, 'The Wedgwoods, Ten Generations of Potters', *Journal of Economic and Business History*, IV (1932); Bladen, 'Potteries in the Industrial Revolution'; E. Surrey Dane, *The Economic History of the Staffordshire Pottery Industry* (M.A. Thesis, Sheffield, 1929); J. C. Wedgwood, *Staffordshire Pottery*.

99   2 *Committee on Orders in Council* (1812), pp. 161, 171; *Factories Inquiry Commission*, I, B2, pp. 1 ff., 78; Thomas, *The Economic Development of*

99 2 *the North Staffordshire Potteries*; Fong, op. cit., pp. 126 ff.; S. Shaw, *History of the Staffordshire Potteries*, p. 30.

99 3 Bray, op. cit., p. 108; *Herculaneum Pottery MSS.* (Picton Library, Liverpool), 380 M.D.47, Minute Book, 3rd December 1806, 2nd April 1816; *Wentworth Woodhouse Muniments*, F.106b, F.107c. Newman to Fitzwilliam, 26th December 1825, G47, *passim*.

100 1 Court, *Rise of the Midland Industries*, pp. 115 ff., 220 ff.; Barker and Harris, op. cit., pp. 112–17, 203–7; J. Campbell, *Political Survey*, p. 27; Aikin, *Manchester*, pp. 312–13; *Committee on Orders in Council* (1812), p. 291; Warner, *Tour*, I, p. 314; *V. C. H. Durham*, II, p. 309–310; Robert Edlington, *A Treatise on the Coal Trade* (1813), pp. 151–2; Saint-Fond, I, p. 136.

100 2 Fong, op. cit., pp. 132–3.

100 3 Court, *Rise of the Midlands Industries*, p. 114; *Factories Inquiry Commission*, I. A1, p. 3; Coleman, *Paper Industry*; Fong, op. cit., p. 123.

CHAPTER 4

104 1 Nicholas Hans, *New Trends in Education in the Eighteenth Century* (1951); R. K. Webb, *The British Working-Class Reader 1790–1848* (1955). Also see W. H. G. Armytage, *Four Hundred Years of English Education* (Cambridge, 1964), Chapter IV: 'Prelude to Take-off, 1732–1790'.

105 1 It was, of course, precisely this openness which led to the attack on privilege, e.g., in the armed forces, within the Civil List, and in the Corporations at this time, and called forth the reform of British institutions beginning in the 1830's.

105 2 E. P. Thompson, *The Making of the English Working Class* (1963), p. 199, quoting 'A Journeyman Cotton Spinner'. In the period 1750–1850, of 132 prominent industrialists, only one-third rose from workmen's or small farmers' families; the rest began from established businesses. Entrepreneurs in the cotton industry, however, had unusually democratic origins, Bendix, op. cit., pp. 24–26.

105 3 Dr. Aikin, of Warrington Academy, began by teaching the Classics, French, 'Grammar, Oratory and Criticism', Logic and History, and later took over the main course of Theology. Turner, *Warrington Academy*, pp. 12–16.

105 4 H. G. Graham, *The Social Life of Scotland in the Eighteenth Century* (1901), pp. 417 ff.

106 1 For John Kelsall, see his *MS. Diary* in Friend's House, Euston Road, especially early 1728, June 1730, February to March 1734, March 1736. For John Dawson of Sedbergh, e.g., E. Hughes (ed.), *Diaries and Correspondence of James Losh*, Vol. 1, *Diary 1811–1823* (Surtees Society, Vol. CLXXI for 1956, 1962), p. XII.

106 2 A. H. John, 'Aspects of English Economic Growth in the First Half of the Eighteenth Century', *Economica*, NS, 28 (1961), p. 189. Also, e.g. H. W. Dickinson and Arthur Lee, 'The Rastricks—Civil Engineers', *Trans.N.S.*, IV (1923–4), p. 50; Barrington Kaye, *The Development of the Architectural Profession in Britain: A Sociological Study* (1960), p. 67.

106 3 On this background, see Lawrence Stone, 'The Educational Revolution in England, 1560–1640', *Past and Present*, 28 (1964).
106 4 Dobbs, *Education and Social Movements*, pp. 67–68, 71; Bouch & Jones, *Lake Counties*, p. 201; Frederic Hill, *National Education, Its Present State and Prospect* (2 vols., 1836), I, p. 241.
107 1 A. J. Taylor, 'The Sub-Contract System in the British Coal Industry', pp. 217–18.
107 2 Cf. W. E. Minchinton, 'The Merchants in England in the Eighteenth Century', in *The Entrepreneur*, p. 5.
108 1 D. Defoe, *Augusta Triumphans*, Vol. XVIII of Tegg ed. (1841), pp. 4–7, 112; Postlethwayt, *Counting House*; R. B. Westerfield, *Middleman*, pp. 395–7; George C. Brauer jun., *The Education of a Gentleman* (New York, 1959), pp. 83–84.
108 2 Campbell, *London Tradesman*, pp. 84–87, also p. 293.
109 1 Raistrick, *Dynasty*, p. 93.
109 2 Josiah Wedgwood, *Letters to Bentley, 1771–1780* (Private Circulation, 1903), W. to B., 8th November 1779, 28th November 1779, 19th December 1779. Also cf., Josiah Wedgwood, *Private Correspondence, 1781–1794* (Private Circulation, 1906), Wedgwood, jun., to Father, 7th March 1790.
110 1 Brian Simon, *Studies in the History of Education, 1780–1870* (1960), p. 36.
110 2 Chester W. New, *Lord Durham, A Biography of John George Lambton, First Earl of Durham* (Oxford, 1929), p. 7.
110 3 W. P. Campbell Stewart, *Quakers and Education* (1953), p. 44.
111 1 J. W. Ashley Smith, *The Birth of Modern Education: The Contribution of the Dissenting Academies 1660–1800* (1954), pp. 133–4. Also, R. H. Tawney, *Religion and the Rise of Capitalism* (1926).
111 2 John William Adamson, *English Education, 1789–1902* (Cambridge, 1930), p. 3; Kelly, *George Birkbeck*, pp. 62–63; Brian Simon, op. cit., pp. 84 ff.
111 3 L. G. Johnson, *The Social Evolution of Industrial Britain* (Liverpool, 1959), pp. 7 and 9.
111 4 Brian Simon, op. cit., p. 18, also 38; D. M. Turner, *History of Science Teaching in England* (1927), p. 43. But the effort behind this should not be underrated. W. W. Rostow, 'Leading Sectors and the Take-off', in Rostow, ed. *The Economics of Take-Off into Sustained Growth* (1963), pp. 16–17.
112 1 F. Musgrove, 'Middle Class Education and Employment in the Nineteenth Century', *Ec.H.R.*, Second Series, XII (1959), p. 100.
112 2 This is in striking contrast with the development in countries which attempt to drive through an industrialization programme in the teeth of social unreadiness: 'The shortage of skills . . . in the case of technicians, engineers, accountants and administrators . . . derive(s) not only from poorly equipped educational systems, but also from problems of motivations and occupational choice. Indeed, a number of developing countries have no absolute shortage of people with advanced education—but they are prepared for traditionally honourable occupations rather than the most urgent needed in industrial enterprises', W. E. Moore, 'Industrialization and Social Change', in Hoselitz and Moore, *Industrialization and Society*, p. 316.

112 3 Wedgwood, *Correspondence*, esp. pp. 16, 132, 547–8, 552–6.
112 4 Musgrove, loc. cit., pp. 100–1; and 'Middle-Class Families and Schools 1780–1880: Inter-Action and Exchange of Function between Institutions', *Sociological Review*, N.S. 7 (1959), 169–72; Ashton, *Peter Stubs*, p. 137; Fleming & Brocklehurst, op. cit., p. 50; Robert E. Schofield, *The Lunar Society of Birmingham. A Social History of Provincial Science and Industry of Eighteenth-Century England* (Oxford, 1963), pp. 131–2, 217, 405.
112 5 Mosgrove, 'Middle-Class Families', p. 169.
112 6 Rosemund Bayne-Powell, *The English Child in the Eighteenth Century* (1939), pp. 65, 77; H. McLachlan, *Warrington Academy, Its History and Influence* (Cheetham Society, Manchester, 1943, N.S. No. 107), pp. 139 ff.
113 1 Conversely, Dr. Aikin of Warrington Academy, one of the leading scholars of the age, had started life in a Merchant's Office, Irene Parker, *Dissenting Academy in England* (Cambridge, 1914), p. 110.
113 2 Bouch & Jones, op. cit., p. 201.
114 1 Hans, op. cit., pp. 38–41; at Manchester, of the 672 boys passing through the Grammar School in the period 1740–65, 28 per cent came from the landed classes and the professions; the remainder were of families of industrial or commercial origins.
114 2 Adamson, *English Education*, p. 47; Simon, op. cit., pp. 103–8. Hughes, *North Country Life*, pp. 364.
115 1 Hans, op. cit., p. 62, *et passim*; Stephen F. Cotgrove, *Technical Education and Social Change* (1958), p. 16.
115 2 Hans, pp. 83, 86; Malachi Postlethwayt, *Universal Dicionary of Trade and Commerce* (3rd ed.), 1766, art. 'British Mercantile College'.
115 3 It may be significant that the Cheadle New Wire Company sent one of its employees to London in 1820 to study chemistry, when some local tuition must have been available, Pendred, 'New Wire Company', p. 109.
116 1 Beresford Worthington, *Professional Accountants, An Historical Sketch* (1895), pp. 25–27; Benjamin Franklin Foster, *The Origin and Progress of Book-Keeping* (1852); Erickson, op. cit., pp. 110–11; James Morrison, *Queries on Bills and Merchants' Accounts* (1818); Solomons, *Studies in Costing*, p. 4, fn. 5; A. C. Littleton and B. S. Yamey, *Studies in the History of Accounting* (1956), p. 302.
117 1 H. McLachlan, *English Education under the Test Acts* (Manchester, 1931) pp. 6–36; Hans, op. cit., pp. 55–59; Parker, op. cit.; E. D. Bebb, *Nonconformity and Social and Economic Life, 1660–1800* (1935), p. 172; H. P. Roberts, 'Non-Conformist Academies in Wales (1662–1862)', *Trans. Hon. Society of Cymmrodorion* (1930).
118 1 Parker, op. cit., p. 122.
118 2 Turner, op. cit., esp. Part II; McLachlan, *Education; idem, Essays and Addresses* (Manchester, 1950); Parker, pp. 105 ff.; Smith, *Modern Education*, pp. 161 ff.; Simon, op. cit., p. 29.
118 3 Joseph Priestley, *An Essay on a Course of Liberal Education for Civil and Active Life* (1765); W. H. Chaloner, 'Dr. Joseph Priestley, John Wilkinson and the French Revolution, 1789–1802', *Trans. R.H.S.*, 5th Ser., VIII (1957); John F. Fulton, 'The Warrington Academy (1757–86),' *Bull. Inst. of the History of Medicine*, I (1933).

118	4	Anthony Lincoln, *Some Political and Social Ideas of English Dissent, 1763–1800* (Cambridge, 1938), pp. 12–13, 16–7; Mathias, *Brewing Industry*, pp. 289–90.
119	1	Allan Ferguson (ed.), *Natural Philosophy Through the 18th Century*, The Philosophical Magazine (London), 150th Anniversary No. (1948), F. Sherwood Taylor, 'Teaching of the Physical Sciences at the end of the Eighteenth Century'; Hans, op. cit., p. 118.
119	2	Turner, op. cit., p. 41.
119	3	Malet, *The Canal Duke*, p. 30; Eric Robinson, 'An English Jacobin, James Watt, jun., 1769–1848', *Cambridge Historical Journal*, XI (1955), p. 350; *Boulton & Watt Letters* (MSS., Royal Cornwall Polytechnic Society, Falmouth), Watt to Wilson, 16th March 1786.
119	4	Douglas McKie, 'The Scientific Periodical from 1665 to 1798', in Ferguson, op. cit.
120	1	Wolf, op. cit., p. 560; E. C. Smith, 'Engineering and Invention in the Eighteenth Century', in Ferguson, op. cit., p. 93.
120	2	Hans, op. cit., pp. 138–41, 145–6; Turner, op. cit., pp. 52–53; A. E. Musson and E. Robinson, 'Science and Industry in the Late Eighteenth Century', *Ec.H.R.*, 2nd Ser., XIII (1960), pp. 230–6, 242; Frank Greenway, 'The Biographical Approach to John Dalton', *Memoirs and Proc. Manchester Lit. & Phil. Soc.*, Vol. 100 (1958–9), pp. 9–10; Meteyard, op. cit., II, 439; Witt Bowden, *The Rise of the Great Manufacturers in England, 1760–1790* (Allentown, Pennsylvania, 1919), p. 6; Michael Brook, 'Dr. Warwick's Chemical Lectures', *Annals of Science*, XI (1956).
120	3	Douglas McKie, 'Scientific Societies to the end of the Eighteenth Century', in Ferguson, op. cit.; R. E. Schofield, 'Membership of the Lunar Society in Birmingham', *Annals of Science*, XII (1956); Eric Robinson, 'The Derby Philosophical Society', ibid., IX (1953).
120	4	Hans, op. cit., p. 158; Kelly, *Birkbeck*, pp. 20 ff.; J. W. Hudson, *The History of Adult Education* (1851); Dobbs, *Education*, pp. 141, 175; Charles Alfons Bennett, *History of Manual and Industrial Education after 1870* (Peoria, Ill., 1926), p. 301; Mabel Tylecote, *The Mechanics' Institutes of Lancashire and Yorkshire before 1851* (Manchester, 1957); James Muir, *John Anderson* (Glasgow, 1950), pp. 8–9, 100; Haber, op. cit., pp. 33.
121	1	Tylecote, op. cit., p. 75, also Appx. II, p. 296; A. Abbott, *Education for Industry and Commerce in England* (1933), p. 15.
121	2	Tylecote, op. cit., p. 9.
121	3	Nasmyth, *Autobiography*, pp. 96, 108–11; McKenzie, *Nielson*, pp. 5–8.
121	4	Muir, op. cit., p. 9; Ure, *Philosophy of Manufactures*, Preface, p. VI; Hill, *National Education*, II, 196.
121	5	This should be compared with present industrializing countries, so many of which use their education system to produce 'intellectuals', but fail to train 'engineers, technicians, managers and . . . organization builders', Harbison & Myers, op. cit., pp. 89, 111. Also Gunnar Myrdal, *An International Economy* (1956), p. 187.
122	1	Ch. 7 below.
122	2	This in itself contributed to high social mobility: 'wide status changes . . . are, and have always been, relatively rare in all societies. High-level managers rarely come from the ranks of

122 2 production workers . . . one significant cause is the fact that the work experience itself is not an adequate means for acquiring the necessary skills. Educational opportunities for adults to up-grade their skills while employed naturally increases chances of promotion'. W. E. Moore, 'Industrialization and Social Change', in Hoselitz & Moore, op. cit., p. 321.

122 4 Robert Robson, *The Attorney in Eighteenth-Century England*, pp. 52–58; Kaye, *Architectural Profession*, pp. 12, 44 ff., 51; McLachlan, *Education*, p. 82; A. M. Carr-Saunders and P. A. Wilson, *The Professions* (Oxford, 1933), p. 293; Bernice Hamilton, 'The Medical Professions in the Eighteenth Century', *Ec.H.R.*, 2nd Ser., IV (1951), p. 141 ff. Cf. also, e.g. (William Halfpenny), *The Builder's Pocket Companion, by Michael Hoare, Carpenter* (1721).

122 5 See Arnold Anderson, 'The Impact of the Educational System on Technological Change and Modernisation' in Hoselitz & Moore, op. cit., p. 261.

122 6 John Gibbons, *Practical Remarks on the Use of the Cinder Pig in the Puddling Furnace; and on the Management of the Forge and the Mill* (1844), pp. 75, 81.

122 7 Dickinson, *James Watt*, p. 47; idem., *Matthew Boulton*, p. 29.

123 1 Dickinson, *James Watt*, pp. 163, 165; *Boulton & Watt Correspondence* (Birmingham Assay Office), Watt to Boulton, 21st June 1784.

123 2 Wedgwood, *Correspondence*, pp. 74, 116; *Boulton & Watt MSS.* (Birmingham Reference Library), G. Gilpin, 14th September 1796; *Boulton and Watt Correspondence* (Birmingham Assay Office), John Gilbert, 15th October 1765; Malet, *Canal Duke*, pp. 10, 53, 137; Dickinson & Lee, 'The Rastricks—Civil Engineers', p. 50; G. F. Tyas, 'Matthew Murray, A Centenary Appreciation', *Trans.N.S.*, VI (1925–6), p. 120.

123 3 Smiles, *Lives*, I, 174 ff., II, 113, 252 ff., IV, 22 ff.

123 4 *Mona Mine MSS.*, No. 2,690.

124 1 Campbell, *London Tradesman*, p. 264; Hower, '*The Wedgwoods*', p. 289; Crump, *Leeds Woollen Industry*, pp. 272 ff., 308; Chambers, *Nottinghamshire*, pp. 131–2; Rothstein, *Silk Industry*, p. 191.

124 2 Hamilton, *Industrial Revolution*, p. 127; Fitton & Wadsworth, op. cit., pp. 98, 105, 111; Owen, *Life of Owen*, p. 101, also 191; *S.C. on Children in Manufactories* (1816), p. 5.

124 3 Gaskell, *Manufacturing Population*, p. 63.

124 4 Owen, *Life of Owen*, pp. 31–32.

124 5 Unwin, *Samuel Oldknow*, p. 126. 'If a more educated and ambitious young man sought such a post at nominal salary', the authors go on to say, 'it was with the intention of learning the business and setting up for himself. Most of Oldknow's managers became prosperous masters.' This problem is treated below, pp. 151–2.

124 6 *Factories Inquiry Commission*, I, A1, 52, 57, A2, 53, 60; *Commission on Children in Factories* (1832), evid. Peter Smart, Q. 7789.

125 1 *Factories Inquiry Commission*, I, p. 187.

125 2 Brassey, *Labour Questions*, p. 126. He added: 'a Board will make appointments upon the faith of testimonials. The private individual will trust personal observation.'

125 3 David Mushet, *Papers on Iron and Steel (1840)*, pp. VI–XII; Clow, *Chemical Revolution*, p. 609.

125 4 The usage was common also in the Public Service, including the productive departments such as the Office of Works and the Dockyards, and survived among early railways. Charles E. Lee: 'The Clerk of the (early Surrey Iron Railway) Company', *Trans.N.S.*, XXVII (1949–51), p. 67.

126 1 *Committee on the Liverpool–Manchester Railway* (1825), p. 671, evid. Thomas Wood.

126 2 Lord, *Capital and Steam Power*, p. 201.

126 3 The distinction between the market-oriented and technique-oriented industries, can be made for entrepreneurs as well as managers. Cf., Court, 'Warwickshire Colliery', pp. 227–8.

126 4 See, Ch. 2 above, also D. C. Coleman, 'London Scrivenors and the Estate Market in the later seventeenth century', *Ec.H.R.*, 2nd Ser., IV (1951), p. 222 and esp. Thompson, *English Landed Society*, pp. 157–8.

126 5 See above, p. 120.

126 6 John Guest, *Historic Notices of Rotherham* (Worksop, 1879), pp. 485, 683.

126 7 See Ch. 6 below. Also, Postlethwayt, *Universal Dictionary*, *s.v.* 'Account' and 'Accountant'; W. E. Minchinton, 'The Merchants in England in the Eighteenth Century', in *The Entrepreneur*, p. 23; Foster, *Book-Keeping; Spencer-Stanhope Muniments* Nos. 60528 and 60529; *Newton Chambers Archives* (MSS., Chapeltown), Correspondence, Scott-Newton early 1811. Extracts in B. S. Yamey, H. C. Edey and Hugh W. Thomson, *Accounting in England and Scotland: 1543–1800: Double Entry in Exposition and Practice* (1963), e.g., pp. 8 ff., 110–12, show the complete lack of interest of accountants in industrial firms.

126 8 *Boulton and Watt Correspondence* (Birmingham Assay Office), Watt to Boulton, 24th January 1774.

127 1 Dunn, *History of the Viewers;* Simpson, 'Mining Records', pp. 77–79.

127 2 Hughes, *North Country Life*, pp. 75–76; Marshall, *Railways to 1830*, p. 30; John, 'Coal and Iron on a Glamorgan Estate', p. 101. This may be seen as an example of Redlich's thesis that managers develop first in the works of the landed classes, who would not stoop to administer them themselves, Fritz Redlich, *Der Unternehmer* (Göttingen, 1964), pp. 205, 331.

127 3 John Curr, the talented and inventive viewer for Norfolk's Sheffield collieries, and George Kirkhouse and W. S. Clark, two of the leading South Wales viewers, for example, came from the North-East. Phillips, *Pioneers of Welsh Coalfield*, p. 186; Fred Bland, 'John Curr, originator of iron tram roads', *Trans.N.S.*, XI (1930–1), p. 121.

128 1 Holland, *Coal Trade*, pp. 293–4.

128 2 J. C., *Compleat Collier*, p. 35; United Colliers' Association, *A Candid Appeal to the Coal Owners and Viewers of Collieries on the Tyne and Wear* (Newcastle, 1826), p. 3; Hughes, 'Eighteenth-Century Estate Agent', p. 97; Benjamin Thompson, *Inventions, Improvements and Practice of B.T.* (Newcastle, 1847), p. 74.

128 3 Thomas Fenwick, *Four Essays on Practical Mechanics* (Newcastle, 1801), *A Theoretical and Practical Treatise on Subterranean Surveying* (Newcastle, 1804), and *A Practical System of the Different Branches of*

128 3 *Natural Philosophy* (Newcastle, 1801); John Curr, *The Coal Viewer and Engine Builder's Practical Companion* (Sheffield, 1797); B. Thompson, op. cit.

128 4 Turner, op. cit., p. 78; Also, Hopkinson, op. cit., p. 398 and Frank Machin, *The Yorkshire Miners, a History* (1958), I, p. 12–17.

128 5 Cf., *Tehidy Estate MSS.*, Memo Book for 1756, Staff Duties: Captain Hocking 'is to attend the Accounts of the several Mines, were in I am an Adventurer and to act on the behalf of myself and my friends'.

129 1 George Abbott, jun., *An Essay on the Mines of England* (1833), pp. 5, 15. For examples of such plural consultancy, see *Copper Committee* (1799), p. 18, evid. John Williams, p. 19, evid. John Vivian, p. 21, evid. Andrew Vivian.

129 2 Esp. A. W. Skempton, 'Engineers of River Navigation', pp. 34–37.

129 3 Paul N. Wilson, 'The Water Wheels of John Smeaton', *Trans.N.S.*, XXX (1955–7); Charles Hadfield, *The Canals of South Wales and the Border* (Cardiff, 1960), p. 20; M. W. Flinn, 'The Travel Diaries of Swedish Engineers of the Eighteenth Century as Sources of Technological History', *Trans.N.S.*, XXXI (1957–9), p. 18; Skempton, 'Engineers', *passim*; F. Williamson, 'George Sorocold of Derby', *Journal Derbyshire Arch. & Nat. Hist. Soc.*, p. 57 (1936).

129 4 *British Transport Commission Archives* (York) ACN/3/13, 9th May 1699. Also, Willan, *River Navigation*, p. 80. Compare the contract for the building of the Stockton and Darlington Railway in 1821: 'the Engineer to be employed, shall have the superintendence and direction of the works, make all the specification for contracts, and tend to the execution and completion of the same', *B.T.C. Archives*, SAD/1/6, Minutes for 25th May 1821.

130 1 Dickinson, *James Watt*, pp. 78–79.

130 2 Colvin, *Biographical Dictionary*, pp. 9–24.

130 2 Smiles, *Lives*, II, p. 350; Rolt, *Telford*, p. 56; Hadfield, *British Canals*, pp. 40, 127;

130 3 Skempton, loc. cit., p. 34; *B.T.C. Archives* (York), SAD/8/51, application George Atkinson, 23rd July 1821, CHN/4/1.

130 4 Smiles, *Lives*, III, pp. 220–1.

130 5 Hadfield, *British Canals*, p. 40; Harley, 'Samuel Whitbread', pp. 178 ff.; A. Stanley Davies, 'First Steam Engine in Wales', *Trans.N.S.*, XVII (1937–8), p. 101.

131 1 Charles Lonsdale, *Letter to the Dundee and Newtyle Railway Company* (Dundee, 1829), prefatory note.

131 2 S. B. Donkin, 'The Society of Civil Engineers (Smeatonians)', *Trans.N.S.*, XVII (1936–7), pp. 52–55; Gibb, *Telford*, pp. 192–4; Rolt, *Telford*, pp. 189–90.

132 1 J. W. Roe, *English and American Tool Builders* (Yale University Press 1916), p. 7; *Boulton and Watt Correspondence* (Birmingham Assay Office), Boulton to Thomas Creighton, 1st October 1791, to H. Holland, 30th August 1801; G. F. Tyas, 'Matthew Murray, A Centenary Appreciation', *Trans.N.S.*, VI (1925–6); *S.C. on Artisans and Machinery* (1824), pp. 250, 322; H. W. Dickinson, 'Joseph Bramah & His Inventions', *Trans.N.S.*, XXII (1941–2), p. 180 and 'Richard Roberts, His Life and Inventions', ibid., XXV (1945–7).

132 2 James Nasmyth, *Autobiography* (1897 ed.), p. 90.

132 3 S. Snell, *A Story of Railway Pioneers* (1921), pp. 1–21; *Dowlais Letters* (MSS., Glamorgan County Record Office), William Taitt to Guest, 24th April 1799; Stanley Mercer, 'Trevithick and the Merthyr Tram Road', *Trans.N.S.*, XXVI (1947–9), p. 91; Jack Simmons, *Parish and Empire*, p. 151; *B.T.C. Archives* (York), LIB(Y)/15/26; *Committee on the Liverpool–Manchester Railway* (1825) evid. George Stephenson, pp. 192–4, Nicholas Wood, p. 211, Francis Giles, p. 380 ff., H. R. Palmer, p. 413, George Leather, pp. 421, 430, Thomas Wood, p. 661.

133 1 Mathias, *Brewing Industry*, p. 31.

133 2 Ure, *Philosophy of Manufactures*, p. 43. Cf., also C. L. Hacker, 'William Strutt of Derby (1756–1830)', *Journ. Derbyshire Arch. & Nat. Hist. Soc.*, p. 80, (1960), p. 50.

133 3 James Montgomery, *The Cotton Spinner's Manual* (Glasgow, 1835) and *The Theory and Practice of Cotton Spinning* (Glasgow, 1833).

134 1 Fitton and Wadsworth, pp. 56–58.

134 2 Owen, *Life of Owen*, p. 36.

134 3 Rowe, *Boulton & Watt*, p. 163; Flinn, *Men of Iron*, p. 233; L. J. Williams, 'A Caernarvonshire Ironmaster and the Seven Years War', *Business History*, II (1959); Birch, 'Haigh Ironworks', p. 324; Robinson, *Smiths of Chesterfield*, pp. 58–59; *Cyfarthfa MSS.*, (National Library of Wales); Box 1, Crawshay to Crawshaw jun., 14th April 1821.

134 4 Muirhead, *James Watt*, p. 263; Insull, *Albion Mill Story*, p. 32; *Boulton and Watt MSS.* (Birmingham Reference Library), Watt jun. to M. R. Boulton, 27th March 1799; Lord, op. cit., p. 164; Dickinson, *James Watt*, p. 111; Cule, *Boulton, Financial History*, p. 38.

134 5 Hadfield, *British Canals*, p. 127; Barker and Harris, p. 206; McKendrick, 'Factory Discipline', p. 51.

135 1 M. R. Bonavia, *The Economics of Transport* (1954 ed.), p. 81.

135 2 Heaton, 'Benjamin Gott', pp. 55–56; *Factories Inquiry Commission*, III, D1, p. 119k, and pp. 125, 146; *Committee on Children in Factories* (1832), evid. John Hall, QQ. 3083, 3087, 3111–12, but see *Lords' Committee, evid. on Factory Bill*, Appx. X, p. 6.

135 3 See p. 83 above. Also *P.R.O.*, ADM.42/153 and 42/236; *B.T.C. Archives* (London), GJC/23/10.

136 1 Thomas C. Cochran, *The Puerto Rican Business Man, A Study in Cultural Change* (Philadelphia, 1959), p. 86. Cf. in general, in industrializing countries, Harbison & Myers, op. cit., p. 27.

136 2 Schoolmasters did move into Counting Houses (e.g. Chappell, *Historic Mellingriffith*, pp. 48–49), but one's confidence is not increased by an application like the following for a clerical post with the Stockton and Darlington Railway Company in 1825: 'I have taught a School upwards of 25 years and for half of that time have been used to public business' . . . *B.T.C. Archives* (York), SAD/8/99.

137 1 Hughes, *North Country Life*, p. 3; Wilkins, *Iron Trade of Wales*, pp. 145, 182; Albert O. Hirschman, *The Strategy of Economic Development* (New Haven, 1958), pp. 153–4.

137 2 Nasmyth, *Autobiography*, p. 136; *Boulton and Watt Correspondence* (Birmingham Assay Office), Watt to Boulton, 28th January 1779.

137 3 John Guest, *Relics and Records of Men and Manufacturers at or in the Neighbourhood of Rotherham* (Rotherham, 1866), p. 56; John, *Walker Family*, pp. 23, 28.

137 4 Crump, *Leeds Woollen Industry*, p. 176; Dickinson, *Matthew Boulton*, pp. 200–1; Cule, *Boulton, Financial History*, p. 184; *Boulton and Watt Correspondence* (Birmingham Assay Office), from A. J. Cabrit, 24th August 1775, Boulton to H. Stieglitz, 2nd May 1790 and to Thomas Loggen, 14th December 1794; McKendrick, 'Josiah Wedgwood'; *Cyfarthfa MSS.*, Crawshay to Benjamin Hall, 6th May 1814.

137 5 Dickinson, *James Watt*, p. 131.

138 1 Wedgwood, *Letters*, pp. 287–8; cf. also, for John Wilkinson, Randall, *The Wilkinsons*, pp. 25–26 and Ch. 6 below.

138 2 *Newton Chambers Archives*, R. Scott to G. Newton, 9th February 1811; *S.C. on Manufactures* (1833), evid. George Smith, QQ. 9242–6. He stressed that his firm had never employed a male book-keeper, but examples of female clerks are rare in industry, cf. Fisher, 'Vermuyden', pp. 95 ff.; Thomas Butler, *Diary, 1796–1799* (1906), p. 374.

138 3 Tylecote, op. cit., pp. 74, 296, appx. II; David Lockwood, *The Black-Coated Worker, A Study in Class Consciousness* (1958), pp. 20–1; F. G. Klingender, *The Condition of Clerical Labour in Britain* (1935), p. 2.

140 1 *P.R.O.*, A.O.1/2447/141, Adm. 42/8 and 42/81; *Galway of Serlby Muniments*, No. 12,850.

140 2 Scott, *Cloth Manufactory*, p. XIII; Quaker Lead Company, *Minutes, passim;* John, *Economic History of South Wales*, II, p. 26; Raistrick 'London Lead Company', p. 124; Meyrick, *History of Cardigan*, p. CCXXIV; Waller, *Value of Mines*, 'Epistle Dedicatory'.

141 1 Hughes, *North Country Life*, p. 74; and 'Eighteenth-Century Estate Agent', pp. 192–3; Parker, *Cokes of Holkham*, p. 109; Malet, *The Canal Duke*, p. 71; *Malley*, op. cit., p. 122.

141 2 *William Brown's Letter Book*, from C. Spedding, 15th June 1755; Flinn, *Men of Iron*, pp. 67, 80, 200.

142 1 Malley, op. cit., appx. II, p. 159.

142 2 Cole, *Robert Owen*, pp. 51, 54; Barker and Harris, op. cit., p. 116; Fitton and Wadsworth, op. cit., p. 49; Rowe, op. cit., p. 100; Pater Methias, 'The Entrepreneur in Brewing'; Lord, op. cit., p. 110; Insull, op. cit., pp. 43, 60, 82–84; Campbell, *Carron Company*, p. 161.

143 1 Cole, *Robert Owen*, p. 68; Addis, *Crawshay Dynasty*, p. 42; Raistrick, *Dynasty*, pp. 228–30; *idem, Two Centuries*, p. 53; *Boulton and Watt Accounts* (Birmingham City Library); *Dowlais Letters*, 24th July 1815; *Cyfarthfa MSS.* (Vol. 1), 16th March 1813; Everard, op. cit., pp. 27, 37, 143; Campbell, *Carron Company*, pp. 181–2, 190; Malet, op. cit., p. 169; Smith, 'Joshua Fields Diary', p. 40; Pease, *Diary*, p. 95; Rolt, *Stephenson*, p. 72; *idem, I. K. Brunel*, p. 21; Lee, *Tyneside Tramroads*, p. 201.

143 2 *Lords Papers*, 1819, II. (99).

144 1 Lloyd, *Old South Wales Ironworks*, p. 82; Devereux, op. cit., pp. 56, 82; Rimmer, 'Shrewsbury Flax Mill', p. 52; *idem, Marshalls*, p. 123; *Nevill MSS.*, Nos. 21, 24th June 1806, 18th May 1807; O. Wood,

144 1 op. cit., pp. 20, 97; *Herculaneum Potteries MSS.*, No. 47, 8th November 1806, 7th December 1813, 7th January 1817.

144 2 *B.T.C. Archives (York)*, SAD/1/28, Stephenson to Edward Pease, 2nd August 1821; SAD/8/51, George Atkinson, 23rd July 1821; *B.T.C. Archives* (London), KAC/23/32, 1806–7, GJC/23/10, 1810–11; Malley, op. cit., p. 24.

144 3 The remainder of this chapter is based on a paper, 'The Genesis of the Managerial Profession: The experience of the Industrial Revolution in Great Britain', published in *Studies in Romanticism*, to which reference should be made for further sources.

146 1 Peter Mathias, *Brewing Industry*, p. 271; *idem*, 'The Entrepreneur in Brewing'; Charles Wilson, 'The Entrepreneur in the Industrial Revolution in Britain', p. 102.

146 2 Clark Kerr, John T. Dunlop, F. H. Harbison and Charles A. Myers, *Industrialism and Industrial Man. The Problems of Labour and Management in Economic Growth* (1962), p. 158.

146 3 *Boulton and Watt Correspondence* (Birmingham Assay Office), Watt to Boulton, 8th May 1794; for the case of the Cramond Slitting Mill, cf. Campbell, *Carron Company*, p. 82.

147 1 Montgomery, *Theory and Practice of Cotton Spinning*, p. 242.

147 2 A. Raistrick, 'The Malham Moor Mines, 1790–1830', *Trans.N.S.*, XXVI (1947–9), p. 72; Barker & Harris, op. cit., p. 88.

147 3 *Mona Mine MSS.*, No. 577, 14th February 1824.

148 1 *Cyfarthfa MSS.*, Crawshay, sen. to Crawshay jun., 17th January 1822; *Dowlais Letters*, Taitt to R. Thompson, 8th February 1794; M. F. Le Play 'Mémoire sur la fabrication de l'acier en Yorkshire', *Annales des Mines*, IV, Ser. III (1843), p. 603.

148 2 John, *Walker Family*, p. 21.

148 3 *Dowlais Letters*, James Wise to J. J. Guest, 10th December 1821.

148 4 Rimmer, *Marshalls*, p. 123.

149 1 Beamish, *Sir Marc I. Brunel*, p. 52; Rolt, *Brunel*, pp. 5, 10–11; H. G. Funkhouser and Helen M. Walker, 'Playfair and His Charts', *Economic History*, III (1935); Hamilton, *Industrial Revolution in Scotland*, pp. 181, 188.

149 2 Rowe, *Boulton & Watt*, pp. 260–2.

150 1 Rolt, *Stephenson*, p. 101; Crump, *Leeds Woollen Industry*, pp. 33–35.

150 2 *Newton Chambers Archives* (Chapeltown). Cf. Letter from G. Newton to R. Scott, 13–12–1798 (ibid.), 'When one Man is possessed of Judgment and undertakes the part of a Manager in the Concern for a small Salary, and another furnishes the whole of the Capital to any amount, it is generally thought that if he is allowed a 5 p.ct. Interest for his Money before the division of Profits, in this Case the Shares ought to be equal; because it is evident that the Profits cannot be divided according to the Capital, which would leave the managing Partner without Profits. . . . In our present Concern capital has been set against Judgment and Management otherwise Mr. (Chambers) in particular could not have maintained his family out of his Profits.'

151 1 John, *Walker Family*, p. 23.

152 1 Interesting, though untypical, was the fate of Richard Nixon of the Little Clifton Foundry, who was induced in 1765 to come to the Seaton Ironworks on the promise of a partnership to teach the

152 1 existing partners, Hicks, Speeding & Co., the coke smelting process. After teaching all he knew, he was sacked without being made a partner, O. Wood, p. 67.

152 2 James Montgomery, *A Practical Detail of the Cotton Manufacture of the U.S.A.* (Glasgow, 1840), p. 147.

153 1 Wilkins, *Iron Trade*, pp. 38–45, 256–7; Elsas, op. cit., p. IX; K. T. Weetch, *Dowlais Ironworks and Its Industrial Community*, 1760–1850 (M.Sc. Thesis, London, 1963), pp. 9 ff.

154 1 Rolt, *Brunel*, p. 7.

155 1 Erickson, *British Industrialists*, p. 52.

157 1 'What Kuznets infers for income differentials may well be valid for schooling also; the initial period of development is accompanied by widening differences amongst strata and localities, only later to be replaced by narrowing differentials'. C. Arnold Anderson, 'The Impact of the Educational System on Technological Change and Modernisation', Hoselitz & Moore, op. cit., p. 262.

157 2 Bendix, *Work and Authority in Industry*, p. 212.

157 3 Harbison & Myers, op. cit., p. 83; Alexander Gerschenkron, *Economic Backwardness in Historical Perspective* (Cambridge, Mass., 1962); Fritz Redlich, 'Business Leadership: Divers Origins and Variant Forms', *Economic Development and Cultural Change*, VI (1957–8). Also see the discussion in vols. 6 and 7 of *Explorations in Entrepreneurial History* between Gerschenkron, Landes, Sawyer and others; John E. Sawyer, 'The Entrepreneur and the Social Order', in Wm. Miller (ed.), *Men in Business, Essays in the History of Entrepreneurship* (Cambridge, Mass., 1952), pp. 9–10; Robert K. Lamb, 'The Entrepreneur and the Community', ibid., p. 116; Arthur H. Cole, 'Entrepreneurship and Entrepreneurial History' in Research Centre in Entrepreneurial History, *Change and the Entrepreneur* (Cambridge, Mass., 1949), p. 90.

CHAPTER 5

161 1 Sombart, *Der Moderne Kapitalismus*, pp. 809 ff., 829–31; and *Hochkapitalismus*, I, pp. 424–30.

161 2 Redford, *Labour Migration*, pp. 18, 20; Smelser, op. cit., p. 105; Garnett, *Tour*, I, p. 23; Ure, *Philosophy of Manufactures*, pp. 15, 21; Fitton & Wadsworth, op. cit., p. 221; Charles Wilson, 'The Entrepreneur', p. 115; Frances Collier, *Family Economy*, p. iii; Dipak Mazumdar, 'Under-Employment in Agriculture and the Industrial Wage Rate', *Economica*, N.S., XXVI (1959).

161 3 Fitzmaurice, *Life of William, Earl of Shelburne* (2nd ed., 1912), I, p. 278; *S.C. on Children in Manufactories* (1816), p. 234.

161 4 *Factories Inquiry Commission*, A1, p. 83, evid. Hugh Miller; Ayton, *Voyage*, II, p. 214; M. G. Jones, *The Charity School Movement* (Cambridge, 1938), p. 208; Anon, 'Some Glasgow Customers of the Royal Bank around 1800', *The Three Banks Review*, 48 (1960), p. 39.

162 1 *Committee on Woollen Manufacture* (1806), evid. Robert Cookson, p. 70, William Child, pp. 103–4, John Atkinson, p. 116; Fong, op. cit., pp. 180–1; Also, A. P. Usher, *An Introduction to the Industrial History of England* (1921), p. 350; Heaton, *Woollen and Worsted Industries*, p. 353.

Notes

162 2 An acute observer in the West Country took it as axiomatic that
the workers, 'if they were not poor, would not submit to (their)
employments'. Charles Hall, *The Effects of Civilization on the People
in European States* (1805), p. 144. Also, Thompson, *The Making of
the English Working Class*, pp. 358–9, 548 ff.

162 3 Usher, op. cit., p. 364.

162 4 For two recent perceptive studies, see Smelser op. cit., and J. F. C.
Harrison, op. cit. For Germany, Wilhelm Brepohl, *Industrievolk
. . . am Ruhrgebiet* (Tübingen, 1957), esp. pp. 97 ff., 138 ff.

162 5 *Committee on Woollen Manufactures* (1806), pp. 145–6.

163 1 For the Continent of Europe, see, Koulisher, *Grande Industrie*, pp.
21–22, 31–33, 46; *idem*, 'Die Ursachen des Übergangs von der
Handarbeit zur Maschinellen Betriebsweise', *Schmollers Jarhrbuch*,
XXX (1906), pp. 41–42; *idem*, *Allgemeine Wirtschaftsgeschichte*, pp.
149–50; John Howard, *An Account of the Principal Lazarettos in Europe*
(Warrington, 1789), and *The State of the Prisons in England and
Wales* (Warrington, 1780); Benjamin Count of Rumford, *Essays,
Political, Economical and Philosophical* (5th ed., 1800) I, p. 38 ff.,
453; Rudolf Forberger, *Die Manufaktur in Sachsen* (Berlin, 1958),
II, pp. 214–19.

163 2 The critical difference was that up to the 1770s, institutional and
legal powers could be recommended to force the poor to labour, as
shown in great detail in Edgar S. Furniss, *The Position of Labour in
a System of Nationalism* (New York, 1957 ed.), chapters 5 and 6.
The new employer demanded free contracts and thus found it
increasingly difficult to justify the use of any power other than
economic necessity to get the poor to labour hard and regularly.
Ibid., pp. 198 ff.

163 3 (Sir H. Mackworth), *Third Report on the State of the Mines at
Bwlchyr Eskir-hyr* (1700), 1st October 1700; Wilkins, *Iron Trade*,
p. 52.

163 4 A. W. Coats, 'Economic Thought and Poor-Law Policy in the
Eighteenth Century', *Ec.H.R.*, 2nd Ser., XIII (1960), p. 47.

164 1 Jones, *Charity School Movement*, pp. 55–57; *Society for Bettering the
Condition and Increasing the Comforts of the Poor*, First Report, No. 4,
Fifth Report, No. 37; Alfred (Samuel Kydd), *The History of the
Factory Movement* (2 vols., 1857), I, pp. 4–5.

164 2 Bouch and Jones, op. cit., p. 305.

165 1 Statement made in 1843, quoted in Smelser, op. cit., p. 187;
Factories Inquiry Commission, I, E, p. 9. His mill, it should be noted,
was in the centre of Manchester, where labour was plentiful.

165 2 Collier, *Family Economy*, p. 124; *House of Lords Committee on Apprentices* (1818–19), p. 200; Unwin, *Samuel Oldknow*, pp. 173–5.

165 3 Professor Habakkuk would add to the causes of an easier labour
supply after 1815, the end of the war, with its demobilization of
400,000 men, and the enlarged immigration from Ireland. H. A.
Habakkuk, *American and British Technology in the Nineteenth Century*
(Cambridge, 1962), pp. 136–7.

165 4 John Brown (ed.), *Memoirs of Robert Blincoe* (Manchester, 1832),
pp. 27–28; Hoskins, op. cit., p. 146; *S.C. on Children in Manufactories* (1816), evid. Sir Robert Peel, p. 138; *Lords' Committee on
Apprentices* (1818–19), Appx. 'An Account of the Cotton and

165   4 Woollen Factories . . . whereof entry has been made . . . for the year 1803 to the last year', 30th April 1819, pp. 48, 50.

166   1 T. S. Ashton, *The Industrial Revolution, 1760–1830* (1948), p. 109.

166   2 W. H. Hutt, 'The Factory System of the Early Nineteenth Century', *Economica*, VI (1926), p. 90; Gras, op. cit., p. 76.

166   3 In T. S. Ashton's monumental understatement: 'it would be wrong to imagine that the ordinary man sought above all continuity of work'. *The Eighteenth Century*. p. 203.

167   1 T. S. Ashton, *Economic Fluctuations in England, 1700–1800* (Oxford, 1959), pp. 173–4.

167   2 Dunn, *View of the Coal Trade*, p. 28; J. Steuart, *Political Economy* (2 vols., 1767), II, p. 558; Hughes, *North Country Life*, p. 254.

167   3 J. D. Chambers, 'Enclosure and Labour Supply in the Industrial Revolution', *Ec.H.R.*, 2nd Ser. V (1953), pp. 338–41; Dobb, *Studies*, p. 277.

167   4 *B.T.C. Archives* (York), CHN/4/1 (Calder & Hebble Navigation), Journal 15th July 1760; Meteyard, op. cit., I, pp. 170–1, 179.

168   1 Ashton, *Peter Stubbs*, p. 49; Scott, *Matthew Murray*, p. 36; *Boulton and Watt Correspondence* (Assay Office), Boulton to H. Holland, 30th August 1801.

168   2 Muirhead, *James Watt*, p. 188; Rowe, *Boulton & Watt*, pp. 60, 162; Marshall, *James Watt*, p. 123; *Boulton and Watt Correspondence* (Birmingham Reference Library), 25th–26th September 1786; *Boulton and Watt Letters* (Falmouth), 21st June 1785, 14th October 1786, 3rd December 1791, 15th November 1792, 21st November 1792, 24th December 1792.

168   3 *Boulton and Watt Correspondence* (Assay Office), 3rd June 1788; Rowe, op. cit., p. 163; Dickinson, *Matthew Boulton*, p. 170.

168   4 Addis, op. cit., pp. 60, 73, 125; *Cyfarthfa MSS.*, Crawshay to Crawshay jun., 19th January 1814; *Dowlais Letters*, Bridge to Taitt, 2nd June 1815; Wedgwood, *Letters to Bentley*, 8th September 1772; Hower, 'The Wedgwoods', p. 300; Beamish, *Sir Marc I. Brunel*, pp. 79–83; *S.C. on Artisans and Machinery* (1824), p. 300.

169   1 *Dowlais Letters*, 22nd March 1801.

170   1 *Boulton and Watt Correspondence* (Assay Office), Peter Atherton, 8th September 1791, Thomas Becket, 17th April 1789, Peter Ewart, 12th December 1791, James Watt jun. to Boulton, 15th June 1801, M. I. Roosevelt, 5th February 1800; *Boulton and Watt Letters* (Falmouth), 17th January 1788, 18th February 1788, 26th February 1796; *Boulton and Watt Correspondence* (Birmingham Reference Library), 2nd January 1796, 6th February 1796, 18th February 1798, 14th November 1798; Rowe, p. 163; Lord, p. 204; *S.C. on Artisans and Machinery* (1824), e.g. pp. 10, 473; W. H. Chaloner and W. O. Henderson, 'Aaron Manby. Builder of the First Iron Steamship', *Trans.N.S.*, XXIX (1953–4 and 1954–5), p. 86; Dodd, *Industrial Revolution*, p. 138.

170   2 *Dowlais Letters*, 7th March 1794. Also, 8th April 1784, 13th June 1785, 8th August 1810, 23rd August 1822, 4th September 1822; Elsas, op. cit., pp. 22–23.

171   1 *Spencer-Stanhope Muniments*, No. 60513; Birch, *Haigh Ironworks*, p. 322; Redford, op. cit., p. 52; Fell, *Iron Industry*, pp. 239, 286–7; Flinn, *Men of Iron*, pp. 40, 235–6.

171 2 *William Brown's Letter Book*, 30th April 1750, 7th February 1755, 1st February 1766.

172 1 Holland, *Coal Trade*, p. 303; Wood, p. 139; Peter L. Payne, 'The Govan Collieries, 1804–1805', *Business History*, III (1961), 83.

172 2 *Mona Mine MSS.*, No. 1282, 15th November 1816, marginal note by Sanderson; Francis, *Smelting of Copper*, p. 120; Rowlands, *Amlwch*, pp. 303–7; Rowe, *Cornwall*, pp. 64, 90; Cule *Boulton*, *Financial History*, pp. 250–1; Jenkins, 'Zinc Industry', pp. 49–50.

173 1 *Co-operative Magazine*, March 1826, pp. 90–91; Cole, *Robert Owen*, p. 70; Mitchell, 'Cotton Industry', p. 107.

173 2 Just as paper makers preferred to train green labour for the new machine processes after 1806, rather than employ skilled hand paper makers. Coleman, *Paper Industry*, p. 303; MacDonald, *Scotland's Shifting Population*, pp. 17–20, 53 ff., 79–82; Garnett, *Tour*, p. 236; *S.C. on Manufactures* (1833) evid. Holdsworth, Q. 5233; Macnab, *New Views of Mr. Owen*, p. 66; G. J. Holyoake, *Self-Help 100 Years Ago* (2nd ed. 1890), p. 129; *Factory Inspector's Reports* (1834), p. 11.

173 3 *Factory Inspector's Reports*, December 1838, Appx. V, p. 98, quoted in Redford, op. cit., p. 19 and MacDonald, op. cit., p. 62; Macnab, pp. 73–74.

173 4 Pinchbeck, op. cit., p. 184; Redford, op. cit., p. 21.

173 5 Horner, *Linen Trade*, p. 252. Arkwright got some of his original female labour in Bakewell in 1777–8 from Manchester. M. H. McKenzie, 'The Bakewell Mill and the Arkwrights', *J. Derbyshire Arch. & Nat. Hist. Soc.*, LXXIX (1959), p. 73, and Robert Thornhill, 'The Arkwright Cotton Mill at Bakewell', ibid., p. 81.

174 1 W. E. Moore, 'Industrialization and Social Change', p. 316.

174 2 MacDonald, op. cit., p. 30; Redford, pp. 116–17; Dodd, op. cit., pp. 284–7; *S.C. on Children in Manufactories* (1816), p. 14.

174 3 W. E. Moore, 'Industrialization and Social Change', p. 313.

175 1 Muirhead, *James Watt*, p. 250; Lord, op. cit., p. 199.

175 2 Marshall, *James Watt*, p. 104.

175 3 Wolf, *Science in the Eighteenth Century*, p. 612; Lord, op. cit., p. 196.

176 1 *Boulton and Watt Correspondence* (Assay Office), Watt to Boulton, 2nd May and 3rd May 1780; Lord, p. 198; Eric Roll, *Boulton and Watt*, p. 195.

176 2 S. Shaw, *Staffordshire*, II, p. 118; Meteyard, II, p. 27; S. Timmins, *Birmingham*, p. 221; Farey, *Steam Engines*, pp. 531–2; Dickinson, *James Watt*, p. 168, and *Matthew Boulton*, p. 171.

176 3 Fleming and Brocklehurst, op. cit., pp. 276–7; Crump, *Leeds Woollen Industry*, pp. 322–3; Insull, op. cit., 28–30; Scott, *Matthew Murray*, pp. 19, 36.

176 4 *S. C. on Artisans and Machinery* (1824), e.g. T. C. Herves.

177 1 Raistrick, *Dynasty*, p. 170; Farey, op. cit., pp. 274–5; John, *South Wales*, p. 63; Hamilton, 'Carron Ironworks', p. 190; Cadell, *Story of the Forth*, pp. 158–9, 188; Clow, *Chemical Revolution*, p. 350; Wilkins, *History of Merthyr Tydfil*, p. 245; Campbell, *Carron Company*, p. 30; Johnson, 'Charcoal Iron Trade', p. 20.

177 2 *Cyfarthfa MSS.*, Crawshay to Crawshay jun., 5th June 1813.

177 3 Raistrick, *Two Centuries*, p. 68.

177   4 Clow, *Chemical Revolution*, p. 139; R. E. Wilson, *A History of the Sheffield Smelting Company Limited, 1760–1960* (1960), pp. 5–7.

177   5 Rolt, *Stephenson*, p. 186; Armytage, *A Social History of Engineering*, p. 119.

178   1 But Wedgwood, it has recently been said, was 'by no means unique; Watt had found millwrights and left skilled engineers; Arkwright had begun with clock-makers, and finished with trained machinists, and George Stephenson was to turn the humble pitmen of Tyneside into the famed architects of the railway world', McKendrick, 'Factory Discipline', p. 38.

178   2 Collier, *Family Economy*, p. 21; Montgomery, *Theory and Practice of Cotton Spinning*, p. 276.

178   3 Pinchbeck, op. cit., pp. 186–7; Rimmer, *Marshalls*, p. 106; *Lords' Committee on Apprentices* (1818–19), evid. John Stewart, p. 194; Gerhart von Schulze-Gävernitz, *Der Grossbetrieb, ein Wirtschaftlicher und Sozialer Fortschritt* (Leipzig, 1892), p. 68.

179   1 Minchinton, *Tinplate Industry*, p. 111; Holland, *Coal Trade*, p. 289; Nasmyth, *Autobiography*, p. 90; Rimmer, *Marshalls*, p. 106.

179   2 It was probably with that type of school in mind that Thompson wrote: 'The eighteenth-century provision for education of the poor—inadequate and patchy as it was—was nevertheless provision for *education* . . . in the counter-revolutionary years, this was poisoned by the dominant attitude of the Evangelicals, that the function of education began and ended with the 'moral rescue' of the children of the poor'. E. P. Thompson, op. cit., p. 377.

180   1 R. K. Webb, *The British Working-Class Reader, 1790–1848* (1955), pp. 13–21; E. D. Lewis, *The Rhonda Valleys,* (1959), p. 31; Gertrude Ward, 'The Education of Child Workers', 1833–1850', *Economic History*, III (1935), p. 110; *Committee on Children in Factories* (1832), evid. Benjamin Bradshaw, Q. 3436; R. H. Greg, *The Factory Question and the 'Ten Hours Bill'* (1837), pp. 35, 62; A. P. Wadsworth, 'The First Manchester Sunday School', *Bulletin of the John Rylands' Library*, XXXIII (1951), p. 320; *S.C. on Children in Manufactories* (1816), Josiah Wedgwood, p. 62, Adam Bogle, p. 168, John Bush, pp. 308–9; *Lords' Committee on Apprentices* (1818–19), evid. Thos. Scott, p. 172, Samuel Fox, p. 181; Adam Henry Robson, *Education of Children Engaged in Industry in England* (1931), esp. pp. 5, 13; *S.C. on Manufactures* (1833), evid. John Marshall, Q. 2521, William Matthews, QQ. 9829–31, 9836; *Lords' Committee on Factory Bill* (1818), evid. John Stewart, p. 186.

180   2 Kelly, *George Birkbeck*, p. 65.

181   1 Bendix, *Work and Authority in Industry*, pp. 203–4.

181   2 Wadsworth and Mann, op. cit. The section following is largely based on my paper: 'Factory Discipline in the Industrial Revolution', *Ec.H.R.* 2nd Ser. XVI (1963), which contains detailed references to sources.

182   1 *William Brown's Letter Book*, Leonard Hartley to Brown, 16th February 1755.

182   2 *S.C. on Children in Manufactories* (1816), evid. William Taylor, p. 259; Ure, *Cotton Manufacture*, II, p. 448; Also, *Factories Inquiry Commission*, II, D2, evid. Peter Ewart, p. 36; J. F. C. Harrison, *Learning and Living*, p. 39.

182   3 Josiah Wedgwood, *Letters to Bentley*, 19th August 1772, 5th July 1776.

183   1 *Council MSS.*, Diary, 13th September 1725; William Bray, *Tour into Derbyshire and Yorkshire*, p. 108; Fitton and Wadsworth, pp. 99–102, 259; Ure, *Philosophy of Manufactures*, p. 344.

183   2 Wadsworth and Mann, p. 391.

184   1 Ure, *Philosophy*, p. 15 and *Cotton Manufacture*, pp. 259, 269; Mantoux, *Industrial Revolution*, p. 376; *Committee on Children in Factories* (1831–2), QQ. 1881–2, 6065–9; Usher, op. cit., p. 350; Gras, op. cit., pp. 85–86.

184   2 Kulischer, *Wirtschaftsgeschichte*, II, p. 459; Court, 'Eighteenth-Century Midlands', p. 94; *Mona Mine MSS.*, No. 2633, pp. 44–45; MacKendrick, 'Discipline', p. 83; Lord, op. cit., pp. 197, 201; Kerr, *et al.* op. cit., p. 200; John Kennedy, *Miscellaneous Papers*, p. 18; E. S. Dane, *Staffordshire Pottery Industry*, p. 14; Jewitt, *The Wedgwoods*, p. 129.

184   3 Rimmer, *Marshalls*, p. 119; Tupling, *Economic History of Rossendale*, p. 221; Belper Round Mills was built like a Benthamite Panopticon prison: an overseer at the centre had a clear view of what went on in all the segments. Fitton and Wadsworth, p. 221.

185   1 Usher, op. cit., p. 346; Kerr, op. cit., p. 193.

187   1 *Factories Inquiry Commission*, I, C1, pp. 44–45, D1, pp. 133, 173–4.

187   2 John Kelsall, *MSS. Diary*, II, end of 10 Mo. 1719.

188   1 *Factories Inquiry Commission*, 2nd Suppl. D1, pp. 69–70.

189   1 595 replied, from 4 districts: A1 (Scotland: 173), B2 (Western: 129), C1 (North-Eastern: 51), D1 (Lancashire: 242).

189   2 *Factories Inquiry Commission*, 2nd Suppl.

189   3 Obviously too low, see above, pp. 186–7.

189   4 See Ch. 2, iii above.

190   1 Crump, *Woollen Industry*, p. 38.

190   2 See p. 161 above.

191   1 E. S. Furniss, op. cit., pp. 100–7, ch. 6; Bendix, op. cit., pp. 36, 63–69, 74–76; A. W. Coats, 'Changing Attitudes to Labour in the Mid-Eighteenth Century', *Ec.H.R.*, 2nd Ser., XI (1958).

191   2 See above, p. 188.

193   1 Max Weber, *The Protestant Ethic and the Spirit of Capitalism* (1930).

193   2 See Section v below.

193   3 Smelser, op. cit., p. 106; Ure, *Philosophy*, pp. 415–16.

193   4 Harris, op. cit., p. 16; Raistrick, 'London Lead Company', p. 156. Much of this section and the next is based on my paper, 'The Factory Village in the Industrial Revolution', *English Historical Review*, LXXIX (1964), which contains detailed references to sources.

194   1 Harrison, *Learning and Living*, p. 40. Mercantilist writers had been waging a similar campaign for at least a century in the national interest, but had made little impact. The local employer could make his wishes much more effectively felt. Furniss, op. cit., pp. 150 ff.

195   1 Fitton and Wadsworth, op. cit., pp. 103, 256; Wadsworth, 'Manchester Sunday Schools', p. 310; *Factories Inquiry Commission*, I, E, p. 24; Elsas, op. cit., p. 71; *S.C. on Children in Manufactories* (1816), evid. Wm. Taylor, p. 260.

195   2 Ibid., p. 23. Compare Charles Hall: 'Leisure in a poor man is thought quite a different thing to what it is in a rich man, and goes by a different name. In the poor it is called idleness, the cause of all mischief'. Op. cit., p. 24.

195   3 *Factories Inquiry Commission*, 2nd Suppl., D1, pp. 69–70. All workers had to attend church at least once every Sunday: *Committee on the Labour of Children in Factories* (1831–2), Q. p. 994.

195   4 K. T. Weetch, *The Dowlais Ironworks and Its Industrial Community 1760–1850* (M.Sc.(Econ.) Thesis, London, 1963), pp. 53, 143 ff.

196   1 Ashton, *The Eighteenth Century*, p. 201. Quotation in Thompson, op. cit., p. 435.

196   2 David Riesman, *The Lonely Crowd. A Study of the Changing American Character* (New Haven, 1950), pp. 115–16; Thompson, op. cit.; Bendix, op. cit., p. 73; Wadsworth and Mann, op. cit., p. 385. Compare the strikingly similar view of Carlyle, quoted below, p. 257.

197   1 From the Standing Instructions to the Staff Supervisor, *Wentworth-Woodhouse Muniments*, No. A1389.

198   1 Smelser, op. cit., p. 105; J. D. Chambers, 'Industrialisation as a factor in Economic Growth in England, 1700–1900', *Contributions to First International Conference of Economic History, Stockholm, 1960* (Paris, 1960), p. 208; Hannah Josephson, *The Golden Threads* (New York, 1949), p. 39. Also, M. Dobb, *Studies in the Development of Capitalism*, p. 266.

198   2 R. A. Lewis, 'Transport for Eighteenth-Century Ironworks', *Economica*, N.S. XVIII (1951).

199   1 Richard Welford, *A History of the Trade and Manufactures of the Tyne, Weir and Tees* (Newcastle and London, 1863), p. 33.

199   2 Daniels, *Early English Cotton Industry*, p. 128.

199   3 Edlington, *Treatise on the Coal Trade*, p. 118; *Boulton and Watt Correspondence* (Assay Office), Boulton to Wm. Keen, 2nd October 1798.

200   1 D. T. Williams, *Swansea*, pp. 175–6, quoting Walter Davies, *General View of Agriculture and Domestic System of South Wales*, I (1815), p. 134–5.

201   1 Collier, *Family Economy*, p. 137; Ure, *Philosophy*, p. 349; Hill, *National Education*, p. 135; *Factories Inquiry Commission*, I, D2, p. 83; and *Suppl. Report* Pt. II.

201   2 *Society for Bettering the Condition and Increasing the Comforts of the Poor*, 4th Report (1798), p. 239; Weetch, op. cit., pp. 53–54.

202   1 *National Library of Wales*, MS. No. 2873, 17th October 1793.

204   1 *Cyfarthfa MSS.*, I, 30th November 1815, 17th January 1816, 5th April 1816; *Dowlais Letters*, 27th September 1800, 26th July, 28th July 1803, 2nd October 1812; Weetch, op. cit., pp. 62–67.

204   2 *Cyfarthfa MSS.*, 19th January 1813, 13th January, 17th January 1816, 12th March 1822, Box 12, Balance Sheet for 1813; *Dowlais Letters*, 22nd January 1813, 9th May 1815, 9th February 1822; *Boulton and Watt Correspondence* (Assay Office), Boulton to John S. Salt, 21st February 1802.

205   1 *Dowlais Letters*, 18th September 1793, 25th April 1799, 4th September 1816, 9th June 1818, 15th September 1820; *Cyfarthfa MSS.*, Box II, 19th January 1828, 19th February 1829.

205 2 O. Wood, op. cit., pp. 21, 120–1.
205 3 Collier, 'Factory Community', p. 117; and *Family Economy*, p. 125; Gorb, op. cit., pp. 136–8; *S.C. on Children in Manufactories* (1816), pp. 279, 357.
206 1 *Mona Mine MSS.*, No. 2553, 5th May 1827, also Nos. 205, 1048, 1374; Rowlands, op. cit., pp. 256, 269; Dodd, *North Wales*, p. 160; *Cyfarthfa MSS.*, 5th February 1817, also 15th June, 30th August 1820, 13th January 1822, Box II, 22nd May 1830, 16th November 1830.
206 2 Ayton, op. cit., II, p. 11.
207 1 E.g. J. Montgomery. *The Theory and Practice of Cotton Spinning* (Glasgow, 1833), pp. 251–2.

CHAPTER 6

209 1 For their recruitment and training, see Chapter 5.
209 2 Conyers Read, 'Lord Burghley's Household Accounts', *Ec.H.R.*, 2nd ser. IX (1956); A. C. Littleton, *Essays in Accountancy* (Urbana, Ill., 1961), pp. 37, 60; Paul V. B. Jones, *The Household of a Tudor Nobleman* (Urbana, Ill., 1917).
210 1 David Solomons, 'The Historical Development of Costing', in Solomons (ed.), *Studies in Costing* (1952), p. 1; F. M. L. Thompson, *English Landed Society*. p. 153; G. E. Mingay, *English Landed Society*, p. 174.
210 2 *Sussex Ironworks Account* (Brit. Mus.), Add. Ms. 33154.
210 3 R. A. C. Parker, *Financial and Economic Affairs*, pp. 9–10. Innumerable examples have survived from the 18th and 19th centuries, often kept in beautiful handwriting, and the available series cover many years. Among those including some industrial interests are *Mona Mine MSS.*, nos. 1271, 1279; *Wentworth-Woodhouse Muniments*, A. 61 ff.; *Middleton of Woollaton Muniments*, C. (a), I. (1).
210 4 Edward Lawrence, *The Duty of a Steward to his Lord* (1727), pp. 133 ff.; George Clarke, *The Landed Man's Assistant, or the Stewards Vade-Mecum* (1715), p. 48; and books listed in Thompson, op. cit., p. 159, footnote.
211 1 R. S. Edwards, 'Some Notes on the Early Literature and Development of Cost Accounting in Great Britain', articles in *The Accountant* XCVII (1937), p. 225; *Middleton of Woollaton MSS.*, M.A. 135; also in this connection, the remarkable farm accounts of Loder, G. E. Fussell (ed.), *Robert Loder's Farm Accounts, 1610–1620* (Camden Soc., 3rd ser., vol. 53, 1936).
211 2 Thompson, op. cit., p. 153, also Mingay, op. cit., *passim*.
211 3 Shipley Colliery MSS., 1824, 1835; also section V on capital below; G. W. Daniels and T. S. Ashton, 'The Records of a Derbyshire Colliery', 127–8. Curiously, in the Middleton of Woollaton Accounts, costs of sinking were kept separate until 1575, and then lumped together with other expenses, loc. cit., Mi.AC., pp. 1–20.
211 4 Cf. *Mona Mine MSS.*, nos. 159, 160, 167, 1544–7; *Wentworth-Woodhouse Muniments*, F.70e, 96, 100, G.94; *Norfolk Muniments* (Sheffield City Library), S.192, S.193; *British Transport Commission Archives*, London, B.C.N./4/364, C.H.N./4/6, 17th June 1784, S.A.D./1/6, Minute Book, 13th July 1830, Report.

212   1 Daniel Defoe, *The Complete English Tradesman* (1747; 1841 Tegg
          ed. vol. 18), pp. 2, 22–23; B. S. Yamey, 'Scientific Book-keeping
          and the Rise of Capitalism', in W. T. Baxter (ed.), *Studies in
          Accounting* (1950), pp. 17–19; J. H. Soltow, 'Scottish Traders in
          Virginia', 88–89; P. Kats, 'Early History of Book-keeping by
          Double Entry', *Journal of Accountancy* (1929), 205, quoting espe-
          cially John Collins (1625–83), *An Introduction to Merchants' Accounts*
          (1652).

212   2 There is now a considerable literature in English about Fra Luca
          Pacioli and later authors of accountancy textbooks, as well as
          about such of the early Italian, Dutch and French accounts as
          have survived. Solomons, loc. cit. pp. 3–4; S. Paul Garner,
          Evolution of Cost Accounting to 1925 (Alabama, 1954), pp. 15–19.

212   3 R. E. Wilson, *Two Hundred Precious Metal Years* (1960), p. 39;
          Gott Papers, Box VI, Annual statement of Partnership Accounts,
          1795–1814; *Spencer-Stanhope Muniments*, Nos. 60458, 60478;
          Littleton, op. cit., p. 66; S. Pigott, *Hollins, A Study of Industry,
          1795–1949* (Nottingham, 1949), p. 33; *Bagshaw MSS.*, p. 490.

213   1 W. T. Baxter, *The House of Hancock: Business in Boston 1724–1775*
          (Cambridge, Mass. 1945), pp. 35, 37, 243; Peter Ramsay, 'Some
          Tudor Merchants' Accounts', in A. C. Littleton and B. S. Yamey,
          Studies in the History of Accounting (1956); Soltow, loc. cit., p. 89;
          L. S. Sutherland, 'The Accounts of an Eighteenth-Century Mer-
          chant', *Econ.H.R.*, III, (1932), p. 375.

213   2 J. G. C. Jackson, 'The History of Methods of Exposition of
          Double-Entry Book-keeping in England', in Littleton and Yamey,
          op. cit., pp. 290 ff.; B. S. Yamey, 'Edward Jones and the Reform
          of Book-keeping, 1795–1810', ibid., p. 313; Solomons, op. cit.,
          p.v.; Benjamin Franklin Foster, *The Origin and Progress of Book-
          keeping* (1852); L. Urwick and E. F. L. Brech, II, p. 21; Garner,
          op. cit., p. 25.

213   3 *Boulton and Watt Correspondence* (Assay Office), 19th August 1796.
213   4 J. Lord, op. cit., p. 132.
214   1 Cf. George Unwin, 'Factory System', p. 216; N. A. H. Stacey,
          English Accountancy. A Study in Social and Economic History. 1800–1954.
          (1954), p. 14.

214   2 B. S. Yamey, 'The Development of Company Accounting Conven-
          tions', *Three Banks Review* 47 (1960), p. 23–24.

215   1 It is sometimes suggested that secrecy was deliberate, to avoid
          giving away advantages in accounting practice or in the business
          practice it described, but, with the possible exception of the
          chemical industries, such secrecy was not usually observed in the
          technical field itself, where it might have been more to the point.
          Edwards, loc. cit., p. 283; Garner, op. cit., p. 39.

216   1 Cf. Hamilton, *Introduction to Merchandise* (1788), quoted in B. S.
          Yamey, H. C. Edey and Hugh W. Thomson, *Accounting in England
          and Scotland, 1543–1800* (1963), pp. 284–5, also ibid.; p. 193.

216   2 *V. C. H. Derbyshire*, p. 332; *Bagshaw Collection*, nos. 378, 379, 388,
          393, 422–3, 479–80. Dylan Pritchard, *Slate Industry*, pp. 59–62;
          Sir F. M. Eden, *The State of the Poor* (1928 ed.), II, p. 627.

217   1 T. C. Barker and J. R. Harris, p. 87; Arthur Raistrick, *Dynasty*,
          pp. 53, 113–15, 131; *William Brown's Letter Book*, 1st April 1752;

217 1 M. W. Flinn (ed.), *Law Book*, Law 57 *et passim*; J. R. Harris, *The Copper Industry*, p. 261; W. P. Kingsford, 'Sir Ambrose Crowley, 43b; Eric Roll, *Boulton and Watt*, p. 245.
217 2 B. Thompson, op. cit., p. 78.
217 3 *S.C. on Manufactures* (1933), Ev. Q. 9138.
218 1 H. W. Dickinson, *John Wilkinson*, pp. 40–41; Wedgwood, *Letters to Bentley*, p. 287, 29th May 1776; Meteyard, II (1866), pp. 188–9; Roll, op. cit. *passim*, J. Lord, op. cit., pp. 126, 140; V. W. Bladen, 'The Potteries', p. 130; *Wentworth-Woodhouse Muniments*, A. 1558, pp. 79–80, A.1558, pp. 79–80; *Caerleon Mills MSS*. (Newport, Mon., Public Library), No. 2; John R. Immer, chapter 7.
218 2 Lord, op. cit., p. 230.
218 3 pp. 240–4.
218 4 Barker and Harris, *St. Helens*, p. 67; H. Heaton, *Yorkshire Woollen and Worsted Industries*, p. 426; Flinn, *Law Book*, p. 73; Samuel Timmins (ed.), *Birmingham*, p. 252.
219 1 Werner Sombart, *Kapitalismus* II, p. 160, based largely on Scott.
219 2 N. K. Hill, 'Accountancy Developments in a Public Utility Company in the Nineteenth Century', *Accounting Research*, VI (1955), p. 385.
219 3 *Boulton and Watt Accounts* (Birmingham City Library), Manufacturing Profit and Loss Accounts, 30th September 1801–30th September 1802.
219 4 (William Hardy) *The Miners' Guide, or Complete Miner, containing the Articles and Customs of the High Peak and Wapentake of Wirksworth, Derbyshire* (Wirksworth, 1810), consists to the extent of one half of advice on the calculations of partnership shares.
220 1 *Mona Mine MSS*. 1333; Thomas S. Peckston, *Gas-Lighting*, p. 100; *Cyfarthfa MSS*., vol. 2, fol. 3; M. Piot, 'Mémoire sur l'exploitation des mines de houille aux environs de Newcastle sur Tyne', *Annales des Mines*, IV Ser., I (1842), pp. 138–9.
220 2 Cf. Everard, op. cit., p. 50; *Committee on Collieries* (1810), Ev. Henry Smith, p. 6.
221 1 For early textbook guidance, cf. Garner, op. cit., pp. 33–35, 43.
221 2 *Wentworth-Woodhouse Muniments*, A. 1556. Cf. also Raistrick, *Coalbrookdale*, p. 53; *Boulton and Watt Correspondence* (Assay Office), Boulton to Thos. Loggan, 14th December 1794; Raistrick and Allen, loc. cit., p. 174; *Spencer-Stanhope Muniments*, 60457 ff.; Parker, *Cokes of Holkham*, pp. 54–55.
221 3 *S.C. on Manufactures* (1833), ev. Samuel Walker, Q. 9569; *S.C. on the Silk Trade*, (1831–2), Ev. John Hall, Q. 6498.
222 1 Quoted B. S. Yamey, 'Scientific Book-keeping', p. 28. Also Garner, op. cit., p. 38.
222 2 Charles Babbage, *Machinery and Manufactures*, pp. 289, 203.
222 3 Campbell, *Carron Company*, p. 63; *Wharncliffe Muniments*, p. 115 also Garner, p. 57.
222 4 W. G. Rimmer, *Marshalls*, p. 122. This advanced departmental, and backward overall, accounting system is typical.
222 5 Quaker Lead Co., *Minutes*, 10th October 1784.
223 1 Garner, op. cit., pp. 49–50.
223 2 *Herculaneum Pottery MSS*., 380 M.D., p. 48.
223 3 Immer, op. cit., p. 195.

224 1 B.T.C. (York) *Archives*, A.C.N./L/32.

224 2 Ibid., S.A.D./8/86.

224 3 *Boulton and Watt Correspondence* (Assay Office), J. Watt, jun. to Boulton, 11th September 1798. Birmingham City Library: Watt to M. R. Boulton, 1st June 1796, M. R. Boulton to Watt, jun., 18th December 1798; *Accounts*, Bundles: Cost Calculations 1802–16, General Expenses 1798–1804; Immer, op. cit., p. 190; Sutherland, loc. cit., pp. 375–6; Mathias, op. cit., p. 471; H. Heaton, 'Benjamin Gott and the Industrial Revolution', p. 62; *Cyfarthfa MSS.*, Box 1, Crawshay, sen. to W. Crawshay, jun., 28th March 1822; *Spencer-Stanhope Muniments*, 60457 ff.; *Norfolk Muniments*, S.196, S.200, S.215–230; Raistrick, 'London Lead Company', Appx. IV, V; Rimmer, op. cit., p. 74; F. J. Monkhouse, 'An Eighteenth-Century Company Promoter', pp. 145–9.

225 1 Bladen, op. cit., p. 127; Hower, 'The Wedgwoods' (1932), p. 305.

225 2 Garner, op. cit., pp. 82–83; Cule, op. cit., p. 290; also his 'Finance and Industry', p. 323; E. W. Cooney, 'Victorian Master Builders', 174–5; *Committee on South Wales Collieries*, Ev. Henry Smith, p. 6; (anon.), *A Practical Inquiry into the Laws of Excavation and Embankment upon Railways* (1840), p.x.; *Committee on Copper Mines*,

226 1 J. W. McConnell, op. cit., pp. 48–49, 52; N. J. Smelser, op. cit., p. 97; J. Montgomery, *Theory and Practice of Cotton Spinning*, pp. 249–50.

226 2 Raistrick, *Quakers*, p. 116, also his *Coalbrookdale*, p. 60; *Kelsall MSS, Diary*, vol. 2; Raistrick and Allen, loc. cit., p. 185.

227 1 Fitton and Wadsworth, pp. 48, 53; Sigsworth, *Black Dyke Mills*, p. 138. Yet by 1846 the firm was successful enough for William Foster, John's son, to write a memorandum on 'How a Great Manufacturer Ought to keep his Books and Prove them', ibid.

227 2 Hartwell, op. cit., p. 637; W. G. Hoskins, *Industry, Trade and People*, p. 37. Cf. also *Caerleon MSS.*, nos. 1–6.

227 3 R. A. C. Parker, op. cit., p. 160; R. E. Wilson, op. cit., p. 12; *Tehidy Estate Papers* (MSS., Redruth), Account Book No. 2, 1776–8; F. Trevithick, *Life of Richard Trevithick* (1872), pp. 57–64.

228 1 A. V. Judges, 'Money, Finance and Banking from the Renaissance to the Eighteenth Century', in Edward Eyre (ed.), *European Civilization, its Origin and Development* (1937), vol. 5, p. 436, footnote; Harold Pollins, 'A Note on Railway Constructional Costs', *Economica*, XIX (1952), pp. 400–1; *Factories Inquiry Commission*, C.1, p. 46 and D.1, p. 109.

228 2 Wedgwood, *Letters to Bentley*, p. 12, 16th February 1771. The reason was then found to be an increase in stocks amounting to £4,000 in London and £1,500 in the Liverpool warehouse.

228 3 Ibid., pp. 89, 92, 23rd and 31st August 1772.

228 4 Roll, op. cit., pp. 98–99; Lord, op. cit., p. 126; Dickinson, *Boulton*, p. 71; Cule, *Financial History*, pp. 15, 24, 178–9; and his 'Boulton and Watt', p. 323.

229 1 Insull, op. cit., p. 55.

229 2 Cadell, op. cit., p. 166; R. H. Campbell, 'The Financing of Carron Company', p. 27; and *Carron Company*, pp. 61, 129.

229 3 (H.E.E.) *Thorncliffe*, No. 2; *Mona Mine MSS.*, 675, 676, 3537,

319

Notes

229 3 3538; Everard, op. cit., p. 108; A. H. John (ed.), *The Walker Family*, p. 12; J. R. Harris, op. cit., pp. 209, 211, 215–17.
230 1 Roll, op. cit., p. 251; Lord, op. cit., p. 200.
230 2 Meteyard, op. cit., II, p. 165.
230 3 *Boulton and Watt Correspondence* (Assay Office), Watt to Boulton ?18th April 1780.
231 1 Raistrick, *Coalbrookdale*, pp. 118–19, 260; Fitton and Wadsworth, op. cit., pp. 238–40; David Mushet, *Papers on Iron and Steel*, p. vii; Crump, op. cit., p. 307. Cf. also Lockwood, *Black-Coated Worker*, p. 19.
231 2 J. A. G. Harley, 'Samuel Whitbread', p. 15; P. Mathias, op. cit., p. 41; Scott, *Matthew Murray*, p. 41, James Watt, jun. to M. R. Boulton, 15th June 1802. 'I wish your own Clerk's and Servants' time wholly occupied in the sale and main object of the work, & every possible simplicity in the Cash & the Accounts of it', William Crawshay ordered in 1816. Letter to William Crawshay, jun., 17th January 1816, *Cyfarthfa MSS.*, vol. 1.
231 3 Lady Charlotte Schreiber, *Extracts from her Journal 1853–1891* (1952), pp. 6–7.
232 1 *Mona Mine MSS.*, e.g. 1, 28, 80.
232 2 *Factories Inquiry Commission*, First Report, B.1, p. 60.
233 1 The present section is based largely on my paper on 'Capital Accounting in the Industrial Revolution', *Yorkshire Bulletin of Economic and Social Research*, XV (1963), to which reference should be made for further sources.
234 1 *Mona Mine MSS.*, No. 3063, Sanderson to Paget, 2nd October 1811.
235 1 The best recent summary of contemporary economic doctrines of capital and profit will be found in G. F. L. Tucker, *Progress and Profit in British Economic Thought, 1650–1850* (Cambridge, 1960), Ch. 5. The quotations are from pp. 78, 87 and 78. The nearest approaches to a modern notion of profit rates will be found in *Spencer-Stanhope Muniments*, 60478, No. 38; Hamilton, *Brass and Copper Industries*, Appx. 7, pp. 359–60; Raistrick, *Two Centuries*, pp. 114, 127. For a recent calculation of profit rates in that period, see F. Crouzet, *La Formation du Capital en Grande-Bretagne*.
235 2 Cf. S. Pollard, 'Fixed Capital in the Industrial Revolution in Britain', *J. Econ. Hist.*, XXIV (1964).
236 1 Raistrick and Allen 'South Yorkshire Ironmasters', p. 185; *B.T.C. Archives* (York), ACN/1/32; *Mona Mine MSS.*, Nos. 2635, 280. As a contrast, it may be noted that some of the best contemporary farm accounts ignored *stocks* at the beginning and the end of their periods, cf. R. A. C. Parker, *Cokes of Holkham*, p. 57.
237 1 *Herculaneum Pottery MSS.*, Minute for 23rd November 1815; Raistrick, *Dynasty*, pp. 277–8. Notions were no clearer at the end of the century, e.g. pp. 244–6; *S.C. on Manufactures* (1833), evid. Wm. Matthews, Q. 9647.
237 2 R. E. Wilson, op. cit., p. 39, referring to 1787. Benjamin Gott began manufacturing, after paying out £34,000 for the share of a deceased partner, with £20,000 'net stock and profit in trade', W. B. Crump, *Leeds Woollen Industry*, p. 255.
237 3 John, *Walker Family*, pp. 14, 16, 25.

237   4   Crump, op. cit., p. 258. For Crawshay, see *Cyfarthfa MSS.*, Vol. I, Crawshay to Benjamin Hall, 26th August 1813.

238   1   *Spencer-Stanhope Muniments*, 60579, No. 24, note dated 14th December 1818; Yamey, Edey & Thompson, op. cit., pp. 197–8, also p. 90.

239   1   *Wentworth-Woodhouse Muniments*, F96; Trevithick, op. cit., p. 38; *Nevill MSS.*, No. 49, Quarter ending 31st March 1808.

240   1   *B.T.C. Archives* (York), e.g. SAD/23/21, Treasurer's Accounts to July, 1825, SAD/1/6, Minute Book, 10th July 1827, 13th July 1830, ACN/1/32, *B.T.C. Archives* (London), BCN/4/364 and 4/365.

240   2   Hill, 'Accountancy Developments', p. 384.

240   3   W. T. Baxter, *The House of Hancock*, p. 243.

240   4   Raistrick, *Dynasty*, pp. 214–15. The property was written down from some £138,000 to some £105,000.

241   1   Ewing Matheson, *The Depreciation of Factories* (4th ed., 1910), preface to 1884 edition. The author went on to state that the extension of fixed capital and joint-stock enterprise had necessitated the introduction of the practice of depreciation.

241   2   George Eyre, the printer, in evidence in 1831. B. W. E. Alford, 'Government expenditure and the growth of the Printing Industry in the Nineteenth Century,' *Ec.H.R.*, 2nd ser. XVII (August 1964), p. 101.

242   1   *Cyfarthfa MSS.* (Vol. I), Crawshay to Benjamin Hall, 6th May 1814. It is significant that in this period of the French Wars, no depreciation allowance, properly speaking, was granted at all on Schedule D Tax. P. K. O'Brien, 'British Incomes in the Early Nineteenth Century'., *Ec.H.R.* 2nd Ser., XII (1959), p. 261.

242   2   *Mona Mine MSS.*, No. 166.

243   1   *S.C. on Manufactures* (1833). evid. Milne, QQ. 10998–11006; *Factories Inquiry Commission*, D2, evid. Greg, p. 30; Insull, op. cit., Appx. B, pp. 82–84.

243   2   *B.T.C. Archives* (London), BCN/4/365 and 366, also, BCN/4/375, showing summaries and significant comparative statements.

244   1   *Nevill MSS.*, No. 21, Minute Book, 30th June 1829; Everard, op. cit, p. 111; also Aire & Calder Navigation in 1819, *B.T.C. Archives* (York), ACN/1/32.

245   1   Phyllis Deane and W. A. Cole, *British Economic Growth 1688–1959* (Cambridge, 1962), p. 301.

245   2   K. H. Burley, 'An Essex Clothier', p. 295; *The Entrepreneur* (Cambridge, Mass. 1957), p. 38. The whole elaborate costing apparatus of the Soho Foundry, i.e. the engine works, built up in 1795–1801, so much in contrast with Matthew Boulton's earlier chaotic pricing, was of course called forth by the fear of competition after the end of the patent period in 1800.

246   1   For an excellent survey, see F. Cruozet, 'La Formation du capital en Grande-Bretagne pendant la Révolution Industrielle'.

246   2   Podmore, *Robert* Owen, p. 642, also pp. 164, 200, 644. Also Harriet Martineau, *Biographical Sketches, 1852–1868* (2nd ed. 1869), pp. 308–9. For the methods used to enable him to produce particularly fine yarn in the first place, cf. Ch. 7, section (i) below.

246   3   N. McKendrick, 'Josiah Wedgwood', 409–12.

Notes

247 1 Baxter, *Studies*, p. 12; Babbage, op. cit., pp. 203–4, 265, 289; George Dodd, *Days at the Factories* (1843), p. 547; Solomons, op. cit., pp. 8–9; A. C. Littleton, *Essays*, p. 68.

248 1 Roll, op. cit., pp. 245–50, 269; Bladen, op. cit., pp. 126–7; W. G. Rimmer, *Marshalls of Leeds*, pp. 122, 150–1; P. Mathias, op. cit., pp. 72–73.

248 2 George O. May, 'The Influence of Accounting on the Development of an Economy'. *The Journal of Accountancy*, LXI (1963), p. 11.

249 1 B. S. Yamey, 'Accounting and the Rise of Capitalism: Further Notes on a Theme by Sombart', in *Studi in Onore di Amintone Fanfani*, VI (Milano, 1962), p. 853.

CHAPTER 7

250 1 Urwick and Brech, *Scientific Management*, II, p. 13.
250 2 *Cyfarthfa MSS.*, Crawshay to Crawshay, jun., 4th February 1813.
250 3 Ch. 1. section (i) above.
251 1 John H. Dales, 'Approaches to Entrepreneurial History', *Explorations in Entrepreneurial History*, I/1 (1948), p. 11, and Karl W. Deutsch, 'A Note on the History of Entrepreneurship, Innovation and Decision Making', ibid., I/5 (1949), p. 10. This view is not really consistent with Schumpeter's and has since been attacked. Donald E. Stout, 'A Pressure Theory of Innovation', ibid., VII/2 (1954); J. A. Schumpeter, 'Economic Theory and Entrepreneurial History', in *Change and the Entrepreneur*, pp. 68–69, and A. H. Cole, 'Entrepreneurship, ibid., pp. 103 ff.

251 2 Insull, *Albion Mill Story*, pp. 30–33, 54; *Boulton and Watt Correspondence* (Falmouth), Boulton to Wilson, 24th January 1786; Lord, pp. 91–93; *Boulton and Watt Correspondence* (Birmingham City Library). Watt to Boulton, 28th March 1786, 13th April, 22nd April 1786.

252 1 Gorb, pp. 134–5. Also Ch. 6, section (vi) above, and Chaloner, 'Owen and Drinkwater', pp. 80, 93–96; Owen, *Life of Owen*, p. 187; Martineau, *Biographical Sketches*, p. 308; *S.C. on Children in Manufactories* (1816), evid. R. Owen, pp. 90–93; Podmore, op. cit., pp. 642 ff.; Urwick and Brech, II, Ch. 4.

253 1 Dennis Chapman, 'William Brown of Dundee, 1791–1864: Management in a Scottish Flax Mill' in *Explorations in Entrepreneurial History*, IV/3 (1952), p. 120, on which the following paragraphs are based.

254 1 Urwick and Brech, II, pp. 25, 38.
254 2 Andrew Ure, *The Cotton Manufacture of Great Britain* (2 vols., 1836), and *Philosophy of Manufactures* (1835); James Montgomery, *The Cotton Spinner's Manual* (Glasgow, 1835), and *The Theory and Practice of Cotton Spinning* (Glasgow, 1833); Benjamin Thompson, *Inventions, Improvements and Practice of B.T.* (Newcastle, 1847); Oliver Evans, *The Young Millwright and Millers' Guide* (Philadelphia, 13th ed., 1834); *B.T.C. Archives* (York), SAD/1/157, 'Hall's Plan for the Better Management of the Stockton & Darlington Railway', 20th November 1830 and SAD/9/97. Letter from Thomas Hill, 2nd July 1825.

254 3 Charles Babbage, *On the Economy of Machinery and Manufactures* (1832, 4th ed. 1835).

322

254 4 Charles Wilson, 'Entrepreneur', p. 103, quoting Mantoux.
255 1 C. Kerr, *et al.*, op. cit., p. 147.
256 1 William Brown, in Chapman, loc. cit., p. 132.
257 1 'Signs of the Times' (1829), quoted in Raymond Williams, *Culture and Society (1780–1950)* (Pelican, 1963 ed.), pp. 86, 87.
257 2 Kerr, op. cit., p. 178.
257 3 Albert O. Hirschman, *The Strategy of Economic Development* (New Haven, 1958), pp. 17, 18.
258 1 Gaskell, *Manufacturing Population*, pp. 45, 53, 54; Ure, *Philosophy of Manufactures*, p. 16; Lord, op. cit., p. 91; Gorb, loc. cit., p. 130.
258 2 Cf. p. 246 above.
260 1 *Mona Mine MSS.*, No. 831, 25th June 1828; Dennis Chapman, op. cit., pp. 127–9; Gibbons, op. cit., pp. 81–82; *B.T.C. Archives*, (York), SAD/1/157, 20th November 1830.
260 2 George Abbott, *Essay on Mines*, p. 144.
260 3 Samuel P. Hays, *The Response to Industrialism, 1885–1914* (Chicago, 1957), p. 49. Cf. also, Ch. 6 section (ii) above.
260 4 Ure, *Cotton Manufacture*, I, p. 272; Fitton and Wadsworth, p. 53; Hartley Coleridge, *The Worthies of Yorkshire and Lancashire* (Leeds, 1836), p. 475, note.
260 5 Kennedy, *Miscellaneous Papers*, p. 18; Smelser, op. cit., p. 102.
261 1 Rimmer, *Marshalls*, p. 119.
261 2 From Letter by James Watt, jun. to T. Wilson, *Boulton and Watt Correspondence* (Falmouth), 27th October 1796; also *Boulton and Watt Correspondence* (Birmingham City Library), M. R. Boulton to Watt jun., 13th October 1797, 7th June 1798; Roll, op. cit., p. 10; G. C. Allen, 'An Eighteenth-Century Combination in the Copper-Mining Industry', *Economic Journal*, XXXIII (1923), p. 75; J. R. Immer, op. cit., pp. 172 ff.
261 3 Wilson and Reader, *D. Napier & Son*, p. 5; Nasymth, *Autobiography*, pp. 125–6.
261 4 Lord, p. 140. Also, Hower, 'The Wedgwoods', p. 299 and McKendrick, 'Factory Discipline', p. 43.
261 5 Bladen, *Potteries*, p. 117; E. S. Dane, op. cit., pp. 17, 18.
262 1 Raistrick *Dynasty*, pp. 124, 257–8; Clow, *Chemical Revolution*, p. 337; Campbell, *Carron Company*, pp. 62, 65; Hall, 'Diary of Joshua Fields' Tour', p. 28; Elsas, op. cit., Evans to Guest, 13th January 1832.
262 2 Pp. 217–8 above.
262 3 *Boulton and Watt Correspondence* (Assay Office), Boulton to J. Robey, 4th January 1794; Roll, op. cit., p. 171. Also, Dickinson, *Matthew Boulton*, pp. 167–8; Shaw, *Staffordshire*, II, p. 119; Cule, *Financial History*, p. 43, note, pp. 299–300; Urwick and Brech, II, p. 28; Immer, op. cit., pp. 54, 59, 119, 289.
263 1 *Mona Mine MSS.*, No. 1056, Treweek to Sanderson, 16th April 1831; Raistrick, *Two Centuries*, p. 73; Dunn, *View of the Coal Trade*, p. 92; Holland, *Coal Trade*, pp. 293–4; Clow, *Chemical Revolution*, p. 369.
263 2 *Cyfarthfa MSS.*, Crawshay to Crawshay, jun., 20th February 1816; Flinn (ed.) *Crowley Law Book*, p. 40 (Law 66).
263 3 Mathias, *Brewing Industry*, p. 40, also, 'The Entrepreneur in Brewing', pp. 34–35.

Notes

264 1 Montgomery, *Theory and Practice of Cotton Spinning*, pp. 14–15, 22–,23.

264 2 Ure *Cotton Manufacture*, I, p. 302; Rimmer, *Marshalls*, pp. 119, 153–4. Also, R. M. Hartwell, *Yorkshire Woollen and Worsted Industry*, pp. 614–15.

264 3 Dodd, *Days at the Factories*, p. 392; James Montgomery, *A Practical Detail of the Cotton Manufacture of the U.S.A.* (Glasgow, 1840), p. 48; also, the account of Blackwall Yard, in Dodd, p. 465.

265 1 *Boulton and Watt Correspondence* (Assay Office), Watt to Boulton, 23rd September 1786.

265 2 Guest, *Rotherham*, p. 685; A. E. Musson, 'James Nasmyth and the Early Growth of Mechanical Engineering', *Ec.H.R.*, 2nd Ser., X (1957), pp. 126–7.

265 3 Lord, p. 143; Bladen, *Potteries*, p. 129; John Thomas, *North Staffordshire Potteries*, p. 524. Also, in general, Court, 'Eighteenth-Century Midlands', and pp. 177 and 250 above.

266 1 John W. Hall, 'The Making and Rolling of Iron', *Trans.N.S.*, VIII (1927–8), p. 44.

266 2 Lord, op. cit., p. 225.

266 3 Ch. 4 above.

267 1 Raistrick, *Dynasty*, pp. 13, 210.

267 2 J. England, 'The Dowlais Ironworks, 1759–93', *Trans. Glamorgan Local History Soc.*, III (1959), pp. 45–47.

268 1 *S.C. of House of Lords on the Wool Trade* (1828), p. 289; Owen, *Life of Owen*, pp. 190–1; Mathias, 'Entrepreneur in Brewing', p. 35, and *The Brewing Industry*, p. 31; Lord, p. 206; Dickinson, *James Watt*, pp. 110, 131; Crump, *Leeds Woollen Industry*, pp. 33–35, 58; Heaton, 'Benjamin Gott', p. 51; *Boulton and Watt Correspondence* (Assay Office), Boulton to Messrs. Isnel, Martin et Fils, 22nd July 1793; Urwick and Brech, II, p. 34; *Dowlais Letters*, Taitt to Thos. Guest, 28th April 1803, and J.J. Guest from London, 7th February 1828; Musson, 'Nasmyth', p. 127.

269 1 *Wm. Brown's Letter Book*, to Carlisle Spedding, 30th July 1754, to James Spedding, 12th April 1764. Cf. also M. Piot in *Annales des Mines* (1842), pp. 145 ff.

269 2 A. J. Taylor, 'Sub-Contract System', pp. 220–1; Also, John, 'Coal and Iron on a Glamorgan Estate', p. 101.

269 3 *Wentworth-Woodhouse Muniments*, No. F.96, F.701, A.1389. Cf. also, Dunn, *View of the Coal Trade*, p. 144; Holland, *Coal Trade*, pp. 293–5.

269 4 This proviso was later dropped.

269 5 Rolt, *Telford*, pp. 40–41, *passim*, also pp. 61, 135. For turnpikes, cf. Devereux, *J. L. MacAdam*, pp. 122–3, and for railways, Brassey, *Labour Question*, pp. 125–6, 137–40.

270 1 *S.C. on Children in Manufactories* (1816), evid. Robert Peel, pp. 135-6; *Factories Inquiry Commission*, I, E, p. 14, Rowland Detroisier; *House of Lords Committee on Apprentices* (1818–19), evid. Archibald Buchanan, p. 76, also Sombart, *Kapitalismus*, II, p. 836; and Ure, *Philosophy of Manufactures*, p. 43.

270 2 Rimmer, *Marshalls*, p. 123.

Abbreviations

B.P.P.	British Parliamentary Papers
Ec.H.R.	Economic History Review
Factories Inquiry Commission	Reports, Evidence and Appendix of the Factories Inquiry Commission, 1833:
	First Report, B.P.P. 1833 (450.) XX
	Second Report, B.P.P. 1833 (519.) XXI
	First Supplementary Report, B.P.P. 1834 (167.) XIX
	Second Supplementary Report, B.P.P. 1834 (167.) XX
J.Ec.H.	Journal of Economic History
J.H.C.	Journals of the House of Commons
P.R.O.	Public Record Office
R.C.	Royal Commission
S.C.	Select Committee
Trans.N.S.	Transactions of the Newcomen Society
Trans.R.H.S.	Transactions of the Royal Historical Society

Index

Academies, Nonconformist, 104, 110, 114–18
Accountancy, 28, 32, 56, 129, 138, 209–49. Education, 112–14, 116, 122–3, 209, 212
Accountants, 27, 126, 136–8, 142, 209, *passim*
Accounting and Management, 215–16, 219 *passim*, 232, 245–9
Agents (Estate), 27–30
Agriculture—*see* 'Estate'
Albion Steam Corn Mill, 20, 98, 134–5, 142, 168, 184, 229, 237–8, 243, 251
Anglesey Copper Mining—*see* Parys Mountain Mines
Arkwright, Sir Richard, 35, 91–92, 106, 134, 168, 178, 183–4, 191–2, 194, 199, 231, 260, 263

Banking, 55, 204
Beatings, 186, 189
Blacklist, 188
Book-keeping, 52, *see also* 'Accountancy'
Boulton, Matthew, 20, 81, 85, 112–13, 119, 122, 137, 146, 149, 168–70, 175–6, 179, 183–4, 187, 200, 203, 218, 222, 225, 246, 257, 261–2, 265
Boulton & Watt, 20, 41, 62, 64, 66–67, 70, 72–73, 78–79, 98, 129, 167, 175, 194, 213, 219, 221, 234, 251–2, 265, 267
Brewing Industry, 28, 47, 97–98, 123, 133, 138
Bridgewater, Duke of, 29–30, 45, 88, 119, 141, 149, 156, 171–2, 183, 198, 268
Building Industry, 45, 85–86

Canal Building, 45, 47, 50, 66–67, 77, 87–88, 98, 135, 172, 183
Capital, 55, 151, 212, 233–45. Capital Accounting, 211, 213, 220, 233–45
Carpet Weaving, 44, 94
Carron Company, 20, 40, 42, 45, 67, 76, 78, 82, 142–3, 145, 152, 154–5, 164, 170–1, 176–7, 194, 198–200, 222, 229, 234, 236, 241–2, 261–2, 265–6
Chemical Industry, 97
Child Labour, 91, 94, 96, 103, 124, 161, 185–9, 270
Civil Engineering, 45, 78, 86–89, 177, 220, 269
Clerical Staff, Numbers, 68, 198, 230–3

Clerks, 85, 106, 115, 121, 125–6, 135–8, 140, 141, 209, 219
Coal Mining, 22, 29–30, 41–42, 45–47, 53–54, 62ff, 107, 127, 154, 171–2, 177, 185, 191, 205, 269. Coal Viewers, 27, 63–65, 68, 88, 123, 127–8, 154, 191, 238, 263, 268
Coalbrookdale Company, 40, 46, 75–76, 78, 88, 122, 132, 143, 152, 156, 176, 198–9, 203, 216, 221, 230, 237, 246, 261, 266–8
Commercial Education, 107–11, 114 *passim*, 126, 213–14
Continental Industry, 48–51, 119–20
Contractors, 86–89, 125, 130–2, 140
Copper Mining, 29, 41, 42, 47, 69–72, 83, 123, 128, 155. Smelting, 53–54, 71–72, 82–84, 123, 155, 172
Cornish Metal Company, 20
'Cost-Book System', 41, 69, 70, 216, 238
Costing and Cost Accounting, 79, 213–14, 217, 219–34, 245, 247–8
Cotton Industry, 21, 35, 40–41, 43, 89–93, 105, 124, 133–4, 173–4, 178, 181–2, 185–6, 225–6
Crowley, Ambrose, 22, 37, 45, 55–60, 134, 141, 167, 170, 191, 195, 199, 216, 218, 240
Cutlery Industry, 35, 45, 82
Cyfarthfa Ironworks, 22, 77–78, 147, 153, 199, 204, 206, 217, 233, 240

Depreciation, 220, 237, 240–4
Dismissals, 187–9, 205, 218
Domestic System, 30–37, 82, 96, 162, 213
Dowlais Ironworks, 44, 77–78, 143, 147–8, 153, 156, 169, 170, 182, 191–2, 195, 200–4, 217, 262, 267
Drunkenness, 184, 187, 193–5, 218

Education—Factory Children, 54, 56, 72–73. Managers—*see* 'Managers', Workers, 121, 179–81, 202
Efficiency, 210
Embezzlement, 33, 68, 163, 184, 210, 212, 218–9
Engineering Industry, 75–76, 78–80, 127, 152, 167–9, 175–6, 180, 199
Engineers—Civil, 86–87, 89, 129–31, 134, 142, 144, 154. Mechanical 131–2, 137. Mining, 69–70, 74, 78,

127, 129, 132. Railway, 132, 154. *See also* 'Coal Viewers'

Entrepreneurship, 2–6, 235, 249–51, 254

Estate (Agricultural), 25ff, 141, 199, 210–11

Etruria, 11, 45, 98–99, 135, 156, 179, 183, 188, 199–200, 261–2

Factory Commission (1833–4), 43, 92 *passim*, 186, 189, 201. Factory Discipline—*see* 'Labour Discipline'. Factory System, 11–12, 34, 90, 162, 166, 197. Factory Villages or Towns, 74, 91, 98, 197–206

Feasts, 182–3

File Making, 33, 37, 82

Fines, 54, 186–7, 189, 203

Foremen, 85, 132, 135, 141, 144, 167, 177–8, 266, 268–9

Framework Knitting, 36, 45, 96

Gas Industry, 45, 89

Glassmaking Industry, 99–100

Gott, Benjamin, 8, 29–31, 36, 43–44, 94, 114, 124, 137, 156, 186, 190, 195, 200, 217, 224, 231, 237, 241, 252, 267

'Grand Alliance', 62

Haddington Cloth Company, 46, 51–53, 140

House Building for Workers, 54, 66, 73, 200–2

Insurance Schemes (workers), 56–57, 202–3

Iron Industry, 22, 31, 40, 44, 46–47, 55–60, 75–78, 134, 146, 152–3, 170–1, 176

Joint-Stock Companies, 12–14, 19–21, 23, 39, 100, 216, 233, 240–1, 268

Labour, Contracts, 191. Discipline, 52, 54, 56–59, 68, 84, 88, 124, 129, 160, 172, 181–92, 193, 196–7, 201, 203, 250–60. Management, 160–208, 257–8. Recruitment, 69, 74, 160–74. Shortage, 167–8, 173, 187. *See also* 'Migration of Workmen', 'Education of Workers'

Lace Industry, 36, 44, 96

Land Owners and Industry, 29–30, 64–65

Large-Scale Enterprise, 9ff, 25ff, 81, 86, 212, 256, 270

Lead Mining and Smelting, 18, 41, 43, 47, 54, 72–74, 82, 177

Leisure, Workers, 56, 182–3, 194–5

Linen Industry, 36, 95

Literacy, 174, 180

Literary and Philosophical Societies, 120

Locomotive Building, 79–80, 128, 132, 152, 176, 265

London Lead Company—*see* 'Quaker Lead Company'

Mackworth, Sir Humphrey, 19, 53–55, 66, 163, 195

Management, Education, 121–2, 132, and Entrepreneurship, 2–6. Large-Scale Units, 6–9, 23–24, 61, 270–1. Practice, Spread of, 27, 78–79, 90, 127–8, 131, 152, 259–70. Problems, 61, 85, 89–90, 103, 207, 212, 250, 254–5, 260, 270–2. Scientific, 79, 158, 207, 233, 249–59, 261

Managers, 104–59. Distrust of, 12ff. Dynasties, 153–6. Education, 104–22, 156–7. Frauds, 15, 17, 19, 21, 58. Numbers, 68, 133–6, 158. Personnel, 41, 106, 133. Profession, 22, 113, 127–9, 133, 153, 157–9, 266. Relations to Owners, 111, 133, 145–8, 150–3, 157–8. Salary, 138–45, 148. Status, 136–57. Training, 122–34, 158, 178

Marshall, John, 80, 95, 143, 146, 148, 178, 179, 184, 186, 187, 191–5, 222, 236–7, 247, 261, 264, 266, 270

Mass Production, 79–80, 112, 262, 265

Mechanics' Institute, 120–1, 138, 181

Merchants, Education, 107–8, 111, 115, 117, 121, 126, 238, and Industrial Revolution, 30–31. Methods of Control and Accountancy, 30–31, 126, 212–13, 221–3, 238, 242, 259

Metal Goods Industry, 80–82

Migration of Workmen, 52, 54, 67, 103, 106, 169–74

Mine Adventurers, 19, 53–55, 140

Mineral and Battery Works, 14–15

Mines, Royal, 14–15, 140. Scotland, 15, 16

Mining Industries, 61–75, 263, 268–9

Monopoly, 14–15, 20–21, 23, 48–49, 59, 62–65, 71, 246

Morals, Working Class, 162, 183, 193–7, 255–6

Nailing Industry, 33, 37, 45, 55, 76, 82

Nepotism, 137, 145–6, 153–4

Newcomen Engine, 62, 64, 66, 67, 69–70, 72, 73, 76, 128, 175. *Also see* 'Steam Engine'

New Lanark, 21, 35, 91–92. 152, 166, 173, 179, 186, 194, 197, 199–201, 206, 234, 246, 252

Oldknow, Samuel, 35, 45, 91, 146, 149, 165, 183–4, 198–9, 204, 206
Outworking, 11, 32–33, 34ff, 56, 81–82, 94. *See also* 'Putting Out'
Owen, Robert, 80, 124, 142–3, 149, 152, 160, 173, 186, 192–5, 197, 201–2, 207, 234, 246, 252, 257, 260, 267

Paper Industry, 11, 22, 100
Parish Apprentices, 164–6, 170, 176, 197
Partnerships, 39, 150–1, 233–5, 241
Parys Mountain Mines, 29, 47, 70–72, 83, 123, 144, 146–7, 155, 168–9, 183, 198–9, 203–6, 225, 229, 232, 234, 236, 242, 259, 263
Peel, Sir Robert, 21, 91, 165, 270
Pensions, 137, 202–3
Piecework Payments, 55, 189–92
Planning of Layout, 263–5
Pottery Industry, 45, 98–99, 123, 133, 152, 177–8
Privileged Manufacture, 48–49, 69
Professions, 104–5, 107, 111, 118, 122, 126–7, 131
Promotion, 124–6, 132
Putting Out, 9, 30ff, 60, 107, 214. *Also see* 'Domestic System', 'Outworking'

Quaker Lead Company, 17–19, 38, 59, 72–73, 82, 123, 140, 148, 155, 177, 193–5, 199, 203, 217, 222, 268

Railway Building, 45–46, 88–89, 125, 127–8, 132, 135, 265
Railway, Works, 53, 63–66, 71, 73–74, 76, 198. *Also see* 'Tramways'
Regularity and Accountancy, 215–18, 262, of Working hours, 161–2, 172, 181, 183–4, 260–2
Religion, 202, 208

Salt Industry, 15, 74
Schools, 105ff, 179–80, 202, of Industry, 162–3, 180
Scientific Education, 105, 108–12, 114–21
Scribbling Mill, 36
Shipbuilding Industry, 84
Silk Industry, 21, 32, 36, 95–96, 123, 185
Slate Quarrying, 47, 74
Smith, Adam, 8, 11–12, 81, 85, 179
Soho Works, 11, 45, 70, 78–82, 89, 102, 123, 132, 137, 142–3, 145, 148–9, 151, 164, 168–70, 175–6, 179, 181–2, 187, 190–1, 194, 198, 200, 203–4, 213, 216, 221–3, 228–30, 234, 242, 247, 251–2, 261–2, 265
Solicitors, 28
Standardization, 79, 181, 265
Steam Engine, 62–63, 66, 71, 73, 76, 78–79, 81, 88, 93, 95, 97–100, 129, 175, 176. *Also see* 'Newcomen Engine' and 'Boulton & Watt'
Stephenson, George, 23, 106, 112, 132, 143, 149, 152, 154, 176, 179. Robert, 80, 112, 132
Sub-Contract, 8, 16, 17, 38ff, 60, 67 74, 79, 81, 85, 88–89, 99, 135, 189, 218, 231
Sunday Schools, 179–80, 193
Swearing, 195

Technical Training, 126–32, 134
Textbooks, 27–28, 111, 116, 120, 126, 128, 133, 207, 210, 213, 238, 241, 254–5, 263
Textile Industry, 35, 178
Tin Mining, 29, 41, 42, 69–71, 128. Plating, 44, 47, 82
Training of Workers, 124–5, 167–9, 174–9
Tramways, 53, 63–64, 70, 74, 77, 198
Tributers, 42, 69
Truck Shops, 180, 194, 203–4
Tucker, Dean, 13, 33, 196
Tut-workers, 42, 69

University Education, 105, 108, 114, 117–19

Watt, James, 81, 87, 114, 122, 126, 128–30, 134, 137, 142, 143, 146, 168, 175–6, 184, 187, 228, 230, 265. *Also see* 'Boulton & Watt'
Weaving, 33–34, 36–37, 92, 94
Wedgwood, Josiah, 45, 98–99, 106, 109, 112, 133–4, 137–8, 153, 156, 167, 168, 172, 177–9, 182–5, 187, 192, 194, 198–9, 217, 224–5, 228, 230, 246–7, 261, 265, 268
Woollen & Worsted Industry, 8, 11, 31, 35–37, 94–95
Workhouses and Factories, 161, 163–4
Workshop, Central, 11–12, 33–35, 48–50, 95
Works Rules, 184–5, 261. Transport, 46–47, 55, 198
Worsted Committees, 33, 218

York Buildings Company, 16–17